THE HARVARD FILE

Compiled by John F. Hamlin

CONTENTS

Published by Air-Britain (Historians) Ltd.

Registered Office: 1 East St., Tonbridge, Kent.

Sales Department: 41 Penshurst Rd., Leigh, Tonbridge, Kent, TN11 8HL

Published in Great Britain by Air-Britain (Historians) Ltd.,
1 East St.,
Tonbridge,
Kent.

ISBN 0 85130 160 6

FRONT COVER:
N7013 of No.20 SFTS, Cranborne, Southern Rhodesia
(R.F.Tagg)

REAR COVER:
Harvard IIb FX292 of No.3 FTS, Feltwell (Ray Hanna via R.C.Sturtivant)

INTRODUCTION

Back in the dark days of 1938, the British Government under Prime Minister Neville Chamberlain at last woke up to the inevitability of conflict with Germany and the need to build up very rapidly a Royal Air Force which would stand a chance of dealing with the situation. The British aircraft industry was, not surprisingly, quite unable to cope with the high volume output suddenly and belatedly demanded of it, and it was therefore decided that aircraft of certain categories should be procured in the United States of America. To carry out this plan, the British Purchasing Commission was formed; it left for Washington in April 1938, complete with a budget of $25 million, which is not much in the aviation world now but was a great deal then. The first of the three aircraft types which the BPC selected that year was an advanced trainer, the North American NA-49, for which an order for 200 (soon doubled), Contract No. 791588/38, was placed in the summer of 1938. The new aircraft, deliveries of which were to begin from North American's Inglewood, California plant as soon as possible, would be known by the RAF as the Harvard Mk.I and would be fitted with some items of British equipment on arrival in the United Kingdom.

The NA-16, which was the ancestor of the NA-49, had first flown in April 1935 at Dundalk, Maryland and North American had received an initial order later that year from the United States Army Air Corps under their designation BT-9. Since then, production of this and other variants had quickly gathered momentum, so that by the time the BPC placed their order more than 400 aircraft had already rolled off the production line for the USAAC, as well as many for export. No major problems were expected, therefore, when the first aircraft, serialled N7000, arrived in England and was taken on charge at the Aeroplane & Armament Experimental Establishment at Martlesham Heath on 3 December 1938 so that a programme of testing could be carried out and Pilots' Notes prepared.

So began the long life-story of the Harvard in British military service, a story which has by no means ended yet.

In 'The Harvard File' the Author has restricted himself to dealing with the histories of the 4760 Harvards which carried British military serial numbers. The major part of the book, Section 9, deals with the service histories of the individual aircraft, but when referring to this listing a number of factors should be borne in mind:

1 The dates shown for movements between units should be treated with respect, as it is often difficult to differentiate in the official records between 'paper' dates and actual movements.
2 Information from official sources is sadly lacking concerning Harvards used overseas. Periods of time during which an aircraft is confirmed as being with a stated unit are shown in ( ) but it should be recognised that a wider time-span could apply.
3 It should be noted that in between periods of service any aircraft would spend time in storage or undergoing repairs at an MU or a civilian contractor's premises, after which it did not necessarily return to its previous unit. Hence the gaps in the dates quoted.
4 The term 'No RAF service' implies that the aircraft spent its entire RAF life in storage before being either struck off charge or sold to a foreign air arm.
5 Code markings known to have been carried are shown in [ ] brackets. This does not imply that the aircraft carried that code all the time it was with the stated unit or that it carried no other codes. Where space allows, however, chan-

Formation of No.3 FTS Harvards from Feltwell in April 1951; the centre aircraft still carries late-wartime style roundels *(Ray Hanna via R.C.Sturtivant)*

ges of code are shown.

Disposals of aircraft to foreign air arms are also mentioned in Section 9 and further details, such as the recipients' serial numbers, are given in Section 11. Also there are details of further transfers between air forces Take as an example a Harvard originally delivered direct to the South African Air Force against the RAF contract. Information on the aircraft's SAAF serial number is shown in Section 9, as are details of its return to the RAF if this occurred. In Section 11, in the listing of all SAAF Harvards, will be found a note of any subsequent sale to, for example, the Portugeuse Air Force, but no information on its extended SAAF history if it remained with that Air Force. In the FAP listing in Section 11 will be found details of the Harvards transferred form the SAAF to the FAP and their subsequent fates if known. FAP Harvards sold onto the United Kingdom civil register are listed in Section 12.

Details of the deliveries of RAF and RN Harvards to the various 'theatres of operation' are given in Section 6, but it should be noted that subsequent movements of aircraft from one part of the world to another were quite common. These movements are shown, where known, in the aircraft listings (Section 9).

Section 7, the schedule of the many units which have operated Harvards, is intended to form a useful item of reference and includes, as far as UK-based and some of the overseas units are concerned, an indication of the maximum number of Harvards on strength at any one time. However, in the case of India- and Middle East-based units, this information is only available from unofficial sources and is therefore not included, only the basic information being given.

ACKNOWLEDGEMENTS

The Author wishes to acknowledge with gratitude the contributions made by a large number of people to the contents of 'The Harvard File'. Prominent in this respect were Ray Sturtivant, who acted as guide and mentor as well as providing a great deal of information; Ken Smy, who contributed the details of the South African Air Force's many Harvards; Malcolm Fillmore and Nigel Kemp, who were prominent in providing details of Harvards on civil registers; and George Burn, for his talented draughtsmanship.

The many other contributors are listed below in alphabetical order. All of them are asked to accept the Author's sincere thanks for their help and encouragement.

Barry Abraham
A. N. Angus
N. J. Arnold
Godfrey M. Ball
W. J. Billingham
W. A. Brent
The Cambridgeshire Collection
Ralph Coombs
Lionel H. Cornwall
Geoff Cruikshank
Noel E. Davidson
David Dews
Ian Dobinson
Jack Douay
Donald P. Eldridge
Aldon P. Ferguson
D. Freeman
John Gee
Rev. Canon P. Goddard
Gp. Capt. J. R. Goodman DFC AFC RAF (Retd)
Brian Goulding ARPS
Jim Halley
Eric Hardy
John Havers
Andy Heape
Dennis Hickin
Gp. Capt. M. E. Hobson
R. G. Hodgson
Canon A. J. Holloway MTh
E. W. Hughes
Paul Jackson
Valentijn Kenens
G. J. Lamplough
G. Latter-Stapley
J. A. Lewney
J. G. Lyne
David Masters
A. W. McDougall
Ministry of Defence (PE)
Ron Moulton
J. Mudd
E. K. Nelson
G. J. Norton
F. E. Oldham
R. D. Parker
Maurice Pickford
A. D. Pickup OBE
V. Platt
G. A. Pott
C. G. Prince
Barry Radley
G. Raymond-Barker
Bruce Robertson
Royal Air Force College, Cranwell
Alan Scholefield
G. A. E. Scott
David J. Smith
Don Smith
Flt. Lt. R. A. Smith (A&AEE)
Robert F. Tagg
Flt. Lt. Andy Thomas
C. J. Wallace
David Watkins
S. Weaver
N. D. Welch
Ray Wilson
J. R. Woods (The Harvard Club)

FT360 of the Headquarters Flight of No.1 FTS Moreton-in-Marsh near the top of a loop *(1 FTS via author)*

ABBREVIATIONS

AACU	Anti Aircraft Cooperation Unit
A&AEE	Aeroplane & Armament Experimental Establishment
AAS	Air Armament School
Aber	Aberdeen
AB&GS	Air Bombing & Gunnery School
ACFE	Air Command Far East
ACSEA	Air Command South East Asia
AES	Aircraft Engineering Services
AFEE	Airborne Forces Experimental Establishment
AFS	Advanced Flying School
AFTU	Airborne Forces Training Unit
AGS	Air Gunnery School
AHQ	Air Headquarters
Alb	Alberta
APC	Armament Practice Camp
APS	Armament Practice School
ARS	Aircraft Repair Section
ASR	Air Sea Rescue
ATA	Air Transport Auxiliary
ATDU	Air Torpedo Development Unit
ATP	Air Transport Pool
ATU	Advanced Training Unit
Avex	Avex Engineering
Av.Tr.	Aviation Traders
BAFSEA	British Air Forces in South East Asia
BAS	Beam Approach School
BC Air	British Commonwealth Air Communications Squadron
BelgAF	Belgian Air Force
BG&NS	Bombing, Gunnery & Navigation School
Birm	Birmingham
BLEU	Blind Landing Experimental Unit
BPC	British Purchasing Commission
Bris	Bristol
Camb	Cambridge
Cam.U	Camouflage Unit
CAOS	Combined Air Observers' School
Cat.	Category
C&CF	Check & Conversion Flight
CF	Communications Flight
CFE	Central Fighter Establishment
CFS	Central Flying School
CFS(B)	Central Flying School (Basic)
CFS(EW)	Central Flying School (Examining Wing)
CGS	Central Gunnery School
CMU	
cr.	crashed
cr.ldd.	crash-landed
CS	Communications Squadron
CU	Communications Unit <u>or</u> Conversion Unit
DBF	Destroyed by fire
DBR	Damaged beyond repair
desp.	despatched
EAAS	Empire Air Armaments School
EANS	Empire Air Navigation School
EATS	Empire Air Training Scheme
ECFS	Empire Central Flying School
Edin	Edinburgh
EFS	Empire Flying School
EFTS	Elementary Flying Training School
ETPS	Empire Test Pilots' School
E&WS	Electrical & Wireless School
FA	Flying accident
FAA	Fleet Air Arm
FAC	Congolese Air Force
FAP	Portuguese Air Force
FCCS	Fighter Command Communications Squadron
FCITF	Fighter Command Instrument Training Flight
FE	Far East
FEAFExS	Far East Air Force Examining Squadron
FEAFTS	Far East Air Force Training Squadron
FECS	Far East Communications Squadron
FEExS	Far East Examining Squadron
FETS	Far East Training Squadron
FF	Ferry Flight
FIS	Flying Instructors' School
Flt	Flight
FPP	Ferry Pilots' Pool
FRS	Flying Refresher School
FSTU	Fighter Support Training Unit
ft	feet
FTCCF	Flying Training Command Communications Flt
FTS	Flying Training School
FTU	Ferry Training Unit
FU	Ferry Unit
GA	Ground accident
GATU	Ground Attack Training Unit
GG	Ground Gunnery
Gp.	Group
Gp. CF	Group Communications Flight
Gp. CS	Group Communications Squadron
HCCS	Home Command Communications Squadron
HCEU	Home Command Examining Unit
HCITF	Home Command Instrument Training Flight
HCU	Heavy Conversion Unit
HKAAF	Hong Kong Auxiliary Air Force
hp	horsepower
HQ	Headquarters
Hw	Helliwells Ltd.
(I)	(India)
IAF	Indian Air Force
IDFAF	Israeli Defence Force Air Force
ItalAF	Italian Air Force
JRTU	Jungle Rescue Training Unit
lbs	pounds weight
Liv	Liverpool
MAAF	Malayan Auxiliary Air Force
Man	Manchester <u>or</u> Manitoba
MEAFITF	Middle East Air Force Instrument Training Flight
MECCU	Middle East Check & Conversion Unit
(Met)	(Meteorological)
METS	Middle East Training School
Mk.	Mark
MLD	Marine Luchtvaartdienst (Dutch Navy)
mls	miles
MoD (PE)	Ministry of Defence (Procurement Executive)
mph	miles per hour
MU	Maintenance Unit
NA	North American Aviation
Nott	Nottingham
NB	New Brunswick
NFT	No further trace
NS	Nova Scotia
NTB	Norwegian Training Base
OCU	Operational Conversion Unit
OFU	Overseas Ferry Unit
Ont	Ontario
OTU	Operational Training Unit
(P)AFU	(Pilots') Advanced Flying Unit
PakAF	Pakistani Air Force
PEI	Prince Edward Island
P>S	Parachute & Glider Training School
PortAF	Portuguese Air Force
PQ	Province of Quebec
(P)RFU	(Pilots') refresher Flying Unit
PRU	Photographic Reconnaissance Unit
PSOC	Presumed Struck Off Charge
PTS	Parachute Training School

RAE	Royal Aircraft Establishment
RAF	Royal Air Force
RAFC	Royal Air Force College
RAFFC	Royal Air Force Flying College
RATG	Rhodesian Air Training Group
RCAF	Royal Canadian Air Force
RCCF	Reserve Command Communications Flight
RCCS	Reserve Command Communications Squadron
RCITF	Reserve Command Instrument Training Flight
R.DanAF	Royal Danish Air Force
retd.	returned
RFS	Reserve Flying School
RFU	Refresher Flying Unit
R.HellAF	Royal Hellenic Air Force
RLG	Relief Landing Ground
RN	Royal Navy
R.NethAF	Royal Netherlands Air Force
R.NorAF	Royal Norwegian Air Force
RNZAF	Royal New Zealand Air Force
RP Trg	Rocket Projectile Training
SAAF	South African Air Force
Sas	Saskatchewan
SF	Station Flight
SFPP	Service Ferry Pilots' Pool
SF Sqdn	Service Ferry Squadron
SFTS	Service Flying Training School
SLAIS	Special Low Attack Instructors' School
SoAC	School of Army Cooperation
SOC	Struck Off Charge
So'ton	Southampton
Sqdn	Squadron
sq.ft.	square feet
SR	Southern Rhodesia
SRAF	Southern Rhodesian Air Force
SS	Sold for scrap
St.And	St. Andrews
TADU	Training Aids Development Unit
TOC	Taken On Charge
TSTU	Transport Support Training Unit
TT	Target Tug
T&WDU	Tactical & Weapons Development Unit
UAS	University Air Squadron
UK	United Kingdom
USAAC	United Staes Army Air Corps
USAAF	United Staes Army Air Force
USN	United States Navy
WAT&CS	West Africa Training & Communications Sqdn
Wg	Wing
YugoAF	Yugoslavian Air Force

The very first Harvard Mk.I, N7000, pictured at A&AEE, Martlesham Heath, 13 January 1939
(Crown copyright, A&AEE Boscombe Down)

NARRATIVE

HARVARD Mark I

As mentioned in the Foreword, the first RAF Harvard, N7000, arrived at A&AEE, Martlesham Heath, in December 1938 and proceeded to undergo a series of test flights to determine its flying characteristics and thus to enable Pilots' Notes to be compiled. The second aircraft N7001, joined the trials in January 1939, but the following month the Mk.I's tendency to spin claimed N7000 as the first Harvard victim when it crashed at Eyke, near Woodbridge in Suffolk, killing both occupants.

By now, Harvards were arriving on these shores in quantity, and Central Flying School received N7002 in January 1939 to enable flying instructors to convert on to this somewhat forbiddding new machine. Deliveries to Flying Training Schools also began in January 1939, 12 FTS at Grantham (Spitalgate) being the first recipient, followed by 2 FTS (Brize Norton) and 10 FTS (Ternhill) in March, 1 FTS (Netheravon) in April and 6 FTS (Little Rissington) in May 1939. In September of that year, apart from continuing deliveries to FTSs, fighter operational training units began to receive Harvards, 11 Gp. Pool at Sutton Bridge and 12 Group Pool at Aston Down each being allocated a small number by the end of the year. These units were retitled 6 OTU and 5 OTU respectively in March 1940. 12 FTS (by now 12 SFTS), the pioneer Harvard user, however, began to relinquish its fourteen aircraft in August 1939 in favour of twin-engined types, and most of the Harvards were passed to 14 SFTS at Kinloss, which also received some new aircraft from November 1939.

Harvards Mk. I began to arrive in Southern Rhodesia for use in the Empire Air Training Scheme in March 1940 specifically to equip 20 SFTS and, later, 22 SFTS, and most of the batch serialled P5916 to P5982 were shipped there direct from the United States, although some may have been trans-shipped in the United Kingdom. In July 1940 it was realized that Great Britain was not the ideal place in which to train pilots, subject as it was to the vagaries of the weather and to enemy action (or even the threat of it) and the Harvard-equipped SFTSs remaining here would therefore be closed down. Withdrawal of the aircraft from these Schools began at once so that they could be shipped to Southern Rhodesia to augment those already there. Special packing was used, and up to the end of 1940 the aircraft were sent to 52 MU at Cardiff for the work to be done. After this, a packing centre was set up at Odiham, where a building contractor well-known locally, Crosby & Co. Ltd., carried out the work. By September 1941, 216 Harvards had been redeployed to Southern Rhodesia and eight to the Middle East, leaving only 35 in service in the United Kingdom.

15 SFTS, a nomadic unit which first received Harvards in September 1939 at Lossiemouth, became by far the main user of the Mk.I, no less than 139 examples passing through its hands before the last one left its South Cerney base in April 1941. At the other end of the scale 5 FTS at Ternhill and 11 FTS at Shawbury each received just one Harvard, which stayed for a matter of a few weeks only, probably due to a policy change.

Although all the SFTSs had relinquished their Harvards by August 1941, a number of OTUs were still taking

Formation of Mk.I Harvards of either No.2 SFTS or No.15 SFTS *(via J.J.Halley)*

An N-serialled Harvard Mk.I of No.8 FTS, Montrose c.1939 *(Sqn Ldr B.A.Hitchings via N.D.Welch)*

small numbers of the type on strength. Prominent among these units was 41 OTU at Old Sarum, the development of 1 School of Army Co-operation, which had used a few Harvards since May 1941. Fighter OTUs which began to use Harvards at this time were 52 OTU at Debden and 53 OTU and 61 OTU at Heston. The Service Ferry Pilots Pool, 1, 2 and 3 Ferry Pilots Pools and the Flying School of the Air Transport Auxiliary were each now provided with a few Mk.I Harvards, and indeed the ATA operated the Mk.I longer than any other UK-based unit, not disposing of its last example until March 1946. Other units which employed Mk.I Harvards in small numbers or singly included a number of second-line Squadrons which used them for training purposes and some Station Flights. One aircraft, N7020, was retained in the United States for use by the British Purchasing Commission.

The Harvard Mk.I, long since supplemented by more up-to-date Marks of the aircraft, remained in service in Southern Rhodesia until November 1945. Two examples in the Middle East were not struck off charge until January 1947, and these appear to have been the last two extant. Unlike other Marks, no Mk.I Harvards, apart from three in South Africa, were sold overseas or preserved.

HARVARD Mark II

In October 1940, while withdrawal of most Harvards Mk.I from service in the United Kingdom was taking place eight Mk.II aircraft with serials in the BD range arrived in England and the first of 20 similar aircraft, carrying AH serials, was received in Canada for use in the Commonwealth Air Training Scheme. The aircraft in the United Kingdom were, however, used for a short time only before five were transferred to Southern Rhodesia along with Mk.I aircraft and two were handed over to the newly-arrived USAAF. Six more Mk.IIs, carrying BJ or BS serials, which arrived in England in November 1940 saw little or no service before being sent on to Rhodesia and six more were lost at sea on the way to the UK.

Bulk deliveries of Mk.II Harvards to Canada began in July 1941 and continued until May 1942, by which time the EATS in Canada had received 305 of this Mark, carrying serials in the AH, AJ and BW ranges. They were allocated to the large number of Service Flying Training Schools operating under the CATS and were used alongside similar RCAF aircraft. The attrition rate was high, and mishaps of varying severity were an everyday occurence. Those SFTSs which were RAF-administered had all closed down by October 1944, and the surviving RAF-serialled Harvards were taken over by the RCAF along with large quantities of other aircraft and equipment.

A further 103 Mk.II Harvards were shipped to Southern Rhodesia via South Africa from August 1941 and were sent to 20 SFTS and 22 SFTS to augment the Mk.I aircraft already there. By the end of the War 40 of these Mk.II Harvards had been written off and 31 more were Struck Off Charge in November 1945, leaving 32 in service or stored. Twelve, including three of those originally used in the United Kingdom, were sold to the Southern Rhodesian Air Force in February 1949 and the last three Harvards of this Mark in Rhodesia were Struck Off Charge by the RAF in December of that year.

Forty-seven Mk.II Harvards were sent to the Middle East, where they had a comparatively short life, the small number of survivors being Presumed SOC in January 1947, while the four in India had all been written off in flying accidents by November 1943. Finally, mention must be made of the 38 aircraft which were shipped direct to New Zealand and were absorbed at once into the Royal New Zealand Air Force.

HARVARD Mark IIa

The introduction of the Mark IIa version of the Harvard allowed the expansion of the Empire Air Training scheme to proceed apace. The first despatches from the USA were to South Africa and the Middle East, both in October 1942, followed by New Zealand in December 1942 and Southern Rhodesia in January 1943. By September 1943 New Zealand had received its allocation of 53 aircraft and the last of 436 aircraft arrived in South Africa that December. These two countries immediately allocated new serial numbers for the Harvards within their own numbering systems, in the case of the SAAF from 7001 upwards. In January 1944 the CATS in Southern Rhodesia took delivery of its 149th and last Mk.IIa Harvard and the following month the last of 100 aircraft arrived in the Middle East. Minor deliveries were made to West Africa and to the Royal Navy in India and Ceylon, but no Mk.IIa aircraft were delivered new to the United Kingdom.

Line-up of Mk.II Harvards at No.31 SFTS, Kingston, Ontario in 1943 *(N.E.Davidson)*

A substantial number of Mk.IIa Harvards remained in Rhodesia after the end of the War and saw further service from late 1947 in the Rhodesian Air Training Group. This task completed, eleven aircraft were sold to the SRAF in 1952/53 and the remaining 45 aircraft were Struck Off Charge as 'Sold' in November 1953, many of them seeing service later in the Belgian Congo with the Belgian Air Force.

South Africa saw a mass exodus of Mk.IIa Harvards after the War. No less than 176 of them were given their original RAF serials back, crated, and shipped to the UK in 1946/47; of these, a large number were then sold to foreign air arms, but the remainder languished at 15 MU, Wroughton, until being sold for scrap in 1950, apart from one aircraft which was used by Wattisham's Station Flight for a time. Of the aircraft remaining in South Africa, twelve were sold to the Dutch Air Force in 1947 for use as a source of spare parts, a few were struck off charge and many others continued in service with the SAAF. A substantial number are indeed still in use in 1988, the oldest one having arrived in South Africa as long ago as October 1942!

In the Middle East the Harvards Mk.IIa went into an early decline, 27 of the remaining aircraft being Struck Off Charge in 1945, 38 in 1946, nine in 1947 and two in 1948, leaving just one to soldier on at Deversoir until November 1950. New Zealand's Mk.IIa Harvards were formally transferred to the RNZAF inventory in September 1946 although a few had already been lost in flying accidents.

HARVARD Mark III

Next in serial number order came the Harvard Mk.III, which, although it had a 24-volt electrical system, was delivered to the same areas as the Mark IIa. Of the 537 Mk.III aircraft which carried British serial numbers, 197 were sent direct to South Africa between December 1943 and August 1944 and 81 went to the Middle East. The EATS in Southern Rhodesia received 70 examples over the eight months from December 1943 to July 1944 and 41 were sent to New Zealand, arriving between November 1943 and November 1944. This Mark was also the favourite of the Royal Navy, which received 143 new aircraft, a few more being transferred from the RAF later.

Post-war, 100 of the Mk.III Harvards used in South Africa were sent to the UK between September 1946 and July 1947, and of these 73 rotted away in MUs until being scrapped in 1950. Just one was used in this country and the other 26 were sold to other air forces. Eleven aircraft remained in South Africa.

Apart from a few aircraft which had been written off earlier, the Harvards Mk.III in Southern Rhodesia were stored there when the EATS closed down at the end of the War and some were brought back into use by the RATG in 1948, remaining in service with 4 FTS until being replaced by Mk.IIb aircraft in 1952. Nineteen of them were Struck Off Charge in September 1952 and a further 45 were stored until being sold, probably for scrap, in November 1953. The aircraft sent to the Middle East, which arrived between January and September 1944, did not, however, remain in service very long. By the end of 1947 only two of the 81 aircraft remained on charge, these lasting to 1950. One example had been returned to the USAAF soon after arrival in the area, and one was returned to the UK in 1947, only to be scrapped.

The Royal Navy continued to use many of their Mk.III Harvards for several years after the War, the last examples being operated by Royal Naval Reserve squadrons until 1956.

HARVARD Mark IIb

Numerically by far the most prolific Mark of the aircraft in British service was the Mk.IIb, built not by North American Aviation, which by 1942 was unable to cope with Harvard production due to the urgency of the P-51 programme, but by Noorduyn Aviation of Canada under licence. There the first examples, in the FE serial batch, were taken on charge in May 1942 to augment the Mk.II aircraft in the Commonwealth Air Training Scheme. Deliveries to Canadian SFTSs continued through to December 1943, by which time 639 of the Mark had been delivered, but 72 of them were shipped to the United Kingdom in March 1944, some after use in Canada but most after a period of storage. As with the Mk.IIa aircraft, the rate of attrition in Canada was high, but a large number of the aircraft survived to be absorbed into the RCAF when the RAF elements of the EATS returned home in the autumn of 1944.

The RAF in India began to receive Harvards of this Mark in February 1943, and deliveries to that area, totalling 507, proceeded at a steady pace until July 1944. Seventeen further aircraft were lost at sea on the way to India. Eleven Mk.IIb Harvards were handed back to the USAAF in India in October 1943 but the rest saw service with 1(I)FTS, various OTUs and a host of other units for the duration of the War. In June 1946 fifteen aircraft were 'recaptured' by the USA and in April 1947 87 survivors were handed over to the Army for scrapping. On the partition of India 82 Harvards were handed over on 25 September 1947 to the Indian Air Force and 29 to the new Pakistan Air Force, and 25 more were 'recaptured' by the USA in November 1947, including the eleven which had been in USAAF hands since 1943. The few remaining aircraft were used by the RAF during its withdrawal from India and were then dumped.

The first Harvards Mk.IIb to arrive in the United Kingdom, FE787 and FE788, were shipped from the USA aboard SS Kaipaki on 9 April 1943, followed by a slow trickle of eight more aircraft until bulk deliveries of FS-serialled Harvards got under way in September 1943. Most ships carrying the Harvards docked on Merseyside, and off-loaded aircraft were taken to Lockheed Aircraft's facility at Speke for basic attention before being sent to either Rootes Securities at Blythe Bridge near Stoke-on-Trent or to Martin Hearn at Hooton Park for modifications to bring them up to British standards. After this procedure, which could take several months, the Harvards were moved to Maintenance Units for storage pending issue to an operating unit. For this reason, it was October 1943 before the first major user of the Mk.IIb, the Air Transport Auxiliary, received its first examples, FH107 and FH115. The Empire Central Flying School received its first aircraft, FS845, in January 1944 but had to wait until June before bulk deliveries began. Meanwhile, shipments from the USA continued at an ever-increasing rate, as did the number of aircraft put into store. Before they could be issued to the RAF, eight Mk.IIb aircraft were handed over to the USAAF at Burtonwood or Warton, and in the same month seven examples were re-shipped to Algiers, probably for use by the Free French Air Force. Two Harvards were sent to the Middle East in the same way in August 1944.

Two units tasked with training flying instructors were next to receive the Mk.IIb, 2 FIS in May and 3 FIS in July 1944, after which deliveries to the FTSs and (P)AFUs began. First of these was 17 SFTS, which received its first Harvard in July 1944, followed in August by 16 SFTS and in September by 5(P)AFU and 9(P)AFU. Several more FTSs began to operate Harvards in the Spring of 1945 as did a further instructors' school, 7 FIS. After the closure of the Empire Air Training Scheme in 1945, pilot training was concentrated in the United Kingdom for the next few years, so that in the summer of 1946 eight FTSs, the CFS and ECFS were equipped with Harvards Mk.IIb. Any major repairs to Harvards which suffered mishaps in the UK were at this time carried out by three main civilian contractors: Helliwells at Walsall, Herts & Essex Aero Club at Broxbourne and Shrager Bros. at Old Warden.

In the Middle East, only one ordinary Mk.IIb, KF222, was received in new condition, and this aircraft appears not to have been used. However, 42 aircraft equipped for target-towing were delivered from January 1945, and one more of the batch, which were selected at random from the final hundred in the KF series, crashed in the USA on a test flight. Four of these target-towing Harvards were shipped to the UK in June 1947 but were not used again before being Struck Off Charge in 1950. Seven were sold to the Royal Hellenic Air Force in February 1947 and the remainder were SOC locally between June 1945 and November 1947.

A large number of Mk.IIb aircraft, however, remained in store, and steps were taken in 1946 to reduce the

33 Harvards from the Central Flying School, Little Rissington can be seen in this shot, taken from another member of the formation, over Farnborough, probably at the 1950 SBAC Show *(Gp.Capt.J.R.Goodman, DFC, AFC, RAF (Retd))*

Line-up of Harvards at No.3 FTS, Feltwell, 1950/51 *(Ray Hanna via R.C.Sturtivant)*

number. In August of that year the first of 116 'new' aircraft was issued to the Dutch Air Force and deliveries to that country continued through to October 1948. Smaller allocations of unused Harvards Mk.IIb were made to the air forces of France, which received 18 in April/May of 1949; Denmark, where eight aircraft were sent between April and June 1947; and Belgium, where Rollason's, who had bought them from the RAF, later sent seven aircraft. Withdrawals fro FTSs and other units in the United Kingdom of used Harvards for disposal overseas accounted for a further 106 aircraft between November 1945, when 23 aircraft left the Norwegian Training Base at Winkleigh for Norway, and October 1949.

A further campaign of equipment disposal in the UK resulted in 151 'as new' Harvards being Struck Off between April 1950 and May 1951. Six FTSs, plus three Flying Refresher Schools, CFS and RAF College, were still operating Harvards Mk.IIb intensively, however, due to a renewed demand for pilots caused by the Korean crisis. Even so, there was still enough surplus stock to allow 64 aircraft, 15 of them not previously used, to be sent to Rhodesia between November 1950 and December 1951 to augment Harvards of earlier Marks in the Rhodesian Air Training Group. Smaller numbers were also shipped from the UK to the Far East and Middle East in the late 1940s and early 1950s to reinforce the RAF in those areas.

By the end of 1953, though, the writing was on the wall for the Harvard, which was due to be replaced by the Hunting Provost trainer with side-by-side seating as the first stage of the Provost/Vampire training sequence. Four of the FTSs had closed down or re-equipped by July 1954, and RAF College had replaced its Harvards with Provosts. By the end of 1954 only 1 FTS at Moreton-in-Marsh and 3 FTS at Feltwell were still using Harvards, the former being in the process of closing down, and in April 1955 the last Harvard in use by an FTS left Feltwell.

The 64 aircraft sent from the UK to boost the RATG were passed through 394 MU to 4 FTS and were used intensively for the next couple of years. In 1953 fourteen of them, plus four shipped from the UK, were sent to Kenya to form 1340 Flight, a unique unit which used Harvards aggressively against the Mau-Mau rebels who were giving trouble at that time. Carrying 20lb bombs in wing racks, the Harvards operated quite effectively until September 1955, by which time ten aircraft remained on strength. Back in Rhodesia, the FTSs were closing down and the last 29 Harvards Mk.IIb were sold for scrap in December 1953.

This was not, and indeed IS not, the end of the story of the Harvard in RAF use. A number of aircraft, some with many hours on the clock, were used intermittently by University Air Squadrons up to May 1957, while in the Far East a few were flown by the Malayan and Hong Kong Auxiliary Air Forces until the same date. The most incredible feat of longevity, however, was made by the two aircraft which are still, at the end of 1988, flown by the MoD(PE) at A&AEE, Boscombe Down, FT375 and KF183; a third, KF314, crashed on 22 February 1982. This venerable pair are used for such tasks as air-to-air photography (for which work, due to the sliding canopy, no aircraft is better suited), and for giving intermediate piston-engined experience to jet pilots who have volunteered to fly the Hurricanes and Spitfires of the Battle of Britain Memorial Flight. Long may they continue to do so!

Preparing the RAF College's last Harvard for its final sortie, at Cranwell in May 1954 *(RAF Cranwell)*

AJ714 of No.20 SFTS, Cranborne, Southern Rhodesia *(Bruce Robertson)*

SERIAL NUMBERS

BRITISH MILITARY SERIAL NUMBERS ALLOCATED TO HARVARDS

RAF serial	Mk.	USAAF serials	Qty	
N7000-7199	I	-	200	
P5783-5982	I	-	200	
AH185-204	II	-	20	
AJ538-987	II	-	450	Originally Ordered by French Air Force
BD130-137	II	-	8	ex RCAF 2521-2528
BJ410,411	II	-	2	ex RCAF 2529,2530
BJ412-415	II	-	4	ex RCAF 2534-2537
BS808	II	-	1	ex RCAF 2538
BW184-207	II	-	24	
DG430,431	II	-	2	
DG432-439	II	-	8	ex RCAF 2539-2546
EX100-846	IIa	41-33073/33819	747	
EX847-999	III	41-33820/33972	153	
EZ100-249	III	41-33973/34122	150	
EZ250-258	III	42-84163/84171	9	
EZ259-278	III	42-84182/84201	20	
EZ279-298	III	42-84282/84301	20	
EZ299-308	III	42-84362/84371	10	
EZ309-328	III	42-84453/84472	20	
EZ329-348	III	42-84543/84562	20	
EZ349-358	III	42-84633/84642	10	
EZ359-378	III	42-84723/84742	20	
EZ379-398	III	42-84803/84822	20	
EZ399-408	III	42-84923/84932	10	
EZ409-428	III	42-85013/85032	20	
EZ429-448	III	42-85103/85122	20	
EZ449-458	III	42-85223/85232	10	
EZ459-799	III	-		Cancelled
FE267-766	IIb	42-464/963	500	
FE767-999	IIb	42-12254/12486	233	
FH100-166	IIb	42-12487/12553	67	
FS661-999	IIb	43-12502/12840	339	
FT100-460	IIb	43-12841/13201	361	
FT955-974	III	42-44538/44557	20	
FX198-497	IIb	43-34615/34914	300	Not in strict order
KE305	III		1	ex USN 26800
KE306	III		1	ex USN 26812
KE307-309	III		3	ex USN 26816-26818
KF100-757	IIb	-	658	Not in strict order
KF758-900	IIb	-		Cancelled
KF901-999	IIb	-	99	
KG100-309	IIb	-		Cancelled

Totals:

Mk.I	400
Mk.II	519
Mk.IIa	747
Mk.IIb	2557
Mk.III	537

	4760

Construction numbers

In the following list, the North American Aviation construction numbers for Harvards Mk.IIa and Mk.III are incomplete and those shown should be treated as provisional. The Noorduyn construction numbers for Mk.IIb aircraft in the FX and KF serial batches were not necessarily in strict order of serial number.

RAF serial	Const. nos.
N7000-7199	49.748-947
P5783-5982	49.1053-1252
AH185-204	66.2747-2766
AJ538-987	76.3508-3957
BD130-137	66.2254-2261
BJ410,411	66.2262,2263
BJ412-415	66.2267-2270
BS808	66.2271
BW184-207	81.4109-4132
DG430,431	66.
DG432-439	66.2272-2279
EX100-224	88.9179-9303
EX225-244	88.9611-9630
EX245-254	88.9641-9650
EX255-264	88.9661-9670
EX265-284	88.9681-9700
EX285-294	88.9721-9730
EX295-304	88.9748-9757
EX305-314	88.9778-9787
EX315-324	88.9808-9817
EX325-334	88.9838-9847
EX335-344	88.9868-9877
EX345-354	88.9913-9822
EX355-364	88.9958-9967
EX365-372	88.10008-10015
EX392-396	88.10108-10112
EX398-401	88.10154-10157
EX421-432	88.10251-10262
EX433-584	88.10528-10677
EX585-619	88.12029-12063
EX633-646	88.12127-12140
EX660-688	88.12326-12354
EX692-705	88.12758-12771
EX741-749	88.13187-13194
EX779-786	88.13598-13605
EX789-796	88.13903-13910
EX811-828	88.14161-14178
EX835-847	88.14371-14383
EX857-868	88.14483-14494
EX873-884	88.14544-14555
EX890-909	88.14657-14676
EX925-946	88.14870-14890
EX972-989	88.15052-15069
EX997-999	88.15122-15124
EZ100-105	88.15125-15130
EZ144-177	88.15334-15367
EZ184-194	88.15688-15698
EZ229-258	88.15856-15885
EZ259-278	88.15896-15915
EZ279-296	88.15996-16013
EZ297,298	88.16081,16082
EZ299-308	88.16143-16152
EZ309-328	88.16234-16253
EZ329-348	88.16324-16343
EZ349-358	88.16414-16423
EZ359-378	88.16504-16523
EZ379-398	88.16584-16603
EZ399-408	88.16704-16713
EZ409-428	88.16794-16813
EZ429-448	88.16884-16903
EZ449-458	88.17004-17013
FE267-999	14.001-733
FH100-166	14.734-800
FS661-999	14A.801-1139
FT100-460	14A.1140-1500
FX198-497	14A.1501-1800
KE305,306	88.11444,11445
KE307-309	88.11460-11462
KF100-757	14A.1801-2458
KF901-999	18.002-100

RAF Harvard instructional airframes

M serial	formerly	date allocated	SOC	
2056M	N7092	7.40		2 SoTT
2123M	N7070	7.40	2.42	Became RCAF A100
2124M	N7096	7.40		Became RCAF A102
2203M	N7129	8.40		15 SFTS Lossiemouth
4913M	FH107	10.44		16 SFTS Newton
4927M	FH115	11.44	7.47	16 SFTS Newton
5015M	FS832	1.45	10.49	17 FTS Cranwell, later 22 FTS
5208M	FS814	4.45	5.54	17 SFTS Cranwell
5250M	FX241	5.45		Churh Lawford
5568M	FX306	8.45		11(P)AFU Calveley
5569M	KF155	8.45		Spitalgate
5768M	FT356	12.45	9.50	Little Rissington
5769M	KF351	1.46	5.50	South Cerney
5770M	FX293	1.46	9.47	1 SoTT, Halton
5771M	FX321	1.46	1.48	1 SoTT, Halton
6161M	KF219	10.46		8 SoTT, Weeton
6276M	FS906	2.47		2 SoTT, Cosford
6312M	FX244	4.47		Little Rissington
6314M	FE866	4.47		Moreton-in-Marsh (see also 6534M)
6316M	KF331	1.47		Reverted to airworthy aircraft 5.47
6521M	EX684	2.48		4 FTS Heany
6522M	EX697	2.48		4 FTS Heany
6530M	FT429	4.48	10.51	Finningley; later Syerston
6534M	FE866	3.48		Cancelled as already 6314M
7107M	FT303	9.53	5.54	2 FTS Cluntoe
7113M	KF513	10.53		3 FTS Feltwell
7116M	KF209	12.53	12.54	3 FTS Feltwell
7229M	KF126	7.55	8.55	Malaya
7554M	FS890	1.58		Little Rissington gate guardian; later to A&AEE at Boscombe Down as a source of spares.(9.73)

Put out to grass! Gate guardian at Little Rissington was FS890, which had been allocated 'maintenance' serial 7554M

(N.D.Welch)

TECHNICAL DETAILS

PERFORMANCE

		Mk.I	Other Marks
Top speed	mph	210	206
Cruising speed	mph	186	180
Landing speed	mph	63	70
Range	mls.	735	730
Initial climb	ft/min	1350	1350
Service ceiling	ft.	23600	23000

DIMENSIONS

Span		43'0"	42'0¼"
Length		27'9"	29'0"
Wing area	sq. ft.		253.7
Weight empty	lbs.	3948	3958

Note: Mk.IIa was a redesign to eliminate the use of aluminium alloy and high-alloy steel. The wings, centre section, fin, rudder, elevators, ailerons, flaps etcetera were made of spot-welded low-alloy steel. Side panels of the forward fuselage and the entire rear fuselage, tailplane etc were covered with plywood, giving a saving of valuable metals of 1246 lbs. Fears of shortages proved groundless, however, so normal structures were reverted to for Mk.IIb and Mk.III.

CONSTRUCTIONAL DETAILS

Mk.I: Model: NA-49
Construction: steel tube, fabric covered.
Engine: 550 hp Pratt & Whitney Wasp R-1340-S3H1 nine-cylinder air-cooled, driving a Hamilton-Standard constant-speed metal airscrew.
Equivalent of USAAC BC-1

Mk.II: Models: NA-66, NA-76 and NA-81
Construction: steel tube, light alloy covered, monocoque rear fuselage.
Engine: 600 hp Pratt & Whitney Wasp R-1340-49 nine-cylinder air-cooled, driving a two-position controllable-pitch metal airscrew.
Equivalent of USAAC AT-6

Mk.IIa: Model: NA-88
Construction: welded low-alloy steel, fabric-covered except for plywood skin on parts of fuselage and tail.
Engine: as Mk.II
Equivalent of USAAF AT-6C-NT

Mk.IIb: (built by Noorduyn Aviation in Canada under licence).
Construction: metal stressed skin; fabric-covered control surfaces.
Engine: 550 hp Pratt & Whitney Wasp R-1340-AN-1 driving Hamilton-Standard constant-speed metal airscrew.
Equivalent of USAAF AT-16-ND

Mk.III: Model; NA-88
Construction: metal stressed skin; fabric-covered control surfaces.
Engine: as Mk.II
24-volt electrical system
Equivalent to USAAF AT-6D-NT

What pulled it along! The engine compartment of Mk.II Harvard BD132 *(Bruce Robertson)*

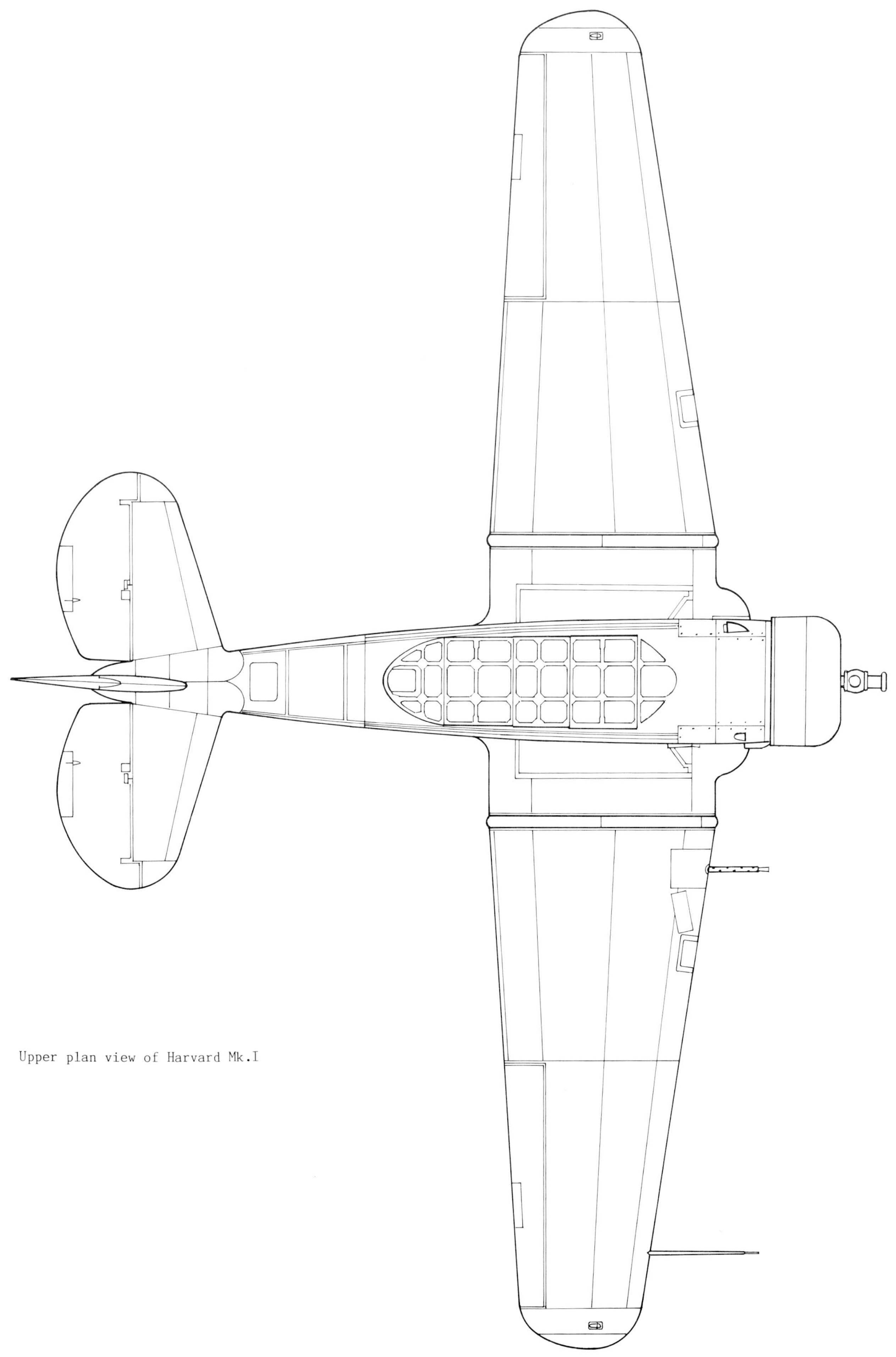

Upper plan view of Harvard Mk.I

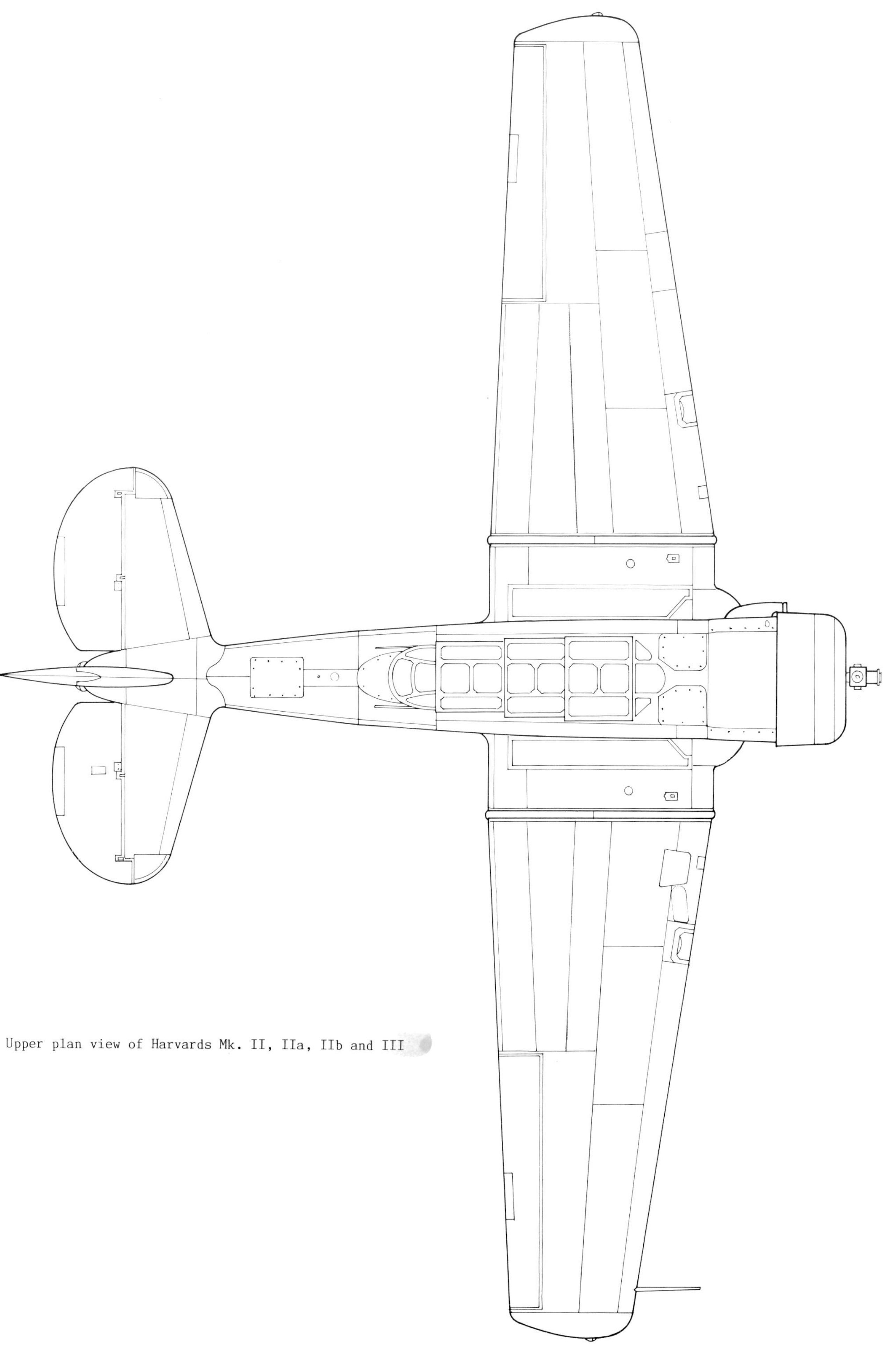

Upper plan view of Harvards Mk. II, IIa, IIb and III

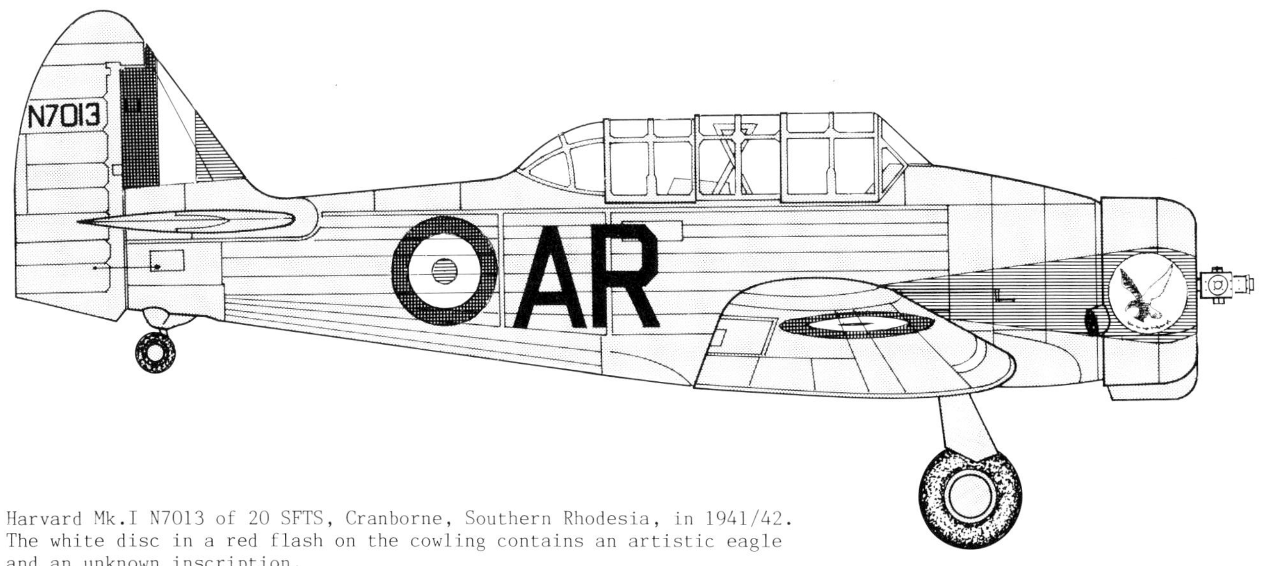

Harvard Mk.I N7013 of 20 SFTS, Cranborne, Southern Rhodesia, in 1941/42. The white disc in a red flash on the cowling contains an artistic eagle and an unknown inscription.

All-yellow Harvard Mk.II AJ930 of 34 SFTS, Medicine Hat, Alberta, part of Canada's enormous contribution to the Empire Air Training Scheme

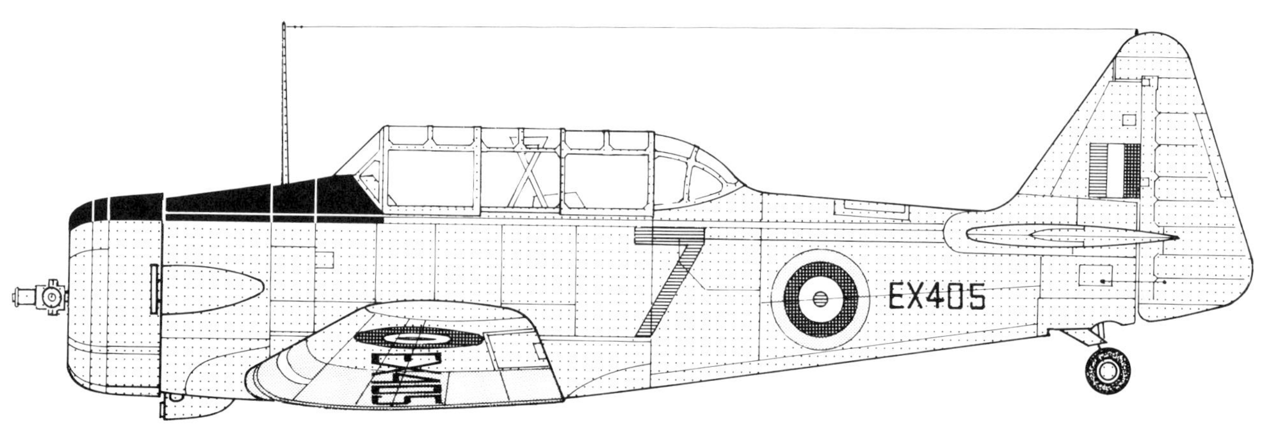

Harvard Mk.IIa EX405 in silver finish while in use by 20 SFTS in Rhodesia.

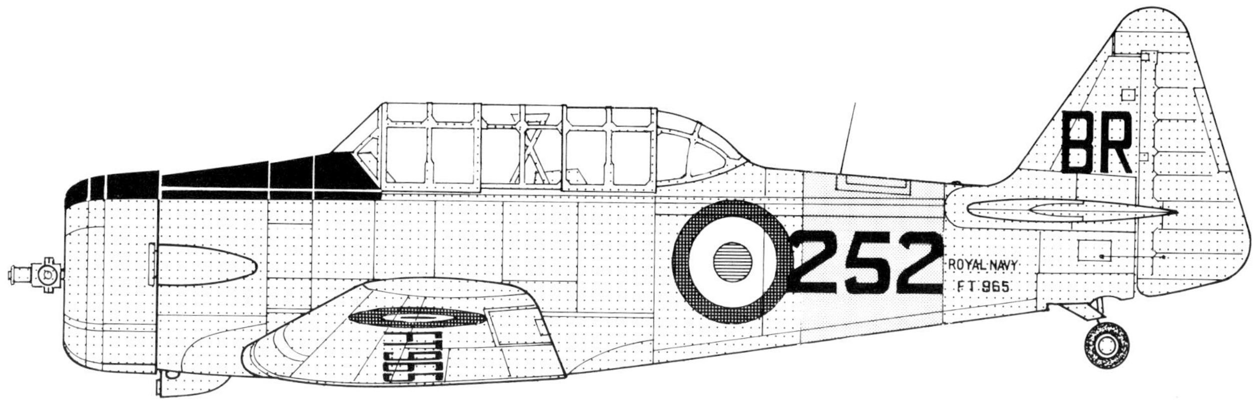

Shown in the postwar silver colour scheme with yellow 'trainer' bands is the Fleet Air Arm's Harvard Mk.III FT965 of 1833 Squadron at Bramcote, 1949.

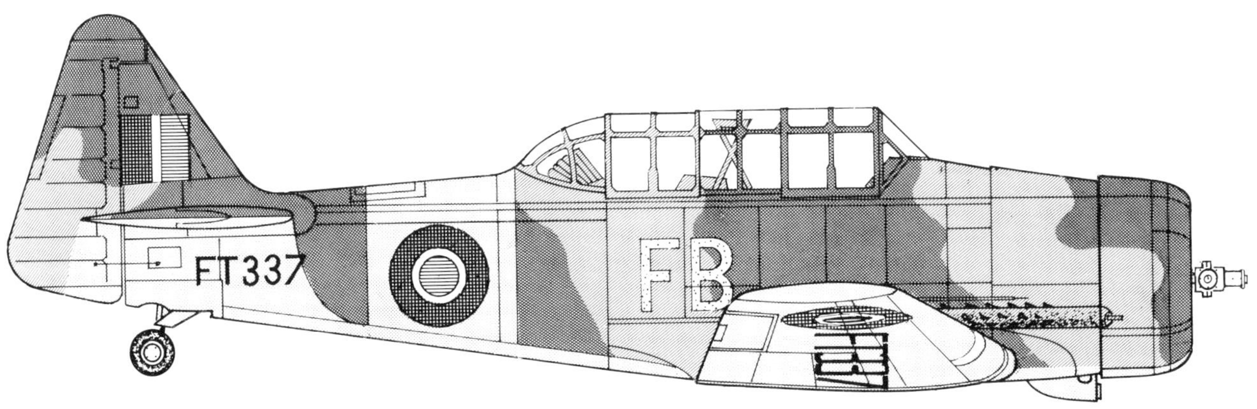

During the late wartime and early postwar period many UK-based Harvards Mk.IIb at Flying Training Schools were camouflaged. FT337 coded FB of 19 FTS, Cranwell, was typical.

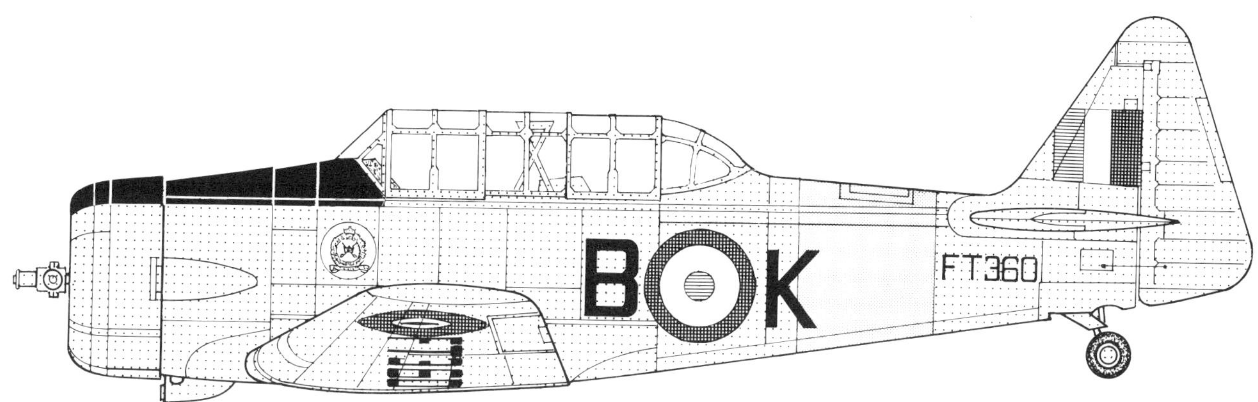

Typical of the Harvard Mk.IIb in use at postwar Flying Training Schools was FT360 of HQ Flight, 1 FTS, Moreton-in-Marsh. Code letters at this FTS were always read from the tailplane forward, so FT360 was K:B. Finish was all-silver with yellow bands and the unit badge on the cowling.

SCHEDULE OF ORIGINAL DELIVERIES

Mk.I

United Kingdom (332 aircraft)

N7000-N7019	12.38- 2.39
N7021-N7199	2.39- 8.39
P5783-P5915	8.39- 7.40

South Africa (3 aircraft)

P5921	12.40
P5928	12.40
P5931	2.40

Southern Rhodesia (64 aircraft)

P5916-P5920	3.40
P5922-P5927	3.40
P5929,P5930	3.40
P5932-P5982	3.40

Retained in USA (1 aircraft)

N7020

Mk.II

United Kingdom (14 aircraft)

BD130-BD137	10.40
BJ410	10.40
BJ412-BJ415	10.40
BS808	

Canada (30 (305 aircraft)

AH185-AH204	10.40-11.40
AJ538-AJ597	7.41- 8.41
AJ643-AJ662	8.41- 9.41
AJ683-AJ702	8.41
AJ723-AJ737	9.41-10.41
AJ753-AJ767	9.41-10.41
AJ788-AJ802	10.41-12.41
AJ823-AJ836	10.41-11.41
AJ847-AJ854	11.41
AJ893-AJ910	11.41-12.41
AJ912-AJ987	11.41- 3.42
BW184-BW203	5.41
BW204-BW207	5.42- 7.42

Crashed in USA (1 aircraft)

AJ911

No trace (1 aircraft)

BJ411

Southern Rhodesia (103 aircraft)

AJ598-AJ642	8.41-
AJ663-AJ682	
AJ703-AJ722	
AJ738-AJ752	
DG430,DG431	11.40
DG434	11.40

Middle East (47 aircraft)

AJ768-AJ782	10.41-
AJ787	
AJ803-AJ822	
AJ837-AJ846	
DG433	

India (4 aircraft)

AJ783-AJ786

New Zealand (38 aircraft)

AJ855-AJ892

Lost at sea (6 aircraft)

DG432
DG435-DG439

Mk.IIa

Southern Rhodesia (149 aircraft)

EX149	
EX157-EX168	1.43- 4.43
EX172	
EX174,EX175	3.43
EX197	3.43
EX241-EX246	1.43- 3.43
EX357-EX359	3.43
EX373-EX379	3.43
EX383-EX389	1.43- 3.43
EX401-EX406	4.43
EX409-EX416	4.43- 5.43
EX418-EX420	4.43- 5.43
EX430	6.43
EX435-EX437	4.43- 5.43
EX490-EX493	5.43
EX510-EX538	4.43- 6.43
EX649-EX658	8.43-12.43
EX669-EX678	8.43-11.43
EX682	9.43
EX684	9.43
EX690,EX691	9.43
EX696-EX700	9.43
EX707	9.43
EX753,EX754	9.43
EX763-EX766	9.43- 1.44
EX768	9.43
EX771	11.43
EX773	11.43
EX777,EX778	9.43
EX780	10.43
EX784-EX786	9.43-11.43
EX788	9.43
EX806	11.43
EX810	11.43
EX812	11.43
EX818	11.43
EX822	11.43
EX824	11.43
EX830	1.44
EX832,EX833	12.43
EX842	1.44
EX845	12.43

Middle East (100 aircraft)

EX100-EX113	10.42?
EX115,EX116	
EX118-EX148	10.42-12.42
EX150-EX156	11.42
EX212	12.42
EX321-EX325	12.42- 7.43
EX369,EX370	7.43
EX689	2.44
EX703	1.44
EX708-EX712	1.44- 2.44
EX714	1.44
EX719-EX728	1.44- 6.44
EX752	2.44
EX756	2.44
EX758,EX759	2.44
EX761,EX762	2.44
EX767	2.44
EX797	2.44
EX800,EX801	2.44
EX807	1.44
EX814	2.44
EX834	1.44
EX839	1.44
EX840	2.44
EX843	2.44
EX844	2.44
EX846	1.44

Ceylon for RN(2 aircraft)

EX641
EX702

South Africa for RN (1 aircraft)

EX683	6.43

India for RN (shipped via Mombassa : 3 aircraft)

EX598
EX609
EX620

The apron at 34 SFTS, Medicine Hat, Alberta, showing a small part of this unit's Harvard fleet (J.R.Walkden)

South Africa (436 aircraft)

EX114	10.42-
EX117	10.42
EX169-EX171	10.42
EX173	10.42
EX176-EX183	10.42
EX196	10.42
EX198-EX211	10.42
EX213-EX240	10.42
EX247-EX320	10.42- 2.43
EX330-EX356	10.42
EX360-EX368	2.43
EX371,EX372	2.43
EX380-EX382	2.43
EX390-EX400	2.43
EX407,EX408	3.43
EX417	3.43
EX429	3.43
EX431-EX434	5.43
EX438-EX489	3.43
EX494-EX497	3.43
EX499	1.43
EX502-EX509	1.43
EX539-EX584	4.43
EX593-EX597	6.43- 8.43
EX599-EX608	6.43- 8.43
EX610-EX619	6.43- 8.43
EX621-EX640	6.43- 8.43
EX642-EX648	6.43- 8.43
EX659-EX668	6.43- 8.43
EX679-EX681	8.43
EX685-EX688	6.43- 8.43
EX692-EX695	6.43- 8.43
EX701	6.43
EX704-EX706	6.43
EX713	6.43
EX715-EX718	6.43
EX729-EX740	6.43- 8.43
EX749-EX751	8.43
EX755	8.43
EX757	8.43
EX760	8.43
EX769,EX770	8.43
EX772	8.43
EX774-EX776	8.43
EX779	
EX781,EX782	
EX787	
EX798,EX799	
EX802-EX805	
EX808,EX809	12.43
EX811	12.43
EX813	12.43
EX815-EX817	12.43
EX819-EX821	12.43
EX823	
EX829	12.43
EX831	12.43
EX835-EX838	12.43
EX841	

New Zealand (53 aircraft)

EX184-EX195	9.42
EX326-EX329	12.42
EX421-EX428	2.43- 3.43
EX585-EX592	5.43
EX741-EX748	8.43
EX783	12.43
EX789-EX796	8.43
EX825-EX828	9.43

West Africa (3 aircraft)

EX498	3.43
EX500,EX501	3.43

14A Harvard Mk.I P5827 of 22 SFTS coded '69'

14B Three Harvards Mk.IIa of 20 SFTS in formation

Mk.III

South Africa (197 aircraft)

EX847	
EX850	12.43
EX855	12.43
EX857,EX858	12.43
EX864	2.44
EX869	12.43
EX871-EX876	12.43
EX878-EX887	
EX889,EX890	12.43
EX892-EX895	12.43
EX898-EX904	12.43
EX909-EX912	12.43
EX914-EX925	12.43- 1.44
EX927	1.44
EX929	12.43
EX931,EX932	12.43- 1.44
EX934,EX935	1.44
EX937	1.44
EX939,EX940	1.44
EX945-EX948	1.44- 2.44
EX950	1.44
EX952-EX955	1.44
EX959,EX960	1.44
EX963,EX964	1.44- 2.44
EX967	2.44
EX969,EX970	1.44
EX972-EX975	2.44
EX977-EX981	2.44
EX985-EX991	2.44
EX993,EX994	2.44
EZ118,EZ119	
EZ123	
EZ131,EZ132	
EZ134-EZ138	3.44
EZ142-EZ147	
EZ149,EZ150	
EZ152	
EZ154,EZ155	
EZ158,EZ159	
EZ161-EZ166	
EZ168,EZ169	
EZ171-EZ176	
EZ178-EZ187	5.44
EZ189	
EZ191-EZ201	5.44- 7.44
EZ203	5.44
EZ205-EZ207	5.44- 7.44
EZ209-EZ211	7.44- 8.44
EZ213 EZ217	
EZ219-EZ221	5.44
EZ224	
EZ226	
EZ229-EZ232	
EZ235-EZ237	5.44- 7.44
EZ240	5.44
EZ247	5.44
EZ251	
EZ254	8.44
EZ256	4.44
EZ259	
EZ289	
EZ292	8.44
EZ294	
EZ307	8.44
EZ309,EZ310	8.44
EZ314,EZ315	8.44
EZ321	8.44
EZ335,EZ336	
EZ338,EZ339	8.44

Crashed in USA (1 aircraft)

EZ223

Retained in USA (1 aircraft)

EZ358

Middle East (81 aircraft)

EX848,EX849	2.44
EX851	2.44
EX856	
EX860	1.44
EX863	
EX888	2.44
EX926	1.44
EX928	2.44
EX930	1.44
EX933	1.44
EX936	1.44
EX938	1.44
EX949	
EX971	3.44
EX982	3.44
EZ100-EZ102	2.44
EZ104-EZ109	2.44
EZ111-EZ115	2.44
EZ117	3.44
EZ120,EZ121	3.44
EZ140,EZ141	3.44
EZ148	
EZ151	3.44
EZ156,EZ157	3.44
EZ160	
EZ170	3.44
EZ202	6.44
EZ249	7.44
EZ263	7.44
EZ313	6.44
EZ319	6.44
EZ322	6.44
EZ325,EZ326	6.44
EZ334	6.44
EZ337	7.44
EZ340	8.44
EZ344	6.44
EZ346	6.44
EZ349	7.44
EZ352-EZ357	6.44- 8.44
EZ384	8.44
EZ387	8.44
EZ389	8.44
EZ392-EZ395	8.44
EZ397,EZ398	8.44
EZ426	
EZ429	
EZ434	
EZ437	
EZ441	9.44
EZ444-EZ446	
EZ450	
EZ452	8.44
EZ454	

New Zealand (41 aircraft)

EX865-EX868	11.43
EX905-EX908	1.44
EX941-EX944	12.43
EX997-EX999	
EZ177	
EZ242-EZ246	.44
EZ297-EZ301	8.44
EZ329-EZ333	8.44
EZ359-EZ363	7.44
EZ439	11.44
EZ449	11.44
EZ453	11.44
EZ455,EZ456	11.44

United Kingdom for RAF (2 aircraft)

FT955
FT958

No trace (1 aircraft)

EZ139

Mk.IIb

Southern Rhodesia (70 aircraft)

EX852-EX854	12.43- 1.44
EX859	1.44
EX861	12.43
EX862	12.43
EX870	12.43
EX877	12.43
EX891	11.43
EX896,EX897	12.43
EX951	2.44
EX956-EX958	1.44- 2.44
EX961,EX962	1.44- 2.44
EX965,EX966	1.44- 2.44
EX968	2.44
EX983,EX984	2.44
EX992	2.44
EX995,EX996	2.44- 4.44
EZ103	2.44
EZ110	5.44
EZ116	5.44
EZ122	5.44
EZ124-EZ130	3.44- 5.44
EZ133	3.44
EZ153	7.44
EZ188	
EZ190	
EZ204	
EZ208	
EZ212	
EZ218	7.44
EZ222	7.44
EZ225	
EZ227,EZ228	
EZ233,EZ234	7.44
EZ238,EZ239	7.44
EZ241	
EZ248	5.44
EZ255	
EZ258	
EZ264	
EZ270	
EZ276	
EZ280	
EZ286,EZ287	
EZ290	
EZ293	
EZ296	
EZ302	
EZ304-EZ306	
EZ308	

India for RN (3 aircraft)

EX913
EX976
EZ432

United Kingdom for RN (133 aircraft)

EZ167
EZ250
EZ252,EZ253
EZ257
EZ260-EZ262
EZ265-EZ269
EZ271-EZ275
EZ277-EZ279
EZ281-EZ285
EZ288
EZ291
EZ295
EZ303
EZ311,EZ312
EZ316-EZ318
EZ320
EZ323,EZ324
EZ327,EZ328
EZ341-EZ343
EZ345
EZ347,EZ348
EZ350,EZ351
EZ364-EZ383
EZ385,EZ386
EZ388
EZ390,EZ391
EZ396
EZ399-EZ425
EZ428
EZ430,EZ431
EZ433
EZ435,EZ436
EZ438
EZ440
EZ442,EZ443
EZ447,EZ448
EZ451
EZ457,EZ458
FT956,FT957
FT959-FT963
FT965-FT974

Malta for RN (1 aircraft)

EZ427

Gibraltar for RN (1 aircraft)

FT964

United States of America for RN (5 aircraft)

KE305-KE309

The complete serial number is not visible in this shot of a Harvard Mk.IIb coded L5 after a belly landing (D.J.Smith)

United Kingdom (1284 aircraft)

FE787,FE788	4.43
FE888	
FH107-FH109	
FH111,FH112	
FH114,FH115	
FS716-FS778	9.43
FS813-FS838	9.43
FS840-FS856	9.43
FS879-FS922	9,43
FT133-FT178	11.43
FT207-FT264	1.44
FT302-FT369	12.43- 3.44
FT375-FT395	3.44- 4.44
FT397-FT460	2.44- 3.44
FX198-FX241	3.44- 4.44
FX243-FX382	3.44- 5.44
FX384-FX400	
FX402-FX404	
FX406-FX444	4.44- 6.44
FX446	
FX450	
FX452,FX453	
FX459	
FX466-FX470	
KF127,KF128	5.44
KF130	5.44
KF133	5.44
KF136	5.44
KF138	5.44
KF140	5.44
KF142	5.44
KF145-KF221	5.44- 6.44
KF223-KF235	5.44- 7.44
KF237-KF402	6.44- 8.44
KF404-KF406	
KF408-KF492	8.44-
KF496-KF498	
KF529	
KF538,KF539	
KF541	
KF547	
KF560-KF757	
KF901,KF902	1.45
KF905-KF907	
KF910,KF911	
KF919,KF920	2.45
KF922	
KF924,KF925	
KF937	
KF943,KF944	3.45
KF947-KF950	
KF953-KF955	
KF958-KF960	
KF962-KF964	
KF966,KF967	
KF972	
KF974	
KF976-KF999	4.45?

United Kingdom for RN (39 aircraft)

KF493
KF495
KF500-KF503
KF505-KF508
KF510,KF511
KF513-KF518
KF520-KF525
KF527,KF528
KF532,KF533
KF535
KF537
KF540
KF543
KF551
KF554-KF559

Canada (639 aircraft)

FE268-FE352	5.42- 7.42
FE383-FE412	8.42
FE433-FE467	9.42
FE498-FE527	10.42
FE553-FE592	11.42
FE618-FE662	11.42-12.42
FE688-FE695	12.42
FE721-FE765	1.43
FE790-FE877	2.43
FE902-FE951	3.43
FE976-FE999	4.43
FH100-FH106	4.43
FH117-FH166	4.43
FS661-FS681	6.43
FS857-FS878	7.43
FS957-FS978	9.43
FT265-FT301	11.43-12.43

Middle East (43 aircraft)

KF222	
KF903,KF904	1.45
KF908	1.45
KF912	1.45
KF913	3.45
KF914-KF918	1.45
KF921	2.45
KF923	1.45
KF926-KF934*	3.45
KF935,KF936	3.45
KF938-KF942	3.45
KF945,KF946	
KF951,KF952	
KF956	
KF957*	
KF961*	
KF965*	
KF968-KF971*	
KF973*	
KF975*	

Note: aircraft sent to the Middle East, except for KF222, equipped for target-towing as Mk.TT. IIb. Those marked with * were shipped via Karachi.

India & Ceylon (507 aircraft)

FE353-FE363	2.43
FE365-FE374	2.43
FE377-FE382	
FE413-FE416	2.43
FE420	2.43
FE422-FE432	2.43
FE468-FE485	2.43- 3.43
FE487-FE492	4.43
FE494-FE496	
FE528	2.43
FE533-FE535	2.43
FE538-FE540	2.43
FE542-FE552	2.43- 5.43
FE593-FE617	4.43- 7.43
FE663-FE687	5.43- 7.43
FE696-FE720	5.43- 8.43
FE766-FE786	8.43
FE789	8.43
FE878-FE887	8.43
FE889-FE901	8.43
FE952-FE975	8.43
FH110	
FH113	
FH116	
FS682-FS715	10.43
FS779-FS812	10.43- 1.44
FS923-FS956	1.44
FS979-FS999	10.43-12.43
FT100-FT132	12.43
FT179-FT206	12.43- 1.44
FT370-FT374	6.44- 7.44

FX242	7.44
FX383	7.44
FX401	7.44
FX445	7.44
FX447-FX449	7.44
FX451	7.44
FX454-458	7.44
FX460-FX465	7.44
FX471-FX497	7.44- 8.44
KF100-KF126	7.44
KF129	7.44
KF131,KF132	7.44
KF134,KF135	7.44
KF137	7.44
KF139	7.44
KF141	7.44
KF143,KF144	7.44

Lost at sea in transit to India and Ceylon (17 aircraft)

FE364
FE375,FE376
FE417-FE419
FE421
FE486
FE493
FE497
FE529-FE532
FE536,KF537
FE541

Far East for RN (2 aircraft)

KF526
KF536

South Africa for RN (1 aircraft)

KF512

Australia for RN (4 aircraft)

KF519
KF530,KF531
KF553

New Zealand (2 aircraft)

KF403	11.44
KF407	11.44

Unknown area for RN (1 aircraft)

KF546

Crashed in USA (4 aircraft)

FT396
FX405
KF236
KF909

India & Ceylon for RN (12 aircraft)

KF494
KF499
KF504
KF509
KF534
KF542
KF544,KF545
KF548-KF550
KF552

No trace (2 aircraft)

FE267
FS839

N7001 of the Aeroplane and Armament Experimental Establishment in all-yellow finish *(via J.J.Halley)*

OPERATING UNITS

In considering the multitude of RAF and RN flying units which used the Harvard, it has been possible to piece together a reasonably comprehensive list of of UK-based units with details of bases, dates, numbers of Harvards on strength and codes carried. This has not always been possible, however, in respect of overseas units, due largely to the lack of surviving official records. While units in Southern Rhodesia and the Far East are fairly well recorded, only an incomplete picture of Harvard users in the India/Ceylon area and in the Middle East can be provided. Known information concerning these two theatres of operation is therefore given in condensed form.

Research into Harvards used in Canada is complicated by the fact that RAF-serialled aircraft were distributed among both RAF-administered units and those of the RCAF. In general, RAF SFTSs in Canada were numbered 31 SFTS and above, and in these units RAF-serialled aircraft predominated, supplemented by RCAF machines. SFTSs numbered below 20 were RCAF units, which used a large percentage of RCAF Harvards with a few RAF-serialled examples to complete their establishments. In view of this, and as no differentiation is made in official records, the number of aircraft shown in the 'Quantity' column of the appropriate table relates to the number of RAF and RCAF aircraft combined. When the RAF left Canada in the autumn of 1944 the complete inventories of each SFTS were taken over by the RCAF, who continued to use the ex-RAF Harvards without renumbering. Aircraft surviving at that time are shown as 'To RCAF' and thus pass out of the scope of this book, other than those examples which eventually found their way to certain European air forces.

R.A.F. in the United Kingdom

UNIT	BASES	MK.	DATES USED	CODES	QTY.	REMARKS
1 FTS/1 SFTS	Netheravon	I	4.39-12.40		52	Alteration in title 9.39
1 FTS	Spitalgate	IIb	6.47- 2.48	FCD to FCF + indiv. ltr.		Re-formed from 17 SFTS
	Oakington	"	11.50-10.51	FCA, FCB + indiv. letter	68	
	Moreton-in-Marsh	"	10.51- 3.55	K, N, O and P + ind. ltr.	40	
2 FTS/2 SFTS	Brize Norton	I	3.39-12.40		46	Alteration intitle 9.39
2 FTS	Chipping Norton	IIb	4.45- 3.46		34	
	Church Lawford	"	7.47- 4.48	FAI to FAK + indiv. ltr.	14	Re-formed from 20 SFTS
	South Cerney	"	4.48- 6.51		36	Merged into CFS(Basic)
	Cluntoe	"	3.53- 6.54	N and P + indiv. letter	27	
3 SFTS	South Cerney	IIb	12.45- 4.46		54	Re-formed from 3(P)AFU
3 SFTS/3 FTS	Feltwell	"	4.46- 4.55	FBP, FBR to FBU + ind.ltr later O, P and R + ind.	44	Alteration in title 4.47
5 FTS	Ternhill	I	1.41- 3.41		1	
6 FTS/6 SFTS	Little Rissington	I	5.39- 8.41		45	Alteration in title 9.39
6 SFTS/6 FTS	"	IIb	12.45- 5.46	FBG to FBJ + indiv. ltr.	55	Re-formed from 6(P)AFU
	Ternhill	"	5.46-12.53	O and P + indiv. letter	42	Alteration in title 5.47
7 SFTS	Peterborough (Westwood)	IIb	3.45- 4.46		40	
7 SFTS/7 FTS	Kirton-in-Lindsey	"	4.46- 4.48	FBA to FBD + indiv. ltr.	60	Alteration in title 1.48
	Cottesmore	"	4.48- 3.54	N, O and P + indiv. ltr.	46	
9 FTS	Wellesbourne Mountford	IIb	6.53- 3.54	M + individual letter	24	
10 FTS/10 FTS	Ternhill	I	3.39-10.40		45	
11 SFTS	Shawbury	I	10.39-12.39		1	
12 FTS	Grantham (Spitalgate)	I	1.39-10.39		14	
14 FTS/14 SFTS	Kinloss	I	7.39- 4.40		41	
14 SFTS	Cranfield	"	4.40-12.40		43	
15 SFTS	Lossiemouth	I	9.39- 4.40		42	
	Middle Wallop	"	4.40- 5.40		36	
	Brize Norton	"	5.40- 8.40		30	Instrument Training Squadron
	South Cerney	"	6.40-10.40		50	Advanced Training Squadron
	Kidlington	"	8.40-			
16 SFTS	Newton	IIb	8.44-11.45	Numerals	77	
17 SFTS	Cranwell	IIb	7.44- 5.45		50	Formerly RAF College
	Grantham (Spitalgate)	"	5.45- 6.47	FCD to FCF + indiv. ltr.	44	Became 1 FTS
19 FTS	Cranwell	IIb	5.45- 4.47	A to H + indiv. letter later FAA to FAF + ind.	102	Became RAF College
20 FTS/20SFTS	Church Lawford	IIb	4.45- 7.47	FAI to FAK + indiv. ltr.	46	Alteration in title 9.46; became 2 FTS
21 FTS	Snitterfield	IIb	5.45- 9.46	FAN, FAP + indiv. letter	52	
22 SFTS	Calveley	IIb	11.45- 5.46	FCI to FCK + indiv. ltr.	27	
	Ouston	"	5.46- 2.48	"	34	
22 SFTS/22 FTS	Syerston	"	2.48- 9.54	" later R, U and Y + ind. letter	52	Alteration in title 2.49
3(P)AFU	South Cerney	IIb	11.45-12.45	Numerals	15	Became 3 FTS
5(P)AFU	Ternhill	IIb	9.44- 5.46	B, E and H + indiv. ltr.	155	Absorbed into 7 SFTS
6(P)AFU	Little Rissington	IIb	10.45-12.45	Letter/number	12	Became 6 SFTS
7(P)AFU	Kirton-in-Lindsey	IIb	10.44-12.44	Numerals	3	

9(P)AFU	Errol	IIb	9.44- 6.45	Numerals	104	
11(P)AFU	Calveley	IIb	12.44- 6.45	Letter/number	62	
21(P)AFU	Moreton-in-Marsh	IIb	12.46- 7.47	FDA, FDC and FDD + individual letter	16	Disbanded to form 1(P)RFU and 2(P)RFU
8 EFTS	Woodley	I	1.40-10.40		2	
18 EFTS	Fairoaks	IIb	7.44- 1.46		1	For use of King Peter of Yugoslavia
ATA	White Waltham/Thame	I	1.41- 3.46	Numerals		
		IIb	10.43- 4.46		18	Initial FTS for ATA pilots
RAFC	Cranwell	IIb	4.47- 6.54	FAA to FAF + indiv. ltr; later A to C + ind. ltr.		
5 RFS	Castle Bromwich	IIb	7.50-10.50		2	
		"	11.52- 5.53		1	
8 RFS	Woodley	IIb	6.50-10.50		1	
11 RFS	Perth	IIb	6.47-12.47		2	
		"	6.50-11.50		12	
		"	11.52- 6.53		4	
		"	4.54- 5.54		1	
14 RFS	Hamble	IIb	11.52- 4.53		1	
16 RFS	Derby (Burnaston)	IIb	7.50-10.50		2	
		"	11.52- 5.53		1	
18 RFS	Fairoaks	IIb	7.50- 8.50		3	
19 RFS	Hooton Park	IIb	7.50- 8.50		1	
		"	5.53- 5.54		2	
22 RFS	Cambridge (Teversham)	IIb	6.47-11.47		2	
		"	6.49-10.49		6	
		"	6.50- 7.50		8	
		"	11.52- 3.54		6	
23 RFS	Usworth	IIb	8.50-10.50		1	
		"	11.52- 5.53		1	
25 RFS	Wolverhampton	IIb	6.50- 8.50		2	
		"	11.52- 2.53		1	
Aberdeen UAS	Dyce	IIb	5.52-11.52		2	
		"	10.55- 5.57		3	
Birmingham UAS	Castle Bromwich	IIb	5.52-11.52		1	
		"	9.55-10.55		1	
		"	2.56- 4.57		2	
Bristol UAS	Filton	IIb	4.53- 4.57		2	
Cambridge UAS	Cambridge (Teversham)	IIb	4.52-11.52		5	
		"	3.54- 4.57		5	
Durham UAS	Usworth	IIb	5.52-11.52		1	
		"	12.55- 5.57		2	
Edinburgh UAS	Turnhouse	IIb	6.52-11.52		1	
		"	5.54- 5.57		2	
Glasgow UAS	Perth	IIb	5.52-11.52		1	
		"	9.55- 5.57		4	
Hull UAS	Brough	IIb	1.56- 5.57		1	
Leeds UAS	Sherburn-in-Elmet	IIb	5.52-11.52		1	
	Yeadon	"	2.56-10.57		2	
Liverpool UAS	Woodvale	IIb	5.54- 4.57		2	
London UAS		IIb	6.47- 6.47		2	
	Booker	"	6.50- ?		1	
		"	11.55-10.56		2	
Manchester UAS	Woodvale	IIb	5.54- 4.57		2	
Nottingham UAS	Newton	IIb	10.52-11.52		1	
		"	3.54- 5.57		4	
Oxford UAS	Abingdon	IIb	6.47-11.47	RUO + individual letter	1	
	Kidlington	"	6.50-10.50		1	
	"	"	6.52- 5.57		3	
Queens UAS	Sydenham	IIb	5.52- 2.56		3	
St. Andrew's UAS	Leuchars	IIb	5.52-11.52		1	
	Crail	"	10.55- 4.57		1	
Southampton UAS	Hamble	IIb	6.52-11.52		1	
	"	"	9.55- 5.57		1	
1 AAS	Manby	I			1	Became EAAS
203 AFS	Keevil	IIb	7.47-10.47	TO + individual letter	7	Formerly 61 OTU
	Chivenor	"	10.47- 7.49	"		
	Stradishall	"	7.49-10.49	"	12	Became 226 OCU

207 AFS	Full Sutton	IIb	11.51- 5.52	M + numeral	4	Formerly 103 FRS
11 AGS	Jurby	IIb	6.47-11.47		2	
APS	Acklington	IIb	11.47- 2.51			
BAS	Watchfield	IIb	6.45- 2.47	FDW + individual letter	8	Disbanded into CFS
CFE	West Raynham	IIb	9.47- 5.49		1	
CFS	Upavon	I	1.39- 6.41		12	
	Little Rissington	IIb	5.46-10.54	FDM to FDO and FDW + ind. ltr; later M and N + individual letter	40	
CFS(B)	South Cerney	IIb	8.51-11.54	O + individual letter	24	
CFS(EW)	Brize Norton	IIb	7.49- 4.50		22	
CGS	Sutton Bridge	I	8.42- 9.42		1	
	Leconfield	IIb	8.46-11.46	FJU and FJX + ind.ltr.	1	
	"	"	6.47- 8.48		1	
	"	"	1.50- 2.51		1	
EAAS	Manby	IIb	10.47- 8.49	FGC + individual letter	16	Became RAFFC
EANS	Shawbury	IIb	1.48- 3.48		1	
ECFS	Hullavington	II			1	
	"	IIb	1.44- 5.46	Single letter; later FCT + individual letter	16	Became EFS
		III	9.44- 7.45			
EFS	Hullavington	IIb	5.46- 9.49	FCT + individual letter	16	Formerly ECFS
ETPS	Farnborough	IIb	- 9.51	Numerals		
1 E&WS	Cranwell	I	11.39-12.41		1	Became 1 SS
FCITF	Tangmere	IIb	8.48- 5.49			
2 FIS	Montrose	IIb	5.44- 7.45		40	
3 FIS	Lulsgate Bottom	IIb	7.44- 8.45		8	
7 FIS	Upavon	IIb	5.45- 5.46		50	
	Little Rissington	"	5.46- 5.46		50	Merged into CFS
FRS	Finningley	IIb	6.49- 4.51		28	Formerly 1(P)RFU; to 101 FRS
101 FRS	Finningley	IIb	4.51-11.51		28	Formerly FRS
102 FRS	North Luffenham	IIb	5.51-12.51		4	
103 FRS	Full Sutton	IIb	5.51-11.51	M + numeral	4	Became 207 AFS
FTU	Abingdon	IIb	9.52- 4.53			Absorbed 1689 Flt
	Benson	"	4.53-11.53			
11 Group Pool	Sutton Bridge	I	9.39- 3.40		1	Became 6 OTU
12 Group Pool	Aston Down	I	10.39- 3.40		6	Became 5 OTU
HCEU	White Waltham	IIb	2.52- 5.57			
HCITF	Honiley	IIb				Formerly RCITF
226 OCU	Bentwaters	IIb	10.48-10.49	TO + individual letter		To Driffield to become 'new' 203 AFS
	Stradishall	"	10.49- 9.51	"	10	Formerly 203 AFS
227 OCU	Andover	IIb	12.47- 1.48		1	Formerly 43 OTU
	Middle Wallop	"	1.48- 4.49		1	
237 OCU	Benson	IIb	7.47- 1.48	LP + numeral	2	Formerly 8 OTU
	Leuchars	"	1.48- 9.50	"	2	
	Benson	"	9.50- 7.51	"	2	
5 OTU	Aston Down	I	3.40-11.40		4	Ex 12 Gp.Pool; became 55 OTU
6 OTU	Sutton Bridge	I	3.40-11.40		6	Ex 11 Gp.Pool; became 56 OTU
8 OTU	Chalgrove	IIb	12.46- 7.47		2	Became 237 OCU
41 OTU	Old Sarum	I	10.41-11.42		11	Formerly 1 SoAC
	Hawarden	"	11.42-11.44		14	
	"	IIb	8.44- 3.45		5	
	Chilbolton	"	3.45- 5.45		2	
43 OTU	Andover	IIb	9.46- 8.47		1	Became 227 OCU
52 OTU	Debden	I	5.41- 8.41		3	
53 OTU	Heston	I	3.41- 5.41		3	
	Kirton-in-Lindsey	IIb	11.44- 2.45		1	
55 OTU	Aston Down	I	11.40- 6.41		1	Formerly 5 OTU
56 OTU	Sutton Bridge	I	11.40- 7.41		6	Formerly 6 OTU
61 OTU	Heston	I	6.41- 4.42		6	
	Rednal	IIb	10.44- 6.45	TO + individual letter	7	
	Keevil	"	6.45- 7.47	"	8	Became 203 AFS
1 P>S	Upper Heyford	IIb	1.48- 3.48		1	

PRU	Benson	I	1.41- 3.41		1	Formerly 2 Cam. Unit
RAFFC	Manby	IIb	8.49- 7.50	FGC + individual letter	3	
RCITF	White Waltham	IIb	8.48- 6.49			
	Honiley	"	6.49- 8.51			Became HCITF
1(P)RFU	Moreton-in-Marsh	IIb	8.47-12.47	FDA, FDC and FDD + individual letter	9	Formed from 21(P)AFU
	Finningley	"	12.47- 5.49	"	16	Became FRS
2(P)RFU	Valley	IIb	8.47- 4.48		14	Formed from 21(P)AFU
1 SoAC	Old Sarum	I	5.41-10.41		4	Became 41 OTU
1 SS	Cranwell	I	12.41- 1.42		1	Formerly 1 E&WS

FCCS	Northolt	IIb	10.46- 2.49		3	
1 FPP		I	4.41-10.41		3	
2 FPP		I	12.40-11.41		1	
	Filton	II	6.42- 8.42		1	
3 FPP	Hawarden	I	8.40- 3.42		3	
FTCCF	Woodley	IIb	2.45- 4.45		1	
	"	"	7.45- 3.53	FKN + individual letter	4	
	White Waltham	"	3.53- 5.54		2	
1 FU	Pershore	IIb	7.46- 8.46		1	
	"	"	11.46- 5.48		3	
12 Gp CF	Hucknall	IIb	10.46-12.46		2	
	Newton	"	12.46- 8.47		2	
	"	"	11.47- 5.49		2	
21 Gp CF	Cranwell	IIb	3.45- 3.46	FKO + individual letter	1	
23 Gp CF	South Cerney	IIb	11.45-10.46		3	
	Halton	"	10.46- 9.47	FKP + individual letter	1	
61 Gp CF	Biggin Hill	IIb	5.51- 6.51		2	
62 Gp CF	Colerne	IIb	6.49-12.49		3	
63 Gp CF	Hooton Park	IIb	7.49- 3.50		2	
64 Gp CF	Linton-on-Ouse	IIb	6.49- 1.50		5	
66 Gp CF	Turnhouse	IIb	12.47- 3.49		1	
	"	"	6.49- 3.50		5	
HCCS	White Waltham	IIb	10.53- 4.54		2	
OFU	Chivenor	IIb	9.50- 3.51		3	
	Abingdon	"	3.51- 2.53	QO + individual letter	3	Became 167 Sqdn
RCCF/RCCS	White Waltham	IIb	6.47- 8.52	RCA + individual letter	5	
SFPP HQ		I	3.41- 5.42		6	
SF Sqdn	Kemble	I	7.41- 6.42		1	
Station Flight	Biggin Hill	IIb	-11.47		1	
"	Church Fenton	IIb	10.46- 5.47		1	
"	Coltishall	I	6.40- 9.42		1	
"	Cranwell	I	5.39-11.39		1	
"	Croughton	II	7.45-10.45		1	
"	Duxford	IIb	10.46-12.47		2	
"	Elmdon	I	11.40- 1.41		1	
"	Feltwell	IIb	4.48-11.49		2	
"	Halton	I	3.42- 8.42		1	
	"	II	7.42- 8.42		1	
	"	IIb	9.47- 1.49		2	
"	Horsham St. Faith	IIb	5.47- 5.50		3	
"	Manston	IIb	4.48- 2.49		2	
	"	"	8.49- 9.50		3	
"	Middle Wallop	IIb	10.46- 8.47		1	
	"	"	10.47- 2.48		1	
"	Northolt	IIb	4.45- 9.46		1	
"	Odiham	IIb	10.46- 6.51	EC	2	
"	Spitalgate	I	4.39-10.39		1	
"	Stoke Orchard	I	10.40-11.40		1	
"	Ternhill	I	4.39- 1.40		3	
"	Thorney Island	IIb	2.48- 5.48		1	

"	Turnhouse	I	6.40- 2.41		1	
"	Watchfield	II	10.40- 2.41		4	
"	Wattisham	IIa	12.47- 7.48		1	
	"	IIb	12.46- 5.47		1	
	"	III	12.47- 7.48		1	
"	Wittering	IIb	2.48-11.48		3	
"	Yatesbury	I	10.40- 2.41		5	
	"	II	11.40-12.40		2	
1689 Flt	Aston Down	IIb	9.45- 4.53	9X + individual letter		
1 Sqdn	Tangmere	IIb	8.47- 8.48	JX + individual letter	9	
5 Sqdn	Chivenor	IIb	2.49- 3.51	7B + individual letter	1	Formerly 595 Sqdn
17 Sqdn	Chivenor	IIb	2.49- 4.51	UT + individual letter		Formerly 691 Sqdn
19 Sqdn	Molesworth	IIb	5.46- 6.46		1	
	Wittering	"	6.46- 9.46		1	
20 Sqdn	Llanbedr	IIb	2.49- 7.49	TH + individual letter	1	
	Valley	"	7.49-10.51		3	
26 Sqdn	Gatwick	I	3.41-12.41		1	
34 Sqdn	Horsham St. Faith	IIb	2.49- 6.52	8Q + individual letter	2	Formerly 695 Sqdn
41 Sqdn	Church Fenton	IIb	8.47- 9.48		9	
46 Sqdn	Digby	I	2.41- 2.41		1	
	Church Fenton	"	2.41- 3.41		1	
	Sherburn-in-Elmet	"	3.41- 5.41		1	
54 Sqdn	Chilbolton	IIb	4.46- 6.46		1	
	Odiham	"	6.46-10.46		1	Detached to Molesworth 9.46
65 Sqdn	Horsham St. Faith	IIb	.46	YT + individual letter		
66 Sqdn	Duxford	IIb	10.46- 8.47		1	
91 Sqdn	Duxford	IIb	3.46-10.46		1	
122 Sqdn	Dalcross	IIb	3.46-10.46		1	
129 Sqdn	Hutton Cranswick	IIb	4.46- 5.46		1	
	Church Fenton	"	6.46-10.46		1	
130 Sqdn	Manston	IIb	3.46- 6.46		1	
	Acklington	"	6.46- 7.46		1	
	Odiham	"	7.46-10.46		1	
141 Sqdn	Grangemouth	I	4.40- 6.40		1	
152 Sqdn	North Weald	I	10.39- 2.40		1	
164 Sqdn	Tangmere	IIb	4.46- 5.46		1	
	Middle Wallop	"	5.46-10.46		1	
165 Sqdn	Duxford	IIb	4.46-10.46		1	
167 Sqdn	Abingdon	IIb	2.53-11.53	QO + individual letter	2	Formerly OFU
242 Sqdn	Church Fenton	I	11.39-11.39		1	
	"	"	2.40- 4.40		1	
247 Sqdn	Chilbolton	IIb	4.46- 6.46		1	
	Odiham	"	6.46-10.46		1	
303 Sqdn	Hethel	IIb	4.46- 8.47		1	
306 Sqdn	Coltishall	IIb	4.46- 5.46		1	
309 Sqdn	Coltishall	IIb	4.46- 8.46		1	
315 Sqdn	Coltishall	IIb	4.46- 5.47		1	
500 Sqdn	West Malling	IIb	4.48-10.53	RAA (later S7) + ind.ltr.	1	
501 Sqdn	Filton	IIb	8.46-11.53	RAB (later SD) + ind.ltr.	3	
502 Sqdn	Aldergrove	IIb	7.48- 7.54	RAC (later V9) + ind.ltr.	4	
504 Sqdn	Wymeswold	IIb	5.48- 9.53	RAD (later TM) + ind.ltr.	3	
541 Sqdn	Benson	IIb	12.47- 3.51	WY + individual letter	3	
587 Sqdn	Weston Zoyland	I	10.44- 6.45	M4 + individual letter	2	
	"	IIb	2.45- 6.46	"	4	
	Tangmere	"	6.46- 6.46	"	4	Disbanded into 691 Sqdn
595 Sqdn	Fairwood Common	IIb	9.46-10.46		2	
	Pembrey	"	10.46-10.47		2	Became 5 Sqdn
600 Sqdn	Biggin Hill	IIb	8.46- 8.53	RAG + individual letter	3	
601 Sqdn	Hendon	IIb	7.46- 3.49	RAH + individual letter	3	
	North Weald	"	3.49- 9.53	HT + individual letter	3	
602 Sqdn	Drem	I	10.39- 6.40		1	
	Abbotsinch/Renfrew	IIb	8.46-10.53	RAI (later LO) + ind.ltr.	4	
603 Sqdn	Prestwick	I	12.39- 6.40		1	
	Turnhouse	IIb	8.46-10.53	RAJ + individual letter		

604 Sqdn	Hendon	IIb	7.46- 3.49	RAK + individual letter	5	
	North Weald	"	3.49- 7.52		3	
605 Sqdn	Honiley	IIb	4.48-10.53	RAL (later NR) + ind.ltr.	3	
607 Sqdn	Ouston	IIb	8.46-10.53	RAN (later LA) + ind.ltr.	4	
608 Sqdn	Thornaby	IIb	4.48-11.53	RAO (later 6T) + ind.ltr.	3	
609 Sqdn	Drem	I	11.39- 6.40		1	
	Church Fenton	IIb	4.48-10.53	RAP (later PR) + ind.ltr.	4	
610 Sqdn	Hooton Park	IIb	8.46-10.53	RAQ (later DW) + ind.ltr.	4	
	Hooton Park	IIb	10.46- 7.51	RAR (later FY) + ind.ltr.	3	
	Woodvale	"	7.51-10.53		3	
612 Sqdn	Dyce	IIb	10.46-10.51	RAS + individual letter	4	
	Edzell	"	10.51-11.52	8W + individual letter	4	
	Dyce	"	11.52- 3.54		2	
613 Sqdn	Ringway	IIb	8.46-10.53	RAT (later Q3) + ind.ltr.	4	
614 Sqdn	Llandow	IIb	9.46- 7.54	RAU (later 7A) + ind.ltr.	3	
615 Sqdn	Kenley	I	6.40- 6.40		1	
	Biggin Hill	IIb	8.46- 6.53	RAV (later V6) + ind.ltr.	4	
616 Sqdn	Finningley	IIb	5.48-11.53	RAW (later YQ) + ind.ltr.	3	
631 Sqdn	Llanbedr	IIb	10.46-10.46		1	
	"	"	11.47- 2.49		1	Became 20 Sqdn
691 Sqdn	Weston Zoyland	IIb	6.46- 7.46	M4 + individual letter	3	
	Fairwood Common	"	7.46-10.46	"	3	
	Chivenor	"	10.46- 2.49	"	3	Became 17 Sqdn
695 Sqdn	Horsham St. Faith	IIb	10.46- 2.49	4M + individual letter	2	Became 34 Sqdn

A&AEE	Martlesham Heath	I	12.38- 9.39	2	
	Boscombe Down	"	9.39- 6.40	1	
	"	II	11.40-12.40	1	
	"	IIb	5.44- date	3	
	"	III			
AFEE	Sherburn-in-Elmet	II	1.43- 2.43	1	For glider-towing trials
	Beaulieu	IIb	10.48-10.50	1	
ATDU	Gosport	IIb	11.47-	1	
BLEU	Martlesham Heath	IIb	2.46- 9.47	1	
2 Cam Unit	Heston	I	1.40- 1.41	1	Became PRU
Handling Sqdn	Hullavington	IIb	10.43- 9.44	1	
	"	III	3.45-10.45	1	
RAE	Farnborough	I			
	"	IIb	12.44- 2.54	3	
TADU	Cardington	II	12.44-10.45	1	

MINOR UNITS IN GERMANY:

84 Gp. CS	Celle	IIb	5.47- 7.47	1
Station Flight	Celle	IIb	10.46- 5.47	2
2 Sqdn	Wunstorf	IIb	5.47- 6.50	3
	Buckeburg	"	6.50- 1.51	3
3 Sqdn	Wunstorf	IIb	4.47- 6.48	1
	Gutersloh	"	6.48- 8.50	1
16 Sqdn	Gutersloh	IIb	6.49- 7.50	2
26 Sqdn	Gutersloh	IIb	- 1.50	1
	Wunstorf	"	1.50- 5.50	1
33 Sqdn	Gutersloh	IIb	2.49- 8.49	2
80 Sqdn	Wunstorf	IIb	4.47- 8.48	2
	Gutersloh	"	8.48- 6.49	2
129 Sqdn	Lubeck	IIb	5.46- 6.46	1
35 Wing	Celle	IIb		
135 Wing	Fassberg	IIb		

ROYAL NAVY

Squadrons:

Squadron	Location	Mark	Dates	Codes
700 Sqdn	Yeovilton	III	8.46- 9.49	Y2 (later VL) + ind.ltr.
701 Sqdn	Heston	III	3.46- 4.46	LO + individual letter
702 Sqdn	Schofields (Australia)	IIb	9.45- 2.46	
709 Sqdn	St. Merryn	IIb	.45- 1.46	S3 + individual letter
	"	III	2.45- 6.45	"
715 Sqdn	St. Merryn	IIb	6.45-11.45	
	"	III	9.45-12.45	
718 Sqdn	Ballyhalbert	III	9.45-10.45	
	Eglinton	"	.46- 3.47	
719 Sqdn	Eglinton	IIb	4.47-11.48	
721 Sqdn	Archerfield (Australia)	III	11.45-12.45	
726 Sqdn	Stamford Hill, S. Africa	III	5.45-11.45	
727 Sqdn	Gosport	IIa	6.47- 7.47	
	"	IIb	7.47- 1.50	GJ + numerals
	"	III	7.47- 1.50	"
728 Sqdn	Hal Far (Malta)	III	8.48-	
729 Sqdn	Coimbatore (Ceylon)	III	5.45- 6.45	
	Pattalam (Ceylon)	"	6.45- 7.45	
	Katukurunda (Ceylon)	"	7.45- 7.46	
732 Sqdn	Drem	III	5.45-11.45	
733 Sqdn	China Bay/Trincomalee (Ceylon)	IIb	12.44-12.45	
736 Sqdn	St. Merryn	III	6.45-11.49	JB + numerals
738 Sqdn	Quonset Point (USA)	III	2.43- 7.43	
	Lewiston (Canada)	"	7.43- 2.45	
	Brunswick (Canada)	"	2.45- 7.45	
748 Sqdn	Dale	III	6.45- 8.45	
	St. Merryn	"	8.45- 2.46	
757 Sqdn	Pattalam (Ceylon)	IIa	10.43- 7.45	P
	Tambaram	"	7.45-11.45	
	"	IIb	7.45-11.45	
	Katukurunda (Ceylon)	"	11.45- 1.46	
758 Sqdn	Hinstock	IIb	3.45- 5.46	U3 + individual letter
	"	III	11.44- 5.46	"
759 Sqdn	Yeovilton	III	3.45- 9.45	Y2, Y3, Y5 and Y6 + individual letter
	Zeals	"	9.45- 1.46	"
	Yeovilton	"	1.46- 2.46	"
760 Sqdn	Zeals	III	4.45- 9.45	Y6 + individual letter
	Lee-on-Solent	"	9.45-12.45	"
	Henstridge	"	12.45- 1.46	"
761 Sqdn	Henstridge	III	11.44- 1.46	
766 Sqdn	Lossiemouth	IIb	1.47-	
	Rattray	III	1.46- 8.46	
	Lossiemouth	"	8.46-11.49	LM + numerals
767 Sqdn	Milltown	IIb	3.49- 8.49	
	"	III	8.48- 8.49	
	Yeovilton	IIb	8.49- 7.50	VL + numerals
	"	III	8.49- 7.50	"
768 Sqdn	Ayr	III	12.43- 1.44	
	Abbotsinch	"	1.44-	
771 Sqdn	Lee-on-Solent	IIb	1.48-	
778 Sqdn	Tangmere	III	12.47- 2.48	
780 Sqdn	Eastleigh	I	9.40-	
	Charlton Horethorne	III	12.43-11.44	U2 + individual letter
	Lee-on-Solent	"	11.44- 1.45	"
	Hinstock	"	3.46- 3.47	"
	Donibristle	"	3.47- 5.47	
	Culdrose	"	5.47-11.49	CW + numerals
	Hinstock	IIb	3.46- 3.47	U2 + individual letter
	Donibristle	"	3.47- 5.47	
	Culdrose	"	5.47-11.49	CW + numerals
781 Sqdn	Lee-on-Solent	IIb	11.47- 2.54	LP + numerals
	"	III	4.53- 5.53	"

782 Sqdn	Donibristle	IIa	5.46- 9.49	
	"	IIb	.48- .49	
	"	III	8.46-11.46	
784 Sqdn	Drem	III	11.45- 1.46	
	Dale	"	1.46- 7.46	
789 Sqdn	Wingfield (S. Africa)	IIa	9.44-11.45	
	"	III	2.45-11.45	
791 Sqdn	Sembawang (Malaya)	IIb	12.45- 5.47	
794 Sqdn	St. Merryn	IIb	6.45- 8.45	
	"	III	1.45- 8.45	
	Eglinton	IIb	8.45- 1.46	
	"	III	8.45- 6.46	
797 Sqdn	Colombo Racecourse (Ceylon)	III	1.44-	
798 Sqdn	Lee-on-Solent	IIb	6.45- 9.45	L3 + individual letter
	"	III	7.44- 9.45	"
	Halesworth	IIb	9.45-10.45	U2 + individual letter
	"	III	9.45-10.45	"
799 Sqdn	Lee-on-Solent	IIb	5.46- 5.48	
	"	III	12.45- 5.48	
	Yeovilton	IIb	5.48-12.51	
	"	III	5.48- 7.51	
	Macrihanish	IIb	12.51- 8.52	MA + numerals
1830 Sqdn	Abbotsinch	IIb	1.50-12.50	AC + numerals
	"	III	1.50-12.50	"
	Donibristle	IIb	12.50-11.52	DO + numerals
	"	III	12.51-11.52	"
	Abbotsinch	IIb	11.52-10.54	AC + numerals
	"	III	11.52- 3.55	"
1831 Sqdn	Stretton	IIb	5.50-11.54	JA (later ST) + numeral
	"	III	6.47- 7.50	"
1832 Sqdn	Culham	IIb	7.47- 7.53	CH + numerals
	"	III	1.48- 7.51	"
	Benson	IIb	7.53- 4.55	
1833 Sqdn	Bramcote	IIb	8.47- 9.50	BR + numerals
	"	III	1.49- 1.55	"
1834 Sqdn	Benson	IIb	10.53- 1.54	
	Yeovilton	"	1.54- 4.55	VL + numerals
1840 Sqdn	Ford	IIb	4.51-12.54	FD + numerals
	"	III	7.52- 2.54	"
1841 Sqdn	Stretton	IIb	8.52- 1.55	ST + numerals
	"	III	7.52- 2.54	"

Transport and communications units:

Ferry Flt	Coimbatore (Ceylon)	IIb		
2 Ferry Flt	Stretton	IIb	7.48-	
	"	III	2.48- 7.48	
4 Ferry Flt	Arbroath	IIb	7.47- 8.47	
Ferry Pool	Anthorn	IIb	8.49-	
"	Yeovilton	IIb		
Station Flight	Anthorn	IIa	4.46- 7.52	AH + numerals
"	Arbroath	IIb	10.50- 5.51	AO + numerals
	"	III	8.51- 7.55	"
"	China Bay (Ceylon)	III	7.45-	
"	Colombo (Ceylon)	IIb	7.45- 8.45	
"	Culdrose	III	12.47- 8.48	CW + numerals
"	Eglinton	IIb	4.47-11.48	JR + numerals
	"	III	6.48- 7.49	"
"	Gosport	III	6.51-11.54	GJ + numerals
"	Hal Far (Malta)	III	3.47- 3.52	HF + numerals
"	Lossiemouth	IIb	11.53-	
	"	III	9.48-	
"	Roborough (for RNEC)	IIb	1.54-12.54	
"	St. Merryn	IIb	.47- .50	
"	Syerston	IIb	1.49- 1.54	
"	Tambaram	IIb	11.45-	
Admiralty Flt	Rochester	IIb	11.49- 1.52	Numerals
	"	III	6.51- 5.55	"

RHODESIA, WEST AFRICA, KENYA

Flying training units:

28 EFTS	Mount Hampden	IIa			few	
4 FTS	Heany	IIa	2.47-10.53	B, D, F, G and H + individual letter	56	Sometimes carried letters SE on engine cowling
	"	IIb	3.52- 8.52	H + numeral	12	
5 FTS	Thornhill	IIa	8.47- 1.48	X + individual letter		
	"	IIb	3.51- 8.53	G + numeral		
20 SFTS	Cranborne	I	7.40-	Two letters		
	"	II	.41- .45	Numerals		
	"	IIa	2.43- .45	Single letter		
	"	III	- .45			
21 SFTS	Kumalo	I			few	
	"	II			few	
22 SFTS	Thornhill	I	3.41- .45	Numerals	105	
	"	II	7.41- .45	"	14	
	"	IIa	1.43- .45			
	"	III	- .45			

Advanced training units:

24 BG&NS	Moffat	I			few	
24 CAOS	Moffat	I			few	
	"	II			few	
CFS (SR)	Norton	IIa	5.44- 9.45		40	Formerly 33 FIS
	"	III	8.44- 9.45			
33 FIS	Belvedere	I	12.41-		2	
	"	II	.42-		13	
	"	IIa	.42- 5.44		1	Renamed CFS (SR)

Transport and communications units:

3 ANS CF	Thornhill	IIa	1.48- 9.51		2	Formed from nucleus of 5 FTS
HQ RATG CF		IIa			few	
Station Flight	Takoradi	IIa			2	
"	Thornhill	IIa			few	
WAT&CS	Accra	IIa			1	

Other units:

1340 Flt	Eastleigh	IIb	3.53- 6.53		4	Anti Mau-Mau operations
	Mwerga	"	6.53- 2.54		9	
	Nanyuki	"	2.54- 4.54		10	
	Eastleigh	"	4.54- 9.55		12	

MIDDLE EAST

Advanced training units:

AB&GS	El Ballah	II			1	
	"	IIa			4	
	"	III			5	
	"	IIb			3	
13 AGS	El Ballah	IIa			1	
	"	III	11.43- 7.45		3	
CGS (ME)	El Ballah	IIa			1	Formerly 1 METS
C&R School		II			1	
C&R Flt, 2 ADU		IIa			2	
11 FIS	Shallufa/El Ballah/ Deversoir/Nicosia	IIa			2	
	"	IIb			2	
MEAF ITF	Shallufa	IIb			5	
1 MECCU	Bilbeis	IIa			3	
	"	III			1	Became 1330 CU
1 METS	El Ballah	II	5.42-		6	
	"	IIa	- 3.43		1	Became CGS (ME)

Unit	Location	Mark	Dates	Remarks	No.	Notes
71 OTU	Ismailia/Gordon's Tree/ Carthago/Ismailia	I	6.41-		2	
	"	II			4	
	"	IIa			20	
	"	III			1	
73 OTU	Sheikh Othman/Abu Suier/ Fayid	II	4.42-11.42		4	
	"	IIa	2.43-	Single letters	25	
	"	III			15	
	"	IIb			1	
74 OTU	Aqir/Rayak/Muqueibila/ Aqir/Petah Tiqvah	II			3	
	"	IIa			5	
	"	III			2	
75 OTU	Gianaclis/Shallufa	IIa			2	
	"	III			1	
5 RFU	Sinello/Perugia/Gando	IIa			1	
1330 CU	Bilbeis	IIa			2	Formerly 1 MECCU
1342 (RP Trg)Flt	Shallufa/El Ballah	IIa			2	
	"	III			1	
1675(H)CU	Lydda/Abu Suier	IIa			1	

<u>Transport and communications units:</u>

Unit	Location	Mark	Dates	No.	Notes
AHQ E. Med. CF	Mariut	IIa		1	
AHQ Levant CF	Lydda	I	- 5.43		Became Lydda CF
Lydda CF	Lydda	I	6.43-		Formerly AHQ Levant CF
Malta ASE & CF		IIa		1	
MECS		IIa		1	
Station Flight	Ismailia	TT.IIb		1	
"	Nicosia	TT.IIb		2	
"	Petah Tiqvah	IIa		2	

<u>Other units</u>:

Unit	Location	Mark	No.
Aden Def. Flt		II	
2 FTLU	Blida	IIb	1
324 Wing		TT.IIb	1
1413 (Met) Flt	Lydda/St. Jean/Lydda	IIa	1

<u>Squadrons</u>:

Unit	Location	Mark	Dates	No.
6 Sqdn	(various airfields)	III		1
	"	IIb		2
8 Sqdn	Khormaksar	IIb	2.48- 7.49	1
32 Sqdn	Nicosia	IIb		2
39 Sqdn	(various airfields)	III		1
43 Sqdn	(various airfields)	IIa		1
73 Sqdn	Tak Ali	IIb	10.49- 9.50	2
84 Sqdn	Habbaniya	IIb	5.49-10.49	1
208 Sqdn	Ein Shemier/Nicosia/Fayid	III	12.47- 5.50	1
	"	IIb		1
213 Sqdn	Deversoir	IIa	12.48- 3.49	1
	"	IIb		1
249 Sqdn	Deversoir	IIa	9.49- 8.50	2
	"	IIb		1
293 Sqdn	Pomigliano	IIb		1
336 Sqdn	Sedes	TT.IIb		1

CANADA

Flying training units:

Unit	Location	Type	Dates	Markings	Number
1 SFTS	Camp Borden, Ont.	II	7.42- .44	Letter + numeral	82
	"	IIb	7.42- .44	"	25
3 SFTS	Calgary, Alb.	IIb	6.44- .44		90
6 SFTS	Dunnville, Ont.	II,IIb	1.41-10.44		105
8 SFTS	Monkton, NB	II,IIb	10.41-1.44		110
	Weyburn, Sas.	"	1.44- 6.44		110
9 SFTS	Summerside, PEI	II	1.41- 7.42		100
	"	?	5.44-11.44		4
10 SFTS	Dauphin, Man.	II	2.41-11.41		95
11 SFTS	Yorkton, Sas.	II	3.41- 1.42		100
12 SFTS	Brandon, Man.	II,IIb	6.44- .44		10
13 SFTS	St. Hubert, PQ	II,IIb	12.41-2.44		100
	North Battleford, Sas.	II	2.44- .44	Letter + numeral	60
		IIb	2.44- .44	"	54
14 SFTS	Aylmer, Ont.	II,IIb	12.42-8.44	Numerals	115
	Kingston, Ont.	"	8.44- .44	"	115
15 SFTS	Claresholm, Alb.	II,IIb	6.44- .44		8
19 SFTS	Vulcan, Alb.	IIb	6.44- .44		4
31 SFTS	Kingston, Ont.	II	10.40- 8.44	Numerals	150
	"	IIb	6.42- 8.44	"	comb.
32 SFTS	Moose Jaw, Sas.	II	9.41-11.42		95
	"	IIb	6.44- 9.44		2
33 SFTS	Carberry, Man.	II	1.41- 5.41		30
	"	IIb	6.44-11.44		2
34 SFTS	Medicine Hat, Alb.	II,IIb	3.41-10.44		108
36 SFTS	Penhold, Alb.	II,IIb	6.44- 9.44		2
37 SFTS	Calgary, Alb.	II	10.42- 3.44		110
	"	IIb	12.42- 3.44		comb.
39 SFTS	Swift Current, Sas.	II	12.41- 9.42		100
41 SFTS	Weyburn, Sas.	II,IIb	.42- 1.44		145

Advanced training units:

Unit	Location	Type	Dates	Number
1 FIS	Trenton, Ont.	II	2.43- .44	26
	"	IIb	2.43- .44	36
2 FIS	Pearce, Alb.	II,IIb	12.43- .44	36

INDIA, CEYLON, BURMA

Flying training units:

Unit	Location	Type	Remarks
1 FTS (I)	Ambala	II	Became 1 FTS (I)
1 SFTS (I)	Ambala	IIb	Absorbed into AFS (I)

Advanced training units:

Unit	Location	Type	Remarks
22 AACU	Santa Cruz and satellites	IIb	
AFS (I)	Ambala	IIb	Formerly 1 AFU
AFTU	Amarda Road		Absorbed into T&WDU
1 AFU	Ambala	IIb	Formed as part of 1 SFTS (I): became AFS (I)
1 AGS (I)	Bairagarh	IIb	Formerly 1 ATU.
20 APC	Ratmalana	IIb	Formerly 1571 (GG) Flt
21 APC	St. Thomas Mount/ Yelahanka/Cholavrum	IIb	Formerly 1572 (GG) Flt
22 APC	Amarda Road/Ranchi	IIb	Formerly 1573 (GG) Flt
23 APC	Salbani/Dhubalia	IIb	
ARS	Karachi	IIb	

1 ATU	Bairagarh	IIb	Became 1 AGS(I)
C&C Flt	Mauripur	IIb	Became 1331 CU
CFS (I)	Ambala	IIb	
3 FSTU	Bhopal	IIb	Absorbed 3 RFU
GATU	Ranchi	IIb	Formerly SLAIS; became part of T&WDU
1(I)OTU	Risalpur	II	Became 151 OTU
151 OTU	Risalpur	II	Formerly 1(I)OTU
	Phaphaman/Risalpur/ Peshawar/Ambala	IIb	Absprbed by AFS(I)
152 OTU	Peshawar	IIb	Absorbed into 151 OTU
3 RFU	Poona/Bhopal	IIb	Formerly ATP; absorbed by 3 FSTU
8 RFU	Yelahanka/Bhopal	IIb	Formerly 1670 CU
SLAIS	Ranchi	IIb	Became GATU
Trg. Flt	Mauripur	IIb	
TSTU	Chaklala/Gujerat	IIb	Formerly 3 PTS; became 1333 CU
1331 CU	Mauripur/Risalpur	IIb	Formerly C&C Flt
1334 CU	Gujerat	IIb	
1571 (GG) Flt	Ratmalana	IIb	Became 20 APC
1572 (GG) Flt	St. Thomas Mount	IIb	Became 21 APC
1573 (GG) Flt	Amarda Road	IIb	Became 22 APC
1670 CU	Yelahanka	IIb	Became 8 RFU
1672 CU	Yelahanka/Kolar	IIb	

<u>Transport and communications units:</u>

AHQ Bengal CU	Barrackpore	IIb	
AHQ India CS	Palam	IIb	Formerly BAFSEA CS
BAFSEA CS	Palam	IIb	Formerly ACSEA CS; became BAFSEA CS
Bengal/Burma CS	Baigachi	IIb	Formerly 3rd TAF CS; became Burma CS
Burma CF/CS	Baigachi/Digri/Mingaladon	IIb	Formerly Bengal/Burma CS
Comm. Flt	Kohat	IIb	
21 FC	Jodhpur/Mauripur	IIb	Became 8 FU
Ferry Flt	Trichinopoly	IIb	
8 FU	Mauripur	IIb	Formerly 21 FC
10 FU	Nagpur	IIb	
1 (I) Gp. CF	Peshawar	IIb	Formerly 223 Gp. CF
2 (I) Gp. CF	Yelahanka/Hindustan	IIb	Formerly 225 Gp. CF
3 (I) Gp. CF	Barrackpore	IIb	Formerly 228 Gp. CF
221 Gp. CF	Imphal/Kalemyo/Monywa/ Meiktila/Mingaladon	IIb	
222 Gp. CF	Ratmalana	IIb	Formerly SF Ratmalana
223 Gp. CF	Chaklala	IIb	Became 1 (I) Gp. CF
224 Gp. CF	Yelahanka/Baigachi	IIb	
225 Gp. CF	Yelahanka	IIb	Became 2 (I) Gp. CF
226 Gp. CF	Chakeri	IIb	
227 Gp. CF	Juhu	IIb	
228 Gp. CF	Alipore/Barrackpore	IIb	Became 3 (I) Gp. CF
231 Gp. CF	Red Road/Alipore	IIb	Absorbed by AHQ Burma
232 Gp. CF	Mingaladon/Comilla	IIb	
HQ ACSEA CS	Ratmalana	IIb	
India CU	Delhi (Willingdon)/Palam	IIb	
36 S.P. Ferry Flt	Ahmedabad	IIb	
Station Flight	Amarda Road	IIb	
"	Kohat	IIb	
"	Koggala	IIb	
"	Negombo	IIb	
"	Ratmalana	IIb	Became 222 Gp. CF
"	Redhills Lake	IIb	
"	St. Thomas Mount	IIb	

3rd TAF CS	Comilla	IIb	Became Bengal/Burma CS
117 Wing CF	Dum Dum		

Other units:

ATP	Poona	IIb	Became 3 RFU
JTRU	Sorbhog	IIb	Became part of T&WDU
1301 Met) Flt	Delhi/Nagpur/Negombo	IIb	
1340 Flt	Sulur/Cannanore	IIb	
166 Wing	Chittagong	IIb	
167 Wing	Ramu/Cox's Bazar	IIb	
168 Wing	Kumbhirgram	IIb	
169 Wing	Feni/Chittagong/Chiringa	IIb	
170 Wing	Imphal	IIb	
900 Wing	Agartala/Comilla	IIb	
908 Wing	Kumbhirgram/Kinmagon/ Hmawbi	IIb	

Squadrons:

In addition to the units listed above, some of the many Squadrons in India Burma and Ceylon which used Harvards from time to time are shown below; all were Mk.IIb aircraft. Due to the paucity of records, it is not possible to quote dates and, therefore, appropriate locations.

5; 11; 17; 18; 20; 22; 27; 28; 30; 31; 34; 42; 45; 52; 60; 62; 67; 79; 81; 82;84; 89; 99; 113; 117; 123; 134; 135; 136; 146; 152; 155; 159; 160; 176; 177; 194; 200; 203; 211; 215; 258; 261; 321; 353; 355; 357; 607; 615; 670; 672; 681; and 684 Squadrons.

FAR EAST

Advanced training units:

APC	Butterworth	IIb	.55- .56
27 APC	Butterworth	IIb	.49- .50
FEAFExS	Seletar	IIb	3.50-11.50
FEAFTrgS	Seletar etc	IIb	

Transport and communications units:

AHQ Malaya CS	Changi	IIb	.46- .47
BC Air CS	Iwakuni	IIb	
FEAF CF/CS	Changi	IIb	6.48- 7.50
	"	"	11.50-12.54
HKCS	Kai Tak	IIb	
HQ ACSEA CS	Kallang	IIb	10.45- 2.46
Station Flight	Butterworth	IIb	
"	Iwakuni	IIb	1.48-10.48
"	Kai Tak	IIb	10.50- 1.51
"	Seletar	IIb	
"	Sembawang	IIb	
"	Tengah	IIb	2.53- 5.56
1315 Flt	Iwakuni	IIb	- 9.48

Other units:

HKAAF	Kai Tak	IIb	12.50- 5.56
HK Ftr. Sqdn	Kai Tak	IIb	.52-
Kuala Lumpur Ftr. Sqdn	Kuala Lumpur	IIb	.51- .55
MAAF		IIb	- 5.57
Malaya Ftr. Sqdn	Butterworth/Tengah	IIb	.49- .51
Penang Ftr. Sqdn	Butterworth	IIb	.51- 4.52
	Penang	"	4.52- .55
Singapore Ftr. Sqdn	Tengah	IIb	.51- .55

Squadrons:

18 Sqdn	Butterworth	IIb	10.47-11.47
33 Sqdn	Changi	IIb	.49- .50
	Kuala Lumpur	"	.50- .50
	Butterworth	"	.50- .50
45 Sqdn	Kuala Lumpur	IIb	5.49- 6.49
60 Sqdn	Tengah etc	IIb	
84 Sqdn	Tengah	IIb	1.48- 6.48
	"	"	5.52- 2.53
267 Sqdn	Kuala Lumpur	IIb	2.54-11.58

AIRCRAFT HISTORIES

N7000
A&AEE 12.38
cr. Eyke, Suffolk, 16.2.39
N7001
A&AEE 1.39- 6.40
desp. S. Rhodesia 8.40
20 SFTS
Collided with P5863, Twentydales Estate, Salisbury, SR, 29.5.42
N7002
CFS 1.39- 6.41
Odiham for S. Rhodesia 8.41
20 SFTS
SOC 7.6.43
N7003
12 FTS 1.39- 8.39
14 FTS 8.39- 9.39
14 SFTS 9.39
cr. ldd. East End, Beds., 31.5.40
N7004
12 FTS [10] 1.39- 8.39
14 FTS 8.39- 9.39
14 SFTS 9.39- 8.40
15 SFTS 8.40-11.40
SFPP 4.41- 1.42
ATA [10] 1.42- 2.43
41 OTU 6.43- 9.44
SOC 30.10.44
N7005
12 FTS 2.39- 8.39
14 SFTS 9.39-12.40
Odiham for S. Rhodesia 2.41
22 SFTS (3.42-10.44)
SOC 31.10.44
N7006
12 FTS 1.39- 8.39
14 SFTS 9.39- 6.40
15 SFTS 6.40- 7.40
Odiham for S. Rhodesia 6.41
20 SFTS
SOC 31.12.43
N7007
12 FTS 2.39- 9.39
11 SFTS 9.39-12.39
desp. S. Rhodesia .40
20 SFTS 8.40- 4.41
SOC 15.4.41
N7008
12 FTS 2.39- 8.39
14 SFTS 9.39- 7.40
15 SFTS 7.40
cr. 2mls W of Chipping Norton, 7.11.40
N7009
12 FTS 2.39- 8.39
14 SFTS 9.39- 7.40
15 SFTS 7.40- 1.41
Odiham for S. Rhodesia 3.41
S. Rhodesia: no record of service
SOC 10.6.42
N7010
12 FTS 2.39- 9.39
14 SFTS 9.39
Overshot Kinloss and cr., Burghead, 15.12.39
N7011
1 SFTS 9.39-10.39
10 SFTS 10.39- 7.40
Odiham for S. Rhodesia 3.41
22 SFTS
SOC 30.4.44
N7012
12 FTS 2.39- 9.39
14 SFTS 9.39- 6.40
15 SFTS 6.40- 2.41
Odiham for S. Rhodesia 2.41
22 SFTS 3.41
Collided with N7133 near Lalapanzi, SR, 27.11.43
N7013
A&AEE 2.39- 5.40
RAE
Odiham for S. Rhodesia 4.41
20 SFTS [AR/86]
22 SFTS
FA Cat.E
N7014
CFS 3.39- 3.40
14 SFTS 3.40- 6.40
15 SFTS 6.40- 8.40
Odiham for S. Rhodesia 3.41
22 SFTS 7.42-
SOC 5.3.45
N7015
CFS 3.39- 6.41
1 SoAC 6.41-10.41
41 OTU 10.41- 6.44
SOC 3.6.44
N7016
CFS 3.39- 9.40
Odiham for S. Rhodesia 2.41
22 SFTS
SOC 5.4.44
N7017
10 FTS 3.39- 9.39
10 SFTS 9.39- 9.40
Odiham for S. Rhodesia 2.41
22 SFTS
SOC 9.8.44
N7018
12 FTS 3.39- 9.39
2 SFTS 9.39- 8.40
15 SFTS 8.40-11.40
Odiham for S. Rhodesia 2.41
20 SFTS
22 SFTS
SOC 2.11.45
N7019
10 FTS 3.39
cr. ldd. Gailey, Staffs., 28.4.39
N7020
Retained in USA for trials
N7021
CFS 3.39- 5.41
1 SoAC 5.41-10.41
41 OTU 10.41- 5.44
PSOC 21.6.47
N7022
CFS 3.39- 5.41
1 SoAC 5.41-10.41
41 OTU 10.41- 5.44
SOC 17.5.44
N7023
10 FTS 3.39- 9.39
10 SFTS 9.39- 1.41
5 SFTS 1.41- 3.41
FPP 3.41- 5.42
ATA 5.42-11.44
SOC 23.11.44
N7024
10 FTS 3.39- 9.39
10 SFTS 9.39- 8.40
desp. S. Rhodesia 8.40
20 SFTS
22 SFTS
SOC 2.11.45
N7025
10 FTS 3.39- 9.39
10 SFTS 9.39- 8.40
desp. S. Rhodesia 8.40
20 SFTS [DD]
22 SFTS
SOC 5.3.45
N7026
10 FTS 3.39- 9.39
10 SFTS 9.39- 8.40
desp. S. Rhodesia 8.40
21 SFTS 12.40-
20 SFTS 3.42-
SOC 5.42
N7027
10 FTS 3.39- 9.39
10 SFTS 9.39-11.40
Odiham for S. Rhodesia 12.40
20 SFTS [69]
22 SFTS
SOC 21.10.44
N7028
10 FTS 3.39- 9.39
10 SFTS 9.39- 8.40
desp. S. Rhodesia 8.40
21 SFTS 10.40-
22 SFTS
SOC 2.11.45
N7029
10 FTS 3.39
cr. ldd. Port Iyfni, N. Wales, 18.11.39
N7030
10 FTS 3.39- 9.39
10 SFTS 9.39- 8.40
desp. S. Rhodesia 8.40
20 SFTS
cr. 13.6.41
N7031
2 FTS 3.39- 9.39
2 SFTS 9.39- 7.40
15 SFTS 7.40-
desp. S. Rhodesia
S. Rhodesia: no record of service
PSOC 1.1.47
N7032
2 FTS [2] 3.39- 9.39
2 SFTS 9.39- 7.40
15 SFTS 7.40- 9.40
Odiham for S. Rhodesia 3.41
22 SFTS
SOC 30.11.43
N7033
2 FTS 3.39- 9.39
2 SFTS 9.39- 7.40
15 SFTS 7.40-12.40
Odiham for ME 3.41
71 OTU 6.41-
SOC 1.12.43
N7034
2 FTS 3.39
cr. on take-off, Brize Norton, 18.10.39
N7035
2 FTS 3.39- 9.39
2 SFTS 9.39- 7.40
15 SFTS 7.40- 2.41
Odiham for S. Rhodesia 2.41
22 SFTS
SOC 9.8.44
N7036
2 FTS 3.39- 9.39
2 SFTS 9.39- 7.40
15 SFTS 7.40- 5.41
Odiham for ME 5.41
71 OTU
SOC 31.8.44
N7037
2 FTS 3.39- 9.39
2 SFTS 9.39- 6.40
15 SFTS 6.40- 2.41
Odiham for S. Rhodesia 2.41
22 SFTS
SOC 2.11.45
N7038
2 FTS 3.39
cr. on take-off, Brize Norton, 1.4.40

The first Harvard I to join an FTS, N7003 of No.12 FTS, Grantham (Spitalgate) early in 1939 *(via J.J.Halley)*

N7039
2 FTS 3.39- 9.39
2 SFTS 9.39- 6.40
15 SFTS 6.40- 8.40
Odiham for S. Rhodesia 3.41
22 SFTS
SOC 7.5.43
N7040
SF Ternhill 4.39- 1.40
8 EFTS 1.40-10.40
15 SFTS 10.40- 3.41
Odiham for S. Rhodesia 6.41
S. Rhodesia: no record of service
SOC 23.7.42
N7041
2 FTS 3.39- 9.39
2 SFTS 9.39-12.40
Odiham for S. Rhodesia 4.41
22 SFTS
FA Cat.E 22.2.44
N7042
1 FTS 4.39- 9.39
1 SFTS 9.39- 4.40
10 SFTS 4.40-10.40
desp. S. Rhodesia
22 SFTS
To S. Africa as synthetic trainer, 11.42
N7043
1 FTS 4.39
cr. near Netheravon, 13.11.39
N7044
1 FTS 4.39- 9.39
1 SFTS 9.39- 6.40
6 SFTS 6.40- 8.40
15 SFTS 8.40- 1.41
1 FPP 4.41-10.41
ATA 3.42- 3.45
SOC 12.3.45
N7045
1 FTS 4.39- 9.39
1 SFTS 9.39- 4.40
CFS 4.40- 6.41
1 SoAC 6.41-10.41
41 OTU 10.41- 8.42
CGS 8.42- 9.42
41 OTU 9.42- 5.44
SOC 27.5.44
N7046
1 FTS 4.39- 9.39
1 SFTS 9.39- 6.40
6 SFTS 6.40- 8.40
15 SFTS 8.40- 3.41
Odiham for S. Rhodesia 3.41
22 SFTS
To S. Africa as synthetic trainer, 11.42
N7047
1 FTS 4.39- 9.39
1 SFTS 9.39- 2.40
10 SFTS 2.40- 9.40
Yatesbury 11.40-12.40
Odiham for S. Rhodesia 3.41
20 SFTS
FA Cat.E 6.4.44
N7048
1 FTS 4.39- 9.39
1 SFTS 9.39- 6.40
15 SFTS 6.40-10.40
Odiham for S. Rhodesia 6.41
22 SFTS
SOC 7.5.43
N7049
1 FTS 4.39- 9.39
1 SFTS 9.39- 6.40
desp. S. Rhodesia 11.40
20 SFTS
SOC 9.8.44
N7050
1 FTS 4.39- 9.39
1 SFTS 9.39-11.40
Odiham for S. Rhodesia 2.41
22 SFTS
SOC 31.8.44
N7051
1 FTS 4.39- 9.39
1 SFTS 9.39- 4.40
10 SFTS 4.40- 8.40
desp. S. Rhodesia 11.40
20 SFTS
22 SFTS
SOC 26.2.43
N7052
1 FTS 4.39- 9.39
1 SFTS 9.39- 3.40
10 SFTS 3.40- 9.40
Yatesbury 11.40- 2.41
Odiham for S. Rhodesia 4.41
20 SFTS [A]
SOC 31.12.43
N7053
1 FTS 4.39- 9.39
1 SFTS 9.39- 3.40
10 SFTS 3.40- 9.40
Odiham for S. Rhodesia 4.41
20 SFTS
cr. Bromley, near Salisbury, SR, 29.4.42
N7054
1 FTS 4.39- 9.39
1 SFTS 9.39-10.39
10 SFTS 10.39
Spun in, Waltham-on-the-Wolds, Leics.,15.4.40
N7055
1 FTS 4.39- 9.39
1 SFTS 9.39-12.40
Odiham for S. Rhodesia 2.41
22 SFTS
SOC 31.7.44
N7056
1 FTS 4.39- 9.39
1 SFTS 9.39- 6.40
Odiham for S. Rhodesia 3.41
22 SFTS
cr. 24.12.41

N7057
1 FTS 4.39- 9.39
1SFTS 9.39- 1.40
6 SFTS 1.40- 6.41
HQ FPP 11.40- 3.42
ATA 8.42- 3.46
SOC 3.10.47
N7058
1 FTS 4.39- 9.39
1 SFTS 9.39- 8.40
15 SFTS 8.40- 2.41
Odiham for S. Rhodesia 2.41
22 SFTS
SOC 12.5.41
N7059
1 FTS 4.39- 9.39
10 SFTS 9.39
cr. ldd. Farndon, Cheshire, 4.1.40
N7060
1 FTS [20] 4.39- 9.39
1 SFTS 9.39- 3.40
10 SFTS 3.40
Collided with Anson N5039 and cr. near Ternhill, 21.3.40
N7061
1 FTS 4.39- 9.39
1 SFTS 9.39- 3.41
Odiham for S. Rhodesia 3.41
20 SFTS
SOC 31.7.44
N7062
1 FTS 4.39- 9.39
1 SFTS 9.39- 6.40
15 SFTS 6.40- 7.40
2 FPP 12.40-11.41
ATA 3.42- 3.45
SOC 22.3.45

N7063
1 FTS 4.39- 9.39
1 SFTS 9.39- 1.40
10 SFTS 1.40-10.40
Odiham for S. Rhodesia 3.41
22 SFTS
Collided with AJ611 and cr., 1.7.42
N7064
1 FTS 4.39
cr. 3mls E of Netheravon, 15.6.39
N7065
1 FTS 4.39- 9.39
1 SFTS 9.39- 3.40
10 SFTS 3.40- 9.40
Odiham for S. Rhodesia 3.41
20 SFTS
SOC 8.8.44
N7066
1 FTS 4.39- 9.39
1 SFTS 9.39- 3.40
10 SFTS 3.40- 9.40
Odiham for ME
ME: no record of service
SOC 1.12.43
N7067
Grantham 4.39
Spun in, Newton, Lincs., 24.9.39
N7068
12 FTS 4.39- 8.39
14 FTS 8.39- 9.39
14 SFTS 9.39- 7.40
15 SFTS 7.40-12.40
Odiham for S. Rhodesia 3.41
22 SFTS
SOC 2.11.45
N7069
12 FTS 4.39- 8.39
14 FTS 8.39- 9.39
14 SFTS 9.39- 2.40
Odiham for S. Rhodesia 4.41
22 SFTS
SOC 4.9.42
N7070
12 FTS 5.39- 8.39
14 FTS 8.39- 9.39
14 SFTS 9.39- 6.40
15 SFTS 6.40
cr. on landing, Bibury, 7.7.40
Became 2123M
N7071
12 FTS 5.39- 9.39
12 SFTS 9.39-10.39
1 SFTS 10.39- 8.40
15 SFTS 8.40-12.40
Odiham for S. Rhodesia 4.41
S. Rhodesia: no record of service
PSOC 1.1.47
N7072
1 FTS 5.39- 9.39
1 SFTS 9.39- 6.40
15 SFTS 6.40- 2.41
Odiham for S. Rhodesia 2.41
22 SFTS - 1.42
20 SFTS 1.42-
NFT
N7073
1 FTS 5.39- 9.39
1 SFTS 9.39- 8.40
15 SFTS 8.40- 1.41
Odiham for S. Rhodesia 1.41
22 SFTS
SOC 5.2.45
N7074
1 FTS 5.39
Spun in, Oare Hill, Marlborough, Wilts., 11.9.39

N7075
1 FTS 5.39- 9.39
1 SFTS 9.39- 4.40
10 SFTS 4.40- 8.40
desp. S. Rhodesia 8.40
22 SFTS
SOC 2.2.44
N7076
1 FTS 5.39- 9.39
1 SFTS 9.39- 1.40
desp. S. Rhodesia 11.40
20 SFTS
cr. near Mount Hampden, SR, 17.3.42
N7077
1 FTS 5.39- 9.39
1 SFTS 9.39-10.39
10 SFTS 10.39
cr. ldd. Llangurig, Montgomeryshire 18.11.39
N7078
1 FTS 5.39- 9.39
1 SFTS 9.39- 9.40
Yatesbury 10.40-12.40
Odiham for S. Rhodesia 12.40
20 SFTS
SOC 10.7.43
N7079
2 SFTS 9.39- 7.40
15 SFTS 7.40- 2.41
Odiham for S. Rhodesia 4.41
22 SFTS
SOC 16.4.42
N7080
2 SFTS 9.39- 7.40
15 SFTS 7.40- 1.41
Odiham for ME 6.41
ME: no record of service
SOC 1.12.43
N7081
6 SFTS 9.39- 9.40
Odiham for S. Rhodesia 5.41
22 SFTS
SOC 9.8.44
N7082
15 SFTS 9.39-12.40
Odiham for S. Rhodesia 3.41
20 SFTS
SOC 11.8.42
N7083
15 SFTS 9.39- 7.40
Odiham for S. Rhodesia 2.41
22 SFTS
SOC 2.11.45
N7084
2 SFTS 9.39- 6.40
15 SFTS 6.40-12.40
Odiham for S. Rhodesia 2.41
22 SFTS
SOC 31.10.44
N7085
15 SFTS 9.39- 1.41
Odiham for S. Rhodesia 3.41
22 SFTS
SOC 2.11.45
N7086
15 SFTS 9.39
Hit Oxford N4786 on take-off from Lossiemouth, 28.9.39
N7087
10 SFTS 1.40- 1.41
Odiham for S. Rhodesia 3.41
20 SFTS [L]
cr. Prince Edward Dam, SR, 19.2.42
N7088
2 SFTS 9.39- 7.40
15 SFTS 7.40-12.40
Odiham for S. Rhodesia 4.41
22 SFTS
SOC 5.1.45
N7089
2 SFTS 9.39- 8.40
15 SFTS 8.40
Hit tree on approach, Weston-on-the-Green, 14.11.40
N7090
2 SFTS 9.39- 7.40
15 SFTS 7.40-11.40
Odiham for S. Rhodesia 5.41
S. Rhodesia: no record of service
SOC 10.7.43
N7091
2 SFTS 9.39- 8.40
15 SFTS 8.40- 3.41
Odiham for S. Rhodesia 3.41
22 SFTS
SOC 1.7.42
N7092
2 SFTS 9.39
cr. ldd. Cosford, 3.12.39
Became 2056M
N7093
2 SFTS 9.39-12.40
Odiham for S. Rhodesia 2.41
22 SFTS
SOC 9.8.44
N7094
2 SFTS 9.39
cr. Black Bourton, Oxon., 5.10.39
N7095
6 SFTS 9.39- 9.40
desp. S. Rhodesia 11.40
20 SFTS
SOC 2.11.45
N7096
6 SFTS 9.39
Undershot, Kidlington, 15.7.40
Became 2124M
N7097
15 SFTS 9.39-10.40
Odiham for S. Rhodesia 2.41
22 SFTS
20 SFTS
SOC 5.3.45
N7098
2 SFTS 9.39- 8.40
15 SFTS 8.40- 2.41
Odiham for S. Rhodesia 4.41
22 SFTS
SOC 31.7.44
N7099
10 FTS 5.39- 9.39
10 SFTS 9.39- 8.40
Odiham for S. Rhodesia
22 SFTS
SOC 29.8.41
N7100
Cranwell 5.39-11.39
1 E&WS 11.39-12.41
1 SS 12.41- 1.42
ATA 1.42- 2.45
SOC 8.2.45
N7101
10 FTS 5.39- 9.39
10 SFTS 9.39
cr. Childs Ercall, Salop, 19.10.39
N7102
10 FTS 5.39- 9.39
10 SFTS 9.39-11.39
desp. S. Rhodesia
20 SFTS
22 SFTS
SOC 9.8.44
N7103
10 FTS 5.39- 9.39
10 SFTS 9.39-11.40
Odiham for S. Rhodesia
22 SFTS
Converted to synthetic trainer, 11.42
N7104
10 FTS 5.39- 9.39
10 SFTS 9.39
cr. 1½mls S of Evesham, 9.11.39
N7105
10 FTS 5.39
cr. in sea off Pwlhelli, 12.9.39
N7106
10 FTS 5.39- 9.39
10 SFTS 9.39
cr. 2½mls SE of Ternhill, 7.6.40
N7107
10 FTS 7.39- 9.39
10 SFTS 9.39- 1.41
Odiham for S. Rhodesia 1.41
22 SFTS
SOC 9.8.44
N7108
10 FTS 7.39- 9.39
10 SFTS 9.39- 9.40
A&AEE 4.41- 4.41
RAE 5.42- 4.44
ATA 4.44- 4.45
SOC 22.4.45
N7109
10 FTS 6.39- 9.39
10 SFTS 9.39- 9.40
15 SFTS 9.40- 2.41
Odiham for S. Rhodesia 8.41
20 SFTS
cr. on M'toko Road, 7mls from Salisbury, SR, 10.1.42
N7110
10 FTS 6.39- 9.39
10 SFTS 9.39-10.40
15 SFTS 10.40- 1.41
20 SFTS
22 SFTS
cr. Wedza District, SR, 29.5.44
N7111
10 FTS 6.39- 9.39
10 SFTS 9.39- 1.41
desp. S. Rhodesia
22 SFTS
20 SFTS
cr. 13.4.43
N7112
10 FTS 6.39- 9.39
10 SFTS 9.39- 8.40
15 SFTS 8.40- 2.41
Odiham 6.41- 8.41
ATA 1.42- 3.44
SOC 17.3.44
N7113
10 FTS 6.39- 9.39
10 SFTS 9.39-12.39
desp. S. Rhodesia
20 SFTS
cr. during formation flying and DBF 11.3.41
N7114
10 FTS 6.39- 9.39
10 SFTS 9.39- 1.40
Odiham for S. Rhodesia 12.40
22 SFTS
20 SFTS
FA Cat. 3 21.6.43
SOC 4.8.43
N7115
10 FTS 6.39- 9.39
10 SFTS 9.39- 9.40
Odiham for S. Rhodesia 3.41
20 SFTS
SOC 31.3.44
N7116
6 FTS 6.39- 9.39
6 SFTS 9.39- 9.40
15 SFTS 9.40- 2.41
Odiham for S. Rhodesia
20 SFTS
SOC 2.11.45
N7117
6 FTS 6.39- 9.39
6 SFTS 9.39- 9.40
SF Stoke Orchard 10.40-11.40
Odiham for S. Rhodesia 11.40
22 SFTS
SOC 31.10.44

N7118
6 FTS 6.39- 9.39
6 SFTS 9.39- 8.40
desp. S. Rhodesia
20 SFTS
SOC 13.5.41
N7119
6 FTS 6.39- 9.39
6 SFTS 9.39-12.40
Odiham for S. Rhodesia 12.40
22 SFTS
SOC 2.11.45
N7120
10 FTS 6.39- 6.39
SF Ternhill 6.39- 1.40
8 EFTS 1.40- 2.41
Odiham for S. Rhodesia 2.41
22 SFTS
SOC 4.12.41
N7121
SF Ternhill 6.39- 6.39
10 FTS 6.39- 9.39
10 SFTS 9.39
cr. 6.12.39
N7122
6 FTS 6.39- 9.39
6 SFTS 9.39- 9.40
desp. S. Rhodesia 11.40
20 SFTS
SOC 2.11.45
N7123
No service in UK
desp. S. Rhodesia
20 SFTS
SOC 25.4.42
N7124
6 FTS 6.39- 9.39
6 SFTS 9.39- 8.40
desp. S. Rhodesia
20 SFTS
SOC 11.8.41
Became 0010M in S. Rhodesia
N7125
6 SFTS 9.39- 8.40
15 SFTS 8.40- 2.41
Odiham for S. RHodesia 2.41
20 SFTS
SOC 2.11.45
N7126
6 SFTS 9.39- 1.40
desp. S. Rhodesia
20 SFTS
cr. and DBF 8.4.43
N7127
6 SFTS 9.39- 4.41
Odiham for S. Rhodesia 5.41
Transferred to ME
71 OTU
PSOC 1.1.47
N7128
6 SFTS 9.39- 8.40
desp. S. Rhodesia 12.40
20 SFTS
SOC 9.8.44
N7129
2 SFTS 9.39- 7.40
15 SFTS 7.40
Undershot, Brize Norton, 5.7.40
Became 2203M
N7130
6 SFTS 9.39- 6.41
Old Sarum 10.41- 1.42
ATA 4.43- 8.44
SOC 14.8.44
N7131
6 SFTS 9.39- 8.40
desp. S. Rhodesia
20 SFTS
cr. near Bromley, SR, 30.9.42
N7132
6 SFTS 9.39
cr. ldd. Brixworth, Northants, 22.11.39

N7133
6 SFTS 9.39- 5.40
Yatesbury 10.40- 2.41
Odiham for S. Rhodesia 2.41
22 SFTS
Collided with N7012 and cr. near Lalapanzi, SR, 27.11.43
N7134
6 SFTS 9.39
cr. ldd. 5mls SW of Daventry, 25.11.39
N7135
2 FTS 6.39- 7.39
14 FTS 7.39- 9.39
14 SFTS 9.39- 6.40
15 SFTS 6.40- 1.41
SFPP 4.41- 1.42
ATA 1.42- 2.45
SOC 9.2.45
N7136
2 FTS 6.39- 9.39
2 SFTS 9.39-12.39
desp. S. Rhodesia
21 SFTS
20 SFTS
SOC 14.2.41
N7137
2 FTS 6.39- 9.39
2 SFTS 9.39- 9.40
15 SFTS 9.40- 2.41
Odiham for S. Rhodesia 2.41
22 SFTS
20 SFTS
SOC 2.7.43
N7138
2 FTS 6.39- 9.39
2 SFTS 9.39- 8.40
15 SFTS 8.40- 1.41
1 FPP 4.41- 5.41
Burtonwood 5.41- 9.41
ATA 1.42- 4.45
SOC 26.4.45
N7139
2 FTS 6.39- 9.39
2 SFTS 9.39
cr. on take-off, Brize Norton, 17.9.39
N7140
2 FTS 6.39- 9.39
2 SFTS 9.39
cr. near Taynton, Oxon, 20.5.40
N7141
2 FTS 6.39- 9.39
2 SFTS 9.39- 2.41
Odiham for S. Rhodesia 2.41
22 SFTS
20 SFTS
SOC 30.4.44
N7142
2 FTS 6.39- 9.39
2 SFTS 9.39- 8.40
15 SFTS 8.40-11.40
SOC 16.11.40
N7143
2 FTS 6.39- 9.39
2 SFTS 9.39- 8.40
15 SFTS 8.40- 4.41
Odiham for S. Rhodesia 4.41
20 SFTS
SOC 5.42
N7144
2 FTS 6.39- 9.39
2 SFTS 9.39
cr. near Chipping Norton, 18.1.40
N7145
2 FTS 6.39- 9.39
2 SFTS 9.39- 8.40
15 SFTS 8.40- 2.41
3 FPP 2.41- 4.42
ATA 4.42- 5.45
SOC 6.5.45
N7146
2 FTS 6.39- 9.39
2 SFTS 9.39- 8.40
15 SFTS 8.40- 2.41
Odiham for S. Rhodesia 2.41
S. Rhodesia: no record of service
SOC 24.9.41
N7147
2 FTS 6.39- 9.39
2 SFTS 9.39- 8.40
15 SFTS 8.40- 3.41
Odiham for S. Rhodesia 3.41
22 SFTS
SOC 7.5.43
N7148
2 FTS 6.39- 9.39
2 SFTS 9.39- 9.40
15 SFTS 9.40-
3 FPP
ATA [5] 3.42-12.44
SOC 19.12.44
N7149
1 FTS 6.39- 9.39
1 SFTS 9.39- 6.40
15 SFTS 6.40-12.40
Odiham for ME 5.41
71 OTU
SOC 29.3.45
N7150
2 FTS 7.39- 9.39
2 SFTS 9.39- 9.40
15 SFTS 9.40- 1.41
Upavon 1.41- 3.41
26 Sqdn 3.41-12.41
41 OTU 12.41- 1.44
SOC 12.1.44
N7151
2 FTS 7.39- 9.39
2 SFTS 9.39-11.40
Odiham for S. Rhodesia 3.41
22 SFTS
SOC 23.11.42
N7152
10 FTS 7.39- 9.39
10 SFTS 9.39- 8.40
desp. S. Rhodesia 11.40
20 SFTS
22 SFTS
SOC 31.12.43
N7153
10 FTS 7.39- 9.39
10 SFTS 9.39- 2.40
desp. S. Rhodesia
S. Rhodesia: no record of service
SOC 8.9.41
N7154
10 FTS 7.39- 9.39
10 SFTS 9.39-
desp. S. Rhodesia
22 SFTS
SOC 2.11.45
N7155
10 FTS 7.39- 9.39
10 SFTS 9.39-11.40
Odiham for S. Rhodesia 3.41
22 SFTS
20 SFTS
SOC 31.12.43
N7156
10 FTS 7.39- 9.39
10 SFTS 9.39- 8.40
desp. S. Rhodesia
22 SFTS
FA Cat.E 29.2.44
N7157
10 FTS 7.39- 9.39
10 SFTS 9.39- 8.40
desp. S. Rhodesia 11.40
20 SFTS
22 SFTS
SOC 5.4.45
N7158
10 FTS 7.39- 9.39
10 SFTS 9.39
cr. 15.7.40

N7159
10 FTS 7.39- 9.39
10 SFTS 9.39
cr. 18.7.40
N7160
10 FTS 7.39- 9.39
10 SFTS 9.39- 8.40
desp. S. Rhodesia 11.40
22 SFTS
SOC 2.11.45
N7161
10 FTS 7.39- 9.39
10 SFTS 9.39- 8.40
desp. S. Rhodesia
20 SFTS
SOC 21.1.42
N7162
15 SFTS 9.39- 1.40
Odiham for S. Rhodesia 1.41
24 CAOS
24 BG&NS
22 SFTS
SOC 5.3.45
N7163
15 SFTS 9.39-12.39
Odiham for S. Rhodesia 3.41
20 SFTS
Collided with P5969 over Prince Edward Dam, SR, 18.2.42
N7164
15 SFTS 9.39- 2.40
desp. S. Rhodesia
20 SFTS
cr. Cranborne, SR, 7.12.42
N7165
15 SFTS 9.39
cr. on approach, Kidlington 29.9.40
N7166
15 SFTS 9.39
Undershot landing, Chipping Norton, 2.10.40
N7167
15 SFTS 9.39- 9.40
Odiham for S. Rhodesia 4.41
22 SFTS
cr. Selukwe, SR, 5.3.44
N7168
15 SFTS 9.39-11.40
Odiham for S. Rhodesia 3.41
22 SFTS
SOC 5.4.45
N7169
CFS 9.39- 5.41
1 SoAC 5.41-10.41
41 OTU 10.41-10.44
SOC 15.10.44
N7170
CFS 9.39- 4.40
Odiham for S. Rhodesia 3.41
22 SFTS
SOC 31.12.43
N7171
CFS 9.39- 3.40
14 SFTS 3.40- 6.40
15 SFTS 6.40-11.40
Odiham for S. Rhodesia 1.41
22 SFTS
SOC 17.7.41
N7172
CFS 9.39-11.40
Odiham for S. Rhodesia 2.41
22 SFTS
FA Cat. 3 9.5.44
N7173
CFS 9.39- 6.41
1 SoAC 6.41-10.41
41 OTU 10.41-10.44
SOC 6.10.44
N7174
CFS 9.39
cr. low flying, Casterley Camp, Wilts., 13.9.40
N7175
11 Gp. Pool 8.39- 3.40
6 OTU 3.40-11.40
56 OTU 11.40- 6.41
Odiham for S. Rhodesia 7.41
22 SFTS
FA Cat.E 4.12.42
N7176
11 Gp. Pool 9.39- 3.40
6 OTU 3.40-11.40
56 OTU 11.40
Destroyed in air raid, Sutton Bridge, 11.5.41
N7177
11 Gp. Pool 8.39- 3.40
6 OTU 3.40-
61 OTU 7.41- 3.42
41 OTU 3.42- 5.44
SOC 27.5.44
N7178
11 Gp. Pool 8.39- 3.40
6 OTU 3.40-
53 OTU 3.41- 5.41
52 OTU 5.41- 7.41
61 OTU 7.41- 3.42
41 OTU 3.42
cr. 4.4.43
N7179
11 Gp. Pool 8.39- 3.40
6 OTU 3.40-
53 OTU 3.41- 5.41
52 OTU 5.41- 8.41
61 OTU 8.41
cr. on take-off, Heston, 24.1.42
N7180
11 Gp. Pool 8.39- 3.40
6 OTU 3.40-
53 OTU 3.41- 5.41
52 OTU 5.41- 7.41
61 OTU 7.41- 3.42
41 OTU 3.42-10.44
587 Sqdn 10.44- 5.45
SOC 18.5.45
N7181
CFS 7.39
cr. on take-off, Upavon, 8.10.39
N7182
CFS 7.39
cr. near Marlborough, 1.11.39
N7183
CFS 7.39- 2.41
Odiham for S. Rhodesia 4.41
20 SFTS
cr. near Marandellas, SR, 24.4.43
N7184
CFS 7.39- 3.40
14 SFTS 3.40- 7.40
15 SFTS 7.40-12.40
Odiham for S. Rhodesia 3.41
22 SFTS
SOC 31.10.44
N7185
CFS 7.39- 1.41
Odiham for S. Rhodesia 5.41
22 SFTS
SOC 10.2.42
N7186
CFS 7.39- 3.40
14 SFTS 3.40-11.40
Odiham for S. Rhodesia 3.41
22 SFTS
PSOC 21.6.47
N7187
1 FTS 7.39- 9.39
1 SFTS 9.39- 2.40
desp. S. Rhodesia
22 SFTS
20 SFTS
cr. 4.8.41
N7188
1 FTS 7.39- 9.39
1 SFTS 9.39- 6.40
15 SFTS 6.40- 2.41
Odiham for S. Rhodesia 2.41
22 SFTS
SOC 7.7.41
N7189
1 FTS 7.39- 9.39
1 SFTS 9.39- 4.40
2 SFTS 4.40- 7.40
15 SFTS 7.40- 2.41
Odiham for S. Rhodesia 5.41
20 SFTS
SOC 9.8.44
N7190
1 FTS 7.39- 9.39
1 SFTS 9.39-12.39
6 SFTS 12.39
Hit tree, Turkdean, Glos., 30.7.41
N7191
1 FTS 8.39- 9.39
1 SFTS 9.39- 6.40
15 SFTS 6.40- 1.41
Odiham for S. Rhodesia 6.41
20 SFTS
FA Cat. 3 8.3.43
N7192
1 FTS 7.39- 9.39
1 SFTS 9.39-12.39
6 SFTS 12.39- 9.40
Odiham for S. Rhodesia 2.41
20 SFTS
22 SFTS
SOC 30.9.44
N7193
1 FTS 7.39- 9.39
1 SFTS 9.39-11.40
Odiham for S. Rhodesia 2.41
22 SFTS
SOC 10.7.42
N7194
1 FTS 7.39- 9.39
1 SFTS 9.39- 6.40
15 SFTS 6.40
cr. Clanfield, Oxon, 1.9.40
N7195
1 FTS 8.39- 9.39
1 SFTS 9.39-11.39
6 SFTS 11.39- 1.41
Odiham for S. Rhodesia 2.41
20 SFTS
22SFTS
SOC 27.2.42
N7196
1 FTS 8.39- 9.39
1 SFTS 9.39- 3.41
Odiham for S. Rhodesia 3.41
22 SFTS
20 SFTS
cr. Wychwood East Farm, Bromley, SR 20.5.44
N7197
1 FTS 8.39- 9.39
1 SFTS 9.39
cr. on take-off, Netheravon, 20.9.39
N7198
1 FTS 8.39- 9.39
1 SFTS 9.39- 6.40
15 SFTS 6.40-10.40
Odiham for S. Rhodesia 3.41
S. Rhodesia: no record of service
PSOC 1.1.47
N7199
1 SFTS 10.39-12.39
desp. S. Rhodesia 8.40
20 SFTS
SOC 1.1.41

****

P5783
6 FTS 8.39- 9.39
6 SFTS 9.39- 7.40
15 SFTS 7.40-11.40
Odiham for S. Rhodesia 2.41
22 SFTS
SOC 31.3.44

P5784
6 FTS 8.39- 9.39
6 SFTS 9.39
cr. on take-off, Hullavington, 14.3.40
P5785
6 FTS 5.39- 9.39
6 SFTS 9.39- 4.41
Odiham for ME 5.41
71 OTU
SOC 31.8.44
P5786
6 FTS 5.39- 9.39
6 SFTS 9.39-12.40
desp. S. Rhodesia
22 SFTS
SOC 9.8.44
P5787
1 FTS 8.39- 9.39
1 SFTS 9.39-12.39
6 SFTS 12.39- 2.41
Odiham for S. Rhodesia 4.41
20 SFTS
22 SFTS
SOC 5.3.45
P5788
1 FTS 8.39- 9.39
1 SFTS 9.39-11.39
6 SFTS 11.39
cr. Haselton, near Cheltenham, 19.8.40
P5789
1 FTS 8.39- 9.39
1 SFTS 9.39-11.39
10 SFTS 11.39-12.39
Elmdon 11.40- 1.41
Odiham for S. Rhodesia 1.41
22 SFTS
SOC 4.8.45
P5790
1 FTS 8.39- 9.39
1 SFTS 9.39- 4.40
2 SFTS 4.40- 2.41
Odiham for S. Rhodesia 2.41
20 SFTS
SOC 30.9.44
P5791
1 FTS 8.39- 9.39
1 SFTS 9.39
Collided with P5792 and cr. 5mls NE of Netheravon, 23.9.39
P5792
1 FTS 8.39- 9.39
1 SFTS 9.39
Collided with P5791 and cr. 5mls NE of Netheravon, 23.9.39
P5793
15 SFTS
Undershot landing, Bibury, 5.8.40
P5794
15 SFTS - 7.40
Odiham for S. Rhodesia 1.41
20 SFTS
22 SFTS
SOC 30.11.44
P5795
14 SFTS 11.39- 6.40
15 SFTS 6.40-11.40
Odiham for S. Rhodesia 4.41
S. Rhodesia: no record of service
PSOC 1.1.47
P5796
14 SFTS 11.39- 6.40
15 SFTS 6.40-12.40
Odiham for S. Rhodesia 1.41
22 SFTS
SOC 5.4.43
P5797
1 FTS 8.39- 9.39
desp. S. Rhodesia
20 SFTS
SOC 31.8.45
P5798
14 SFTS 11.39- 8.40
15 SFTS 8.40- 2.41
Odiham for S. Rhodesia 2.41
20 SFTS
cr. New Martinsthorpe RLG, SR, 4.12.43
P5799
14 SFTS 11.39- 9.40
desp. S. Rhodesia
20 SFTS
22 SFTS
SOC 2.11.45
P5800
14 SFTS 11.39- 6.40
15 SFTS 6.40- 2.41
Odiham for S. Rhodesia 6.41
Transferred to ME
71 OTU
PSOC 1.1.47
P5801
14 SFTS 11.39
cr. Alves, Morayshire, 16.12.39
P5802
14 SFTS 11.39- 7.40
15 SFTS 7.40- 1.41
Odiham for S. Rhodesia 4.41
22 SFTS
PSOC 1.1.47
P5803
14 SFTS 11.39-
15 SFTS
Broke up in mid-air near Upper Heyford, 18.9.40
P5804
14 SFTS 11.39- 5.40
desp. S. Rhodesia
20 SFTS
cr. 16.6.41
P5805
14 SFTS 11.39- 6.40
15 SFTS 6.40- 2.41
Odiham for S. Rhodesia 4.41
22 SFTS
FA Cat.E 28.5.42
P5806
14 SFTS 11.39- 6.40
15 SFTS 6.40-11.40
SOC 21.11.40
P5807
14 SFTS 11.39
cr. ldd. near Northampton, 18.4.40
P5808
14 SFTS 11.39- 6.40
15 SFTS 6.40- 2.41
Odiham for S. Rhodesia 2.41
22 SFTS
20 SFTS
FA Cat.E 4.12.43
P5809
14 SFTS 11.39-12.40
Odiham for S. Rhodesia 3.41
22 SFTS
NFT
P5810
No service in UK
desp. S. Rhodesia
S. Rhodesia: no record of service
SOC 5.6.43
P5811
14 SFTS 11.39- 8.40
15 SFTS 8.40-11.40
Odiham for S. Rhodesia 1.41
20 SFTS
22 SFTS
SOC 2.11.45
P5812
14 SFTS 11.39- 3.42
Halton Trg. Flt 3.42- 8.42
41 OTU 1.43- 9.44
SOC 12.5.45
P5813
14 SFTS 11.39
cr. ldd. W. Crawley, Bucks. 31.5.40
P5814
15 SFTS 2.40- 2.41
Odiham for S. Rhodesia 2.41
22 SFTS
FA Cat. 3 15.2.43
P5815
15 SFTS 1.40-10.40
Odiham for S. Rhodesia 12.40
20 SFTS
FA Cat. 3 12.5.43
P5816
15 SFTS 1.40- 5.40
14 SFTS 5.40- 8.40
desp. S. Rhodesia
20 SFTS
33 FIS
SOC 7.5.43
P5817
15 SFTS 1.40- 5.40
14 SFTS 5.40
Collided with Oxford N4638 and cr. near Bozeat, Northants., 10.6.40
P5818
15 SFTS 1.40- 2.41
Odiham 4.41- 7.41
41 OTU 6.42-10.44
SOC 10.10.44
P5819
15 SFTS 1.40- 2.40
Yatesbury 11.40-12.40
Odiham for S. Rhodesia 1.41
22 SFTS
SOC 15.3.42

P5790 of either No.1 FTS or No.2 SFTS *(via J.J.Halley)*

P5820
15 SFTS 1.40
cr. 1dd. Ambergate, near Birkenhead 8.1.40
P5821
15 SFTS 1.40-12.40
Odiham for S. Rhodesia 2.41
20 SFTS
22 SFTS
SOC 2.11.45
P5822
15 SFTS 1.40- 5.40
14 SFTS 5.40- 6.40
15 SFTS 6.40- 7.40
Odiham for S. Rhodesia 12.40
20 SFTS
SOC 5.2.45
P5823
14 SFTS 1.40- 6.40
15 SFTS 6.40- 1.41
Odiham for S. Rhodesia 3.41
22 SFTS
SOC 31.10.44
P5824
14 SFTS 1.40- 7.40
15 SFTS 7.40- 4.41
Odiham for S. Rhodesia 6.41
20 SFTS
SOC 2.11.45
P5825
14 SFTS 1.40- 5.40
15 SFTS 5.40-11.40
Odiham for S. Rhodesia 3.41
22 SFTS
Collided with AJ613 and cr. 12.3.43
P5826
14 SFTS 1.40- 7.40
15 SFTS 7.40- 2.41
Odiham for S. Rhodesia 2.41
20 SFTS
cr. near Belvedere Camp, Salisbury, SR, 6.4.42
P5827
14 SFTS 1.40- 7.40
15 SFTS 7.40-12.40
Odiham for S. Rhodesia 2.41
22 SFTS [69]
SOC 30.9.43
P5828
15 SFTS 2.40
cr. on approach, Weston-on-the-Gr'n 23.11.40
P5829
15 SFTS 2.40- 5.40
14 SFTS 5.40- 6.40
15 SFTS 6.40-12.40
Odiham for S. Rhodesia 2.41
20 SFTS
33 FIS
CFS(SR)
SOC 30.11.44
P5830
2 Cam U 1.40- 2.41
PRU 2.41- 4.41
Odiham for S. Rhodesia 4.41
22 SFTS
SOC 9.8.44
P5831
15 SFTS 2.40-11.40
Odiham for S. Rhodesia 3.41
22 SFTS
SOC 2.11.45
P5832
15 SFTS 11.39- 2.40
Odiham for S. Rhodesia 5.41
S. Rhodesia: no record of service
PSOC 1.1.47
P5833
15 SFTS 12.39- 2.41
Odiham for S. Rhodesia 2.41
22 SFTS
cr. Fort Victoria, SR, 13.4.44
P5834
15 SFTS 12.39- 2.41
Odiham for S. Rhodesia 2.41
20 SFTS
SOC 31.12.43
P5835
6 SFTS 1.40- 4.41
Odiham for S. Rhodesia
22 SFTS
FA Cat.E 12.6.44
P5836
2 SFTS 12.39- 7.40
Odiham for S. Rhodesia 2.41
22 SFTS
SOC 5.3.45
P5837
2 SFTS 12.39- 8.40
1 FPP 12.40- 5.42
ATA 4.43- 5.44
SOC 23.5.44
P5838
2 SFTS 12.39- 7.40
15 SFTS 7.40- 4.41
desp. S. Rhodesia
S. Rhodesia: no record of service
PSOC 1.1.47
P5839
6 SFTS 1.40- 9.40
desp. S. Rhodesia
S. Rhodesia: no record of service
PSOC 1.1.47
P5840
6 SFTS 1.40-12.40
Odiham for S. Rhodesia 1.41
22 SFTS
SOC 30.12.43
P5841
6 SFTS 1.40
Spun in, Tingewick, Bucks., 8.6.40
P5842
6 SFTS 1.40
Spun in, Oddington, Oxon, 18.5.40
P5843
15 SFTS 11.39- 2.41
desp. ME 11.41
ME: no record of service
PSOC 1.1.47
P5844
15 SFTS 11.39- 8.40
Odiham for S. Rhodesia 1.41
22 SFTS
SOC 2.11.45
P5845
15 SFTS 12.39- 2.41
Odiham for S. Rhodesia 2.41
22 SFTS
20 SFTS
FA Cat. 3 14.5.44
P5846
15 SFTS 11.39-12.40
Odiham for S. Rhodesia 2.41
22 SFTS
FA Cat.E 3.4.44
P5847
15 SFTS 11.39- 1.41
Odiham for S. Rhodesia 6.41
20 SFTS
SOC 5.3.45
P5848
15 SFTS 11.39
Hit chimney while low flying, Fochabers, 9.1.40
P5849
15 SFTS [S] 12.39- 2.41
Odiham for S. Rhodesia 4.41
20 SFTS
22 SFTS
SOC 31.12.43
P5850
6 SFTS 1.40
cr. Kingham Hill, Oxon, 27.8.40
P5851
6 SFTS 1.40- 2.41
Odiham for S. Rhodesia 3.41
22 SFTS
cr. 24.3.42
P5852
6 SFTS 11.39- 4.40
Odiham for S. Rhodesia 1.41
22 SFTS
SOC 21.7.44
P5853
6 SFTS 11.39- 7.40
Odiham for S. Rhodesia 12.40
22 SFTS
SOC 30.9.44
P5854
2 SFTS 9.39- 7.40
15 SFTS 7.40- 2.41
Odiham for S. Rhodesia 2.41
22 SFTS
SOC 7.5.43
P5855
6 SFTS 9.39- 9.40
desp. S. Rhodesia
22 SFTS
NFT
P5856
6 SFTS 9.39- 8.40
desp. S. Rhodesia
20 SFTS
cr. Gadzema, SR, 17.2.41
P5857
10 SFTS 9.39- 8.40
desp. S. Rhodesia
20 SFTS
SOC 2.11.45
P5858
10 SFTS 9.39-10.40
15 SFTS 10.40- 2.41
Odiham for S. Rhodesia 2.41
20 SFTS
SOC 2.11.45
P5859
1 SFTS 10.39- 8.40
15 SFTS 8.40- 4.41
HQ FPP 4.41- 3.42
ATA 8.42
FA Cat.E 17.3.44
P5860
1 SFTS 10.39-10.41
41 OTU 10.41-
PSOC 21.6.47
P5861
1 SFTS 10.39-11.39
10 SFTS 11.39- 3.40
desp. S. Rhodesia
20 SFTS
DBF, Cranborne, SR, 27.2.41
P5862
12 Gp. Pool 11.39
Spun in, Aston Down, 26.1.40
P5863
1 SFTS 10.39-11.39
6 SFTS 11.39- 9.40
15 SFTS 9.40-12.40
Odiham for S. Rhodesia 4.41
20 SFTS
Collided with N7001, Twentydales Estate, near Salisbury, SR,29.5.42
P5864
12 Gp. Pool 10.39- 3.40
5 OTU 3.40
Spun in, Wilforton, Hereford 9.4.40
P5865
242 Sqdn 11.39-11.39
609 Sqdn 11.39- 6.40
615 Sqdn 6.40- 6.40
609 Sqdn 6.40- 6.40
15 SFTS 6.40-12.40
Odiham for S. Rhodesia 3.41
22 SFTS
SOC 5.4.45
P5866
603 Sqdn 12.39- 6.40
Turnhouse 6.40- 2.41
46 Sqdn 2.41-12.41
61 OTU 1.42- 4.42
41 OTU 4.42-10.44
587 Sqdn 10.44- 6.45
SOC 26.6.45

P5867
602 Sqdn 10.39- 6.40
Coltishall 6.40- 9.42
ATA 4.43
FA Cat.E 17.3.44
P5868
152 Sqdn 10.39- 2.40
242 Sqdn 2.40- 4.40
141 Sqdn 4.40- 6.40
desp. S. Rhodesia
20 SFTS
cr. Inkomo bombing range, SR, 1.10.42
P5869
12 Gp. Pool 10.39- 3.40
5 OTU 3.40-11.40
55 OTU 11.40- 6.41
61 OTU 6.41- 1.42
41 OTU 4.41-11.44
SOC 7.5.45
P5870
12 Gp. Pool 10.39- 3.40
5 OTU 3.40
cr. on approach, Aston Down, 9.6.40
P5871
12 Gp. Pool 10.39
Spun in near Chalford, Glos., 21.11.39
P5872
12 Gp. Pool 10.39- 3.40
5 OTU 3.40-11.40
55 OTU 11.40- 5.41
52 OTU 5.41- 7.41
61 OTU 7.41- 4.42
41 OTU 4.42- 4.44
SOC 10.4.44
P5873
6 SFTS [T] 11.39- 9.40
15 SFTS 9.40- 1.41
Odiham for S. Rhodesia 2.41
22 SFTS
SOC 5.2.45
P5874
6 SFTS 11.39-12.40
Odiham for S. Rhodesia 12.40
22 SFTS - 2.43
20 SFTS 2.43- 8.44
SOC 9.8.44
P5875
6 SFTS 11.39- 9.40
15 SFTS 9.40-12.40
Odiham for S. Rhodesia 2.41
22 SFTS
SOC 2.11.45
P5876
No service in UK
desp. S. Rhodesia
20 SFTS
cr. Inkomo bombing range, SR, 25.8.41
P5877
2 SFTS 12.39- 8.40
15 SFTS 8.40- 2.41
Odiham for S. Rhodesia 2.41
S. Rhodesia: no record of service
SOC 31.10.44
P5878
2 SFTS 1.40- 6.40
15 SFTS 6.40- 3.41
Odiham for S. Rhodesia 5.41
S. Rhodesia: no record of service
SOC 9.8.44
P5879
6 SFTS 11.39- 1.41
Odiham for S. Rhodesia 2.41
22 SFTS - 1.42
SOC 7.1.42
P5880
6 SFTS 11.39- 1.41
Odiham for S. Rhodesia 2.41
20 SFTS
cr. 12.8.41
P5881
6 SFTS 11.39- 1.41
Odiham for S. Rhodesia 2.41
22 SFTS - 6.41
SOC 11.6.41
P5882
10 SFTS 11.39- 8.40
desp. S. Rhodesia
S. Rhodesia: no record of service
PSOC 1.1.47
P5883
10 SFTS 11.39- 8.40
Odiham for S. Rhodesia 12.40
22 SFTS
20 SFTS
cr. Inkomo bombing range, SR,5.1.43
P5884
10 SFTS 11.39
cr. on take-off, Ternhill, 4.7.40
P5885
15 SFTS 11.39- 5.40
14 SFTS 5.40
Spun in near Brockworth, Glos. and DBF, 19.9.40
P5886
15 SFTS 11.39- 8.40
Odiham for S. Rhodesia 2.41
22 SFTS - 2.43
20 SFTS 2.43-
SOC 30.11.44
P5887
15 SFTS 11.39- 8.40
Odiham for S. Rhodesia 1.41
20 SFTS
22 SFTS
SOC 2.7.45
P5888
15 SFTS 11.39-11.40
Odiham for ME 5.41
71 OTU 6.41-
SOC 1.1.44
P5889
15 SFTS 11.39- 2.41
Odiham for S. Rhodesia 2.41
22 SFTS
SOC 20.10.41
P5890
15 SFTS 11.39
Spun in, Farley Mount, Hants, 20.5.40
P5891
10 SFTS 6.40- 8.40
15 SFTS 8.40- 9.40
Odiham for S. Rhodesia 1.41
22 SFTS
SOC 13.1.43
P5892
15 SFTS 12.39- 2.41
Odiham for S. Rhodesia 6.41
22 SFTS
20 SFTS
SOC 27.2.42
P5893
15 SFTS 11.39-12.40
Odiham for ME 4.41
71 OTU 6.41-
PSOC 1.1.47
P5894
2 SFTS 11.39- 8.40
15 SFTS 8.40- 2.41
Odiham for S. Rhodesia
S. Rhodesia: no record of service
PSOC 1.1.47
P5895
2 SFTS 5.40- 8.40
Odiham for S. Rhodesia 2.41
22 SFTS
SOC 29.7.43
P5896
10 SFTS 11.39- 5.40
desp. S. Rhodesia
20 SFTS
cr. and DBF 19.8.41
P5897
2 SFTS 11.39- 5.40
3 FPP 10.40- 5.41
HQ FPP 5.41- 5.42
ATA 4.43- 3.45
SOC 29.3.45
P5898
2 SFTS 11.39- 9.40
15 SFTS 9.40- 2.41
Odiham for S. Rhodesia 2.41
20 SFTS
SOC 30.11.43
P5899
2 SFTS 12.39-10.40
15 SFTS 10.40- 2.41
Odiham for S. Rhodesia 2.41
22 SFTS
SOC 9.8.44
P5900
2 SFTS 6.40- 9.40
15 SFTS 9.40-12.40
Odiham for S. Rhodesia 1.41
20 SFTS
22 SFTS
SOC 2.11.45
P5901
2 SFTS 6.40- 7.40
15 SFTS 7.40
cr. on take-off, Windrush, 25.7.40
P5902
15 SFTS 1.40- 5.40
14 SFTS 5.40- 6.40
15 SFTS 6.40- 1.41
Odiham for S. Rhodesia 3.41
22 SFTS
SOC 5.1.45
P5903
2 SFTS 6.40- 9.40
15 SFTS 9.40-11.40
Odiham for S. Rhodesia 3.41
20 SFTS
NFT
P5904
14 SFTS 3.40- 6.40
15 SFTS 6.40-12.40
Odiham for S. Rhodesia 1.41
22 SFTS - 9.43
SOC 1.9.43
P5905
14 SFTS 3.40- 6.40
15 SFTS 6.40- 2.41
Odiham for S. Rhodesia 2.41
22 SFTS
SOC 2.2.44
P5906
14 SFTS 3.40- 8.40
15 SFTS 8.40- 2.41
1 FPP 4.41- 6.41
ATA 12.41 5.45
SS (Coley) 2.49
P5907
15 SFTS 1.40- 6.40
10 SFTS 6.40- 8.40
desp. S. Rhodesia
20 SFTS
SOC 30.11.43
P5908
6 SFTS 6.40- 9.40
Odiham for S. Rhodesia 1.41
22 SFTS
SOC 2.11.45
P5909
No service in UK
desp. S. Rhodesia 8.40
20 SFTS
NFT
P5910
No service in UK
desp. S. Rhodesia 8.40
20 SFTS
cr. near Inkomo bombing range, SR, 9.12.40
P5911
6 SFTS 6.40- 1.41
ATA 1.41- 2.44
SOC 17.3.44

P5912
6 SFTS 6.40-12.40
Odiham for S. Rhodesia 12.40
20 SFTS
SOC 2.11.45
P5913
6 SFTS [D] 6.40- 9.40
Odiham for S. Rhodesia 1.41
22 SFTS
SOC 31.7.44
P5914
6 SFTS 6.40- 9.40
desp. S. Rhodesia 11.40
20 SFTS
33 FIS
SOC 9.8.44
P5915
3 FPP 8.40-12.41
ATA 12.41- 1.44
SOC 17.3.44
P5916
20 SFTS 4.40-
Collided with P5982 and cr.,11.7.41
P5917
20 SFTS 4.40-
22 SFTS
SOC 2.11.45
P5918
20 SFTS 4.40
cr. 26.5.41
P5919
20 SFTS 4.40
Collided with P5940 and cr. 5.11.42
P5920
20 SFTS 4.40-
SOC 5.3.45
P5921
Direct to SAAF 3.40
P5922
20 SFTS 4.40
cr. 10mls NE of Marandellas, SR, 14.9.44
P5923
20 SFTS [6] 4.40-
SOC 7.6.43
P5924
20 SFTS 4.40-
SOC 15.3.42
P5925
20 SFTS 4.40-
SOC 4.5.45
P5926
20 SFTS 4.40-
SOC 31.8.44
P5927
20 SFTS 3.40
cr. near Greendale, Salisbuty, SR, 26.2.43
P5928
Direct to SAAF 3.40
P5929
20 SFTS 4.40
FA Cat.E 8.3.43
P5930
20 SFTS 4.40
cr. near Goromonzi, SR, 17.12.40
P5931
Direct to SAAF 3.40
P5932
20 SFTS 4.40-
NFT
P5933
22 SFTS 4.40-
FA Cat.E 2.9.43
P5934
20 SFTS 3.40-
SOC 5.3.45
P5935
20 SFTS 5.40-
22 SFTS
SOC 2.11.45
P5936
20 SFTS 3.40-
SOC 29.2.44

P5937
20 SFTS 4.40-
SOC 31.7.44
P5938
20 SFTS
Collided with P5941 and cr.30.10.40
P5939
20 SFTS
cr. on take-off, Cranborne, SR, 25.3.41
P5940
20 SFTS 7.40
Collided with P5919 and cr. 5.11.42
P5941
20 SFTS 4.40
cr. Sebastopol RLG, SR, 7.12.43
P5942
20 SFTS 4.40
cr. Trelawney, near Salisbury, SR, 9.6.42
P5943
20 SFTS 4.40
Spun in near Cleveland Dam, SR, 14.10.40
P5944
20 SFTS
SOC 23.10.41
P5945
22 SFTS - 2.43
20 SFTS 2.43-
SOC 4.5.45
P5946
20 SFTS 4.40-
SOC 30.11.43
P5947
20 SFTS
22 SFTS - 2.43
20 SFTS 2.43-
SOC by 1.45
P5948
22 SFTS
NFT
P5949
20 SFTS
cr. 24.7.41
P5950
20 SFTS
cr. near Rock Farm, Norton, SR, 13.3.42
P5951
20 SFTS
cr. Salisbury, SR 20.6.41
P5952
20 SFTS [10]
SOC 2.11.45
P5953
20 SFTS
SOC by 3.44
P5954
20 SFTS
cr. 35mls from Marandellas, SR, 16.12.43
P5955
20 SFTS
SOC by 4.44
P5956
20 SFTS
SOC by 3.44
P5957
20 SFTS
cr. 28.1.41
P5958
20 SFTS
cr. Grove Farm, near Salisbury, SR, 26.9.43
P5959
20 SFTS
SOC by 9.44
P5960
20 SFTS
33 FIS
CFS(SR)
SOC 2.11.45

P5961
20 SFTS
NFT
P5962
20 SFTS [S]
cr. Headlands District, SR, 15.3.44
P5963
20 SFTS
cr. on Marandellas Rd., Salisbury, SR,3.10.40
P5964
20 SFTS
cr. Glenforest Farm, near Salisbury SR, 11.11.40
P5965
20 SFTS
NFT
P5966
20 SFTS
SOC for conversion to instructional airframe for SAAF 8.11.42
P5967
20 SFTS
NFT
P5968
20 SFTS
33 FIS
CFS(SR)
SOC by 11.44
P5969
20 SFTS
SOC 5.1.45
P5970
20 SFTS
SOC by 9.44
P5971
20 SFTS
NFT
P5972
20 SFTS
Collided with P5977 and cr. near Ruwa , 5.10.40
P5973
20 SFTS
22 SFTS
NFT
P5974
20 SFTS
22 SFTS
SOC by 4.44
P5975
22 SFTS
20 SFTS
SOC 4.8.45
P5976
20 SFTS
NFT
P5977
20 SFTS
Collided with P5972 and cr. near Ruwa, 5.10.40
P5978
20 SFTS
SOC 5.3.45
P5979
20 SFTS
cr. ldd. Hillside, SR, 28.9.40
P5980
20 SFTS
NFT
P5981
20 SFTS
cr. 9mls E of Norton, SR, 15.12.41
P5982
20 SFTS 3.40-
Collided with P5916 and cr. 11.7.41

****

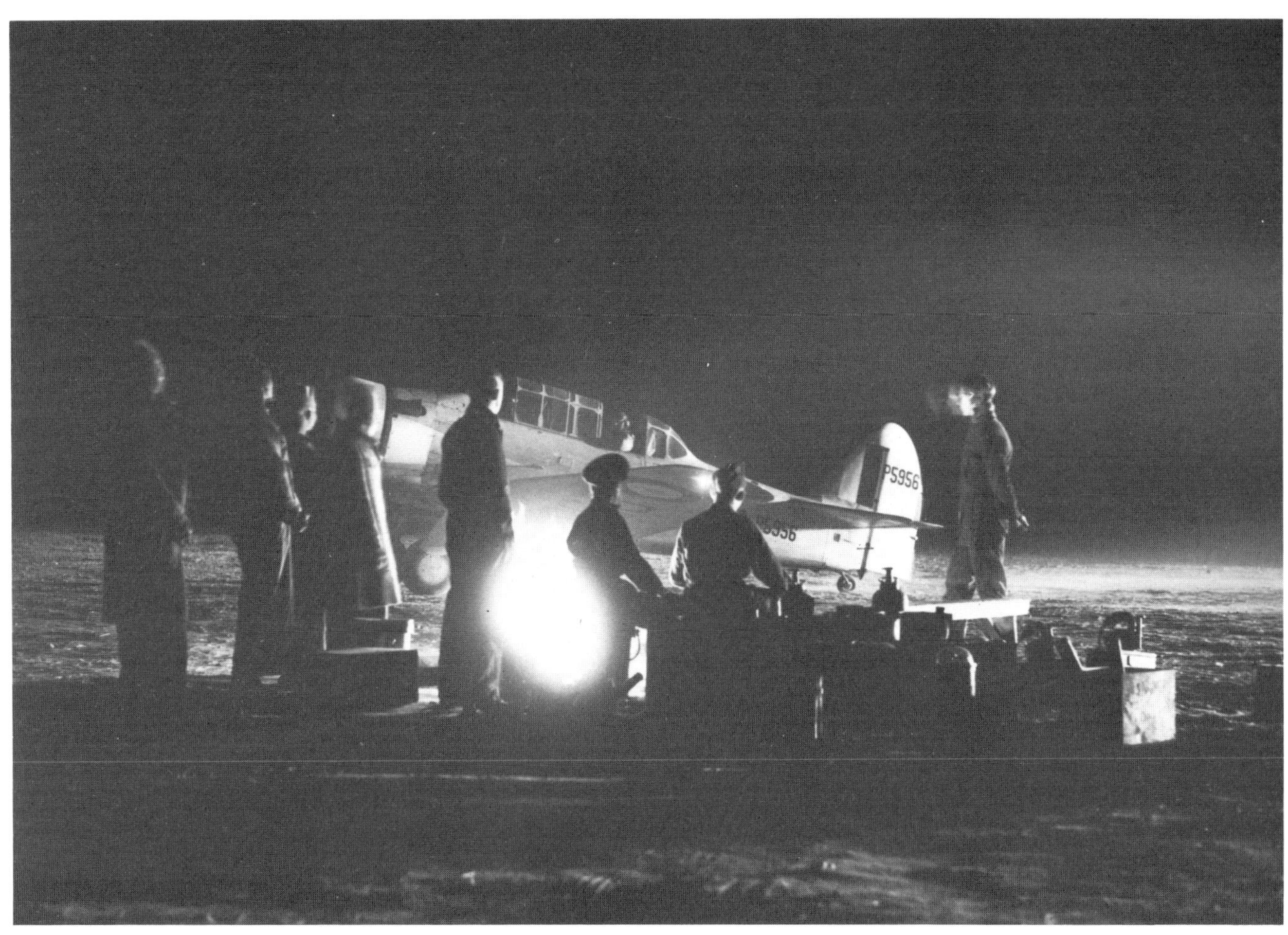

Nocturnal shot of P5956 in Southern Rhodesia, probably at No.20 SFTS, Cranborne *(via J.J.Halley)*

AH185
13 SFTS
31 SFTS
To RCAF
AH186
13 SFTS
To RCAF
AH187
9 SFTS
31 SFTS
To RCAF
AH188
9 SFTS
41 SFTS
To RCAF
AH189
31 SFTS
9 SFTS
To RCAF
AH190
9 SFTS 1.41-
41 SFTS
cr. near Hume, Sas., 2.1.44
AH191
9 SFTS 2.41-
41 SFTS
To RCAF
AH192
31 SFTS
8 SFTS - 2.43
14 SFTS 2.43-
To RCAF
AH193
31 SFTS
9 SFTS 1.41-
To RCAF
AH194
31 SFTS
9 SFTS 2.41-
41 SFTS
34 SFTS
To RCAF
AH195
31 SFTS 11.40- 1.41
SOC 21.2.41
AH196
9 SFTS 1.41-
cr. near Cavendish, PEI, 1.6.41
AH197
31 SFTS 1.41-
9 SFTS
DBR in accident, Summerside, 9.4.41
AH198
9 SFTS 1.41-
To RCAF
AH199
9 SFTS
13 SFTS
To RCAF
AH200
9 SFTS 2.41-
To RCAF
AH201
31 SFTS
9 SFTS 3.41-
2 SFTS
FA Cat.E 7.1.44
AH202
9 SFTS
cr. in snowstorm 4mls N of Summerside, PEI, 11.1.42
AH203
31 SFTS
9 SFTS
To RCAF
AH204
9 SFTS 1.41-
****
AJ538
31 SFTS
cr. in St. Lawrence River 3.5.44
AJ539
31 SFTS
To RCAF
AJ540
31 SFTS (10.41- 7.44)
To RCAF
AJ541
31 SFTS (7.42- 8.43)
To RCAF
AJ542
31 SFTS
Collided with AJ549 and cr.,11.6.42
AJ543
31 SFTS (10.41-
cr. on take-off, Gananoque RLG, 14.9.42
AJ544
31 SFTS (9.42- 5.43)
To RCAF
AJ545
31 SFTS (10.41- 7.43)
To RCAF
AJ546
31 SFTS (6.42- 8.43)
To RCAF
AJ547
31 SFTS
Cr. on take-off, Gananoque RLG, 3.12.43
AJ548
31 SFTS (10.41- 7.43)
SOC 26.8.43
AJ549
31 SFTS
Collided with AJ542 and cr.,11.6.42

AJ574, a typical Mk.II of No.31 SFTS *(via R.C.Sturtivant)*

AJ550
31 SFTS (10.41-11.43)
To RCAF
AJ551
31 SFTS (10.42- 3.43)
To RCAF
AJ552
31 SFTS (4.42-11.42)
To RCAF
AJ553
31 SFTS
To RCAF
AJ554
31 SFTS (4.43-12.43)
To RCAF
AJ555
31 SFTS (4.42- 7.43)
To RCAF
AJ556
31 SFTS
FA Cat.B 23.6.43
AJ557
31 SFTS (8.42- 5.43)
To RCAF
AJ558
31 SFTS (10.42-10.43)
To RCAF
AJ559
31 SFTS
Collided with AJ572 and cr.,23.2.42
AJ560
31 SFTS (10.41- 6.44)
To RCAF
AJ561
31 SFTS (4.42- 8.43)
To RCAF
AJ562
31 SFTS (10.41-11.43)
To RCAF
AJ563
31 SFTS (10.41-
cr. on take-off, Gananoque RLG, 20.9.43

AJ564
31 SFTS (10.41- 7.43)
To RCAF
AJ565
31 SFTS (10.41-12.43)
To RCAF
AJ566
31 SFTS
To RCAF
AJ567
31 SFTS (10.41- 7.44)
To RCAF
AJ568
31 SFTS
To RCAF
AJ569
31 SFTS
SOC 19.11.43
AJ570
31 SFTS (10.41- 6.43)
To RCAF
AJ571
31 SFTS (10.41- 7.43)
To RCAF
AJ572
31 SFTS (10.41-
Collided with AJ559 and cr.,23.2.42
AJ573
31 SFTS [20]
To RCAF
AJ574
31 SFTS [37] (10.41-12.42)
To RCAF
AJ575
31 SFTS (10.41- 7.44)
To RCAF
AJ576
31 SFTS (10.41-11.43)
To RCAF
AJ577
31 SFTS (10.42- 9.43)
To RCAF

AJ578
31 SFTS (10.41- 5.43)
To RCAF
AJ579
31 SFTS (10.41- 8.43)
To RCAF
AJ580
31 SFTS
To RCAF
AJ581
31 SFTS (10.42- 6.44)
To RCAF
AJ582
31 SFTS (10.41-11.41)
39 SFTS (12.41-
31 SFTS [45] (6.42-10.43)
To RCAF
AJ583
31 SFTS (10.41- 8.43)
To RCAF
AJ584
31 SFTS (10.41-10.43)
To RCAF
AJ585
31 SFTS (6.42- 6.44)
To RCAF
AJ586
31 SFTS (10.41- 9.43)
To RCAF
AJ587
31 SFTS (2.43- 9.43)
14 SFTS
To RCAF
AJ588
31 SFTS
To RCAF
AJ589
31 SFTS (7.42- 2.44)
To RCAF
AJ590
31 SFTS
cr. during aerobatics 11.10.42

AJ591
31 SFTS [54]
To RCAF
AJ592
31 SFTS
To RCAF
AJ593
31 SFTS (10.41- 8.43)
14 SFTS
To RCAF
AJ594
31 SFTS (10.42- 1.44)
To RCAF
AJ595
31 SFTS (6.42-10.43)
To RCAF
AJ596
31 SFTS (5.42- 5.44)
To RCAF
AJ597
31 SFTS
cr. in St. Lawrence River, 28.7.42
AJ598
22 SFTS 1.42-
20 SFTS
SOC 2.11.45
AJ599
20 SFTS - 3.42
22 SFTS [31] 3.42-12.43
26 EFTS 12.43-
SOC 20.11.45
AJ600
22 SFTS
cr. 9.1.42
AJ601
20 SFTS
22 SFTS
SOC 12.8.48
AJ602
22 SFTS
SOC
AJ603
20 SFTS
SOC 9.8.44
AJ604
20 SFTS [AK]
FA Cat. 3 14.7.43
AJ605
33 FIS
CFS(SR)
SOC 2.11.45
AJ606
22 SFTS
SOC 2.11.45
AJ607
20 SFTS
To SRAF 24.2.49
AJ608
20 SFTS
22 SFTS
SOC 30.11.44
AJ609
22 SFTS
SOC 2.11.45
AJ610
22 SFTS
20 SFTS
FA Cat. 3 14.6.43
AJ611
22 SFTS
Collided with Harvard Mk.I N7063 and cr., 1.7.42
AJ612
22 SFTS
SOC 14.9.42
AJ613
20 SFTS
33 FIS
22 SFTS
SOC 28.11.46
AJ614
33 FIS
CFS(SR) [614]
SOC 2.11.45

AJ615
22 SFTS
SOC 31.12.43
AJ616
22 SFTS [23] (9.42- 5.44)
SOC 12.8.48
AJ617
20 SFTS
SOC 2.11.45
AJ618
20 SFTS
cr. in Portuguese E. Africa 30.9.43
AJ619
22 SFTS
SOC 12.8.48
AJ620
20 SFTS
SOC 2.11.45
AJ621
22 SFTS 2.42-
20 SFTS
To SRAF 2.49
AJ622
22 SFTS
SOC 14.7.44
AJ623
22 SFTS
24 CAOS
SOC 2.11.45
AJ624
20 SFTS
CFS(SR)
SOC 7.44
AJ625
27 EFTS - 2.44
22 SFTS 2.44
SOC 2.11.45
AJ626
20 SFTS
SOC 30.9.44
AJ627
33 FIS
20 SFTS
FA Cat.E 12.5.45
AJ628
20 SFTS
22 SFTS
SOC 12.8.48
AJ629
22 SFTS
SOC 5.2.45
AJ630
22 SFTS
33 FIS - 5.44
CFS(SR) 5.44-
22 SFTS
SOC 12.8.48
AJ631
20 SFTS
SOC 29.12.49
AJ632
22 SFTS (4.42-11.43)
SOC 2.11.45
AJ633
22 SFTS
FA Cat. 3 23.9.42
AJ634
20 SFTS
cr. Hatfield, Salisbury, SR 23.1.42
AJ635
22 SFTS
SOC 7.6.44
AJ636
22 SFTS
20 SFTS
SOC 2.11.45
AJ637
22 SFTS
20 SFTS
SOC 8.7.44
AJ638
20 SFTS
cr. Lovedale Farm, nr. Salisbury SR 14.5.42

AJ639
20 SFTS
22 SFTS
SOC 8.8.44
AJ640
22 SFTS
SOC 2.11.45
AJ641
20 SFTS
SOC 31.10.44
AJ642
22 SFTS 2.42-
20 SFTS
SOC 2.11.45
AJ643
31 SFTS
Collided with AJ645 and cr., 2.2.43
AJ644
31 SFTS (2.42-11.43)
To RCAF
AJ645
31 SFTS
Collided with AJ643 and cr., 2.2.43
AJ646
31 SFTS (6.42- 4.43)
13 SFTS
cr. near Marieville, Que., 31.10.43
AJ647
31 SFTS (12.42- 5.44)
To RCAF
AJ648
31 SFTS
To RCAF
AJ649
31 SFTS
cr. in Gananoque Lake, 17.5.42
AJ650
31 SFTS (12.42- 7.43)
To RCAF
AJ651
31 SFTS
cr. dive-bombing on Millhaven range 13.4.42
AJ652
31 SFTS
To RCAF
AJ653
31 SFTS
To RCAF
AJ654
31 SFTS
To RCAF
AJ655
31 SFTS [73]
To RCAF
AJ656
31 SFTS
To RCAF
AJ657
Canada: no record of service
SOC 16.3.43
AJ658
31 SFTS
To RCAF
AJ659
31 SFTS (2.43- 1.44)
To RCAF
AJ660
31 SFTS
To RCAF
AJ661
31 SFTS
To RCAF
AJ662
31 SFTS [80]
To RCAF
AJ663
20 SFTS
SOC 4.5.45
AJ664
20 SFTS
SOC 3.7.45
AJ665
22 SFTS
SOC 28.11.46

A wintry Ontario landscape as AJ662 carries out a training sortie from No.31 SFTS (via R.C.Sturtivant)

AJ666
20 SFTS
SOC 2.11.45

AJ667
22 SFTS 2.42-
To SRAF 2.49

AJ668
20 SFTS
SOC 2.11.45

AJ669
20 SFTS
FA Cat. 3 14.4.42

AJ670
22 SFTS
SOC 2.11.45

AJ671
22 SFTS 2.42-
33 FIS
SOC 2.2.44

AJ672
20 SFTS
cr. on take-off, Cranborne, SR, 15.12.41

AJ673
20 SFTS - 3.42
22 SFTS [40] 3.42-
3 ANS
SOC 5.8.48

AJ674
S. Rhodesia: no record of service
SOC 30.9.43

AJ675
22 SFTS
SOC 2.11.45

AJ676
22 SFTS 2.42-
SOC 2.11.45

AJ677
22 SFTS
SOC 28.11.46

AJ678
21 SFTS - 3.44
22 SFTS 3.44-
SOC 28.12.49

AJ679
20 SFTS
SOC 2.11.45

AJ680
20 SFTS
FA.Cat. 3 7.4.43

AJ681
20 SFTS
SOC 2.11.45

AJ682
22 SFTS 2.42-
cr. Umvuma, SR 10.4.44

AJ683
31 SFTS
cr. in Lake Ontario, 8.11.42

AJ684
31 SFTS
Collided with FE437 and cr., 8.2.43

AJ685
31 SFTS (5.42- 9.43)
To RCAF

AJ686
31 SFTS (4.43- 7.44)
To RCAF

AJ687
31 SFTS
cr. in flames, Millhaven range, 19.12.43

AJ688
31 SFTS
To RCAF

AJ689
31 SFTS
To RCAF

AJ690
31 SFTS
cr. in Lake Ontario, 8.5.43

AJ691
31 SFTS
SOC 11.6.42

AJ692
31 SFTS [90]
To RCAF

AJ693
31 SFTS
cr. in Lake Ontario, 29.9.43

AJ694
31 SFTS
cr. 1ml NW of Kingston, Ont., afld. 20.4.42

AJ695
31 SFTS (10.41-11.43)
SOC 4.8.44

AJ696
31 SFTS (10.41- 5.43)
To RCAF

AJ697
31 SFTS
cr. 24.1.42

AJ698
31 SFTS
Cat.A 21.9.41

AJ699
31 SFTS [97]
cr. in Lake Ontario 3.9.43

AJ700
31 SFTS
To RCAF

AJ701
31 SFTS
cr. in Lake Ontario 20.11.41

AJ702
31 SFTS
DBF after undershooting, Kingston, 28.1.43

AJ703
22 SFTS
31 FIS - 5.44
CFS(SR) 5.44-
SOC 12.8.48

AJ704
22 SFTS [97] 2.42-
SOC 12.8.48

AJ705
22 SFTS 2.42-
cr. 10.6.42

AJ706
20 SFTS - 3.42
22 SFTS 3.42-
To SRAF 28.2.49

AJ707
33 FIS
SOC 12.8.48

AJ708
20 SFTS
22 SFTS 1.42-
FA Cat.E 2.3.45

AJ709
20 SFTS - 3.42
22 SFTS 3.42-
SOC 12.8.48

AJ710
20 SFTS
SOC 2.11.45

AJ711
22 SFTS 2.42-
SOC 2.11.45

AJ712
20 SFTS
SOC 31.10.44

AJ713
20 SFTS
cr. Nyamaroya Reserve, SR, 2.8.43

AJ714
20 SFTS [85]
SOC 30.11.43

AJ715
20 SFTS [E]
cr. Pendennis RLG, SR, 4.4.42

AJ716
22 SFTS
FA Cat.E 12.3.43

AJ673 of No.20 SFTS, Cranborne, Southern Rhodesia (C.J.Wallace)

AJ717
20 SFTS
SOC 9.8.44
AJ718
20 SFTS - 3.42
22 SFTS 3.42-
To SRAF 2.49
AJ719
20 SFTS - 3.42
22 SFTS 3.42-
SOC 3.7.45
AJ720
20 SFTS
To SRAF 2.49
AJ721
20 SFTS
SOC 2.11.45
AJ722
20 SFTS
SOC 4.8.45
AJ723
32 SFTS
37 SFTS
13 SFTS
NFT
AJ724
32 SFTS 9.41-
34 SFTS
To RCAF
AJ725
34 SFTS
cr. 10mls S of Walsh, Alb. 19.10.43
AJ726
31 SFTS [6]
32 SFTS
34 SFTS
To RCAF
AJ727
32 SFTS
34 SFTS
Collided with RCAF 2731 and cr.
3mls NW of Redcliff, Alb., 4.12.42
AJ728
13 SFTS
cr. 7mls N of Richard, Sas.,6.12.44
AJ729
13 SFTS
To RCAF
AJ730
32 SFTS (10.41- 4.42)
34 SFTS (1.43- 3.44)
To RCAF
AJ731
32 SFTS 9.41-
To RCAF
AJ732
32 SFTS
cr. 25mls SW of Moose Jaw, 25.7.42
AJ733
32 SFTS (12.41- 8.42)
To RCAF
AJ734
32 SFTS
34 SFTS
To RCAF
AJ735
32 SFTS
To RCAF
AJ736
32 SFTS
34 SFTS
To RCAF
AJ737
32 SFTS
34 SFTS
cr. near Seven Persons, Alb. 1.7.44
AJ738
22 SFTS
SOC 2.11.45
AJ739
20 SFTS
SOC 28.11.46
AJ740
20 SFTS [32]
SOC 2.11.45

AJ741
20 SFTS
22 SFTS
To SRAF 24.2.49
AJ742
22 SFTS
SOC 2.11.45
AJ743
33 FIS
FA Cat. 3 1.11.43
AJ744
20 SFTS
SOC 31.3.42
AJ745
20 SFTS
22 SFTS
SOC 30.11.44
AJ746
20 SFTS
SOC 31.12.49
AJ747
20 SFTS
cr. near New Martinsthorpe RLG, SR,
11.8.42
AJ748
20 SFTS
22 SFTS
SOC 2.11.45
AJ749
20 SFTS
cr. Werza, SR, 29.12.42
AJ750
20 SFTS
SOC 2.11.45
AJ751
20 SFTS
SOC 31.3.42
AJ752
33 FIS
22 SFTS
To SRAF 2.49
AJ753
Canada: no record of service
To RCAF
AJ754
32 SFTS
To RCAF
AJ755
32 SFTS
Collided with RCAF 2637 and cr.
22mls E of Wymark, 25.7.42
AJ756
34 SFTS
32 SFTS - 9.44
13 SFTS 9.44-
NFT
AJ757
32 SFTS
To RCAF
AJ758
39 SFTS
37 SFTS
34 SFTS
To RCAF
AJ759
37 SFTS
FA Cat.E 10.12.42
AJ760
39 SFTS
34 SFTS
To RCAF
AJ761
34 SFTS
Collided on ground with AJ828,
22.1.42
AJ762
39 SFTS
37 SFTS
To RCAF
AJ763
34 SFTS
cr. $\frac{1}{2}$ml S of Hobson RLG 8.12.41

AJ764
37 SFTS
34 SFTS
To RCAF
AJ765
37 SFTS (12.42- 2.44)
34 SFTS
To RCAF
AJ766
39 SFTS
cr. in Lake Montague, Sas., 6.9.42
AJ767
37 SFTS
34 SFTS
Cat.A 10.9.44
AJ768
73 OTU -10.42
74 OTU 10.42-
SOC 29.3.45
AJ769
73 OTU -11.42
Aden FD Flt 11.42-
71 OTU
SOC 31.1.46
AJ770
73 OTU -11.42
71 OTU 11.42-
SOC 31.5.45
AJ771
71 OTU
Collided with AJ808 and cr. 3mls S
of Summit, 29.10.42
AJ772
73 OTU
SOC 31.5.45
AJ773
Middle East: no record of service
SOC 31.8.44
AJ774
73 OTU
To S. Rhodesia
20 SFTS
FA Cat.E 13.7.43
AJ775
Middle East: no record of service
Lost 11.9.42
AJ776
1 METS
SOC 31.5.45
AJ777
Middle East: no record of service
SOC 31.1.46
AJ778
73 OTU
DBR in accident 11.5.42
AJ779
71 OTU
DBR in accident 9.5.42
AJ780
Middle East: no record of service
SOC 31.5.45
AJ781
1 METS
73 OTU
AB&GS
SOC 31.1.46
AJ782
AB&GS
SOC 31.5.45
AJ783
1 OTU(I) 7.42-
151 OTU 7.42

AJ783
1 OTU(I) - 7.42
151 OTU 7.42-
Hit obstruction while low flying,
Risalpur, 10.11.43
AJ784
1 OTU(I) - 7.42
151 OTU 7.42-
SOC 30.4.43

AJ777 of an unrecorded unit in India; one of only four Mk.II Harvards to reach that area *(Air-Britain)*

AJ785
152 OTU
151 OTU
cr. 7mls NW of Risalpur, 31.7.42
AJ786
1 OTU(I) - 7.42
151 OTU 7.42-
SOC 31.8.44
AJ787
India: no record of service
SOC 31.5.45
AJ788
37 SFTS
34 SFTS
To RCAF
AJ789
34 SFTS
cr. 8mls SSE of Saskatoon, Sas., 8.1.42
AJ790
39 SFTS
37 SFTS [79]
34 SFTS
To RCAF
AJ791
Canada: no record of service
To RCAF
AJ792
34 SFTS
To RCAF
AJ793
39 SFTS
37 SFTS
34 SFTS
cr. Medicine Hat, Alb., 2.3.44
AJ794
39 SFTS
37 SFTS
13 SFTS
To RCAF

AJ795
39 SFTS
37 SFTS
To RCAF
AJ796
39 SFTS
37 SFTS
Collided with RCAF Crane 8127 of 3 SFTS and cr. in Victoria Park, Calgary, 28.8.43
AJ797
34 SFTS
SOC 27.12.44
AJ798
39 SFTS
37 SFTS
34 SFTS
To RCAF
AJ799
39 SFTS
37 SFTS
34 SFTS
To RCAF
AJ800
37 SFTS
13 SFTS
Cat.A 2.8.44
AJ801
41 SFTS (3.42- 1.44)
To RCAF
AJ802
39 SFTS
37 SFTS
2 Sqdn RCAF
To RCAF
AJ803
71 OTU
1 MECCU
FA Cat.E 29.10.43

AJ804
Middle East: no record of service
PSOC 1.1.47
AJ805
335 Sqdn
1 METS
SOC 1.10.43
AJ806
AB&GS
SOC 31.5.45
AJ807
Middle East: no record of service
SOC 8.4.43
AJ808
71 OTU
Collided with AJ771 and cr. 3mls N of Summit, 29.10.42
AJ809
1 MECCU
To FFAF 12.43
Retd. to RAF 4.44
SOC 22.2.45
AJ810
73 OTU
SOC 1.3.44
AJ811
71 OTU - 4.43
SOC 31.5.45
AJ812
73 OTU
80 Sqdn
SOC 1.1.44
AJ813
1 METS
C&R School
To FFAF 12.43
AJ814
73 OTU [J]
SOC 31.5.45

AJ815
71 OTU
AB&GS
SOC 26.4.45
AJ816
74 OTU
SOC 1.12.43
AJ817
1 METS
74 OTU
SOC 31.5.45
AJ818
71 OTU
1 METS
Rayak
To FFAF 1.44
AJ819
71 OTU
SOC 31.5.45
AJ820
1 METS
73 OTU
SOC 26.4.45
AJ821
1 METS
SOC 25.1.45
AJ822
No RAF service
To R.Egypt.AF 4.44
cr. and retd. to RAF
SOC 31.5.45
AJ823
37 SFTS
13 SFTS
2 FIS(C) 9.44-
To RCAF
AJ824
39 SFTS
37 SFTS
13 SFTS
To RCAF
AJ825
39 SFTS
To RCAF
AJ826
39 SFTS
cr. 5mls NE of McMahon, Sas.,8.5.42
AJ827
39 SFTS
37 SFTS
To RCAF
AJ828
34 SFTS
Collided on ground with AJ761; DBR 22.1.42
AJ829
34 SFTS
37 SFTS
To RCAF
AJ830
39 SFTS
37 SFTS
13 SFTS
34 SFTS
To RCAF
AJ831
37 SFTS
To RCAF
AJ832
37 SFTS
To RCAF
AJ833
39 SFTS
To RCAF
AJ834
39 SFTS
34 SFTS
To RCAF
AJ835
37 SFTS
13 SFTS
34 SFTS
To RCAF
AJ836
39 SFTS
37 SFTS
Cat.A 6.10.42
AJ837
71 OTU
SOC 22.2.45
AJ838
74 OTU
To R.Egypt.AF 11.43
AJ839
74 OTU
Spun in, El Kusseir, 11.11.42
AJ840
74 OTU
CGS(ME)
To USAAF 3.44
AJ841
74 OTU
154 Sqdn
SOC 25.4.46
AJ842
74 OTU
To R.Egypt.AF 4.44
Retd. to RAF 8.44
SOC 21.5.45
AJ843
73 OTU
1 METS
SOC 31.5.45
AJ844
Middle East: no record of service
SOC 31.5.45
AJ845
Middle East: no record of service
SOC 31.1.46
AJ846
1 METS
73 OTU
SOC 29.8.46
AJ847
37 SFTS
13 SFTS
To RCAF
AJ848
39 SFTS
37 SFTS
To RCAF
AJ849
39 SFTS
37 SFTS
13 SFTS
To RCAF
AJ850
39 SFTS
Cat.A 15.1.42
AJ851
39 SFTS
37 SFTS
To RCAF
AJ852
39 SFTS
37 SFTS
To RCAF
AJ853
39 SFTS
37 SFTS
To RCAF
AJ854
39 SFTS
37 SFTS
Cat.A 15.12.42
AJ855 to AJ892
Direct to RNZAF
AJ893
41 SFTS
8 SFTS - 6.44
12 SFTS 6.44-
To RCAF
AJ894
39 SFTS
37 SFTS
cr. Conrick, Alb., 1.8.43
AJ895
37 SFTS
To RCAF
AJ896
39 SFTS
13 SFTS
To RCAF
AJ897
39 SFTS
37 SFTS
13 SFTS
To RCAF
AJ898
39 SFTS
34 SFTS
Cat.A 4.12.42
AJ899
39 SFTS
37 SFTS
cr. and DBF 8.1.44
AJ900
39 SFTS
37 SFTS
To RCAF
AJ901
39 SFTS
37 SFTS
To RCAF
AJ902
39 SFTS
37 SFTS
To RCAF
AJ903
39 SFTS
37 SFTS
13 SFTS
To RCAF
AJ904
Canada: no record of service
To RCAF
AJ905
39 SFTS
37 SFTS
To RCAF
AJ906
39 SFTS
13 SFTS
To RCAF
AJ907
Canada: no record of service
To RCAF
AJ908
39 SFTS
37 SFTS
To RCAF
AJ909
39 SFTS
34 SFTS
To RCAF
AJ910
39 SFTS
37 SFTS
To RCAF
AJ911
cr. in USA before delivery
AJ912
39 SFTS
37 SFTS
Collided with AJ953 and cr.2½mls E of Conrick, Alb., 7.1.43
AJ913
39 SFTS
To RCAF
AJ914
39 SFTS
To RCAF
AJ915
39 SFTS
37 SFTS
To RCAF
AJ916
41 SFTS
Cat.A 22.6.43
AJ917
39 SFTS
37 SFTS
To RCAF

AJ918
41 SFTS
To RCAF
AJ919
41 SFTS
8 SFTS
To RCAF
AJ920
39 SFTS
13 SFTS
To RCAF
AJ921
39 SFTS
To RCAF
AJ922
41 SFTS [15]
To RCAF
AJ923
32 SFTS
34 SFTS
To RCAF
AJ924
41 SFTS
To RCAF
AJ925
41 SFTS
To RCAF
AJ926
41 SFTS
To RCAF
AJ927
39 SFTS
8 SFTS
Collided with RCAF 2896 and cr. 23.3.44
AJ928
41 SFTS
To RCAF
AJ929
41 SFTS
To RCAF
AJ930
39 SFTS
34 SFTS [39]
13 SFTS
To RCAF
AJ931
41 SFTS
To RCAF
AJ932
41 SFTS
To RCAF
AJ933
41 SFTS
To RCAF
AJ934
41 SFTS
To RCAF
AJ935
41 SFTS
To RCAF
AJ936
41 SFTS
To RCAF
AJ937
41 SFTS
37 SFTS
To RCAF
AJ938
41 SFTS (7.42-12.43)
To RCAF
AJ939
41 SFTS
To RCAF
AJ940
41 SFTS
To RCAF
AJ941
41 SFTS
To RCAF
AJ942
41 SFTS
32 SFTS
34 SFTS
To RCAF

AJ943
41 SFTS - 7.43
37 SFTS 7.43-
AJ944
41 SFTS (11.42-10.43)
To RCAF
AJ945
37 SFTS (1.43-10.43)
13 SFTS
To RCAF
AJ946
39 SFTS
cr. 5mls SE of Swift Current, Sas., 16.3.42
AJ947
41 SFTS
To RCAF
AJ948
39 SFTS (1.42- 6.42)
37 SFTS (4.43- 1.44)
13 SFTS
To RCAF
AJ949
39 SFTS
37 SFTS
13 SFTS
To RCAF
AJ950
Canada: no record of service
To RCAF
AJ951
39 SFTS (3.42- 8.42)
37 SFTS
To RCAF
AJ952
39 SFTS
37 SFTS (11.42- 1.44)
13 SFTS (4.44-11.44)
To RCAF
AJ953
37 SFTS
Collided with AJ912 and cr. 2½mls E of Conrick, Alb., 7.1.43
AJ954
39 SFTS
34 SFTS
To RCAF
AJ955
39 SFTS
To RCAF
AJ956
39 SFTS
Cat.A 8.8.43
AJ957
39 SFTS
37 SFTS
13 SFTS
To RCAF
AJ958
39 SFTS
37 SFTS (11.42-10.43)
13 SFTS
To RCAF
AJ959
37 SFTS
Cat.A 7.7.44
AJ960
39 SFTS
37 SFTS (6.43- 1.44)
To RCAF
AJ961
39 SFTS
37 SFTS
To RCAF
AJ962
39 SFTS
37 SFTS [47] (6.43-11.43)
To RCAF
AJ963
39 SFTS
34 SFTS
To RCAF
AJ964
39 SFTS (1.42- 5.42)
To RCAF

AJ965
39 SFTS
37 SFTS (5.43- 9.43)
13 SFTS
To RCAF
AJ966
39 SFTS (1.42- 9.42)
37 SFTS
cr. 10mls WSW of Midnapore, Alb., 31.12.43
AJ967
39 SFTS
37 SFTS
To RCAF
AJ968
39 SFTS
37 SFTS
13 SFTS
To RCAF
AJ969
37 SFTS (6.43- 1.44)
To RCAF
AJ970
39 SFTS
41 SFTS
FA Cat.E 2.1.44
AJ971
39 SFTS
37 SFTS (5.43-10.43)
13 SFTS
To RCAF
AJ972
37 SFTS (1.43- 9.43)
Cat.A 2.9.44
AJ973
39 SFTS
37 SFTS
13 SFTS
To RCAF
AJ974
39 SFTS
37 SFTS [59] (1.43- 9.43)
To RCAF
AJ975
39 SFTS (1.42- 6.42)
37 SFTS (11.42-10.43)
2 FIS(C)
cr. on take-off, Pearce, Alb., 28.9.44
To RCAF as inst. airframe A.434
AJ976
39 SFTS
37 SFTS (5.43- 1.44)
To RCAF
AJ977
39 SFTS
37 SFTS (4.43- 9.43)
To RCAF
AJ978
39 SFTS
37 SFTS (2.43-10.43)
13 SFTS
To RCAF
AJ979
39 SFTS (1.42- 6.42
AJ979
39 SFTS (1.42- 6.42)
13 SFTS
NFT
AJ980
39 SFTS (1.42- 5.42)
37 SFTS
13 SFTS
To RCAF
AJ981
37 SFTS (9.43- 1.44)
34 SFTS
To RCAF
AJ982
39 SFTS
cr. 1ml N of Swift Current, Sas., 29.7.42

No.37 SFTS in Canada operated AJ962 among many others *(RAF Museum)*

AJ983
39 SFTS
37 SFTS (10.42- 9.43)
To RCAF
AJ984
39 SFTS
37 SFTS (8.43- 1.44)
13 SFTS
To RCAF
AJ985
39 SFTS
37 SFTS
To RCAF
AJ986
37 SFTS (3.43- 1.44)
13 SFTS
To RCAF
AJ987
37 SFTS
NFT

****

BD130
AFEE 1.43- 2.43
ECFS
TADU 12.44- 7.45
Croughton 7.45-10.45
SS (Coley) 2.49
BD131
Watchfield 10.40- 2.41
Odiham for S. Rhodesia 3.41
21 SFTS
20 SFTS
To SRAF 2.49
BD132
Watchfield 10.40- 2.41
Odiham for S. Rhodesia 2.41
33 FIS [15]
CFS(SR)
To SRAF 2.49
BD133
Watchfield 10.40- 2.41
Odiham for S. Rhodesia 2.41
22 SFTS - 8.44
26 EFTS 8.44-
SOC 2.11.45
BD134
A&AEE 11.40-12.40
Odiham for S. Rhodesia 12.40
20 SFTS
22 SFTS -12.43
26 EFTS 12.43- 2.44
22 SFTS 2.44-
To SRAF 2.49
BD135
Watchfield 10.40- 2.41
Odiham for S. Rhodesia 2.41
20 SFTS - 3.42
22 SFTS 3.42-12.42
SOC 1.1.43
BD136
SF Sqdn 7.41- 6.42
2 FF 6.42- 8.42
To USAAF at Bovingdon 15.9.42
BD137
Halton 7.42- 8.42
To USAAF at Bovingdon 8.42

****

BJ410
No service in UK
Odiham for S. Rhodesia 1.41
22 SFTS
FA Cat. 3 10.12.43
BJ411
No trace
BJ412
No service in UK
Odiham for S. Rhodesia 1.41
22 SFTS
SOC 2.11.45
BJ413
Yatesbury 11.40-12.40
Odiham for S. Rhodesia 1.41
FA Cat. 3 29.7.42
BJ414
No service in UK
Odiham for S. Rhodesia 12.40
desp. ME
71 OTU 3.42
Collided with Hurricane Z4869, 17.3.42
BJ415
Yatesbury 11.40-12.40
Odiham for S. Rhodesia 1.41
20 SFTS
cr. Mazoe, near Salisbury, SR, 7.7.42

****

BS808
No service in UK
Odiham for S. Rhodesia 12.40
20 SFTS
SOC 12.8.48

****

Seen at A&AEE during the short time it spent there in December 1940 is Mk.II Harvard BD134 *(via J.J.Halley)*

BW184
11 SFTS -11.41
13 SFTS
To RCAF
BW185
11 SFTS -10.41
Cat.A 25.5.43
BW186
8 SFTS - 2.43
14 SFTS 2.43- 4.44
To RCAF
BW187
11 SFTS - 1.42
8 SFTS 1.42-
Cat.A 13.6.42
BW188
5 B&GS 5.41-
41 SFTS
To RCAF
BW189
14 SFTS 2.44-
To RCAF
BW190
13 SFTS (1.42- 3.43)
31 SFTS
To RCAF
BW191
13 SFTS
Collided with BW192 and cr. 12.6.43
BW192
10 SFTS
13 SFTS
Collided with BW191 and cr. 12.6.43
BW193
13 SFTS
SOC 18.10.43
BW194
Canada: no record of service
Cat.A 31.10.41
BW195
8 SFTS
14 SFTS 3.44- 8.44
To RCAF

BW196
11 SFTS -10.41
8 SFTS
To RCAF
BW197
Canada: no record of service
To RCAF
BW198
11 SFTS -11.41
SOC 24.2.44
BW199
14 SFTS 9.43-
To RCAF
BW200
11 SFTS
To RCAF
BW201
11 SFTS -11.41
8 SFTS 11.41-
To RCAF
BW202
11 SFTS - 1.42
1 SFTS(C)
To RCAF
BW203
11 SFTS - 1.42
33 SFTS 1.42-
41 SFTS -11.43
To RCAF
BW204
39 SFTS
13 SFTS (4.44-10.44)
To RCAF
BW205
34 SFTS
cr. in S. Saskatchewan River at Estuary, Sas., 12.6.44
BW206
13 SFTS
14 SFTS 2.43-
To RCAF
BW207
10 SFTS
13 SFTS
14 SFTS
To RCAF

DG430
S. Rhodesia: no record of service
To SRAF 2.49
DG431
S. Rhodesia: no record of service
PSOC 1.1.47
DG432
Reported lost at sea 1.41
DG433
71 OTU (10.43- 4.44)
(carried its former RCAF serial)
NFT
DG434
22 SFTS (10.43- 4.44)
(carried its former RCAF serial)
NFT
DG435 to DG439 inclusive
Reported lost at sea 1.41

****

EX100
71 OTU [30]
73 OTU
SOC 22.2.45
EX101
71 OTU [18]
Collided with EX324 and cr. 4mls S of Summit, 29.12.42
EX102
71 OTU
75 OTU
1342 Flt
SOC 28.11.46
EX103
73 OTU
SOC 22.2.45
EX104
71 OTU
SOC 29.3.45
EX105
71 OTU
1413 Flt
SOC 9.5.46

EX106
71 OTU
SOC 29.5.47

EX107
71 OTU
SOC 28.11.46

EX108
71 OTU
SOC 31.8.44

EX109
71 OTU - 4.43
SOC 28.11.46

EX110
71 OTU
Hit high ground, Kasfareet, 31.7.43

EX111
71 OTU
73 OTU [F]
SOC 6.7.45

EX112
71 OTU
73 OTU [L]
SOC 28.11.46

EX113
71 OTU
73 OTU [Q]
SOC 28.11.46

EX114
Direct to SAAF (7095) 11.42

EX115
71 OTU
SOC 28.11.46

EX116
73 OTU [N]
SOC 22.3.45

EX117
Direct to SAAF (7096) 11.42

EX118
73 OTU [T]
SOC 31.5.45

EX119
1 MECCU
SOC 29.3.45

EX120
73 OTU
1 MECCU
SOC 31.5.45

EX121
73 OTU [Z]
DBR in accident 16.3.44

EX122
73 OTU [U]
SOC 31.5.45

EX123
73 OTU [A]
SOC 22.2.45

EX124
73 OTU [B]
SOC 28.11.46

EX125
73 OTU [V]
SOC 31.5.45

EX126
249 Sqdn
73 OTU [Y]
Collided with EX767 and cr. 3.10.44

EX127
Malta ASR&CF 5.43-
SOC 31.8.44

EX128
73 OTU
SOC 21.6.45

EX129
73 OTU
SOC 23.9.44

EX130
73 OTU [D]
SOC 31.5.45

EX131
74 OTU
SOC 28.11.46

EX132
73 OTU
SOC 28.11.46

EX133
C&R Flt, 2 ADU
SOC 1.12.43

EX134
73 OTU
SOC 28.11.46

EX135
74 OTU
SOC 31.8.44

EX136
73 OTU [E]
SOC 28.11.46

EX137
SF Petah Tiqva
SOC 26.2.48

EX138
73 OTU [M]
SOC 31.5.45

EX139
73 OTU [G]
SOC 28.11.46

EX140
CGS(ME) - 6.43
73 OTU 6.43-
1 MECCU
SOC 31.5.45

EX141
74 OTU
SF Petah Tiqva
cr. in sea off Palestine during aerobatics, 27.7.45

EX142
C&R Flt, 2 ADU
1 MECCU
SOC 21.6.45

EX143
71 OTU
DBR in accident, Ismailia, 14.8.43

EX144
71 OTU
SOC 28.11.46

EX145
71 OTU
SOC 28.11.46

EX146
71 OTU
SOC 28.11.46

EX147
71 OTU
SOC 28.11.46

EX148
71 OTU
73 OTU
SOC 31.5.45

EX149
33 FIS
NFT

EX150
73 OTU [H]
SOC 28.11.46

EX151
73 OTU [Z]
SOC 31.5.45

EX152
74 OTU
To R.Egypt.AF 4.44
Retd. to RAF
SOC 29.3.45

EX153
73 OTU [S]
SOC 28.11.46

EX154
73 OTU [R]
PSOC 1.1.47

EX155
73 OTU
Collided with Hurricane Z4839 and cr. 12mls W of Abu Sueir, 30.8.43

EX156
73 OTU
To R.Egypt.AF 3.44
Retd. to RAF 8.44
SOC 28.11.46

EX157
20 SFTS
SOC 9.8.44

EX158
22 SFTS 3.43-
SOC 30.9.44

EX159
20 SFTS [3]
4 FTS [92/G:N]
Sold 30.11.53

EX160
20 SFTS [C]
4 FTS
To SRAF 5.52

EX161
22 SFTS 2.43-
20 SFTS
4 FTS [H:A]
Hit cables and DBR, 20.1.53

EX162
22 SFTS 3.43-
20 SFTS
SOC 1.3.46

EX163
RATG HQ CF 2.43-
28 EFTS
20 SFTS
FA Cat.E 2.7.43

EX164
S. Rhodesia: no record of service
SOC 30.4.44

EX165
33 FIS - 5.44
CFS(SR) 5.44-
SOC 9.8.44

EX166
20 SFTS
SOC 2.11.45

EX167
22 SFTS 3.43-
20 SFTS
4 FTS
Collided with EX818 and cr. 4mls S of Bambesi, SR, 25.3.53

EX168
20 SFTS
4 FTS
cr. Imbesu Park, near Bulawayo, SR, 19.5.48

EX169
Direct to SAAF (7131) 11.42

EX170
Direct to SAAF (7132) 11.42

EX171
Direct to SAAF (7133) 11.42

EX172
22 SFTS
20 SFTS
cr. 90mls N of Concession, SR, 3.2.44

EX173
Direct to SAAF (7134) 11.42

EX174
22 SFTS 3.43-
SOC 30.11.43

EX175
22 SFTS [44] 3.43-
20 SFTS
SOC 1.3.46

EX176
Direct to SAAF (7135) 11.42

EX177
Direct to SAAF (7136) 11.42
Retd. to RAF: arr. UK 10.46
To R.Hell.AF 5.47

EX178
Direct to SAAF (7046) 11.42

EX179
Direct to SAAF (7047) 11.42

EX180
Direct to SAAF (7050) 11.42

EX181
Direct to SAAF (7045) 11.42
Retd. to RAF: arr. UK 9.46
To Belg.AF 3.47

EX182
Direct to SAAF (7051) 11.42
EX183
Direct to SAAF (7049) 11.42
EX184 to EX195
Direct to RNZAF(1016 to 1017) 9.42
EX196
Direct to SAAF (7052) 11.42
EX197
33 FIS
CFS(SR)
20 SFTS
4 FTS
DBR in accident, Heany, SR, 3.9.53
EX198
Direct to SAAF (7053) 11.42
EX199
Direct to SAAF (7054) 11.42
Retd. to RAF: arr. UK 1.47
SS 8.50
EX200
Direct to SAAF (7055) 11.42
Retd. to RAF: arr. UK 1.47
SS 8.50
EX201
Direct to SAAF (7056) 11.42
EX202
Direct to SAAF (7057) 11.42
Retd. to RAF: arr. UK 11.46
SS 8.50
EX203
Direct to SAAF (7058) 11.42
EX204
Direct to SAAF (7059) 11.42
EX205
Direct to SAAF (7060) 11.42
EX206
Direct to SAAF (7048) 11.42
EX207
Direct to SAAF (7061) 11.42
Retd. to RAF: arr. UK 10.46
SS 8.50
EX208
Direct to SAAF (7001) 11.42
EX209
Direct to SAAF (7002) 11.42
Retd. to RAF: arr. UK 11.46
SS 8.50
EX210
Direct to SAAF (7003) 11.42
EX211
DIrect to SAAF (7004) 11.42
EX212
ME: no record of service
SOC 31.10.46
EX213
Direct to SAAF (7005) 11.42
EX214
Direct to SAAF (7006) 11.42
Retd. to RAF: arr. UK 12.46
SS 8.50
EX215
Direct to SAAF (7008) 11.42
EX216
Direct to SAAF (7009) 11.42
EX217
Direct to SAAF (7010) 11.42
Retd. to RAF: arr. UK 1.47
SS 8.50
EX218
Direct to SAAF (7011) 11.42
EX219
Direct to SAAF (7012) 11.42
EX220
Direct to SAAF (7013) 11.42
Retd. to RAF: arr. UK 1.47
SS 8.50
EX221
Direct to SAAF (7014) 11.42
Retd. to RAF: arr. UK 10.46
To R.Hell.AF 3.47
EX222
Direct to SAAF (7015) 11.42

EX162, a Mk.IIa, being readied for a training sortie in Southern Rhodesia (via J.J.Halley)

EX223
Direct to SAAF (7016) 11.42
Retd. to RAF: arr. UK 11.46
To R.Hell.AF 3.47
EX224
Direct to SAAF (7017) 11.42
EX225
Direct to SAAF (7018) 11.42
Retd. to RAF: arr. UK 10.46
SS 8.50
EX226
Direct to SAAF (7019) 11.42
Retd. to RAF: arr. UK 10.46
SS 8.50
EX227
Direct to SAAF (7020) 11.42
EX228
DIrect to SAAF (7021) 11.42
Retd. to RAF: arr. UK 11.46
To R.Hell.AF 3.47
EX229
Direct to SAAF (7022) 11.42
EX230
Direct to SAAF (7007) 11.42
Retd. to RAF: arr. UK 11.46
To Belg.AF 3.47
EX231
Direct to SAAF (7092) 11.42
EX232
Direct to SAAF (7085) 11.42
EX233
Direct to SAAF (7086) 11.42
EX234
Direct to SAAF (7088) 11.42
Retd. to RAF: arr. UK 12.46
SS 8.50
EX235
Direct to SAAF (7093) 11.42
Retd. to RAF: arr. UK 11.46
SS 8.50
EX236
Direct to SAAF (7089) 11.42
Retd. to RAF: arr. UK 11.46
To R.Hell.AF 4.47
EX237
Direct to SAAF (7090) 11.42
Retd. to RAF: arr UK 1.47
SS 8.50
EX238
Direct to SAAF (7087) 11.42
Retd. to RAF: arr. UK 11.46
SS 8.50
EX239
Direct to SAAF (7094) 11.42
Retd. to RAF: arr. UK 11.46
To Belg.AF 2.47
EX240
Direct to SAAF (7091) 11.42

EX241
20 SFTS
cr. Kabanga, near Gwelo, SR,27.7.43
EX242
22 SFTS 2.43-
SOC for conversion to inst. a'frame 30.11.44
EX243
22 SFTS 2.43- .45
SOC 5.4.46
EX244
22 SFTS 3.43-
cr. and DBR 16.6.44
EX245
22 SFTS 2.43-
4 FTS [81/G:C]
To Belg.AF 11.53
EX246
22 SFTS [69] 3.43-
4 FTS 3.49-
To SRAF 5.52
EX247
Direct to SAAF (7137) 11.42
EX248
Direct to SAAF (7138) 11.42
EX249
Direct to SAAF (7139) 11.42
Retd. to RAF: arr. UK 11.46
To R.Hell.AF 3.47
EX250
Direct to SAAF (7140) 11.42
EX251
Direct to SAAF (7141) 11.42
Retd. to RAF: arr. UK 11.46
To Belg.AF 5.47
EX252
Direct to SAAF (7142) 11.42
EX253
Direct to SAAF (7097) 11.42
Retd. to RAF: arr. UK 11.46
To R.Hell.AF 3.47
EX254
Direct to SAAF (7098) 11.42
Retd. to RAF: arr.UK 11.46
To Belg.AF 2.47
EX255
Direct to SAAF (7099) 11.42
Retd. to RAF: arr. UK 11.46
SS 8.50
EX256
Direct to SAAF (7264) 3.43
To R.Neth.AF for spares 2.47
EX257
Direct to SAAF (7100) 11.42
Retd. to RAF: arr. UK 11.46
To R.Hell.AF 3.47

EX258
Direct to SAAF (7101) 11.42
Retd. to RAF: arr. UK 11.46
To Ital.AF 5.49
EX259
Direct to SAAF (7102) 11.42
Retd. to RAF: arr. UK 11.46
To R.Hell.AF 5.47
EX260
Direct to SAAF (7103) 11.42
EX261
Direct to SAAF (7104) 11.42
EX262
Direct to SAAF (7105) 11.42
EX263
Direct to SAAF (7106) 11.42
EX264
Direct to SAAF (7107) 11.42
Retd. to RAF: arr. UK 10.46
To Belg.AF 2.47
EX265
Direct to SAAF (7108) 11.42
EX266
Direct to SAAF (7109) 11.42
Retd. to RAF: arr. UK 11.46
SS 8.50
EX267
Direct to SAAF (7110) 11.42
EX268
Direct to SAAF (7111) 11.42
EX269
Direct to SAAF (7112) 11.42
Retd. to RAF: arr. UK 11.46
To Ital.AF 5.49
EX270
Direct to SAAF (7113) 11.42
Retd. to RAF: arr. UK 10.46
SS 8.50
EX271
Direct to SAAF (7171) 2.43
EX272
Direct to SAAF (7165) 2.43
Retd. to RAF: arr. UK 11.46
SS 8.50
EX273
Direct to SAAF (7184) 2.43
Retd. to RAF: arr. UK 11.46
To Belg.AF 2.47
EX274
Direct to SAAF (7194) 2.43
Retd. to RAF: arr. UK 11.46
SS 8.50
EX275
Direct to SAAF (7164) 2.43
Retd. to RAF: arr. UK 11.46
To Belg.AF 5.47
EX276
Direct to SAAF (7177) 2.43
EX277
Direct to SAAF (7166) 2.43
EX278
Direct to SAAF (7169) 2.43
Retd. to RAF: arr. UK 11.46
To Ital.AF 5.49
EX279
Direct to SAAF (7195) 2.43
Retd. to RAF: arr. UK 10.46
To R.Dan.AF 11.46
EX280
Direct to SAAF (7167) 2.43
Retd. to RAF: arr. UK 11.46
SS 8.50
EX281
Direct to SAAF (7172) 2.43
EX282
Direct to SAAF (7196) 2.43
Retd. to RAF: arr. UK 11.46
To R.Hell.AF 3.47
EX283
Direct to SAAF (7163) 2.43
Retd. to RAF: arr. UK 11.46
SS (Coley) 2.50
EX284
Direct to SAAF (7197) 2.43
EX285
Direct to SAAF (7075) 2.43
Retd. to RAF: arr. UK 10.46
To R.Dan.AF 11.46
EX286
Direct to SAAF (7170) 2.43
EX287
Direct to SAAF (7168) 2.43
EX288
Direct to SAAF (7181) 2.43
Retd. to RAF: arr. UK 11.46
SS 8.50
EX289
Direct to SAAF (7183) 2.43
Retd. to RAF: arr. UK 10.46
SS 8.50
EX290
Direct to SAAF (7198) 2.43
EX291
Direct to SAAF (7199) 2.43
Retd. to RAF: arr. UK 11.46
To R.Hell.AF 5.47
EX292
Direct to SAAF (7182) 2.43
Retd. to RAF: arr. UK 10.46
To Belg.AF 3.47
EX293
Direct to SAAF (7200) 2.43
EX294
Direct to SAAF (7076) 11.42
EX295
Direct to SAAF (7077) 11.42
Retd. to RAF: arr. UK 10.46
To Belg.AF 2.47
EX296
Direct to SAAF (7078) 11.42
EX297
Direct to SAAF (7079) 11.42
Retd. to RAF: arr. UK 11.46
SS 8.50
EX298
Direct to SAAF (7080) 11.42
EX299
Direct to SAAF (7081) 11.42
Retd. to RAF: arr. UK 10.46
To R.Hell.AF 3.47
EX300
Direct to SAAF (7082) 11.42
EX301
Direct to SAAF (7083) 11.42
Retd. to RAF: arr. UK
To Ital.AF 5.49
EX302
Direct to SAAF (7084) 11.42
EX303
Direct to SAAF (7143) 11.42
Retd. to RAF: arr. UK 10.46
To Belg.AF 2.47
EX304
Direct to SAAF (7114) 11.42
EX305
Direct to SAAF (7115) 11.42
Retd. to RAF: arr. UK 10.46
To Belg.AF 4.47
EX306
Direct to SAAF (7116) 11.42
Retd. to RAF: arr. UK 10.46
SS 8.50
EX307
Direct to SAAF (7117) 11.42
Retd. to RAF: arr. UK 10.46
SS 8.50
EX308
Direct to SAAF (7118) 11.42
Retd. to RAF: arr. UK 11.46
To R.Hell.AF 5.47
EX309
Direct to SAAF (7119) 11.42
EX310
Direct to SAAF (7120) 11.42
EX311
Direct to SAAF (7121) 11.42
EX312
Direct to SAAF (7122) 11.42
EX313
Direct to SAAF (7123) 11.42
Retd. to RAF: arr. UK
To R.Hell.AF 7.47
EX314
Direct to SAAF (7124) 11.42
EX315
Direct to SAAF (7125) 11.42
EX316
Direct to SAAF (7126) 11.42
EX317
Direct to SAAF (7127) 11.42
EX318
Direct to SAAF (7128) 11.42
Retd. to RAF: arr. UK 9.46
To Belg.AF 2.47
EX319
Direct to SAAF (7129) 11.42
Retd. to RAF: arr. UK
SS 8.50
EX320
Direct to SAAF 11.42
Retd. to RAF: arr. UK 10.46
To R.Hell.AF 5.47
EX321
71 OTU
SOC 23.2.45
EX322
13 AGS
71 OTU
73 OTU
SOC 28.11.46
EX323
71 OTU
cr. ldd. Ismailia 3.6.43
EX324
71 OTU
Collided with EX101 and cr. 4mls S of Summit, 29.12.42
EX325
71 OTU
SOC 29.3.45
EX326 to EX329
Direct to RNZAF (1018 to 1021) 12.42
EX330
Direct to SAAF (7150) 12.42
EX331
Direct to SAAF (7073) 10.42
EX332
Direct to SAAF (7151) 12.42
Retd. to RAF: arr. UK
To Ital.AF 5.49
EX333
Direct to SAAF (7147) 12.42
EX334
Direct to SAAF (7074) 10.42
EX335
Direct to SAAF (7072) 10.42
EX336
Direct to SAAF (7148) 12.42
EX337
Direct to SAAF (7069) 10.42
Retd. to RAF: arr. UK
SS 8.50
EX338
Direct to SAAF (7065) 10.42
Retd. to RAF: arr. UK
SS 8.50
EX339
Direct to SAAF (7070) 10.42
Retd. to RAF: arr. UK
SS (Coley) 2.50
EX340
Direct to SAAF (7071) 10.42
Retd. to RAF: arr. UK 10.46
To R.Hell.AF 3.47
EX341
Direct to SAAF (7146) 12.42
EX342
Direct to SAAF (7062) 10.42
EX343
Direct to SAAF (7153) 12.42
EX344
Direct to SAAF (7161) 12.42

EX345
Direct to SAAF (7155) 12.42
EX346
Direct to SAAF (7154) 12.42
EX347
Direct to SAAF (7158) 12.42
Retd. to RAF: arr. UK
To R.Hell.AF 3.47
EX348
Direct to SAAF (7160) 12.42
Retd. to RAF: arr. UK
SS 8.50
EX349
Direct to SAAF (7067) 10.42
Retd. to RAF: arr. UK
SS 8.50
EX350
Direct to SAAF (7157) 12.42
EX351
Direct to SAAF (7068) 10.42
EX352
Direct to SAAF (7023) 12.42
EX353
Direct to SAAF (7149) 12.42
Retd. to RAF: arr; UK
SS 8.50
EX354
Direct to SAAF (7156) 12.42
EX355
Direct to SAAF (7024) 12.42
EX356
Direct to SAAF (7025) 12.42
Retd. to RAF: arr. UK 11.46
SS 8.50
EX357
20 SFTS
cr. 4mls S of Hunyani, SR, 15.8.44
EX358
20 SFTS [35]
4 FTS [B:A]
cr. at 2010S;2924E, SR, 25.9.52
EX359
20 SFTS
4 FTS [H:B] 8.48-
Collided with EX700 and cr. near Bushtik, SR,15.10.52
EX360
Direct to SAAF (7173) 12.42
Retd. to RAF: arr. UK
SF Wattisham 12.47-
SOC 20.7.48
EX361
Direct to SAAF (7174) 12.42
EX362
Direct to SAAF (7186) 12.42
Retd. to RAF: arr. UK
SS 8.50
EX363
Direct to SAAF (7162) 12.42
Retd. to RAF: arr. UK 11.46
SS 8.50
EX364
Direct to SAAF (7066) 12.42
EX365
Direct to SAAF (7152) 10.42
EX366
Direct to SAAF (7064) 12.42
Retd. to RAF: arr. UK
SS 8.50
EX367
Direct to SAAF (7063) 10.42
EX368
Direct to SAAF (7159) 12.42
EX369
71 OTU
cr. ldd. Ismailia 25.6.43
EX370
71 OTU
SOC 26.4.46
EX371
Direct to SAAF (7187) 12.42
Retd. to RAF: arr. UK 10.46
To Belg.AF 2.47
EX372
Direct to SAAF (7188) 12.42

EX373
20 SFTS
4 FTS [B:S] 12.48-
To SRAF 3.52
EX374
20 SFTS
22 SFTS
4 FTS [86] 1.50-
To Belg.AF 11.53
EX375
20 SFTS
22 SFTS [11]
4 FTS [B:B] 6.47-
Collided with EX535 and cr. near Bulawayo, SR, 18.5.50
EX376
22 SFTS 2.43-
20 SFTS
SOC 10.45
EX377
22 SFTS 3.43-
SOC 9.8.44
EX378
22 SFTS 2.43-
20 SFTS
4 FTS 8.48-
cr. Whites Run, SR, 19.2.51
EX379
33 FIS
CFS(SR)
20 SFTS [J]
4 FTS 8.48-
To Belg.AF 11.53
EX380
Direct to SAAF (7144) 1.43
EX381
Direct to SAAF (7145) 1.43
EX382
Direct to SAAF (7175) 12.42
Retd. to RAF: arr. UK 11.46
To R.Hell.AF 3.47
EX383
22 SFTS [A:9] 2.43-
SOC 31.3.44
EX384
22 SFTS 3.43-
20 SFTS
4 FTS 6.48
cr. ldd. Bushtik Road, SR, 20.7.48
EX385
22 SFTS 2.43-
4 FTS [F:B] 10.48-12.52
To SRAF 2.53
EX386
22 SFTS 2.43-
4 FTS 8.48
Undershot landing, Heany, SR, 25.11.49
EX387
22 SFTS 2.43-
NFT
EX388
20 SFTS
CFS(SR)
4 FTS 9.48
Hit tree while low flying 18mls NNW of Shabani, SR, 21.2.49
EX389
22 SFTS 2.43-
SOC 1.3.46
EX390
Direct to SAAF (7189) 12.42
Retd. to RAF: arr. UK 11.46
To Ital.AF 5.49
EX391
Direct to SAAF (7190) 12.42
Retd. to RAF: arr. UK 11.46
SOC 4.9.54
EX392
Direct to SAAF (7185) 12.42
EX393
Direct to SAAF (7179) 12.42
Retd. to RAF: arr. UK 10.46
To Belg.AF 5.47

EX394
Direct to SAAF (7191) 12.42
Retd. to RAF: arr. UK 10.46
SS 8.50
EX395
Direct to SAAF (7192) 12.42
Retd. to RAF: arr. UK 10.46
SS 8.50
EX396
Direct to SAAF (7305) 7.43
EX397
Direct to SAAF (7180) 12.42
Retd. to RAF: arr. UK 11.46
To Ital.AF 5.49
EX398
Direct to SAAF (7176) 12.42
EX399
Direct to SAAF (7193) 12.42
EX400
Direct to SAAF (7178) 12.42
Retd. to RAF: arr. UK 10.46
To R.Dan.AF 12.46
EX401
28 EFTS
20 SFTS
4 FTS [B:D]
To SRAF 4.53
EX402
20 SFTS
cr. 20mls NE of Que Que, SR, 1.7.44
EX403
28 EFTS [7]
20 SFTS
SOC 4.4.46
EX404
20 SFTS
cr. Hopley Farm, near Salisbury, SR 18.11.43
EX405
20 SFTS
5 FTS [X:C]
4 FTS [B:U/52] 12.47
To Belg.AF 11.53
EX406
HQ RATW 6.43-
22 SFTS 9.44-
FA Cat.E 24.11.44
EX407
Direct to SAAF (7203) 3.43
EX408
Direct to SAAF (7043) 1.43
EX409
22 SFTS 7.44-
FA Cat.E 22.2.45
EX410
20 SFTS
22 SFTS 7.44-
SOC 7.6.46
EX411
CFS(SR)
20 SFTS
4 FTS [B:L/B:T]
cr. ldd. Heany, SR, 1.7.53
EX412
20 SFTS
22 SFTS
4 FTS 3.49-
FA Cat.5s 14.8.53
EX413
20 SFTS
SOC 2.11.45
EX414
22 SFTS
4 FTS
To SRAF 4.52
EX415
20 SFTS
cr. 8mls W of Sipolilo, SR, 11.9.44
EX416
22 SFTS 6.44-
4 FTS [D:K/H:K] 1.48-
Sold 11.53

Racks ready for practice bombs are visible in this shot of No.20 SFTS Harvard IIa EX405 (F.F.Smith via R.C.Sturtivant)

EX417
Direct to SAAF (7026) 1.43
Retd. to RAF: arr. UK 12.46
SS 8.50
EX418
20 SFTS
4 FTS [H:F] 7.48-
DBR in heavy landing, Heany, SR, 19.6.53
EX419
33 FIS
CFS(SR)
4 FTS [B:R/H:87] 4.48-
To Belg.AF 11.53
EX420
22 SFTS 6.44-
4 FTS [57/G:E] 1.48- 4.48
5 FTS [X:E]

EX420
22 SFTS 6.44-
4 FTS - 1.48
5 FTS [X:E] 1.48- 5.48
3 ANS [X:E] 4.48- 7.48
4 FTS [57/SEG:E] 7.48-
To Belg.AF 11.53
EX421 to EX428
Direct to RNZAF (NZ1022 to NZ1029) 3.43
EX429
Direct to SAAF (7204) 3.43
EX430
20 SFTS
4 FTS 8.48-
cr. Somabula, SR, 27.10.48
EX431
Direct to SAAF (7275) 4.43
Retd. to RAF: arr. UK 11.46
To R.Hell.AF 6.47
EX432
Direct to SAAF (7276) 4.43

EX433
Direct to SAAF (7272) 4.43
EX434
Direct to SAAF (7267) 4.43
Retd. to RAF: arr. UK 10.46
SS 8.50
EX435
20 SFTS
22 SFTS
SOC 4.4.46
EX436
20 SFTS
4 FTS [B:F/H:60]
To Belg.AF 11.53
EX437
20 SFTS
4 FTS [B:N/G:F] 12.47
Sold 11.53
EX438
Direct to SAAF (7027) 1.43
Retd. to RAF: arr. UK 11.46
To Belg.AF 2.47
EX439
Direct to SAAF (7282) 4.43
Retd. to RAF: arr. UK 10.46
To Belg.AF
EX440
Direct to SAAF (7265) 4.43
Retd. to RAF: arr. UK 11.46
SS 8.50
EX441
Direct to SAAF (7274) 4.43
Retd. to RAF: arr. UK 10.46
To R.Hell.AF 5.47
EX442
Direct to SAAF (7207) 3.43
Retd. to RAF: arr. UK 10.46
To R.Hell.AF 3.47
EX443
Direct to SAAF (7202) 3.43

EX444
Direct to SAAF (7028) 1.43
EX445
Direct to SAAF (7201) 3.43
EX446
Direct to SAAF (7029) 1.43
EX447
Direct to SAAF (7206) 3.43
EX448
Direct to SAAF (7030) 1.43
Retd. to RAF: arr. UK 10.46
To Belg.AF 5.47
EX449
Direct to SAAF (7209) 3.43
Retd. to RAF: arr. UK 12.46
SS 8.50
EX450
Direct to SAAF (7208) 3.43
Retd. to RAF: arr. UK 12.46
SS 8.50
EX451
Direct to SAAF (7211) 3.43
EX452
Direct to SAAF (7031) 1.43
Retd. to RAF: arr. UK 12.46
SS 8.50
EX453
Direct to SAAF (7266) 4.43
EX454
Direct to SAAF (7032) 1.43
EX455
Direct to SAAF (7033) 1.43
EX456
Direct to SAAF (7283) 4.43
EX457
Direct to SAAF (7034) 1.43
EX458
Direct to SAAF (7035) 1.43
Retd. to RAF: arr. UK 11.46
SS 8.50

EX459
Direct to SAAF (7036) 1.43
EX460
Direct to SAAF (7205) 3.43
EX461
Direct to SAAF (7210) 3.43
Retd. to RAF: arr. UK 10.46
To Belg.AF 2.47
EX462
Direct to SAAF (7037) 1.43
EX463
Direct to SAAF (7278) 4.43
EX464
Direct to SAAF (7277) 4.43
EX465
Direct to SAAF (7279) 4.43
Retd. to RAF: arr. UK 11.46
SS 8.50
EX466
Direct to SAAF (7038) 1.43
Retd. to RAF: arr. UK 10.46
To Ital.AF 5.49
EX467
Direct to SAAF (7039) 1.43
EX468
Direct to SAAF (7040) 1.43
EX469
Direct to SAAF (7273) 4.43
EX470
Direct to SAAF (7299) 5.43
EX471
Direct to SAAF (7298) 5.43
Retd. to RAF: arr. UK 11.46
To R.Hell.AF 3.47
EX472
Direct to SAAF (7301) 5.43
EX473
Direct to SAAF (7041) 1.43
EX474
Direct to SAAF (7044) 1.43
EX475
Direct to SAAF (7296) 5.43
EX476
Direct to SAAF (7295) 4.43
Retd. to RAF: arr. UK 11.46
To Belg.AF 2.47
EX477
Direct to SAAF (7042) 1.43
Retd. to RAF: arr. UK 12.46
SS (Coley) 2.50
EX478
Direct to SAAF (7300) 5.43
Retd. to RAF: arr. UK
SS 8.50
EX479
Direct to SAAF (7297) 5.43
Retd. to RAF: arr. UK 10.46
SS 8.50
EX480
Direct to SAAF (7212) 3.43
EX481
Direct to SAAF (7213) 3.43
Retd. to RAF: arr. UK 10.46
SS 8.50
EX482
Direct to SAAF (7214) 3.43
EX483
Direct to SAAF (7215) 3.43
Retd. to RAF: arr. UK
SS 8.50
EX484
Direct to SAAF (7216) 3.43
Retd. to RAF: arr. UK
SS 8.50
EX485
Direct to SAAF (7217) 3.43
EX486
Direct to SAAF (7218) 3.43
Retd. to RAF: arr. UK 11.46
To R.Hell.AF 3.47
EX487
Direct to SAAF (7219) 3.43
Retd. to RAF: arr. UK
SS 8.50

EX488
Direct to SAAF (7220) 3.43
EX489
Direct to SAAF (7221) 3.43
Retd. to RAF: arr. UK 10.46
To Ital.AF .49
EX490
20 SFTS
22 SFTS [73]
Collided with EX512 and cr. 4mls NE of Inkomo RLG, SR, 24.6.44
EX491
22 SFTS 7.43-
20 SFTS
22 SFTS
4 FTS [H:54] 6.48-
Sold 11.53
EX492
20 SFTS
CFS(SR)
SOC 4.1.46
EX493
22 SFTS 7.43-
20 SFTS
22 SFTS
20 SFTS
SOC 1.3.46
EX494
Direct to SAAF (7222) 3.43
EX495
Direct to SAAF (7223) 3.43
EX496
Direct to SAAF (7255) 3.43
EX497
Direct to SAAF (7256) 3.43
EX498
349 Sqdn 3.43
FA Cat.E 19.9.43
BBOC 21.6.45
WACS 6.45
To Belg. Congo 8.45
EX499
Direct to SAAF (7253) 3.43
EX500
SF Takoradi 3.43
349 Sqdn
To Belg. Congo 8.45
SOC 30.10.47
EX501
SF Takoradi 3.43
349 Sqdn
FA Cat.E 27.10.44
To Belg. Congo 8.45
EX502
Direct to SAAF (7257) 3.43
Retd. to RAF: arr. UK 12.46
SS 8.50
EX503
Direct to SAAF (7254) 3.43
Retd. to RAF: arr. UK 11.46
SS (Coley) 2.50
EX504
Direct to SAAF (7258) 3.43
Retd. to RAF: arr. UK 11.46
To Ital.AF 5.49
EX505
Direct to SAAF (7259) 3.43
EX506
Direct to SAAF (7262) 3.43
EX507
Direct to SAAF (7260) 3.43
EX508
Direct to SAAF (7261) 3.43
Retd. to RAF: arr. UK
SS 8.50
EX509
Direct to SAAF (7263) 3.43
Retd. to RAF: arr. UK 12.46
SS 8.50
EX510
22 SFTS 6.44-
4 FTS [D] 12.47-
5 FTS [X:B]
4 FTS [F:I/H:51]
Sold 11.53

EX511
22 SFTS
4 FTS 1.48-
cr. ldd. Whites Run RLG, SR, 28.3.49
EX512
20 SFTS
Collided with EX490 and cr. 4mls NE of Inkomo RLG, SR, 24.6.44
EX513
20 SFTS
4 FTS
5 FTS [X:O] 11.47-12.47
4 FTS 12.47
FA Cat.5c 14.3.50
EX514
28 EFTS
20 SFTS
5 FTS [X:N]
4 FTS [D:A] 12.48-
cr. 22mls SE of Bulawayo, SR, 15.7.51
EX515
20 SFTS
SOC 9.8.44
EX516
20 SFTS
SOC 4.4.46
EX517
CFS(SR)
4 FTS [B:P]
cr. ldd. 4mls W of Essexvale, SR, 8.9.53
EX518
22 SFTS 6.44-
20 SFTS
5 FTS [X:D]
4 FTS [D:B] 12.47-
cr. ldd. 6mls E of Heany, SR, 1.8.49
EX519
20 SFTS
CFS(SR)
4 FTS
To SRAF 5.52
EX520
? SFTS
4 FTS
To SRAF 7.52
EX521
20 SFTS
3 ANS [X:A]
4 FTS 8.49-11.50
SOC 28.3.51
EX522
20 SFTS
4 FTS [D:N/G:M] 1.48-
To SRAF 7.52
EX523
20 SFTS [P]
5 FTS [X:G]
4 FTS [D:C] 12.47-
cr. Meilloo, SR, 16.7.48
EX524
22 SFTS 10.43-
SOC 3.3.44
EX525
20 SFTS
4 FTS [H:63] 7.48-
To Belg.AF 11.53
EX526
33 FIS
CFS(SR)
20 SFTS
5 FTS
cr., out of fuel, Chileka, Nya., 10.5.47
EX527
20 SFTS
SOC 9.8.44
EX528
22 SFTS [25] 11.44-
RATW CF
4 FTS [D:C]
3 ANS
4 FTS [H:41]
To Belg.AF 11.53

EX529
22 SFTS 6.44-
4 FTS [F:J] 7.48-
Sold 11.53
EX530
22 SFTS 7.43-
5 FTS [X:F]
4 FTS
cr. Meilloo Ranges, SR, 14.2.51
EX531
33 FIS
CFS(SR)
4 FTS [B]
cr. ldd. Heany, SR, 23.8.49
EX532
33 FIS
20 SFTS
22 SFTS [29] 12.44-
5 FTS [X:P] 11.47-
4 FTS
3 ANS [X:P]
4 FTS
Spun in, 4mls E of Bushtik, SR, 24.12.52
EX533
22 SFTS 7.43-
4 FTS [H:N] 3.48-
Sold 11.53
EX534
20 SFTS [T]
4 FTS [B:O/H:68] 7.48-
To Belg.AF 11.53
EX535
33 FIS
CFS(SR)
4 FTS 2.48-
Collided with EX375 and cr. near Bulawayo, SR, 18.5.50
EX536
22 SFTS 1.44-
20 SFTS
4 FTS 3.48-
cr. ldd. Whites Run RLG, SR, 25.1.49

EX537
20 SFTS
cr. near Beatrice, SR, 16.11.43
EX538
22 SFTS 7.43-
SOC 4.12.45
EX539
Direct to SAAF (7284) 4.43
EX540
Direct to SAAF (7270) 4.43
Retd. to RAF: arr. UK 1.47
SS 8.50
EX541
Direct to SAAF (7281) 4.43
EX542
Direct to SAAF (7269) 4.43
Retd. to RAF: arr. UK 10.46
To Belg.AF 4.47
EX543
Direct to SAAF (7280) 4.43
EX544
Direct to SAAF (7268) 4.43
Retd. to RAF: arr. UK 10.46
To Belg.AF 2.47
EX545
Direct to SAAF (7271) 4.43
EX546
Direct to SAAF (7286) 4.43
Retd. to RAF: arr. UK 12.46
To Belg.AF 5.47
EX547
Direct to SAAF (7288) 4.43
Retd. to RAF: arr. UK 11.46
To Belg.AF 2.47
EX548
Direct to SAAF (7292) 4.43
EX549
Direct to SAAF (7293) 4.43
EX550
Direct to SAAF (7236) 3.43
Retd. to RAF: arr. UK 12.46
To Belg.AF 5.47

EX551
Direct to SAAF (7239) 3.43
Retd. to RAF: arr. UK 10.46
To Belg.AF 2.47
EX552
Direct to SAAF (7229) 3.43
Retd. to RAF: arr. UK 11.46
To R.Hell.AF 3.47
EX553
Direct to SAAF (7289) 4.43
EX554
Direct to SAAF (7230) 3.43
EX555
Direct to SAAF (7287) 4.43
Retd. to RAF: arr. UK 11.46
SS 8.50
EX556
Direct to SAAF (7226) 3.43
Retd. to RAF: arr. UK 11.46
SS 8.50
EX557
Direct to SAAF (7233) 3.43
Retd. to RAF: arr. UK 1.47
SS 8.50
EX558
Direct to SAAF (7235) 3.43
Retd. to RAF: arr. UK 10.46
To R.Hell.AF 4.47
EX559
Direct to SAAF (7228) 3.43
EX560
Direct to SAAF (7227) 3.43
EX561
Direct to SAAF (7224) 3.43
EX562
Direct to SAAF (7225) 3.43
Retd. to RAF: arr. UK 11.46
SS 8.50
EX563
Direct to SAAF (7290) 4.43
Retd. to RAF: arr. UK 12.46
SS 8.50
EX564
Direct to SAAF (7294) 4.43

EX510 of postwar No.4 FTS, Heany, Southern Rhodesia, carries code F:I and the letters SE signifying single-engined! *(D.Watkins)*

EX514 of No.20 SFTS, Cranborne, Southern Rhodesia with chequerboard marking on upper rear fuselage *(via R.C.Sturtivant)*

EX565
Direct to SAAF (7240) 3.43
Retd. to RAF: arr. UK 11.46
SS 8.50
EX566
Direct to SAAF (7238) 3.43
EX567
Direct to SAAF (7232) 3.43
Retd. to RAF: arr. UK 9.46
To Belg.AF 2.47
EX568
Direct to SAAF (7285) 4.43
Retd. to RAF: arr. UK 10.46
To R.Hell.AF 3.47
EX569
Direct to SAAF (7234) 3.43
Retd. to RAF: arr. UK 11.46
SS (Coley) 2.50
EX570
Direct to SAAF (7231) 3.43
EX571
Direct to SAAF (7291) 4.43
EX572
Direct to SAAF (7241) 3.43
EX573
Direct to SAAF (7242) 3.43
Retd. to RAF: arr. UK 11.46
SS 8.50
EX574
Direct to SAAF (7237) 3.43
Retd. to RAF: arr. UK 1.47
SS 8.50
EX575
Direct to SAAF (7251) 3.43
EX576
Direct to SAAF (7252) 3.43
EX577
Direct to SAAF (7250) 3.43
EX578
Direct to SAAF (7245) 3.43
Retd. to RAF: arr. UK 12.46
SS 8.50
EX579
Direct to SAAF (7249) 3.43
Retd. to RAF: arr. UK 11.46
To R.Hell.AF 8.47
EX580
Direct to SAAF (7248) 3.43
EX581
Direct to SAAF (7247) 3.43
Retd. to RAF: arr. UK 1.47
To Ital.AF 5.49
EX582
Direct to SAAF (7243) 3.43

EX583
Direct to SAAF (7246) 3.43
EX584
Direct to SAAF (7244) 3.43
EX585 to EX592
Direct to RNZAF (NZ1030 to NZ1037) 5.43
EX593
Direct to SAAF (7302) 7.43
Retd. to RAF: arr. UK 11.46
SS 8.50
EX594
Direct to SAAF (7378) 6.43
EX595
Direct to SAAF (7379) 6.43
EX596
Direct to SAAF (7380) 6.43
Retd. to RAF: arr. UK 11.46
SS 8.50
EX597
Direct to SAAF (7381) 6.43
Retd. to RAF: arr. UK 10.46
To R.Hell.AF 3.47
EX598
Del'd. to Coimbatore, India, via Mombassa, for RN
NFT
EX599
Direct to SAAF (7335) 6.43
EX600
Direct to SAAF (7382) 6.43
EX601
Direct to SAAF (7383) 6.43
EX602
Direct to SAAF (7384) 6.43
Retd. to RAF: arr. UK 10.46
To Belg.AF 3.47
EX603
Direct to SAAF (7336) 6.43
Retd. to RAF: arr. UK 10.46
SS 8.50
EX604
Direct to SAAF (7317) 6.43
EX605
Direct to SAAF (7385) 6.43
EX606
Direct to SAAF (7386) 6.43
EX607
Direct to SAAF (7387) 6.43
Retd. to RAF: arr. UK 1.47
SS 8.50
EX608
Direct to SAAF (7388) 6.43

EX609
757 Sqdn 6.45- 7.45
NFT
EX610
Direct to SAAF (7303) 7.43
EX611
Direct to SAAF (7337) 6.43
Retd. to RAF: arr. UK 10.46
SS 8.50
EX612
Direct to SAAF (7389) 6.43
Retd. to RAF: arr. UK 11.46
To R.Hell.AF 6.47
EX613
Direct to SAAF (7390) 6.43
Retd. to RAF: arr. UK 12.46
SS 8.50
EX614
Direct to SAAF (7338) 6.43
Retd. to RAF: arr. UK 12.46
SS 8.50
EX615
Direct to SAAF (7339) 6.43
Retd. to RAF: arr. UK 11.46
To R.Hell.AF 3.47
EX616
Direct to SAAF (7340) 6.43
Retd. to RAF: arr. UK 12.46
SS 8.50
EX617
Direct to SAAF (7341) 6.43
Retd. to RAF: arr. UK 10.46
To R.Hell.AF 3.47
EX618
Direct to SAAF (7391) 6.43
EX619
Direct to SAAF (7342) 6.43
EX620
757 Sqdn 8.44- 4.45
desp. UK
SOC 10.1.50
EX621
Direct to SAAF (7343) 6.43
EX622
Direct to SAAF (7392) 6.43
EX623
Direct to SAAF (7344) 6.43
Retd. to RAF: arr. UK 10.46
To Belg.AF 2.47
EX624
Direct to SAAF (7345) 6.43
Retd. to RAF: arr. UK 10.46
To R.Hell.AF 4.47
EX625
Direct to SAAF (7304) 7.43
EX626
Direct to SAAF (7306) 7.43
EX627
Direct to SAAF (7325) 6.43
Retd. to RAF: arr. UK 12.46
SS 8.50
EX628
Direct to SAAF (7326) 6.43
Retd. to RAF: arr. UK 10.46
SS 8.50
EX629
Direct to SAAF (7327) 6.43
EX630
Direct to SAAF (7346) 6.43
EX631
Direct to SAAF (7347) 6.43
EX632
Direct to SAAF (7348) 6.43
EX633
Direct to SAAF (7349) 6.43
Retd. to RAF: arr. UK 11.46
To Belg.AF 2.47
EX634
Direct to SAAF (7319) 6.43
EX635
Direct to SAAF (7316) 6.43
EX636
Direct to SAAF (7350) 6.43
EX637
Direct to SAAF (7307) 7.43

EX638
Direct to SAAF (7351) 6.43
EX639
Direct to SAAF (7352) 6.43
EX640
Direct to SAAF (7353) 6.43
EX641
Del'd. to Ceylon for RN
NFT
EX642
Direct to SAAF (7354) 6.43
EX643
Direct to SAAF (7355) 6.43
EX644
Direct to SAAF (7308) 7.43
EX645
Direct to SAAF (7356) 6.43
EX646
Direct to SAAF (7357) 6.43
EX647
Direct to SAAF (7358) 6.43
Retd. to RAF: arr. UK 10.46
To R.Hell.AF 3.47
EX648
Direct to SAAF (7359) 6.43
EX649
S. Rhodesia: no record of service
FA Cat.E 13.1.45
EX650
22 SFTS 10.44-
SOC 4.9.45
EX651
22 SFTS 10.44-
4 FTS [H:50] 10.52-
To Belg.AF 11.53
EX652
20 SFTS
SOC 4.9.45
EX653
20 SFTS
SOC 15.2.45
EX654
22 SFTS 10.44-
4 FTS
Sold 11.53
EX655
22 SFTS 10.44-
4 FTS [H:96]
To Belg.AF 11.53
EX656
22 SFTS
4 FTS [H:77] 12.48-
To Belg.AF 11.53
EX657
22 SFTS 10.44-
4 FTS [H:80]
To Belg.AF 11.53
EX658
22 SFTS 12.44-
4 FTS
Sold 11.53
EX659
Direct to SAAF (7311) 6.43
EX660
Direct to SAAF (7309) 7.43
Retd. to RAF: arr. UK 9.46
To Belg.AF 2.47
EX661
Direct to SAAF (7315) 6.43
Retd. to RAF: arr. UK 12.46
To Belg.AF 3.47
EX662
Direct to SAAF (7313) 6.43
EX663
Direct to SAAF (7318) 6.43
EX664
Direct to SAAF (7361) 7.43
EX665
Direct to SAAF (7314) 6.43
EX666
Direct to SAAF (7360) 6.43
EX667
Direct to SAAF (7312) 6.43
EX668
Direct to SAAF (7310) 6.43

EX669
20 SFTS
4 FTS 12.48-
Overshot into ditch, Whites Run RLG
SR, 12.5.49
EX670
S. Rhodesia: no record of service
SOC 9.8.44
EX671
22 SFTS
4 FTS [H:55]
To Belg.AF 11.53
EX672
22 SFTS
4 FTS 3.48-
cr. 27mls from Bulawayo, SR,16.7.48
EX673
20 SFTS
4 FTS [B:O]
Sold 11.53
EX674
20 SFTS
SOC 4.9.45
EX675
20 SFTS
4 FTS [D:D] 1.49-
cr. ldd. 2½mls NE of Heany, SR,
18.4.50
EX676
20 SFTS
4 FTS [H:48]
Sold 11.53
EX677
CFS(SR)
4 FTS [H:97]
Sold 11.53
EX678
22 SFTS 7.44-
4 FTS [H:64]
To Belg.AF 11.53
EX679
Direct to SAAF (7328) 6.43
EX680
Direct to SAAF (7329) 6.43
Retd. to RAF: arr. UK 10.46
To Belg.AF 5.47
EX681
Direct to SAAF (7330) 6.43
EX682
22 SFTS 10.44-
CFS(SR)
4 FTS [H:69] 9.48-
To Belg.AF 11.53
EX683
789 Sqdn [H] 9.44- 4.45
SOC 14.1.50
EX684
20 SFTS
Became 6521M 2.48
EX685
Direct to SAAF (7331) 6.43
EX686
Direct to SAAF (7332) 6.43
EX687
Direct to SAAF (7320) 8.43
To RN in S. Africa
789 Sqdn 9.44- 1.45
desp. UK
727 Sqdn (6.47-7.47)
SOC 12.8.49
EX688
Direct to SAAF (7333) 6.43
EX689
71 OTU
SOC 31.5.48
EX690
20 SFTS
4 FTS
Sold 11.53
EX691
S. Rhodesia: no record of service
SOC 1.2.45
EX692
Direct to SAAF (7321) 8.43

EX693
Direct to SAAF (7334) 6.43
EX694
Direct to SAAF (7362) 7.43
EX695
Direct to SAAF (7363) 7.43
EX696
22 SFTS 10.44-
20 SFTS
4 FTS 12.48
Engine cut on overshoot; cr. 8mls
NE of Bulawayo, SR, 26.11.52
EX697
20 SFTS
Became 6522M 28.2.48
EX698
22 SFTS 10.44-12.44
CFS(SR) 12.44-
4 FTS [H:61]
To Belg.AF 11.53
EX699
CFS(SR)
4 FTS
To Belg.AF 11.53
EX700
20 SFTS
4 FTS [F:M] 12.48-
Sold 11.53
EX701
Direct to SAAF (7364) 7.43
EX702
757 Sqdn 12.43-
NFT
EX703
MECS
SOC 25.9.47
EX704
Direct to SAAF (7365) 7.43
EX705
Direct to SAAF (7406) 7.43
EX706
Direct to SAAF (7407) 7.43
EX707
20 SFTS
CFS(SR)
5 FTS [XH]
4 FTS [D:E]
cr. ldd. Heany, SR, 24.9.49
EX708
73 OTU [M]
SOC 28.11.46
EX709
71 OTU
SOC 27.10.44
EX710
71 OTU
SOC 29.5.47
EX711
71 OTU
1675 CU
SOC 28.11.46
EX712
To USAAF in ME 2.44
Retd. to RAF
AB&GS
SOC 28.11.46
EX713
Direct to SAAF (7322) 8.43
EX714
ME: no record of service
SOC 22.2.45
EX715
Direct to SAAF (7366) 7.43
Retd. to RAF: arr. UK 10.46
SS 8.50
EX716
Direct to SAAF (7367) 7.43
EX717
Direct to SAAF (7368) 7.43
EX718
Direct to SAAF (7372) 11.43
EX719
74 OTU
SOC 28.11.46

EX720
5 RFU
SOC 21.6.45
EX721
71 OTU
73 OTU [K]
SOC 28.11.46
EX722
To USAAF in ME 2.44
EX723
71 OTU
SOC 29.5.47
EX724
74 OTU
SOC 28.11.46
EX725
73 OTU [D]
SOC 28.11.46
EX726
ME: no record of service
SOC 31.5.45
EX727
74 OTU
SOC 28.11.46
EX728
71 OTU
73 OTU [S]
SOC 28.11.46
EX729
Direct to SAAF (7373) 11.43
Retd. to RAF: arr. UK 11.46
To R.Hell.AF 5.47
EX730
Direct to SAAF (7374) 11.43
EX731
Direct to SAAF (7375) 11.43
Retd. to RAF: arr. UK 11.46
To Ital.AF 5.49
EX732
Direct to SAAF (7369) 7.43
EX733
Direct to SAAF (7323) 8.43
EX734
Direct to SAAF (7376) 11.43
Retd. to RAF: arr. UK 11.46
SS 8.50
EX735
Direct to SAAF (7324) 8.43
EX736
Direct to SAAF (7370) 7.43
Retd. to RAF: arr. UK 11.46
To R.Hell.AF 3.47
EX737
Direct to SAAF (7393) 11.43
EX738
Direct to SAAF (7394) 11.43
Retd. to RAF: arr. UK
SS 8.50
EX739
Direct to SAAF (7371) 7.43
EX740
Direct to SAAF (7377) 11.43
EX741 to EX748
Direct to RNZAF (NZ1038 to NZ1045) 8.43
EX749
Direct to SAAF (7397) 10.43
EX750
Direct to SAAF (7398) 10.43
EX751
Direct to SAAF (7395) 11.43
Retd. to RAF: arr. UK 11.46
SS 8.50
EX752
74 OTU
SOC 29.5.47
EX753
CFS(SR)
5 FTS [XJ]
4 FTS [B:K]
To SRAF 3.52
Retd. to RAF 6.52
4 FTS [H:56] 6.52
To Belg.AF 11.53

EX754
20 SFTS [18]
SOC 4.4.46
EX755
Direct to SAAF (7399) 10.43
EX756
ME: no record of service
SOC (to USAAF ?) 26.9.46
EX757
Direct to SAAF (7396) 11.43
Retd. to RAF: arr. UK 11.46
SS 8.50
EX758
71 OTU
73 OTU [Y]
SOC (to USAAF ?) 26.9.46
EX759
AB&GS
SOC 29.5.47
EX760
Direct to SAAF (7400) 10.43
Retd. to RAF: arr. UK 10.46
To Belg.AF 4.47
EX761
75 OTU
1342 Flt
AB&GS
SOC 28.11.46
EX762
AB&GS
SOC 28.11.46
EX763
22 SFTS 10.43-
FA Cat.E 19.1.44
EX764
22 SFTS
SOC 7.44
EX765
20 SFTS
5 FTS [XM]
4 FTS [B:V]
SOC 5.1.50
EX766
20 SFTS
4 FTS
cr. 2020S;2855E 22.10.48
EX767
73 OTU [K]
Collided with EX126 and cr. 3.10.44
EX768
33 FIS
CFS(SR)
20 SFTS
cr. 23.11.45
EX769
Direct to SAAF (7401) 10.43
EX770
Direct to SAAF (7402) 10.43
EX771
20 SFTS
4 FTS [H:75]
To Belg.AF 11.53
EX772
Direct to SAAF (7403) 10.43
EX773
20 SFTS
5 FTS [XL]
4 FTS
Sold 11.53
EX774
Direct to SAAF (7404) 10.43
EX775
Direct to SAAF (7408) 7.43
EX776
Direct to SAAF (7405) 10.43
EX777
20 SFTS
4 FTS [H:44]
Colldided with FT164 on landing, Heany, SR, 13.4.53
EX778
20 SFTS [60]
4 FTS
Sold 11.53

EX779
Direct to SAAF (7409) 7.43
Retd. to RAF: arr. UK 9.46
To Belg.AF 2.47
EX780
20 SFTS
SOC 4.9.45
EX781
Direct to SAAF (7410) 7.43
EX782
Direct to SAAF (7411) 7.43
EX783
Direct to RNZAF (NZ1070) 12.43
EX784
22 SFTS 8.44-
4 FTS [H:62]
To Belg.AF 11.53
EX785
CFS(SR)
4 FTS
Sold 11.53
EX786
20 SFTS
4 FTS [D:G]
To SRAF 3.52
EX787
Direct to SAAF (7412) 7.43
EX788
20 SFTS
4 FTS
To Belg.AF 11.53
EX789 to EX796
Direct to RNZAF (NZ1046 to NZ1053) 8.43
EX797
ME: no record of service
SOC 31.5.45
EX798
Direct to SAAF (7413) 11.43
EX799
Direct to SAAF (7414) 11.43
EX800
73 OTU [H]
SOC 28.11.46
EX801
73 OTU [O]
SOC 31.5.45
EX802
Direct to SAAF (7415) 11.43
EX803
Direct to SAAF (7416) 11.43
EX804
Direct to SAAF (7417) 11.43
EX805
Direct to SAAF (7418) 11.43
EX806
22 SFTS 8.44-
4 FTS
Sold 11.53
EX807
73 OTU [C]
SOC 31.5.45
EX808
Direct to SAAF (7500) 12.43
EX809
Direct to SAAF (7462) 12.43
Retd. to RAF: arr. UK 12.46
SS 8.50
EX810
20 SFTS
SOC 5.2.46
EX811
Direct to SAAF (7463) 12.43
EX812
20 SFTS
4 FTS 9.48-
Sold 11.53
EX813
Direct to SAAF (7464) 12.43
EX814
AHQ E.Med.CF
213 Sqdn [AK:K] 12.48- 3.49
249 Sqdn 9.49- 8.50
SOC 22.11.50

No.4 FTS's final type of coding is seen on EX818 *(E.W.Hughes)*

EX815
Direct to SAAF (7465) 12.43
EX816
Direct to SAAF (7455) 12.43
EX817
Direct to SAAF (7471) 12.43
EX818
20 SFTS
RATW CF
4 FTS [B:Z/H:65]
Collided with EX167 and cr. 4mls S of Bembesi, SR, 25.3.53
EX819
Direct to SAAF (7466) 12.43
EX820
Direct to SAAF (7467) 12.43
Retd. to RAF: arr. UK 10.46
SS 8.50
EX821
Direct to SAAF (7470) 12.43
Retd. to RAF: arr. UK 12.46
To Belg.AF 5.47
EX822
33 FIS
CFS(SR)
SOC 4.12.45
EX823
Direct to SAAF (7468) 12.43
Retd. to RAF: arr. UK 10.46
To Belg.AF 4.47
EX824
22 SFTS 8.44- 8.44
CFS(SR) 8.44- 4.45
PSOC 1.1.47
EX825 to EX828
Direct to RNZAF (NZ1054 to NZ1057) 9.43
EX829
Direct to SAAF (7456) 12.43

EX830
CFS(SR)
4 FTS [B:E]
cr. ldd. 2mls E of Heany, SR, on overshoot, 17.2.49
EX831
Direct to SAAF (7457) 12.43
EX832
22 SFTS [32] 7.44- 8.44
CFS(SR) 8.44-
5 FTS [XK]
4 FTS [D:H] 12.47-
cr. ldd. Heany, SR, 5.7.49
EX833
33 FIS
CFS(SR)
SOC 4.4.46
EX834
73 OTU [X]
SOC 28.11.46
EX835
DIrect to SAAF (7458) 12.43
Retd. to RAF: arr. UK
To Ital.AF 5.49
EX836
Direct to SAAF (7459) 12.43
Retd. to RAF: arr. UK1.47
NFT
EX837
Direct to SAAF (7460) 12.43
EX838
Direct to SAAF (7461) 12.43
EX839
73 OTU [Z]
SOC 28.11.46
EX840
73 OTU [Q/U]
SOC 26.9.46

EX841
Direct to SAAF (7428) 11.43
EX842
22 SFTS 7.44-
4 FTS [B:W]
Spun in near Heany, SR, 1.8.50
EX843
73 OTU [F]
SOC 29.5.47
EX844
73 OTU [F]
SOC 27.7.44
EX845
CFS(SR)
4 FTS [D:J] 12.47-
To SRAF 3.52
EX846
74 OTU
SOC 31.5.45
EX847
Direct to SAAF (7429) 11.43
EX848
ME: no record of service
SOC 28.11.46
EX849
1330 CU
SOC 29.8.46
EX850
Direct to SAAF (7451) 11.43
Retd. to RAF: arr. UK 12.46
SS (Coley) 2.50
EX851
73 OTU [O]
SOC 28.11.46
EX852
S. Rhodesia: no record of service
SOC 30.9.52

EX853
S. Rhodesia: no record of service
SOC 30.9.52
EX854
4 FTS
Sold 11.53
EX855
Direct to SAAF (7448) 11.43
Retd. to RAF: arr. UK 10.46
SS 8.50
EX856
1330 CU
1 MECCU
Wrecked in gale 14.5.45
EX857
Direct to SAAF (7449) 11.43
EX858
Direct to SAAF (7444) 11.43
Retd. to RAF: arr. UK 12.46
SS 8.50
EX859
CFS(SR)
cr. 5mls E of Norton, SR, 5.4.45
EX860
71 OTU
75 OTU
1342 Flt
SOC 28.11.46
EX861
S. Rhodesia: no record of service
SOC 30.9.52
EX862
4 FTS
Sold 11.53
EX863
ME: no record of service
SOC 28.11.46
EX864
Direct to SAAF (7419) 11.43
EX865 to EX868
Direct to RNZAF (NZ1058 to NZ1061) 11.43
EX869
Direct to SAAF (7450) 11.43
EX870
4 FTS
Sold 11.53
EX871
Direct to SAAF (7472) 11.43
EX872
Direct to SAAF (7420) 11.43
EX873
Direct to SAAF (7430) 11.43
EX874
Direct to SAAF (7473) 12.43
EX875
Direct to SAAF (7453) 11.43
Retd. to RAF: arr. UK 1.47
SF Wattisham 12.47-
SOC 20.7.48
EX876
Direct to SAAF (7484) 12.43
EX877
S. Rhodesia: no record of service
SOC 2.7.45
EX878
Direct to SAAF (7421) 11.43
EX879
Direct to SAAF (7422) 11.43
Retd. to RAF: arr. UK 10.46
SS 8.50
EX880
Direct to SAAF (7423) 11.43
Retd. to RAF: arr. UK 1.47
SS 8.50
EX881
Direct to SAAF (7424) 11.43
EX882
Direct to SAAF (7425) 11.43
Retd. to RAF: arr. UK 11.46
SS 8.50
EX883
Direct to SAAF (7432) 11.43
Retd. to RAF: arr. UK 11.46
SS 8.50
EX884
Direct to SAAF (7426) 11.43
EX885
Direct to SAAF (7433) 11.43
EX886
Direct to SAAF (7427) 11.43
Retd. to RAF: arr. UK
SS 8.50
EX887
Direct to SAAF (7454) 11.43
EX888
ME: no record of service
SOC 28.11.46
EX889
Direct to SAAF (7440) 11.43
EX890
Direct to SAAF (7445) 11.43
EX891
4 FTS
Sold 11.53
EX892
Direct to SAAF (7431) 11.43
EX893
Direct to SAAF (7446) 11.43
EX894
Direct to SAAF (7441) 11.43
EX895
Direct to SAAF (7434) 11.43
Retd. to RAF: arr. UK 10.46
To R.Dan.AF 11.46
EX896
4 FTS
Sold 11.53
EX897
4 FTS
Sold 11.53
EX898
Direct to SAAF (7447) 11.43
EX899
Direct to SAAF (7435) 11.43
EX900
Direct to SAAF (7442) 11.43
Retd. to RAF: arr. UK 1.47
SS 8.50
EX901
Direct to SAAF (7436) 11.43
EX902
Direct to SAAF (7437) 11.43
Retd. to RAF: arr. UK 11.46
SS 8.50
EX903
Direct to SAAF (7474) 12.43
EX904
Direct to SAAF (7438) 11.43
EX905 to EX908
Direct to RNZAF (NZ1066 to NZ1069) 1.44
EX909
Direct to SAAF (7475) 12.43
EX910
Direct to SAAF (7476) 12.43
Retd. to RAF: arr. UK 11.46
To Belg.AF 2.47
EX911
Direct to SAAF (7485) 12.43
EX912
Direct to SAAF (7477) 12.43
EX913
797 Sqdn
Transferred India to Malta
728 Sqdn
NFT
EX914
Direct to SAAF (7443) 11.43
Retd. to RAF: arr. UK 1.47
SS 8.50
EX915
Direct to SAAF (7439) 11.43
EX916
Direct to SAAF (7478) 12.43
EX917
Direct to SAAF (7479) 12.43
EX918
Direct to SAAF (7480) 12.43
EX919
Direct to SAAF (7486) 12.43
EX920
Direct to SAAF (7481) 12.43
EX921
Direct to SAAF (7452) 11.43
EX922
Direct to SAAF (7469) 12.43
EX923
Direct to SAAF (7483) 12.43
Retd. to RAF: arr. UK 1.47
SS 8.50
EX924
Direct to SAAF (7482) 12.43
EX925
Direct to SAAF (7489) 1.44
Retd. to RAF: arr. UK 10.46
To R.Dan.AF 11.46
EX926
73 OTU [T]
SOC 29.5.47
EX927
Direct to SAAF (7490) 1.44
Retd. to RAF: arr. UK 1.47
SS 8.50
EX928
ME: no record of service
SOC 28.11.46
EX929
Direct to SAAF (7487) 12.43
Retd. to RAF: arr. UK 1.47
SS 8.50
EX930
ME: no record of service
SOC 28.11.46
EX931
Direct to SAAF (7491) 1.44
EX932
Direct to SAAF (7488) 12.43
EX933
To USAAF in ME 3.44
EX934
Direct to SAAF (7492) 1.44
EX935
Direct to SAAF (7504) 12.43
EX936
ME: no record of service
SOC 28.11.46
EX937
Direct to SAAF (7493) 1.44
Retd. to RAF: arr. UK 9.46
To Belg.AF 2.47
EX938
73 OTU [G]
SOC 28.11.46
EX939
Direct to SAAF (7505) 12.43
Retd. to RAF: arr. UK 10.46
To Belg.AF 4.47
EX940
Direct to SAAF (7494) 1.44
Retd. to RAF: arr. UK 11.46
To Belg.AF 5.47
EX941 to EX944
Direct to RNZAF (NZ1062 to NZ1065) 12.43
EX945
Direct to SAAF (7514) 2.44
Retd. to RAF: arr. UK 12.46
SS 8.50
EX946
Direct to SAAF (7501) 12.43
Retd. to RAF: arr. UK 10.46
To Belg.AF 4.47
EX947
Direct to SAAF (7502) 12.43
Retd. to RAF: arr. UK 1.47
SS 8.50
EX948
Direct to SAAF (7503) 12.43
Retd. to RAF: arr. UK 10.46
SS 8.50
EX949
ME: no record of service
SOC 29.5.47

EX950
Direct to SAAF (7495) 12.43
Retd. to RAF: arr. UK 10.46
SS 8.50
EX951
S. Rhodesia: no record of service
SOC 30.4.52
EX952
Direct to SAAF (7496) 12.43
EX953
Direct to SAAF (7497) 12.43
Retd. to RAF: arr. UK 11.46
SS 8.50
EX954
Direct to SAAF (7498) 12.43
EX955
Direct to SAAF (7499) 12.43
EX956
3 ANS [8] -10.48
4 FTS
Sold 11.53
EX957
S. Rhodesia: no record of service
SOC 30.9.52
EX958
4 FTS
Sold 11.53
EX959
Direct to SAAF (7509) 12.43
Retd. to RAF: arr. UK 10.46
To Belg.AF 2.47
EX960
Direct to SAAF (7506) 12.43
EX961
20 SFTS [76]
5 FTS -12.47
4 FTS
Sold 11.53
EX962
S. Rhodesia: no record of service
PSOC 1.1.47
EX963
Direct to SAAF (7515) 2.44
EX964
Direct to SAAF (7507) 12.43
Retd. to RAF: arr. UK 11.46
SS 8.50
EX965
4 FTS
Sold 11.53
EX966
S. Rhodesia: no record of service
SOC 30.9.52
EX967
Direct to SAAF (7516) 2.44
Retd. to RAF: arr. UK 1.47
SS 8.50
EX968
20 SFTS
4 FTS
Sold 11.53
EX969
Direct to SAAF (7508) 12.43
EX970
Direct to SAAF (7510) 2.44
EX971
73 OTU [N]
208 Sqdn 12.47-
SOC 10.5.50
EX972
Direct to SAAF (7517) 2.44
Transferred to RN and retd. to UK
718 Sqdn 10.45-
NFT
EX973
Direct to SAAF (7518) 2.44
EX974
Direct to SAAF (7531) 1.44
Retd; to RAF: arr. UK 9.46
To Belg.AF 2.47
EX975
Direct to SAAF (7519) 2.44
EX976
To RN in India via S. Africa 4.44
No service in India
Retd. to UK by 1.47
No service in UK
To Port.AF 3.56
EX977
Direct to SAAF (7520) 2.44
Retd. to RAF: arr. UK
SS 8.50
EX978
Direct to SAAF (7521) 2.44
Retd. to RAF: arr. UK 1.47
SS 8.50
EX979
Direct to SAAF (7522) 2.44
Retd. to RAF: arr. UK 1.47
SS 8.50
EX980
Direct to SAAF (7523) 2.44
EX981
Direct to SAAF (7524) 2.44
Retd. to RAF: arr. UK 10.46
SS 8.50
EX982
73 OTU [D]
SOC 28.11.46
EX983
cr. en route from Cape Erection Unit in SA to S. Rhodesia 2.44
EX984
4 FTS
Sold 11.53
EX985
Direct to SAAF (7525) 2.44
Retd. to RAF: arr. UK 11.46
SS 8.50
EX986
Direct to SAAF (7511) 2.44
Retd. to RAF: arr. UK 1.47
SS 8.50
EX987
Direct to SAAF (7512) 2.44
Retd. to RAF: arr. UK 10.46
SS 8.50
EX988
Direct to SAAF (7513) 2.44
Retd. to RAF: arr. UK 10.46
SS 8.50
EX989
Direct to SAAF (7530) 1.44
EX990
Direct to SAAF (7526) 2.44
EX991
Direct to SAAF (7532) 3.44
Retd. to RAF: arr. UK 10.46
SS 8.50
EX992
20 SFTS
4 FTS
Sold 11.53
EX993
Direct to SAAF (7527) 2.44
Retd. to RAF: arr. UK 10.46
To Belg.AF 3.47
EX994
Direct to SAAF (7528) 2.44
Retd. to RAF: arr. UK 10.46
To Belg.AF 5.47
EX995
S. Rhodesia: no record of service
SOC 30.9.52
EX996
S. Rhodesia: no record of service
Sold 11.53
EX997 to EX999
Direct to RNZAF (NZ1071 to NZ1073)

****

EZ100
73 OTU
Retd. to USAAF 8.46
EZ101
ME: no record of service
SOC 28.11.46
EZ102
AB&GS
Overturned on landing, El Ballah, 31.3.45
EZ103
4 FTS
Sold 11.53
EZ104
ME: no record of service
Retd. to USAAF 8.46
EZ105
ME: no record of service
SOC 29.8.46
EZ106
74 OTU
PSOC 1.1.47
EZ107
ME: no record of service
Retd. to USAAF 8.46
EZ108
ME: no record of service
SOC 28.11.46
EZ109
73 OTU [A]
SOC 28.11.46
EZ110
4 FTS
Sold 11.53
EZ111
73 OTU [B]
SOC 28.11.46
EZ112
74 OTU
73 OTU [U]
SOC 28.11.46
EZ113
ME: no record of service
SOC 29.5.47
EZ114
ME: no record of service
SOC 31.5.45
EZ115
73 OTU
Retd. to USAAF 8.46
EZ116
4 FTS
Sold 11.53
EZ117
73 OTU [G]
Retd. to USAAF 8.46
EZ118
Direct to SAAF (7566) 3.44
Retd. to RAF: arr. UK
SS 8.50
EZ119
Direct to SAAF (7567) 3.44
Retd. to RAF: arr. UK 1.47
SS 8.50
EZ120
ME: no record of service
SOC 25.1.45
EZ121
ME: no record of service
SOC 28.11.46
EZ122
S. Rhodesia: no record of service
SOC 30.9.50
EZ123
Direct to SAAF (7568) 3.44
Retd. to RAF for RN: arr. UK 1.46
757 Sqdn 6.45- 7.45
SOC 16.1.50
EZ124
4 FTS
Sold 11.53
EZ125
4 FTS
Sold 11.53

EZ126
4 FTS
Sold 11.53
EZ127
4 FTS
Sold 11.53
EZ128
4 FTS
Sold 11.53
EZ129
4 FTS
Sold 11.53
EZ130
4 FTS
Sold 11.53
EZ131
Direct to SAAF (7533) 3.44
Retd. to RAF: arr. UK 1.47
SS 8.50
EZ132
Direct to SAAF (7569) 3.44
EZ133
4 FTS
Sold 11.53
EZ134
Direct to SAAF (7539) 2.44
Retd. to RAF: arr. UK 12.46
SS 8.50
EZ135
Direct to SAAF (7541) 3.44
Retd. to RAF: arr. UK

EZ136
Direct to SAAF (7534) 2.44
Retd. to RAF: arr. UK 1.47
SS 8.50
EX137
Direct to SAAF (7535) 2.44
Transferred to RN in S. Africa 2.45
789 Sdqn 3.45- 8.45
Retd. to UK
RAE (.48)
SOC 14.1.50
EZ138
Direct to SAAF (7529) 3.44
EZ139
No trace
EZ140
73 OTU [T]
SOC 28.11.46
EZ141
ME: no record of service
SOC 29.8.46
EZ142
Direct to SAAF (7536) 2.44
Retd. to RAF: arr. UK 1.47
SS 8.50
EZ143
Direct to SAAF (7570) 3.44
EZ144
Direct to SAAF (7571) 3.44
EZ145
Direct to SAAF (7572) 3.44
EZ146
Direct to SAAF (7573) 3.44
EZ147
Direct to SAAF (7574) 3.44
Retd. to RAF: arr. UK 10.46
SS 8.50
EZ148
ME: no record of service
SOC 28.11.46
EZ149
Direct to SAAF (7575) 3.44
Retd. to RAF: arr. UK 1.47
SS 8.50
EZ150
Direct to SAAF (7537) 2.44
Retd. to RAF: arr. UK 10.46
To R.Dan.AF 11.46
EZ151
ME: no record of service
SOC 28.11.46

EZ152
Direct to SAAF (7538) 2.44
Retd. to RAF: arr. UK 10.46
To R.Dan.AF 11.46
EZ153
20 SFTS -11.47
SOC 8.12.52
EZ154
Direct to SAAF (7540) 2.44
EZ155
Direct to SAAF (7576) 3.44
EZ156
ME: no record of service
SOC 31.5.45
EZ157
73 OTU [R/D]
SOC 28.11.46
EZ158
Direct to SAAF (7577) 3.44
Retd. to RAF: arr. UK 1.47
SS 8.50
EZ159
Direct to SAAF (7546) 3.44
Retd. to RAF: arr. UK 10.46
SS 8.50
EX160
13 AGS (mod. as T.T.III)
SOC 28.11.46
EZ161
Direct to SAAF (7547) 3.44
Retd. to RAF: arr. UK
SS (Coley) 2.50
EZ162
Direct to SAAF (7548) 3.44
Retd. to RAF: arr. UK 9.46
To Belg.AF 2.47
EZ163
Direct to SAAF (7549) 3.44
EZ164
Direct to SAAF (7550) 3.44
EZ165
Direct to SAAF (7551) 3.44
EZ166
Direct to SAAF (7552) 3.44
Retd. to RAF: arr. UK 1.47
SS 8.50
EZ167
758 Sqdn [U2X] 3.45- 4.45
794 Sqdn [N] 6.45- 7.45
736 Sqdn 7.45- 1.46
SOC 21.3.56
EZ168
Direct to SAAF (7533) 3.44
Retd. to RAF: arr. UK 1.47
SS 8.50
EZ169
Direct to SAAF (7542) 3.44
Retd. to RAF: arr. UK
SS 8.50
EZ170
13 AGS
SOC 28.11.46
EZ171
Direct to SAAF (7554) 3.44
Transferred to RN in S. Africa 1.45
desp. UK
782 Sqdn
766 Sqdn [235:LM]
SOC 14.1.50
EZ172
Direct to SAAF (7543) 3.44
Retd. to RAF: arr. UK 12.46
SS (Coley) 2.50
EZ173
Direct to SAAF (7544) 3.44
EZ174
Direct to SAAF (7555) 3.44
Retd. to RAF: arr. UK 9.46
To Belg.AF 2.47
EZ175
Direct to SAAF (7556) 3.44
Loaned to RN in S. Africa and retd.
Retd. to RAF: arr. UK 1.47
SS 8.50

EZ176
Direct to SAAF (7557) 3.44
EZ177
Direct to RNZAF (NZ1079)
EZ178
Direct to SAAF (7558) 3.44
Transferred to RN in S. Africa 2.45
789 Sqdn 2.45- 4.45
desp. UK
766 Sqdn 9.46-10.46
NFT
EZ179
Direct to SAAF (7559) 3.44
EZ180
Direct to SAAF (7545) 3.44
Retd. to RAF: arr. UK 1.47
SS 8.50
EZ181
Direct to SAAF (7560) 3.44
Retd. to RAF: arr. UK 1.47
SS 8.50
EZ182
Direct to SAAF (7561) 3.44
Retd. to RAF: arr. UK 12.46
SS 8.50
EZ183
Direct to SAAF (7562) 3.44
Retd. to RAF: arr. UK 12.46
SS 8.50
EZ184
Direct to SAAF (7584) 5.44
EZ185
Direct to SAAF (7585) 5.44
Retd. to RAF: arr. UK 10.46
SS 8.50
EZ186
Direct to SAAF (7563) 3.44
Retd. to RAF: arr. UK 9.46
To Belg.AF 2.47
EZ187
Direct to SAAF (7617) 5.44
Retd. to RAF: arr. UK 1.47
SS 8.50
EZ188
4 FTS
Sold 11.53
EZ189
Direct to SAAF (7615) 5.44
EZ190
4 FTS
Sold 11.53
EZ191
Direct to SAAF (7599) 4.44
Retd. to RAF: arr. UK 1.47
SS 8.50
EZ192
Direct to SAAF (7600) 4.44
Retd. to RAF: arr. UK 10.46
SS 8.50
EZ193
Direct to SAAF (7564) 3.44
Retd. to RAF: arr. UK 12.46
SS 8.50
EZ194
Direct to SAAF (7601) 4.44
EZ195
Direct to SAAF (7565) 3.44
Retd. to RAF: arr. UK 1.47
SS 8.50
EZ196
Direct to SAAF (7586) 5.44
Retd. to RAF: arr. UK
SS 8.50
EZ197
Direct to SAAF (7602) 4.44
Retd. to RAF: arr. UK 1.47
SS 8.50
EZ198
Direct to SAAF (7616) 5.44
Retd. to RAF: arr. UK 1.47
SS 8.50
EZ199
Direct to SAAF (7603) 4.44
Retd. to RAF: arr. UK 10.46
SS 8.50

EZ200
Direct to SAAF (7587) 5.44
Retd. to RAF: arr. UK 12.46
SS (Coley) 2.50
EZ201
Direct to SAAF (7588) 5.44
EZ202
ME: no record of service
SOC 28.11.46
EZ203
Direct to SAAF (7589) 5.44
Retd. to RAF: arr. UK
SS (Coley) 2.50
EZ204
5 FTS 11.47-
Sold 11.53
EZ205
Direct to SAAF (7604) 4.44
Retd. to RAF: arr. UK 1.47
SS 8.50
EZ206
Direct to SAAF (7590) 5.44
Retd. to RAF: arr. UK 1.47
SS 8.50
EZ207
Direct to SAAF (7591) 5.44
EZ208
S. Rhodesia: no record of service
SOC 30.9.52
EZ209
Direct to SAAF (7610) 5.44
Retd. to RAF: arr. UK 1.47
SS 8.50
EZ210
Direct to SAAF (7605) 4.44
Retd. to RAF: arr. UK 10.46
To Belg.AF 4.47
EZ211
Direct to SAAF (7620) 6.44
Transferred to RN in S. Africa 1.45
789 Sqdn 1.45- 3.45
Desp. UK
NFT
EZ212
4 FTS
395 MU CF 12.50-11.52
4 FTS 9.53-
Sold 11.53
EZ213
Direct to SAAF (7592) 5.44
EZ214
Direct to SAAF (7578) 4.44
Retd. to RAF: arr. UK 9.46
To Belg.AF 2.47
EZ215
Direct to SAAF (7579) 4.44
Retd. to RAF: arr. UK
SS 8.50
EZ216
Direct to SAAF (7580) 4.44
EZ217
Direct to SAAF (7581) 4.44
EZ218
22 SFTS 9.44-12.44
CFS(SR) 12.44-
4 FTS
Sold 11.53
EZ219
Direct to SAAF (7593) 5.44
Retd. to RAF: arr. UK 1.47
SS 8.50
EZ220
Direct to SAAF (7582) 4.44
Retd. to RAF: arr. UK 10.46
To R.Dan.AF 11.46
EZ221
Direct to SAAF (7594) 5.44
Retd. to RAF: arr. UK 10.46
To R.Dan.AF 11.46
EZ222
22 SFTS 9.44-
4 FTS
Sold 11.53

EZ223
Remained in USA
cr. 30.11.44
EZ224
Direct to SAAF (7614) 5.44
EZ225
4 FTS
Sold 11.53
EZ226
Direct to SAAF (7613)
EZ227
4 FTS
Sold 11.53
EZ228
4 FTS
Sold 11.53
EZ229
Direct to SAAF (7606) 4.44
EZ230
Direct to SAAF (7583) 4.44
Retd. to RAF: arr. UK 9.46
SS 8.50
EZ231
Direct to SAAF (7595) 5.44
Retd. to RAF: arr. UK 12.46
SS 8.50
EZ232
Direct to SAAF (7608) 4.44
EZ233
20 SFTS
5 FTS 11.47-
Sold 11.53
EZ234
CFS(SR)
5 FTS 11.47-
SOC 30.9.52
EZ235
Direct to SAAF (7596) 4.44
Retd. to RAF: arr. UK 12.46
SS 8.50
EZ236
Direct to SAAF (7609) 5.44
EZ237
Direct to SAAF (7607) 4.44
Retd. to RAF: arr. UK 1.47
NFT
EZ238
4 FTS 4.50- 2.52
Kumalo CF 2.52-
4 FTS
Sold 11.53
EZ239
CFS(SR)
SOC 30.9.52
EZ240
Direct to SAAF (7597) 5.44
Transferred to RN in S. Africa 1.45
726 Sqdn 2.45- 9.45
desp. UK
1832 Sqdn 11.47-10.48
700 Sqdn 10.48- 5.49
780 Sqdn [204:CW]
781 Sqdn 4.53- 5.54
SOC 5.54
EZ241
4 FTS
Sold 11.53
EZ242 to EZ246
Direct to RNZAF (NZ1074 to NZ1078) .44
EZ247
Direct to SAAF (7598) 5.44
Retd. to RAF: arr. UK 1.47
SS 8.50
EZ248
20 SFTS
4 FTS
Sold 11.53
EZ249
73 OTU
SOC 28.11.46
EZ250
732 Sqdn 9.45-10.45
SOC 14.1.50

EZ251
Direct to SAAF (7621) 6.44
EZ252
780 Sqdn 6.46-12.46
766 Sqdn [238:LM] 3.48- 7.49
SOC 10.1.50
EZ253
798 Sqdn 1.46- 3.46
780 Sqdn 3.46- 5.46
727 Sqdn 4.49- 5.49
SF Arbroath [903:AO] 5.50-
799 Sqdn 4.51- 5.51
1841 Sqdn [204:JA] 7.52- 1.54
SOC 19.2.54
EZ254
Direct to SAAF (7619) 6.44
Transferred to RN in S. Africa 1.45
desp. UK 10.45
766 Sqdn 9.46- 1.47
SOC 14.1.50
EZ255
? SFTS [19]
5 FTS
SOC 30.9.52
EZ256
Direct to SAAF (7630) 6.44
Retd. to RAF: arr. UK 10.46
To Belg.AF 2.47
EZ257
758 Sqdn 2.45-
732 Sqdn [D] 7.45-10.45
SOC 14.1.50
EZ258
S. Rhodesia: no record of service
SOC 30.9.52
EZ259
Direct to SAAF (7631) 6.44
Transferred to RN in S. Africa 1.45
desp. UK
766 Sqdn [247:LM] 1.49-
SOC 1.1.50
EZ260
758 Sqdn [U3MM] 12.44- 7.45
732 Sqdn [S] 7.45-12.45
784 Sqdn 12.45- 1.46
732 Sqdn 8.46-11.46
766 Sqdn 11.46-10.47
736 Sqdn [201] 11.47- 2.49
SOC 3.50
EZ261
Eglinton 8.45-10.45
NFT
EZ262
700/799 Sqdn 11.47- 3.49
cr. ldd. Yeovilton 3.3.49
EZ263
ME: no record of service
SOC 28.11.46
EZ264
CFS(SR)
4 FTS
Sold 11.53
EZ265
798 Sqdn .45- 3.46
780 Sqdn 3.46- 7.46
SOC 14.1.50
EZ266
798 Sqdn 10.45- 3.46
780 Sqdn 3.46- 7.46
SOC 13.1.50
EZ267
798 Sqdn
Eglinton 2.46-
SOC 14.1.50
EZ268
748 Sqdn [W] 11.45- 2.46
SOC 3.56
EZ269
RN: no record of service
SOC 14.1.50
EZ270
S. Rhodesia: no record of service
SOC 30.9.52

Mk.III EZ306 of No.20 SFTS, Cranborne, Southern Rhodesia *(J.G.Lyne)*

EZ271
780 Sqdn 4.46- 5.46
NFT
EZ272
799 Sqdn 12.45- 2.46
1830 Sqdn [202:AC] 1.49- 9.50
SOC 18.5.53
EZ273
718 Sqdn 10.45-11.45
758 Sqdn 5.46- 5.46
780 Sqdn 5.46- 8.46
SOC 11.5.51
EZ274
709 Sqdn [S3N] 2.45- 6.45
798 Sqdn [N] 8.45-
766 Sqdn [G] 4.46- 5.46
SOC 3.56
EZ275
798 Sqdn 10.45-12.45
759 Sqdn 12.45- 2.46
766 Sqdn [B] 2.46-12.46
1831 Sqdn 6.46-11.47
desp. Malta
SF Hal Far 4.49- 3.50
retd. UK
SOC 5.56
EZ276
S. Rhodesia: no record of service
SOC 30.9.52
EZ277
758 Sqdn 12.44- 4.45
732 Sqdn 6.45- 7.45
718 Sqdn 9.45-11.45
NFT
EZ278
794 Sqdn 12.44- 4.45
758 Sqdn [U3VV] 1.46- 6.46
SF Abbotsinch 10.47- 4.49
Admiralty Flt [204] 7.54- 5.55
SOC 6.56

EZ279
4 FF 3.47- 6.47
NFT
EZ280
CFS(SR)
SOC 30.9.52
EZ281
1832 Sqdn [202:CH] 3.50- 2.51
To Port.AF 3.56
EZ282
RN: no record of service
SOC
EZ283
758 Sqdn
780 Sqdn 5.46- 7.46
SOC 10.1.50
EZ284
700 Sqdn [203:VL] 4.46- 9.47
SOC 23.10.48
EZ285
759 Sqdn 12.45- 1.46
780 Sqdn 5.46-
766 Sqdn 9.46-11.46
desp. Malta
SF Hal Far 5.49- 6.52
NFT
EZ286
22 SFTS 11.44-
20 SFTS
SOC 30.9.52
EZ287
4 FTS
Sold 11.53
EZ288
799 Sqdn 4.46- 5.46
desp. Malta
SF Hal Far 5.49
cr. ldd. Hal Far 8.7.49
EZ289
Direct to SAAF (7612) 5.44
Retd. to RAF: arr. UK 12.46
SS 8.50

EZ290
22 SFTS 11.44-12.44
CFS(SR) 12.44-
SOC 30.9.52
EZ291
759 Sqdn 1.46- 2.46
1830 Sqdn 6.47- 4.50
SOC 22.6.50
EZ292
Direct to SAAF (7622) 6.44
Retd. to RAF: arr. UK 10.46
To Belg.AF 3.47
EZ293
20 SFTS
4 FTS
SOC 30.9.52
EZ294
Direct to SAAF (7611) 5.44
Retd. to RAF: arr. UK 1.47
SS 8.50
EZ295
SF St. Merryn 1.49- 6.49
SOC 19.5.50
EZ296
22 SFTS 11.44-12.44
CFS(SR) 12.44-
SOC 30.9.52
EZ297 to EZ301
Direct to RNZAF (NZ1080 to NZ1084) 8.44
EZ302
20 SFTS
4 FTS
Sold 11.53
EZ303
SF St. Merryn 12.45- 2.46
To Port.AF 3.56
EZ304
22 SFTS 10.44-
4 FTS
Sold 11.53

EZ305
- 22 SFTS 10.44-
- 4 FTS
- Sold 11.53

EZ306
- 22 SFTS 11.44-
- 20 SFTS [28]
- 4 FTS
- Sold 11.53

EZ307
- Direct to SAAF (7623) 6.44
- Retd. to RAF: arr. UK 10.46
- To Belg.AF 5.47

EZ308
- 20 SFTS
- 4 FTS
- Sold 11.53

EZ309
- Direct to SAAF (7624) 6.44
- Retd. to RAF: arr. UK 10.46
- SS 8.50

EZ310
- Direct to SAAF (7625) 6.44
- Retd. to RAF: arr. UK 9.46
- To Belg.AF 2.47

EZ311
- RN: no record of service
- SOC

EZ312
- 759 Sqdn 12.45- 2.46
- 746 Sqdn 2.46- 3.46
- To Port.AF 3.56

EZ313
- 13 AGS
- Retd. to USAAF 8.46

EZ314
- Direct to SAAF (7626) 6.44

EZ315
- Direct to SAAF (7618) 6.44

EZ316
- Lee-on-Solent 11.45- 2.46
- Rattray 2.46- 8.47
- 1831 Sqdn [203:JA] 8.47- 9.49
- 799 Sqdn 2.51- 6.51
- SF Gosport [GJ] 6.51- 9.55
- SOC 9.55

EZ317
- 798 Sqdn 1.45
- NFT

EZ318
- 799 Sqdn 5.46-
- 1832 Sqdn [205:CH] 7.47-11.49
- 780 Sqdn 1.50- 2.50
- SOC 21.2.50

EZ319
- 73 OTU [W]
- Retd. to USAAF 7.46

EZ320
- 798 Sqdn 6.45- 8.45
- 1832 Sqdn 9.47- 5.48
- SOC 27.11.48

EZ321
- Direct to SAAF (7627) 6.44
- Retd. to UK 12.46
- SS 8.50

EZ322
- AB&GS
- SOC 28.11.46

EZ323
- 794 Sqdn 1.46- 2.46
- desp. Malta
- SF Hal Far 5.49-11.50
- SOC 31.12.51

EZ324
- 780 Sqdn 4.46- 5.46
- 766 Sqdn 1.47-
- SOC 10.1.50

EZ325
- 73 OTU [B]
- 208 Sqdn
- cr. on landing, Aqir, 29.8.46

EZ326
- ME: no record of service
- SOC 28.11.46

EZ327
- 736 Sqdn [202:JB] 11.45- 7.48
- SOC 16.1.50

EZ328
- 759 Sqdn 1.46- 3.46
- 766 Sqdn 4.46- 5.47
- SOC 10.1.50

EZ329 to EZ333
- Direct to RNZAF (NZ1085 to NZ1089) 8.44

EZ334
- 73 OTU [J]
- SOC 28.11.46

EZ335
- Direct to SAAF (7632) 6.44
- Retd. to RAF: arr. UK 9.46
- To Belg.AF 2.47

EZ336
- Direct to SAAF (7633) 6.44

EZ337
- 73 OTU
- SOC 31.5.45

EZ338
- Direct to SAAF (7628) 6.44

EZ339
- Direct to SAAF (7629) 6.44
- Retd. to RAF: arr. UK 10.46
- To R.Dan.AF 11.46

EZ340
- 74 OTU
- Retd. to USAAF 7.46

EZ341
- 784 Sqdn 11.45- 6.46
- To Port.AF 3.56

EZ342
- 700 Sqdn 7.49- 7.50
- SOC 5.56

EZ343
- 794 Sqdn 2.46- 6.46
- 766 Sqdn 12.47-
- SOC 14.1.50

EZ344
- 73 OTU [Z]
- SOC 28.11.46

Gosport Station Flight Mk.II Harvard EZ316 photographed in July 1953 *(via R.C.Sturtivant)*

Camouflaged Mk.III EZ400 of RNAS Culdrose's Station Flight (via R.C.Sturtivant)

EZ345
758 Sqdn [U3WW] 12.45- 5.46
780 Sqdn [U2B] 5.46-12.46
1833 Sqdn [U2B] 7.47-11.49
799 Sqdn 2.51- 5.51
SF Anthorn [AH] 5.51- 7.54
SOC 6.56
EZ346
ME: no record of service
Retd. to USAAF 7.46
EZ347
798 Sqdn [L3R] 7.44- 6.45
SOC 21.3.56
EZ348
798 Sqdn 3.46- 3.46
780 Sqdn 3.46- 9.46
desp. Malta
SF Hal Far [911:HF] 3.47- 2.52
SOC 6.2.52
EZ349
ME: no record of service
SOC 29.8.46
EZ350
798 Sqdn 10.44-
NFT
EZ351
RN: no record of service
SOC 14.1.50
EZ352
73 OTU
Retd. to USAAF 7.46
EZ353
ME: no record of service
Retd. to USAAF 7.46
EZ354
13 AGS
11 FIS
Retd. to USAAF 7.46
EZ355
ME: no record of service
SOC 28.11.46
EZ356
73 OTU [S]
SOC 28.11.46
EZ357
43 Sqdn
6 Sqdn 3.48- 7.48
39 Sqdn [39] 7.48- 7.49
SOC 22.11.50
EZ358
Retained in USA on special duties
SOC 1.1.47
EZ359 to EZ363
Direct to RNZAF (NZ1090 to NZ1094) 7.44

EZ364
758 Sqdn [U3RR] 2.45- 5.45
794 Sqdn 5.45- 6.45
736 Sqdn 6.45- 1.46
766 Sqdn [238:LM] 4.46- 2.48
782 Sqdn 2.48- 4.49
799 Sqdn 3.51- 6.51
Admiralty Flt [203] 6.51- 7.54
SOC 5.56
EZ365
RN: no record of service
SOC
EZ366
SF Ballyhalbert 10.45-
794 Sqdn 2.46- 4.46
Admiralty Flt [204] 6.51- .52
SOC 15.9.54
EZ367
758 Sqdn
798 Sqdn 12.45- 3.46
780 Sqdn 3.46- 4.46
SOC 10.1.50
EZ368
RN: no record of service
SOC
EZ369
758 Sqdn
NFT
EZ370
RN: no record of service
SOC
EZ371
798 Sqdn [L3K] 5.45- 2.46
Eglinton
799 Sqdn 4.48- 5.48
SOC 18.5.53
EZ372
799 Sqdn 4.51- 5.51
1840 Sqdn [221:FD] 7.52- 2.54
SOC 21.1.55
EZ373
758 Sqdn 2.45- 3.45
732 Sqdn 6.45-11.45
784 Sqdn [T] 11.45- 7.46
1830 Sqdn [279:AC] 7.53- 3.55
1832 Sqdn 3.55- 5.55
SOC 5.56
EZ374
780 Sqdn [U2D] 4.46-10.46
1833 Sqdn 7.47- 4.48
SOC 18.5.53
EZ375
758 Sqdn [U3JJ] 3.45- 6.45
794 Sqdn 6.45- 6.45
736 Sqdn [M] 6.45-10.45
799 Sqdn 4.51- 6.51
SOC 5.56

EZ376
798 Sqdn [U3X] 10.45- 3.46
758 Sqdn [U2X] 3.46- 5.46
758 Sqdn [U2X] 5.46- 6.46
781 Sqdn 4.53- 5.53
1830 Sqdn [238:AC/ 206:AC] 12.53-11.54
SOC 5.56
EZ377
780 Sqdn 4.46- 5.46
NFT
EZ378
759 Sqdn [Y5F] 4.45-11.45
766 Sqdn 9.46- 4.48
SOC 30.12.49
EZ379
798 Sqdn [U2F] 9.45- 3.46
758 Sqdn [U2F] 3.46- 6.46
1831 Sqdn [204:JA] 10.47-10.48
SOC 21.3.56
EZ380
798 Sqdn [4Z] 10.45-11.45
799 Sqdn 11.45- 5.46
766 Sqdn 9.46-11.46
NFT
EZ381
798 Sqdn [U2S] 10.45-11.45
780 Sqdn [U2S] 3.46- 6.46
1833 Sqdn .49
NFT
EZ382
798 Sqdn 3.45-
766 Sqdn 9.46-
NFT
EZ383
1830 Sqdn [207:AC] 2.48- 4.50
SOC 15.5.50
EZ384
ME: no record of service
SOC 30.5.46
EZ385
780 Sqdn 6.46- 8.46
NFT
EZ386
766 Sqdn 1.46-
1832 Sqdn [201:CH] 7.47- 1.51
SOC 5.7.51
EZ387
ME: no record of service
SOC 29.5.47
EZ388
798 Sqdn 10.45- 3.46
758 Sqdn 3.46-
782 Sqdn 12.47- 1.48
SF Eglinton [903:JR] 2.48- 4.49
SOC 13.3.50
EZ389
ME: no record of service
SOC 29.5.47
EZ390
758 Sqdn 1.46- 5.46
780 Sqdn 5.46- 7.46
SOC 10.1.50
EZ391
761 Sqdn 12.45- 1.46
SOC 14.1.50
EZ392
73 OTU [S]
SOC 28.11.46
EZ393
AB&GS
SOC 29.5.47
EZ394
ME: no record of service
SOC 28.11.46
EZ395
AB&GS
SOC 29.5.47
EZ396
798 Sqdn [U2K] 10.45- 3.46
1833 Sqdn [U2K] 10.47-11.48
SOC 3.56
EZ397
AB&GS
SOC 28.11.46

EZ398
73 OTU [V]
SOC 28.11.46
EZ399
758 Sqdn
SOC 14.1.50
EZ400
736 Sqdn 12.45- 1.46
SF Culdrose [900:CW] 12.47- 9.48
Admiralty Flt 10.54- 5.55
SOC 5.56
EZ401
SF Anthorn 3.50- 3.51
To Port.AF 3.56
EZ402
1831 Sqdn [202:JA] 1.48- 1.50
SOC 25.1.50
EZ403
761 Sqdn [Z] 11.44- 4.46
766 Sqdn [245:LM] 2.48- 4.48
To Port.AF 3.56
EZ404
700 Sqdn 4.46- 5.46
727 Sqdn [202:GJ] 7.47- 2.49
SOC 21.3.56
EZ405
1831 Sqdn [203:JA/ 203:ST] 1.50- 1.51
SOC 18.5.53
EZ406
759 Sqdn [Y2Z] 4.45-10.45
SF Hal Far 12.47
Collided with Vampire and cr., 25.10.48
EZ407
784 Sqdn 11.45- 9.46
790 Sqdn 9.46-12.46
To Port.AF 3.56
EZ408
794 Sqdn 2.46- 5.46
1831 Sqdn [202:JA] 11.49- 1.50
SOC 14.1.50
EZ409
766 Sqdn 6.47-12.47
SF Lossiemouth 9.48
SOC 10.1.50
EZ410
780 Sqdn 9.48-
SOC 14.1.50
EZ411
758 Sqdn 12.44-
NFT
EZ412
RN: no record of service
SOC 14.1.50
EZ413
736 Sqdn 11.45- 8.46
741 Sqdn [S] 8.46-11.47
736 Sqdn 11.47-10.48
767 Sqdn 10.48- 7.50
SOC 5.56
EZ414
RN: no record of service
SOC 14.1.50
EZ415
RN: no record of service
SOC 14.1.50
EZ416
799 Sqdn 12.45- 5.46
SOC 14.1.50
EZ417
RN: no record of service
SOC 14.1.50
EZ418
1832 Sqdn [201:CH] 7.47- 8.49
SOC 16.1.50
EZ419
732 Sqdn 8.45-10.45
NFT
EZ420
St. Merryn 12.45- 4.46
766 Sqdn [J] 4.46- 7.47
To Port.AF 3.56
EZ421
758 Sqdn [U30] 12.45- 3.46
780 Sqdn [U30] 3.46- 3.47
To Port.AF 3.56
EZ422
794 Sqdn [F] 8.45- 1.46
NFT
EZ423
760 Sqdn 4.45-10.45
SF Eglinton
Spun in, Maydown, 25.6.48
EZ424
759 Sqdn [Y3Y] 3.45-11.45
701 Sqdn [LOE] 3.46- 4.46
SOC 14.1.50
EZ425
759 Sqdn [Y6Q] 3.45-10.45
2 FF - 7.48
SOC 10.1.50
EZ426
ME: no record of service
SOC 28.11.46
EZ427
SF Hal Far 2.47- 1.52
SOC 6.2.52
EZ428
701 Sqdn 1.46- 2.46
799 Sqdn 4.51- 6.51
Admiralty Flt [205] 6.51- .54
SOC 22.7.54
EZ429
73 OTU
SOC 28.11.46
EZ430
No RN service
Transferred to RAF 1.45
ECFS
Hdlg. Sqdn 3.45-10.45
Retd. to RN 1.46
No record of further service
SOC 14.1.50
EZ431
798 Sqdn 6.45- 7.45
782 Sqdn 5.46-
766 Sqdn 1.48- 4.49
To Port.AF 3.56
EZ432
SF China Bay
desp. UK
780 Sqdn 6.46-11.46
SF Arbroath [905:AO] 7.51
Undershot; cr. ldd. Arbroath, 22.10.54
EZ433
759 Sqdn [Y3U] 3.45- 5.45
782 Sqdn
766 Sqdn 11.46-12.47
SOC 10.1.50
EZ434
ME: no record of service
DBR in accident and SOC 28.11.44
EZ435
759 Sqdn [Y6C] 4.45-11.45
NFT
EZ436
798 Sqdn
4 FF 6.47-
SF Hal Far [913:HF] 12.47- 6.52
SOC 23.6.52
EZ437
73 OTU [P]
SOC 28.11.46
EZ438
759 Sqdn [Y3P] 11.45- 4.46
766 Sqdn [A] 4.46- 2.47
1833 Sqdn [253:BR] 9.49- 5.51
To Port.AF 3.56
EZ439
Direct to RNZAF (NZ1095) 11.44
EZ440
766 Sqdn 6.47- 2.48
SOC 19.5.50
EZ441
ME: no record of service
SOC 29.8.46
EZ442
727 Sqdn [GP2Z]
SOC 14.1.50
EZ443
RN: no record of service
SOC 14.1.50
EZ444
73 OTU
SOC 28.11.46
EZ445
11 FIS
SOC 28.11.46
EZ446
ME: no record of service
SOC 29.5.47
EZ447
700 Sqdn [Y2M]
NFT

Cocooned on a carrier deck in October 1947 is EZ406, latterly of No.759 Squadron and now on the way to Malta *(FAA Museum)*

No.700 Squadron of the Fleet Air Arm operated Mk.III Harvard EZ447, shown here after coming to grief
(via R.C.Sturtivant)

EZ448
732 Sqdn 8.45-11.45
SOC 23.4.49
EZ449
Direct to RNZAF (NZ1096) 11.44
EZ450
73 OTU [I]
SOC 28.11.46
EZ451
No RN service
To Port.AF 3.56
EZ452
73 OTU [W]
SOC 13.9.45
EZ453
Direct to RNZAF (NZ1097) 11.44
EZ454
73 OTU [C]
SOC 31.12.47
EZ455
Direct to RNZAF (NZ1098) 11.44
EZ456
Direct to RNZAF (NZ1099) 11.44
EZ457
RN: no record of service
SOC 14.1.50
EZ458
RN: no record of service
SOC 14.1.50

****

FE267
No trace
FE268
31 SFTS (6.42- 5.44)
SOC 16.11.44
FE269
31 SFTS [98] (1.42- 5.44)
To RCAF
FE270
31 SFTS (3.42- 5.44)
14 SFTS [96]
To RCAF
FE271
31 SFTS (3.42- 7.43)
To RCAF
FE272
31 SFTS
14 SFTS
To RCAF
FE273
31 SFTS [22] (10.42- 7.43)
14 SFTS
To RCAF
FE274
31 SFTS (6.42- 8.44)
14 SFTS
To RCAF
FE275
31 SFTS (6.43- 5.44)
TO RCAF
FE276
31 SFTS [100] (11.42-)
14 SFTS (11.43-)
To RCAF
FE277
31 SFTS [105] (10.42- 6.43)
To RCAF
FE278
41 SFTS (6.42- 7.43)
To RCAF
FE279
41 SFTS [83] (8.42- 4.43)
To RCAF
FE280
41 SFTS
To RCAF
FE281
41 SFTS (4.43-10.43)
To RCAF
FE282
41 SFTS
To RCAF
FE283
41 SFTS (4.43- 1.44)
To RCAF
FE284
133 Sqdn RCAF
34 SFTS
cr. Little Plume, Alberta, 12.8.44)
FE285
133 Sqdn RCAF
34 SFTS [29]
To RCAF
FE286
133 Sqdn RCAF
14 SFTS
To RCAF
FE287
41 SFTS
To RCAF
FE288
31 SFTS
cr. in L. Ontario, 15.6.42
FE289
31 SFTS
34 SFTS [67]
14 SFTS
To RCAF
FE290
31 SFTS (11.42- 6.44)
14 SFTS
To RCAF
FE291
31 SFTS (7.42- 7.44)
14 SFTS
SOC 22.9.44
FE292
31 SFTS (7.42- 7.44)
14 SFTS
To RCAF

FE293
31 SFTS (12.43- 8.44)
14 SFTS
To RCAF
FE294
31 SFTS
1 FIS
To RCAF
FE295
31 SFTS (1.43- 8.44)
14 SFTS
To RCAF
FE296
31 SFTS [9] (7.42- 6.44)
14 SFTS
To RCAF
FE297
31 SFTS
FA Cat.E 9.7.43
FE298
31 SFTS
desp. India 5.44
60 Sqdn
Missing off Burmese coast, 13.6.45
FE299
31 SFTS (12.42- 7.44)
To RCAF
FE300
41 SFTS (8.42- 1.44)
To RCAF
FE301
41 SFTS
Collided with FE349 and cr.,23.6.43
FE302
41 SFTS (6.42- 9.43)
To RCAF
FE303
41 SFTS
cr. 3½mls NNE of Weyburn, Sas., 30.7.42
FE304
41 SFTS [85]
DBF 13.9.43
FE305
41 SFTS
SOC 27.8.42
FE306
41 SFTS (11.42- 6.43)
To RCAF
FE307
13 SFTS
3 SFTS
133 Sqdn RCAF
34 SFTS [14]
To RCAF
FE308
133 Sqdn RCAF
34 SFTS
Caught fire in air and cr. 5mls W of Bowhill, Alberta, 28.9.42
FE309
34 SFTS
To RCAF
FE310
133 Sqdn RCAF
To RCAF
FE311
135 Sqdn RCAF
SOC 19.2.43
FE312
135 Sqdn RCAF
166 Sqdn RCAF
3 SFTS
To RCAF
FE313
135 Sqdn RCAF
166 Sqdn RCAF
3 SFTS
To RCAF
FE314 (11.42- 1.44)
41 SFTS
To RCAF
FE315 (9.42- 6.43)
41 SFTS
To RCAF

Probably belonging to No.73 OTU, EZ454 at rest in the Middle East (Harry Holmes via R.C.Sturtivant)

FE316
41 SFTS (8.42- 1.44)
To RCAF
FE317
41 SFTS [25]
To RCAF
FE318
41 SFTS
cr. Halbrite RLG after engine failure, 19.10.43
FE319
41 SFTS (12.42- 1.44)
8 SFTS
To RCAF
FE320
41 SFTS (8.42- 9.43)
To RCAF
FE321
Canada: no record of service
SOC 7.10.42

FE322
41 SFTS (4.43- 1.44)
To RCAF
FE323
41 SFTS (5.43- 1.44)
To RCAF
FE324
41 SFTS
SOC 25.11.43
FE325
41 SFTS (8.42-12.43)
To RCAF
FE326
41 SFTS (1.43- 6.43)
To RCAF
FE327
1 SFTS (9.43-10.44)
To RCAF

FE296 of No.31 SFTS waits at the holding point at Kingston, Ontario while RCAF Anson 7099 lands (via R.C.Sturtivant)

FE328
31 SFTS [60] (8.42- 6.43)
14 SFTS
To RCAF
FE329
1 SFTS
cr. near Edenvale RLG, 15.7.42
FE330
1 SFTS
To RCAF
FE331
31 SFTS (11.42- 5.44)
To RCAF
FE332
31 SFTS (1.43- 6.43)
13 SFTS
desp. UK 4.44
No service in UK
To R.Neth.AF 2.47
FE333
14 SFTS
13 SFTS (6.44- 9.44)
34 SFTS
To RCAF
FE334
6 SFTS
SOC 2.11.42
FE335
6 SFTS
To RCAF
FE336
6 SFTS
SOC 12.11.42
FE337
41 SFTS (5.43-12.43)
To RCAF
FE338
41 SFTS [38] (10.42-11.43)
To RCAF
FE339
41 SFTS (4.43-11.43)
To RCAF
FE340
41 SFTS (4.43-12.43)
8 SFTS
SOC 11.4.44
FE341
41 SFTS (5.43-10.43)
To RCAF
FE342
41 SFTS (8.42- 4.43)
To RCAF
FE343
41 SFTS [84]
cr. in R. Missouri, N. Dakota, USA, 20.12.43
FE344
41 SFTS
1 SFTS
To RCAF
FE345
41 SFTS
SOC 28.3.44
FE346
41 SFTS (3.43-12.43)
To RCAF
FE347
41 SFTS
To RCAF
FE348
41 SFTS
To RCAF
FE349
41 SFTS (11.42- 6.43)
Collided in mid-air with FE301, 23.6.43
FE350
41 SFTS
To RCAF
FE351
41 SFTS (8.43-11.43)
To RCAF
FE352
41 SFTS
8 SFTS
cr. on take-off, Weyburn, Sas., 3.2.44
FE353
152 OTU
Hit ground during practice forced landing, Risalpur, 18.10.43
FE354
151 OTU
SLAIS
AFS(I)
To IAF 9.47
FE355
152 OTU
ACSEA CS
228 Gp. CF
SOC 24.4.47
FE356
151 OTU
SOC 24.4.47
FE357
Bengal CU
SOC 24.4.47
FE358
1 SFTS(I)
cr. in slow roll, Roorkee, 21.8.44
FE359
151 OTU
SOC 9.8.45
FE360
3 RFU - 9.44
1 AGS 9.44-
SOC 24.4.47
FE361
1 SFTS(I)
1 AFU [1]
IAF Display Flt
cr. ldd. Sarawa, 2.3.45
FE362
151 OTU
152 OTU
C&CF
1331 CU
SOC 24.4.47
FE363
India: no record of service
'Recaptured' by USA 6.46
FE364
Lost at sea en route to Colombo, 9.42
FE365
151 OTU
cr. during aerobatica, Tavu, 19.4.43
FE366
SF Ratmalana
1670 CU
8 RFU
SOC 19.7.45
FE367
1 AFU (12.43- 2.44)
SOC 24.4.47
FE368
1 SFTS(I)
Collided with FE681 on approach to Ambala, 4.7.44
FE369
152 OTU
SOC 26.9.46
FE370
1 SFTS(I) 4.43-
168 Wing
Missing 20.3.45
FE371
1 SFTS(I)
22 APC
3(I)Gp. CF
cr. 12mls W of Belar 6.1.47
FE372
1 SFTS(I)
SOC 24.4.47
FE373
1 SFTS(I)
82 Sqdn
To Pak.AF 9.47
FE374
151 OTU
1 SFTS(I)
AFS(I)
To IAF 9.47
FE375
Lost at sea en route to Colombo, 9.42
FE376
Lost at sea en route to Colombo, 9.42
FE377
151 OTU
SOC 24.4.47
FE378
151 OTU
1 SFTS(I)
1 AFU
ACSEA CS
SOC 24.4.47
FE379
1 SFTS(I)
'Recaptured' by USA 6.46
FE380
1 SFTS(I)
AFS(I)
SOC 31.7.47
FE381
152 OTU
cr. while low flying, Campbellpur, 6.2.43
FE382
1 SFTS(I) -11.43
1 AFU 11.43-
SOC 24.4.47
FE383
1 OTU
13 SFTS
To RCAF
FE384
1 OTU
13 SFTS
To RCAF
FE385
1 OTU
To RCAF
FE386
1 OTU
SOC 19.1.43
FE387
1 OTU
SOC 30.1.42
FE388
1 OTU
To RCAF
FE389
Canada: no record of service
SOC 26.12.42
FE390
1 OTU
To RCAF
FE391
1 OTU
To RCAF
FE392
1 OTU
SOC 2.2.43
FE393
1 OTU
SOC 20.4.44
FE394
Canada: no record of service
SOC 12.1.43
FE395
1 OTU
desp. UK 3.44
No service in UK
To R.Neth.AF for spares 12.46
FE396
1 OTU
13 SFTS
To RCAF

FE397
1 OTU
SOC 23.1.43
FE398
1 OTU
SOC 28.6.44
FE399
1 OTU
SOC 24.12.43
FE400
1 OTU
To RCAF
FE401
1 OTU
13 SFTS
To RCAF
FE402
1 OTU
To RCAF
FE403
1 SFTS
cr. Camp Borden, Ont., 12.12.43
FE404
39 SFTS
13 SFTS
To RCAF
FE405
39 SFTS
37 SFTS
13 SFTS
To RCAF
FE406
39 SFTS
37 SFTS (12.42-12.43)
To RCAF
FE407
39 SFTS
32 SFTS
34 SFTS
To RCAF
FE408
37 SFTS
3 SFTS
To RCAF
FE409
37 SFTS (6.43-12.43)
13 SFTS
3 SFTS
To RCAF
FE410
37 SFTS (10.43- 1.44)
13 SFTS (7.44-)
3 SFTS
To RCAF
FE411
37 SFTS
cr. Rockyford, Alberta, 16.6.43
FE412
37 SFTS
To RCAF
FE413
84 Sqdn
1 SFTS(I) 4.43-
1 AFU [17]
To Pak.AF 9.47
FE414
1 SFTS(I)
'Recaptured' by USA 6.46
FE415
84 Sqdn
3 TAF CS
3 RFU
224 Gp. CF
desp. FE
84 Sqdn 1.48- 6.48
FECS 6.48- 5.56
MAAF 11.56- 5.57
SOC 17.5.57
FE416
170 Wing -11.44
166 Wing 11.44-
SOC 28.3.46
FE417
Lost at sea en route to Colombo, 9.42
FE418
Lost at sea en route to Colombo, 9.42
FE419
Lost at sea en route to Colombo, 9.42
FE420
SF Ratmalana
ACSEA CF
SOC 25.10.45
FE421
Lost at sea en route to Colombo, 9.42
FE422
152 OTU
176 Sqdn
155 Sqdn
227 Gp. CF
Undercarriage collapsed on landing, Agra, 2.2.46
FE423
AFTU
SF Colombo [A]
SOC 24.4.47
FE424
1 SFTS(I) 4.43-
1 AFU [15]
To IAF 9.47
FE425
1 SFTS(I)
cr. 6mls from Ambala 5.4.43
FE426
168 Wing
152 OTU
60 Sqdn
SOC 13.6.46
FE427
3 RFU (6.44- 8.44)
SOC 24.4.47
FE428
1 SFTS(I)
1 AFU (12.43- 2.44)
SOC 24.4.47
FE429
CFS(I(
1 SFTS(I)
1 AFU (12.43- 2.44)
To IAF 9.47
FE430
India: no record of service
SOC 24.4.47
FE431
1 SFTS(I)
SOC 27.6.46
FE432
1 SFTS(I)
159 Sqdn
1 SFTS(I)
cr. on overshoot, Ambala, 30.5.46
FE433
1 SFTS(C)
To RCAF
FE434
1 SFTS(C)
To RCAF
FE435
Canada: no record of service
To RCAF
FE436
14 SFTS 12.42- .44
To RCAF
FE437
31 SFTS
1 SFTS
To RCAF
FE438
14 SFTS (2.44- 8.44)
To RCAF
FE439
41 SFTS
SOC 3.11.42
FE440
41 SFTS
37 SFTS
13 SFTS
To RCAF
FE441
41 SFTS (1.43- 9.43)
To RCAF
FE442
41 SFTS (11.42- 4.43)
8 SFTS
To RCAF
FE443
41 SFTS
To RCAF
FE444
41 SFTS
FA Cat.E 25.10.42
FE445
41 SFTS [47]
To RCAF
FE446
41 SFTS
To RCAF
FE447
34 SFTS - 8.44
36 SFTS 8.44-
To RCAF
FE448
34 SFTS
FE Cat.E 11.9.43
FE449
36 SFTS
To RCAF
FE450
34 SFTS
To RCAF
FE451
2 FIS(C)
To RCAF
FE452
34 SFTS (5.44- 8.44)
To RCAF
FE453
34 SFTS
To RCAF
FE454
32 SFTS
34 SFTS
To RCAF
FE455
34 SFTS
cr. 10mls SW of Medicine Hat, Alb., 15.11.42
FE456
34 SFTS
To RCAF
FE457
129 Sqdn RCAF
To RCAF
FE458
Canada: no record of service
cr. Shubenacadie Lake 9.43
FE459
Canada: no record of service
SOC 9.6.44
FE460
Loaned to RN at Dartmouth NS
To RCAF
FE461
34 SFTS
cr. 5mls E of Dunmore, Alb.,27.4.43
FE462
41 SFTS
To RCAF
FE463
41 SFTS (10.42- 1.44)
To RCAF
FE464
1 SFTS(C)
CFS(C)
To RCAF
FE465
1 SFTS(C) (11.42- .44)
To RCAF
FE466
1 SFTS(C)
DBR in accident 17.11.44

FE467
1 SFTS(C) [K8]
To RCAF
FE468
1 SFTS(I)
Abandoned in spin, Hardalpur,8.3.44
FE469
1 SFTS(I)
1 AFU
Hit tree while low flying,
Magarpura, 2.11.44
FE470
C&CF
1331 CU
SOC 24.4.47
FE471
1 SFTS(I)
cr. on overshoot, Amabala, 13.5.46
FE472
1 SFTS(I)
To Pak.AF 9.47
FE473
8 RFU
SOC 24.4.47
FE474
10 Sqdn IAF
SOC 24.4.47
FE475
1 SFTS(I)
1 AFU
cr. in river, Rupar, 26.7.44
FE476
1 SFTS(I)
684 Sqdn
'Recaptured' by USA 11.47
FE477
1 SFTS(I)
1 AFU
SOC 11.12.44
FE478
1 SFTS(I)
SOC 31.12.43
FE479
1 SFTS(I)
'Recaptured' by USA 13.6.46
FE480
1 SFTS(I)
1 AFU
Collided with FE551 over Shahabad
and cr., 7.6.44
FE481
1 SFTS(I)
cr. 3mls N of Amabala 28.4.43
FE482
1 SFTS(I)
AFS (I)
To IAF 9.47
FE483
151 OTU
AFS(I)
To IAF 9.47
FE484
1 SFTS(I)
1 AFU
Abandoned in spin 5mls SE of
Patiala, 14.7.45
FE485
3 RFU
AFS(I)
ATP Poona
SOC 27.6.46
FE486
Lost at sea en route to Bombay 5.43
FE487
1 SFTS(I)
1 AFU
AFTU
SOC 1.6.47
FE488
151 OTU
152 Sqdn
SOC 31.7.44
FE489
151 OTU
SLAIS - 8.44
SOC 24.4.47
FE490
India: no record of service
SOC 27.3.47
FE491
1 SFTS(I)
SOC 24.4.47
FE492
ARS Karachi
cr. ldd. 15mls S of Drigh Rd.1.2.43
FE493
Lost at sea en route to Bombay 5.43
FE494
1 SFTS(I)
SOC 24.4.47
FE495
1 AFU [12]
'Recaptured' by USA 10.46
FE496
1 SFTS(I)
SOC 24.4.47
FE497
Lost at sea en route to Bombay 5.43
FE498
1 OTU
DBR in accident 1.6.43
FE499
13 SFTS
To RCAF
FE500
1 OTU
To RCAF
FE501
1 OTU
SOC 18.11.43
FE502
1 OTU
To RCAF
FE503
1 OTU
To RCAF
FE504
Canada: no record of service
To RCAF
FE505
1 OTU
14 SFTS
TO RCAF
FE506
6 SFTS
SOC 11.10.44
FE507
Canada: no record of service
To RCAF
FE508
6 SFTS
To RCAF
FE509
6 SFTS
16 SFTS
To RCAF
FE510
6 SFTS
16 SFTS
To RCAF
FE511
6 SFTS
To RCAF
FE512
6 SFTS
To RCAF
FE513
Canada: no record of service
To RCAF
FE514
1 FIS(C)
To RCAF
FE515
1 FIS(C)
To RCAF
FE516
CFS(C)
To RCAF
FE517
CFS(C)
To RCAF
FE518
Canada: no record of service
To RCAF
FE519
1 SFTS(C)
1 FIS(C)
1 SFTS(C)
To RCAF
FE520
1 SFTS(C)
To RCAF
FE521
1 SFTS(C)
To RCAF
FE522
123 Sqdn RCAF
To RCAF
FE523
123 Sqdn RCAF
To RCAF
FE524
1 OTU
To RCAF
FE525
Canada: no record of service
To RCAF
FE526
Canada: no record of service
To RCAF
FE527
Canada: no record of service
To RCAF
FE528
3 RFU
1 AFU
SOC 24.4.47
FE529
Lost at sea en route to Bombay 5.43
FE530
Lost at sea en route to Bombay 5.43
FE531
Lost at sea en route to Bombay 5.43
FE532
Lost at sea en route to Bombay 5.43
FE533
1 SFTS(I)
cr. ldd. Nagla, 4.7.44
FE534
1 SFTS(I)
Hit by Tiger Moth DE870 while
parked, Ambala, 22.2.44
FE535
India: no record of service
SOC 26.9.46
FE536
Lost at sea en route to Bombay 5.43
FE537
Lost at sea en route to Bombay 5.43
FE538
1 SFTS(I) 7.43-
SOC 24.4.47
FE539
1 SFTS(I)
1 AFU
Hit house and cr., Wazirabad, nr.
Amabala, 6.1.44
FE540
1 AFU
SOC 13.6.46
FE541
Lost at sea en route to Bombay 5.43
FE542
ATP Poona
3 RFU
SOC 23.1.45
FE543
1 SFTS(I)
21 FC
SOC 24.4.47

FE544
1 SFTS(I)
1 AFU
1 SFTS(I)
SOC 24.4.47
FE545
ATP Poona
cr. ldd. Lohegoan 5.1.44
FE546
AFS(I)
cr. ldd. Lalror Station, 6.11.46
FE547
1571 Flt
146 Sqdn
SOC 27.2.47
FE548
1 SFTS(I)
1 AFU
Hit house and cr., Ambala City, 20.12.43
FE549
1 SFTS(I)
cr. 8mls NW of Ambala, 4.8.43
FE550
44th Airborne Divn
SOC 24.4.47
FE551
1 SFTS(I)
1 AFU
1 SFTS(I)
Collided with FE480 over Shahabad, 7.6.44
FE552
India: no record of service
SOC 11.7.46
FE553
CFS(C)
1 FIS(C)
cr. Murray Township, Ont., 28.5.43
FE554
1 SFTS(C)
To RCAF
FE555
1 SFTS(C)
To RCAF
FE556
CFS(C)
To RCAF
FE557
CFS(C)
1 FIS(C)
To RCAF
FE558
6 SFTS
DBR in accident 27.6.44
FE559
1 FIS(C)
To RCAF
FE560
Canada: no record of service
To RCAF
FE561
1 SFTS(C)
cr. Elmvale, Ont., 20.5.43
FE562
1 FIS(C)
To RCAF
FE563
1 SFTS(C)
To RCAF
FE564
6 SFTS
31 SFTS
To RCAF
FE565
Canada: no record of service
To RCAF
FE566
Canada: no record of service
To RCAF
FE567
1 FIS(C)
31 SFTS
To RCAF
FE568
Canada: no record of service
To RCAF
FE569
31 SFTS
To RCAF
FE570
Canada: no record of service
To RCAF
FE571
31 SFTS [21]
14 SFTS
To RCAF
FE572
1 FIS(C) (10.43- 4.44)
To RCAF
FE573
1 FIS(C)
1 SFTS
DBR in accident 17.3.44
FE574
Canada: no record of service
To RCAF
FE575
31 SFTS
14 SFTS
To RCAF
FE576
Canada: no record of service
To RCAF
FE577
31 SFTS (6.43- 7.44)
To RCAF
FE578
1 FIS(C)
To RCAF
FE579
1 FIS(C) (10.43-12.44)
To RCAF
FE580
Canada: no record of service
To RCAF
FE581
1 SFTS(C)
To RCAF
FE582
6 SFTS
DBR in accident 26.8.44
FE583
1 SFTS(C)
To RCAF
FE584
1 SFTS(C)
To RCAF
FE585
Canada: no record of service
To RCAF
FE586
31 SFTS (11.43- 7.44)
SOC (DBR at Noorduyn) 31.8.44
FE587
1 SFTS(C)
cr. S of Christian Is., Georgia Bay, 18.4.43
FE588
Canada: no record of service
To RCAF
FE589
Canada: no record of service
To RCAF
FE590
1 SFTS(C)
To RCAF
FE591
16 SFTS
To RCAF
FE592
1 SFTS(C)
To RCAF
FE593
ATP Poona
AFTU
607 Sqdn
SOC 5.1.45
FE594
1 AGS(I)
1 SFTS(I)
21 FC
SOC 24.4.47
FE595
151 OTU
SOC 24.4.47
FE596
SF Amarda Road
GATU
AFTU
36 SP Ferry Flt
DBR in accident 27.9.45
FE597
ATP Poona
To IAF 9.47
FE598
ATP Poona
cr. ldd. Poona 18.12.43
FE599
SF Amarda Road
AFTU
21 FC
SOC 11.7.46
FE600
ATP Poona
42 Sqdn
SOC 24.4.47
FE601
320 MU
Spun in on test flight 2mls SE of Rehi, 3.4.43
FE602
SF Amarda Road
AFTU
SOC 24.4.47
FE603
1 SFTS(I)
Abandoned after engine failure near Ambala,23.4.46
FE604
Trg. Flt. Mauripur
C&CF
1331 CU
1 SFTS(I)
SOC 24.4.47
FE605
1 SFTS(I)
SOC 7.5.47
FE606
SF Amarda Road
6 Sqdn IAF
SOC 1.6.47
FE607
1571 Flt
AFTU
23 APC
SOC 1.1.45
FE608
ATP Poona
SOC 24.4.47
FE609
5 Sqdn
200 Sqdn
160 Sqdn
45 Sqdn 1.48- 6.48
SF Negombo 6.48- .50
desp. Hong Kong .50
SF Kai Tak 10.50- 2.51
HKAAF 2.51
cr. in sea 9mls W of Kai Tak, 28.4.52
FE610
1 AGS(I)
PSOC 1.1.47
FE611
No RAF service
To USAAF in India 10.43
FE612
1571 Flt
SOC 28.9.44

FE613
27 Sqdn
10 FU
SOC 30.5.46
FE614
3 RFU
45 Sqdn
cr. during low inverted run, Monierkal, 14.5.45
FE615
1571 Flt
89 Sqdn
757 Sqdn [V] 12.44- 5.45
17 Sqdn
20 APC
SOC 24.4.47
FE616
1 AFU
To IAF 9.47
FE617
1571 Flt
89 Sqdn
'Recaptured' by USA 11.47
FE618
36 OTU
1 OTU
To RCAF
FE619
Canada: no record of service
To RCAF
FE620
126 Sqdn RCAF
DBR in accident 21.11.44
FE621
Canada: no record of service
To RCAF
FE622
14 SFTS 12.42-
36 OTU
To RCAF
FE623
Canada: no record of service
To RCAF
FE624
Canada: no record of service
To RCAF
FE625
130 Sqdn RCAF
To RCAF
FE626
128 Sqdn RCAF
To RCAF

FE627
1 OTU
To RCAF
FE628
130 Sqdn RCAF
To RCAF
FE629
Canada: no record of service
To RCAF
FE630
Canada: no record of service
To RCAF
FE631
Canada: no record of service
To RCAF
FE632
1 OTU
To RCAF
FE633
41 SFTS
To RCAF
FE634
Canada: no record of service
To RCAF
FE635
41 SFTS
SOC 25.10.43
FE636
41 SFTS [10]
To RCAF
FE637
41 SFTS
To RCAF
FE638
41 SFTS
To RCAF
FE639
41 SFTS
To RCAF
FE640
41 SFTS
To RCAF
FE641
124 Sqdn RCAF
To RCAF
FE642
41 SFTS
To RCAF
FE643
14 SFTS (1.43- 7.44)
To RCAF
FE644
14 SFTS 12.42-
To RCAF
FE645
14 SFTS
To RCAF
FE646
31 SFTS
14 SFTS (4.43- 4.44)
To RCAF
FE647
31 SFTS
14 SFTS
DBR in accident 24.10.44
FE648
31 SFTS
To RCAF
FE649
14 SFTS
cr. $\frac{1}{2}$ml N of St. Thomas, Sas., 13.3.44

FE650
31 SFTS
14 SFTS
To RCAF
FE651
14 SFTS
To RCAF
FE652
14 SFTS
To RCAF
FE653
14 SFTS 12.42-
To RCAF
FE654
14 SFTS 12.42-
To RCAF
FE655
14 SFTS 12.42-
To RCAF
FE656
14 SFTS 12.42-
To RCAF
FE657
14 SFTS 12.42-
To RCAF
FE658
14 SFTS 12.42-
To RCAF
FE659
14 SFTS 12.42-
To RCAF
FE660
14 SFTS 12.42-
To RCAF
FE661
14 SFTS [72] 12.42-
To RCAF
FE662
14 SFTS
Collided with RCAF Harvard 3209 on approach, Aylmer, Ont., 4.1.44
FE663
ATP Poona
3 RFU
SOC 24.4.47
FE664
151 OTU
AFS(I)
3 RFU
To IAF 9.47
FE665
India: no record of service
'Recaptured' by USA 11.47
FE666
9 Sqdn IAF
SOC 19.7.45
FE667
AFTU
3 RFU
SOC 21.6.45
FE668
C&CF
1331 CU
SOC 24.4.47
FE669
India: no record of service
PSOC 1.1.47
FE670
3 Sqdn IAF
CF Kohat
SOC 11.12.44
FE671
151 OTU
21 FC
1331 CU
SOC 24.4.47
FE672
1 SFTS(I)
cr. on take-off, Ambala, 9.6.44
FE673
India: no record of service
SOC 19.6.47
FE674
ATP Poona
Engine caught fire; cr. near Poona, 1.9.43

FE675
146 Sqdn
GATU
SLAIS
cr. ldd. while lost, Karu, 14.3.45
FE676
No RAF service
To USAAF in India 11.10.43
FE677
1571 Flt
757 Sqdn 5.45-
20 APC
SF Koggala for 205(FB) Sqdn 6.48-11.49
SF Negombo 11.49-10.50
SF Kai Tak 10.50-12.50
HKAAF 12.50-
SOC 9.1.58
FE678
ATP Poona
cr. 16mls N of Poona 13.8.43
FE679
India: no record of service w. RAF
Transferred to RN 1.45
757 Sqdn 1.45- 4.45
Retd. to RAF
NFT
FE680
AFTU
3 RFU
SOC 24.4.47
FE681
1 SFTS(I)
DBR in accident 4.7.44
FE682
1 SFTS(I)
SOC 28.9.44

FE683
1571 Flt
10 FU
20 APC
cr. in sea off Ceylon during aerobatics, 27.8.45
FE684
No RAF service
To USAAF in India 10.43
FE685
No RAF service
To USAAF in India 10.43
Retd. to RAF
355 Sqdn
To IAF 9.47
FE686
No RAF service
To USAAF in India 10.43
FE687
20 APC
5 Sqdn
To Pak.AF 9.47
FE688
31 SFTS
To RCAF
FE689
Canada: no record of service
To RCAF
FE690
31 SFTS
To RCAF
FE691
31 SFTS
To RCAF
FE692
Canada: no record of service
To RCAF
FE693
1 FIS(C)
To RCAF
FE694
31 SFTS
14 SFTS
To RCAF
FE695
6 SFTS
To RCAF
FE696
No RAF service
To USAAF in India 10.43
FE697
ATP Poona
'Recaptured' by USA 11.47
FE698
AHQ Malaya CS
cr. in sea off Moulmein, Burma, 4.5.46
FE699
No RAF service
To USAAF in India 10.43
FE700
No RAF service
To USAAF in India 10.43
FE701
No RAF service
To USAAF in India 10.43
FE702
1572 Flt
1 AFU
21 APC
cr. on take-off, Sambre, 5.4.44
FE703
1572 Flt
21 APC
261 Sqdn
672 Sqdn
'Recaptured' by USA 11.47
FE704
1 SFTS(I) 7.43-
1 AFU
SOC 24.4.47
FE705
1572 Flt
SOC 24.4.47

FE706
607 Sqdn
84 Sqdn
SOC 24.4.47
FE707
67 Sqdn
231 Gp. CS
SOC 24.4.47
FE708
1572 Flt
To Pak.AF 9.47
FE709
India: no record of service
SOC 31.8.44
FE710
India: no record of service
SOC 31.8.44
FE711
ATP Poona
To IAF 9.47
FE712
224 Gp. CS
1 SFTS(I)
Hit by FE424 while taxying, Ambala, 30.5.46
FE713
1571 Flt
757 Sqdn 5.45-
ACSEA CS
20 APC
'Recaptured' by USA 11.47
FE714
ATP Poona
SOC 30.5.46
FE715
89 Sqdn
SOC 26.6.47
FE716
No RAF service
To USAAF in India 10.43
FE717
No RAF service
To USAAF in India 10.43
FE718
ATP Poona
3 RFU
Hit tree while low flying, Hingangaon, 16.5.44
FE719
3 RFU
1 SFTS(I)
cr. 15mls NE of Jullundur, 19.6.46
FE720
135 Sqdn
6 Sqdn IAF 1.44-
SOC 24.4.47
FE721
14 SFTS 9.43-
cr. during practice forced landing, 15.5.44
FE722
14 SFTS 9.43-
To RCAF
FE723
31 SFTS
To RCAF
FE724
14 SFTS 9.43-
To RCAF
FE725
31 SFTS
To RCAF
FE726
14 SFTS 10.43-
To RCAF
FE727
14 SFTS 9.43-
To RCAF
FE728
31 SFTS
To RCAF
FE729
1 FIS(C)
To RCAF

FE730
Canada: no record of service
To RCAF
FE731
1 FIS(C)
cr. 3mls N of Brockville, Ont., 29.6.44
FE732
6 SFTS
cr. 7mls NW of Dunnville, Ont., 29.11.43
FE733
1 SFTS(C)
2 FIS(C)
To RCAF
FE734
Canada: no record of service
To RCAF
FE735
31 SFTS
To RCAF
FE736
31 SFTS
To RCAF
FE737
Canada: no record of service
To RCAF
FE738
14 SFTS 1.44-
1 SFTS
To RCAF
FE739
31 SFTS
1 SFTS(C)
To RCAF
FE740
1 SFTS(C)
DBR in accident 18.5.44
FE741
1 FIS(C)
To RCAF
FE742
1 SFTS(C)
To RCAF
FE743
1 SFTS(C)
To RCAF
FE744
1 SFTS(C)
cr. near Lafontaine, Ont., 21.3.44
FE745
1 SFTS(C)
To RCAF
FE746
Canada: no record of service
To RCAF
FE747
Canada: no record of service
To RCAF
FE748
31 SFTS
To RCAF
FE749
Canada: no record of service
To RCAF
FE750
No service in Canada
desp. UK 3.44
No service in UK
To R.Neth.AF 5.47
FE751
Canada: no record of service
To RCAF
FE752
Canada: no record of service
To RCAF
FE753
31 SFTS
14 SFTS
To RCAF
FE754
Canada: no record of service
To RCAF

At A&AEE Boscombe Down in December 1943 for flame-damping trials was FE788. Note letter 'P' in a circle signifying a prototype!
(Crown copyright, A&AEE Boscombe Down)

FE755
14 SFTS 1.44- 4.44
desp. UK 5.44
9(P)AFU 4.45- 6.45
5(P)AFU 6.45-11.45
22 SFTS [FCI:F] 11.45- 2.49
22 FTS 2.49- 7.50
" 12.50- 8.54
Sold Hw spares 3.55

FE756
No service in Canada
desp. UK 3.44
9(P)AFU [T:44] 9.44- 6.45
5(P)AFU 6.45-12.45
St. Mawgan 10.46-11.46
1 FU 11.46- 8.47
Pershore 1.48- 5.48
Manston 5.48- 6.48
2 FTS [FAK:N] 1.49- 7.49
CFS(EW) 7.49- 6.50
3 FTS 6.50- 8.50
2 FTS 8.50- 4.51
1 FTS 4.51
Collided with FS815 during aerobatics and cr. 1ml S of Graveley, 2.7.51

FE757
1 SFTS(C)
cr. near Penetanguishine, Ont., 12.12.43

FE758
No service in Canada
desp. UK 3.44
No service in UK
To R.Neth.AF 4.47

FE759
1 SFTS(C)
Hit tree and cr., Edenvale range, 5.9.44

FE760
No service in Canada
desp. UK 3.44
No service in UK
To. R.Dan.AF 5.47

FE761
No service in Canada
desp. UK 3.44
9(P)AFU 10.44--6.45
5(P)AFU 6.45-11.45
22 SFTS [FCJ:A] 11.45- 2.49
22 FTS 2.49-12.49
2 FTS 12.49
cr. ldd. 2mls E of Southam, 6.6.50

FE762
31 SFTS
To RCAF

FE763
1 SFTS(C)
SOC 23.11.44

FE764
31 SFTS [85]
To RCAF

FE765
1 SFTS(C) [84]
cr. 3mls N of Edenvale RLG, 28.11.43

FE766
20 Sqdn
60 Sqdn
To Pak.AF 9.47

FE767
20 Sqdn
'Recaptured' by USA 11.47

FE768
1 SFTS(I) 8.43-
SOC 24.4.47

FE769
227 Gp. CF
Undercarriage collapsed on landing, Agra, 1.2.46

FE770
34 Sqdn
221 Gp. CF
1572 Flt
Bengal/Burma CS
'Recaptured' by USA 11.47

FE771
151 OTU
135 Sqdn
SOC 26.9.46

FE772
SF Amarda Road
60 Sqdn 7.46- 5.49
SF Sembawang 5.49- 8.49
33 Sqdn 8.49- 2.51
MAAF 2.51- 1.57
SOC 4.57

FE773
3 TAF CS
SOC 30.5.46

FE774
81 Sqdn
60 Sqdn
SOC 22.2.45

FE775
BAFSEA CS
AHQ(I)CS 3.46-
To IAF 9.47
FE776
258 Sqdn
cr. ldd. Bangaon, 20.3.45
FE777
22 APC
3(I)Gp. CF
'Recaptured' by USA 11.47
FE778
228 Gp. CF
Hit van while taxying, Barrackpore, 6.4.46
FE779
152 Sqdn
261 Sqdn
SOC 24.4.47
FE780
607 Sqdn
134 Sqdn
11 Sqdn
21 FC
SOC 30.5.46
FE781
81 Sqdn
SOC 27.6.46
FE782
1571 Flt
SOC 31.7.46
FE783
AFS(I)
SOC 24.4.47
FE784
India: no record of service
PSOC 1.1.47
FE785
2 Sqdn IAF - 4.44
3 Sqdn IAF 4.46-10.46
2(I)Gp. CF [H]
SOC 27.2.47
FE786
11 Sqdn
SOC 11.7.46
FE787
No RAF service
To R.Neth.AF 5.47
FE788
A&AEE 12.43-
SOC 4.9.54
FE789
17 Sqdn
Missing in bad weather, 3.6.45
FE790
Canada: no record of service
To RCAF
FE791
123 Sqdn RCAF
To RCAF
FE792
123 Sqdn RCAF [F]
To RCAF
FE793
Canada: no record of service
To RCAF
FE794
Canada: no record of service
To RCAF
FE795
Canada: no record of service
To RCAF
FE796
Canada: no record of service
To RCAF
FE797
8 SFTS
To RCAF
FE798
No service in Canada
desp. UK 3.44
No service in UK
To R.Dan.AF 1.47

FE799
41 SFTS 4.43-
desp. UK 3.44
16 SFTS 8.44-11.45
3(P)AFU 11.45-12.45
3 SFTS 12.45- 4.47
3 FTS [FBU:B] 4.47- 9.50
SOC 14.9.50
FE800
41 SFTS 4.43-
desp. UK 3.44
16 SFTS 8.44- 7.45
16 FTS 3.46- 4.46
To R.Dan.AF 12.46
FE801
Canada: no record of service
To RCAF
FE802
No service in Canada
desp. UK 3.44
9(P)AFU 9.44- 6.45
5(P)AFU 6.45- 4.46
SOC 4.10.50
FE803
41 SFTS
To RCAF
FE804
41 SFTS
8 SFTS
33 SFTS
To RCAF
FE805
No service in Canada
desp. UK 3.44
US Embassy, London 8.46-
Retd. to USA
FE806
8 SFTS
cr. on take-off, Weyburn 12.5.44
FE807
34 SFTS
To RCAF
FE808
37 SFTS (6.43- 1.44)
13 SFTS
To RCAF
FE809
Canada: no record of service
To RCAF
FE810
Canada: no record of service
To RCAF
FE811
13 SFTS
To RCAF
FE812
Canada: no record of service
To RCAF
FE813
34 SFTS
To RCAF
FE814
37 SFTS
To RCAF
FE815
34 SFTS
To RCAF
FE816
Canada: no record of service
To RCAF
FE817
13 SFTS (5.44-12.44)
To RCAF
FE818
34 SFTS
To RCAF
FE819
37 SFTS
FA Cat.E 6.11.43
FE820
Canada: no record of service
To RCAF
FE821
37 SFTS
To RCAF

FE822
13 SFTS
To RCAF
FE823
Canada: no record of service
To RCAF
FE824
37 SFTS (8.43- .44)
To RCAF
FE825
37 SFTS (10.43- .44)
To RCAF
FE826
13 SFTS (6.44- .44)
To RCAF
FE827
34 SFTS [52]
To RCAF
FE828
37 SFTS
To RCAF
FE829
34 SFTS
To RCAF
FE830
34 SFTS [38]
To RCAF
FE831
13 SFTS
To RCAF
FE832
14 SFTS 2.43- 5.43
6 SFTS 5.43-
To RCAF
FE833
14 SFTS 2.43- 5.43
6 SFTS 5.43-
To RCAF
FE834
14 SFTS 2.43- 5.43
6 SFTS 5.43-
To RCAF
FE835
14 SFTS 2.43- 5.43
6 SFTS 5.43-
To RCAF
FE836
14 SFTS 2.43- 6.43
31 SFTS 6.43-
To RCAF
FE837
14 SFTS 2.43- 6.43
31 SFTS [26] 6.43-
To RCAF
FE838
14 SFTS 3.43- 6.43
31 SFTS 6.43
cr. near Sharbot Lake, Ont., 30.11.43
FE839
14 SFTS 2.43-
To RCAF
FE840
14 SFTS 2.43-
To RCAF
FE841
14 SFTS 2.43- 8.44
To RCAF
FE842
6 SFTS
To RCAF
FE843
34 SFTS
To RCAF
FE844
6 SFTS
To RCAF
FE845
Canada: no record of service
To RCAF
FE846
6 SFTS
To RCAF

FE847
Canada: no record of service
To RCAF
FE848
13 SFTS
To RCAF
FE849
13 SFTS
To RCAF
FE850
Canada: no record of service
To RCAF
FE851
Canada: no record of service
To RCAF
FE852
13 SFTS
To RCAF
FE853
13 SFTS
To RCAF
FE854
13 SFTS
To RCAF
FE855
Canada: no record of service
To RCAF
FE856
Canada: no record of service
To RCAF
FE857
6 SFTS
To RCAF
FE858
13 SFTS
To RCAF
FE859
13 SFTS (9.43- .44
desp. UK via USAAF Fort Dix 3.44
No service in UK
SOC 11.7.46
FE860
13 SFTS
To RCAF
FE861
13 SFTS
To RCAF
FE862
41 SFTS -10.43
5 B&GS 10.43
DBR in accident 3.6.44
FE863
41 SFTS
8 SFTS
To RCAF
FE864
41 SFTS
3 B&GS
To RCAF
FE865
Canada: no record of service
To RCAF
FE866
No service in Canada
desp. UK via USAAF Fort Dix 3.44
9(P)AFU 9.44- 6.45
5(P)AFU 6.45-12.45
22 SFTS [FCI:L] 12.45
Overshot, Ouston, 5.12.46
Became 6314M 4.47
FE867
No service in Canada
desp. UK via USAAF Fort Dix 4.44
No service in UK
To R.Dan.AF 1.47
FE868
34 SFTS
cr. on take-off, Medicine Hat, Alb. 3.11.43
FE869
34 SFTS
To RCAF
FE870
Canada: no record of service
To RCAF

FE871
Canada: no record of service
To RCAF
FE872
34 SFTS
To RCAF
FE873
1 FIS(C) [97]
13 SFTS
To RCAF
FE874
34 SFTS
To RCAF
FE875
34 SFTS
To RCAF
FE876
34 SFTS
To RCAF
FE877
34 SFTS [16]
To RCAF
FE878
8 FU
Hit tree, low flying near Jodhpur, 25.6.45
FE879
1(I)Gp. CF
To Pak.AF 9.47
FE880
681 Sqdn
615 Sqdn
SOC 24.4.47
FE881
1 SFTS(I) 8.43-
20 Sqdn
SOC 27.6.46
FE882
146 Sqdn
1 Sqdn IAF
2(I)Gp. CF
SOC 26.6.47
FE883
607 Sqdn
AFS(I)
To IAF 9.47
FE884
166 Wing 1.44-
30 Sqdn
SOC 21.6.45
FE885
ACSEA CS
SOC 5.7.45
FE886
1 AGS(I)
SOC 27.6.46
FE887
SLAIS
SOC 24.4.47
FE888
No RAF service
To R.Neth.AF 9.46
FE889
1 SFTS(I) 8.43-
cr. on landing, Ambala, 29.1.45
FE890
3 TAF CS
SOC 31.7.44
FE891
152 OTU
cr. near Peshawar, 28.12.43
FE892
151 OTU
SOC 24.4.47
FE893
908 Wing
SOC 31.8.44
(but still active in 6.45)
FE894
169 Wing
177 Sqdn
SOC 30.5.46
FE895
17 Sqdn
SOC 24.4.47

FE896
3 RFU
SOC 11.7.46
FE897
1 AGS(I)
3 RFU
desp. FE
28 Sqdn
GA Cat.E 2.4.48
SOC 11.8.49
FE898
1571 Flt
DBR in accident 18.10.45
FE899
ATP Poona
3 RFU
SOC 24.4.47
FE900
1 SFTS(I) 8.43-
cr. 1ml N of Amabala 15.2.44
FE901
21 FC
1571 Flt
3 FSTU
SOC 1.6.47
FE902
Canada: no record of service
To RCAF
FE903
Canada: no record of service
DBR in accident 22.4.43
FE904
41 SFTS 4.43-
desp. India 3.44
India: no record of service
SOC 11.7.46
FE905
41 SFTS 4.43-
To RCAF
FE906
41 SFTS 4.43-
desp. UK via USAAF Fort Dix 3.44
17 SFTS 8.44-11.46
CFS 11.46-12.46
21(P)AFU 12.46- 2.47
RAFC [FAA:G] 2.47-11.49
3 FTS [FBU:G] 11.49
cr. Manea, Cambs., 1.6.51
FE907
41 SFTS 4.43-
desp. UK via USAAF Fort Dix 3.44
17 SFTS
To R.Neth.AF 8.46
FE908
41 SFTS 4.43-
desp. UK via USAAF Fort Dix 3.44
5(P)AFU 11.44- 4.45
7 SFTS [FBB:T] 4.45- 1.48
7 FTS 1.48- 9.50
2 FTS 9.50-12.50
CFS 12.50- 7.52
6 FTS 7.52-11.53
SS (AES) 5.57
FE909
41 SFTS 4.43-
desp. UK via USAAF Fort Dix 3.44
5(P)AFU - 5.45
19 FTS [BB] 5.45- 4.47
RAFC [FAA:L] 4.47-10.47
Sold Hw spares
FE910
41 SFTS 4.43-
desp. UK via USAAF Fort Dix 3.44
16 SFTS 8.44-11.45
3(P)AFU 11.45- 3.46
6 SFTS [FBG:I] 3.46- 5.47
6 FTS 5.47
Engine cut on overshoot, Ternhill, 12.3.51
FE911
34 SFTS
DBR in accident 5.6.44
FE912
Canada: no record of service
To RCAF

FE913
Canada: no record of service
To RCAF
FE914
Canada: no record of service
To RCAF
FE915
1 FIS(C) [81]
34 SFTS
To RCAF
FE916
Canada: no record of service
DBR in accident 23.8.43
FE917
3 SFTS
To RCAF
FE918
Canada: no record of service
To RCAF
FE919
13 SFTS
To RCAF
FE920
Canada: no record of service
To RCAF
FE921
34 SFTS
cr. Whitlash, Montana, USA, during low-level aerobatics, 17.1.44
FE922
34 SFTS
To RCAF
FE923
34 SFTS
To RCAF
FE924
34 SFTS
To RCAF
FE925
Canada: no record of service
To RCAF
FE926
Canada: no record of service
To RCAF
FE927
Canada: no record of service
To RCAF
FE928
Canada: no record of service
To RCAF
FE929
34 SFTS
To RCAF
FE930
Canada: no record of service
To RCAF
FE931
34 SFTS
To RCAF
FE932
Canada: no record of service
To RCAF
FE933
Canada: no record of service
To RCAF
FE934
14 SFTS
To RCAF
FE935
Canada: no record of service
To RCAF
FE936
Canada: no record of service
To RCAF
FE937
41 SFTS
1 SFTS(C)
To RCAF
FE938
1 SFTS(C)
To RCAF
FE939
1 SFTS(C)
To RCAF
FE940
1 SFTS(C)
To RCAF
FE941
1 SFTS(C)
To RCAF
FE942
1 SFTS(C)
To RCAF
FE943
1 SFTS(C)
cr. near Little Lake, Ont., 19.2.44
FE944
1 SFTS(C)
To RCAF
FE945
1 SFTS(C)
To RCAF
FE946
1 SFTS(C)
cr. ldd. Arnold, Ont., 22.9.43
FE947
Canada: no record of service
To RCAF
FE948
Canada: no record of service
desp. UK 3.44
17 SFTS 8.44-11.46
CFS 11.46-12.46
21(P)AFU 12.46- 7.47
1(P)RFU 7.47- 1.48
3 FTS [FBU:D] 1.48- 3.49
2 FTS 3.49- 4.49
3 FTS 4.49- 5.49
7 FTS [O:Q] 12.51- 8.53
2 FTS 8.53- 5.54
1 FTS [P:N] 5.54- 3.55
SS (Avex) 5.57
FE949
31 SFTS
To RCAF
FE950
31 SFTS
To RCAF
FE951
CFS(C)
To RCAF
FE952
1571 Flt
23 APC
To IAF 9.47
FE953
FF Trichinopoly
607 Sqdn
7 Sqdn IAF
cr. ldd. while lost, Kanbalu, Burma 4.4.45
FE954
India: no record of service
To IAF 9.47
FE955
SF Amarda Road
SOC 30.5.46
FE956
1 SFTS(I)
cr. ldd 6mls NE of Patalia, 4.4.44
FE957
SF Amarda Road
681 Sqdn
20 APC
'Recaptured' by USA 11.47
FE958
1 SFTS(I) 8.43-
cr. on landing, Ambala, 5.9.46
FE959
1571 Flt
757 Sqdn 5.45-
45 Sqdn 1.48-
SF Negombo 6.48- 7.51
MAAF 11.52- 5.57
SOC 11.12.57
FE960
1 SFTS(I)
AFTU
SOC 24.4.47
FE961
3 RFU
cr. while low flying 10mls ENE of Poona, 29.7.44
FE962
3 TAF CS
79 Sqdn
DBR in accident 4.44
FE963
CFS(I)
SOC 24.4.47
FE964
1 AFU [16]
SOC 24.4.47
FE965
607 Sqdn
1340 Flt
cr. ldd. on fire near Colitattu, Malabar, 5.12.45
FE966
211 Sqdn
'Recaptured ' by USA 11.47
FE967
2 Sqdn IAF
SOC 29.3.45
FE968
60 Sqdn
1 Sqdn IAF
SOC 24.4.47
FE969
605 Sqdn
'Recaptured' by USA 11.47
FE970
1 SFTS(I)
607 Sqdn
SOC 24.4.47
FE971
3 Sqdn IAF
AFS(I)
DBR in accident 18.7.47
FE972
ACSEA CS
1 SFTS(I)
SOC 24.4.47
FE973
(124 RSU)
Hit trees on approach, Silchar West 24.3.44
FE974
900 Wing
To IAF 9.47
FE975
22 AACU
Spun in, Landhi, 29.9.44
FE976
2 FIS(C)
3 SFTS
To RCAF
FE977
2 FIS(C)
To RCAF
FE978
8 SFTS
cr. 3mls S of Cody, NB, 19.10.43
FE979
Canada: no record of service
To RCAF
FE980
3 SFTS
To RCAF
FE981
13 SFTS 6.44-
To RCAF
FE982
Canada: no record of service
To RCAF
FE983
8 SFTS
cr. 7mls N of Monkton, NB, 11.11.43
FE984
2 FIS(C)
To RCAF

FE985
8 SFTS
13 SFTS
To RCAF
FE986
8 SFTS
2 FIS(C)
To RCAF
FE987
8 SFTS
31 SFTS
To RCAF
FE988
Canada: no record of service
To RCAF
FE989
8 SFTS
2 FIS(C)
To RCAF
FE990
8 SFTS
13 SFTS
To RCAF
FE991
31 SFTS
To RCAF
FE992
31 SFTS
14 SFTS
To RCAF
FE993
34 SFTS
To RCAF
FE994
8 SFTS
2 FIS(C)
To RCAF
FE995
8 SFTS
Missing 1.12.43
FE996
8 SFTS
To RCAF
FE997
Canada: no record of service
To RCAF
FE998
8 SFTS
35 SFTS
To RCAF
FE999
2 FIS(C)
To RCAF

****

FH100
8 SFTS
To RCAF
FH101
3 SFTS
To RCAF
FH102
8 SFTS
To RCAF
FH103
8 SFTS
To RCAF
FH104
14 SFTS 2.44-
To RCAF
FH105
13 SFTS
35 SFTS
To RCAF
FH106
32 SFTS 6.44- 9.44
13 SFTS 9.44-
To RCAF
FH107
ATA 10.43-10.44
Montrose 10.44-11.44
16 SFTS 11.44-11.45
21 SFTS 11.45-
Became 4913M
FH108
No RAF service
To R.Neth.AF 4.48
FH109
No RAF service
To R.Dan.AF 4.47
FH110
151 OTU
SOC 28.9.44
FH111
5(P)AFU 1.45- 5.45
19 FTS 5.45
FA Cat.E 25.7.45
FH112
A&AEE 10.43- 6.44
SOC 14.6.44
FH113
176 Sqdn
To IAF 9.47
FH114
5(P)AFU 2.45- 4.45
7 SFTS 4.45- 5.46
To R.Dan.AF 12.46
FH115
ATA [O/A:H] 10.43-11.44
2 FIS 11.44-11.44
16 SFTS 11.44-
Became 4927M
SOC 7.7.47
FH116
India CU
SOC 24.4.47
FH117
35 SFTS
13 SFTS
To RCAF
FH118
Canada: no record of service
To RCAF
FH119
13 SFTS
To RCAF

Monsoon-time view of FH113 of No.176 Squadron at Baigachi in 1946 *(J.Witcombe via A.Thomas)*

FH120
8 SFTS
cr. on approach, Monkton NB, 8.12.43

FH121
7 SFTS(C)
DBR in accident, 19.10.44
FH122
8 SFTS
To RCAF
FH123
31 SFTS 12.43- 8.44
14 SFTS 8.44-
To RCAF
FH124
2 FIS(C)
To RCAF
FH125
14 SFTS
To RCAF
FH126
2 FIS(C)
To RCAF
FH127
8 SFTS - 1.44
14 SFTS 1.44-
To RCAF
FH128
15 SFTS
cr. 6mls E of Staveley, Alb.28.8.44
FH129
35 SFTS
13 SFTS
To RCAF
FH130
13 SFTS
To RCAF
FH131
8 SFTS
3 SFTS(C)
To RCAF
FH132
2 FIS(C)
To RCAF
FH133
32 SFTS 6.44-
To RCAF
FH134
34 SFTS
To RCAF
FH135
13 SFTS
To RCAF
FH136
34 SFTS [B9:F]
35 SFTS
To RCAF
FH137
31 SFTS
To RCAF
FH138
Canada: no record of service
To RCAF
FH139
Canada: no record of service
To RCAF
FH140
8 SFTS 7.43-
13 SFTS
35 SFTS
To RCAF
FH141
8 SFTS 7.43-
To RCAF
FH142
8 SFTS 7.43-
To RCAF
FH143
8 SFTS 7.43-
To RCAF
FH144
8 SFTS 7.43-
To RCAF

FH145
8 SFTS 7.43-
35 SFTS
To RCAF
FH146
8 SFTS 7.43-
To RCAF
FH147
8 SFTS 7.43-
To RCAF
FH148
8 SFTS 7.43-
To RCAF
FH149
8 SFTS 7.43-
To RCAF
FH150
13 SFTS
To RCAF
FH151
8 SFTS 7.43-
To RCAF
FH152
7 B&GS
To RCAF
FH153
8 SFTS 7.43-
14 SFTS 2.44-
To RCAF
FH154
8 SFTS
35 SFTS
To RCAF
FH155
Canada: no record of service
To RCAF
FH156
Canada: no record of service
To RCAF
FH157
Canada: no record of service
To RCAF
FH158
Canada: no record of service
To RCAF
FH159
8 SFTS 5.43-
To RCAF
FH160
8 SFTS 5.43-
14 SFTS 2.44-
To RCAF
FH161
2 WS
DBR in accident 21.9.44
FH162
8 SFTS 5.43-
To RCAF
FH163
8 SFTS 5.43-
To RCAF
FH164
8 SFTS 5.43
DBR in accident 1.9.43
FH165
8 SFTS 5.43-
To RCAF
FH166
8 SFTS 5.43-
14 SFTS
To RCAF

****

FS661
19 SFTS 6.44-
To RCAF
FS662
13 SFTS
cr. and DBF 17.8.43
FS663
13 SFTS
To RCAF

FS664
13 SFTS
cr. near St. Angele de Mannoir, 10.9.43
FS665
13 SFTS
14 SFTS
To RCAF
FS666
13 SFTS 10.43-
To RCAF
FS667
13 SFTS 10.43-
19 SFTS
To RCAF
FS668
13 SFTS
To RCAF
FS669
13 SFTS
To RCAF
FS670
13 SFTS
To RCAF
FS671
Canada: no record of service
To RCAF
FS672
13 SFTS
To RCAF
FS673
Canada: no record of service
To RCAF
FS674
13 SFTS
To RCAF
FS675
13 SFTS
TO RCAF
FS676
Canada: no record of service
To RCAF
FS677
3 SFTS [H31]
To RCAF
FS678
Canada: no record of service
To RCAF
FS679
13 SFTS
To RCAF
FS680
13 SFTS
To RCAF
FS681
Canada: no record of service
To RCAF
FS682
28 Sqdn
2(I)Gp. CF [D]
To IAF 9.47
FS683
134 Sqdn
SOC 24.4.47
FS684
136 Sqdn
SOC 31.5.45
FS685
757 Sqdn 7.44- 5.45
SOC 7.5.47
FS686
India: no record of service
SOC 24.4.47
FS687
India: no record of service
SOC 21.6.45
FS688
SF Jessore
159 Sqdn
'Recaptured' by USA 11.47
FS689
167 Wing
BAFSEA CS
'Recaptured' by USA 11.47

FS690
7 Sqdn IAF
cr. ldd. out of fuel, 2350N:8420E, 12.6.44
FS691
123 Sqdn
SOC 24.4.47
FS692
9 Sqdn IAF
SOC 22.2.45
FS693
3 RFU
BAFSEA CS
AFS(I)
To IAF 9.47
FS694
151 OTU
'Recaptured' by USA 11.47
FS695
155 Sqdn
PSOC 1.1.47
FS696
India: no record of service
SOC 7.5.47
FS697
SF Palam
To IAF 9.47
FS698
169 Wing
27 Sqdn
60 Sqdn
Engine failed; aband'd 2218N:8802E, 6.12.44
FS699
5 Sqdn
SOC 27.9.45
FS700
1 SFTS(I)
To IAF 9.47
FS701
4 Sqdn IAF
SOC 24.4.47
FS702
AFS(I)
To Pak.AF 9.47
FS703
India CU
ACSEA CS
PSOC 1.1.47
FS704
India: no record of service
SOC 26.9.46
FS705
3 RFU
SOC 24.4.47
FS706
9 Sqdn IAF
SOC 24.4.47
FS707
67 Sqdn
7 Sqdn IAF
To IAF 9.47
FS708
353 Sqdn
11 Sqdn
FF Trichinopoly
SOC 24.4.47
FS709
82 Sqdn
cr. ldd. Tulihal, 2.4.45
FS710
215 Sqdn
cr. out of fuel 2mls E of Sandeshall, 9.9.44
FS711
151 OTU
232 Gp. CS
To Pak.AF 9.47
FS712
42 Sqdn
SOC 19.6.47
FS713
1 SFTS(I)
SOC 18.10.45

FS714
India CU
BAFSEA CS
ACSEA CS
SOC 24.4.47
FS715
3 RFU
1340 Flt
SOC 24.4.47
FS716
No RAF service
To R.Neth.AF 1.47
FS717
No RAF service
To R.Neth.AF 2.48
FS718
A&AEE
ETPS
cr. on fire, Millbrook, Beds., 29.7.46
FS719
No RAF service
To R.Neth.AF 11.47
FS720
91 Sqdn 3.46-10.46
FCCS 10.46- 4.48
SOC 30.4.51
FS721
No RAF service
To. R.Dan.AF 4.47
FS722
ATA
11(P)AFU 5.45- 6.45
21 FTS 6.45- 9.46
SOC 4.10.50
FS723
ATA 5.44- 5.45
To R.Neth.AF 1.48
FS724
No RAF service
To. R.Neth.AF 10.47
FS725
20 FTS 4.45- 7.47
2 FTS [FAI:F] 7.47
cr. ldd. Church Lawford, 9.1.48
FS726
No RAF service
To R.Neth.AF 7.47
FS727
No RAF service
To. R.Neth.AF
FS728
No RAF service
To R.Neth.AF 11.47
FS729
SOC on arrival in UK 5.9.43
FS730
2 FTS 4.45- 5.45
To R.Neth.AF 4.48
FS731
No RAF service
To R.Neth.AF 1.48
FS732
19 FTS 5.45- 5.46
1 FTS 7.52- 1.55
SS (AES) 5.57
FS733
ATA 5.44- 3.45
To R.Neth.AF 10.47
FS734
NTB 2.45-11.45
To R.Nor.AF 11.45
FS735
3 FTS [FBT:L] 3.46
Spun in during aerobatics, 1ml SW of Upwood, 17.9.49
FS736
RAE
22 RFS 6.50- 7.50
19 RFS 7.50- 8.50
11 RFS 8.50-11.50
1 FTS 2.51
Hit tree and DBR, Moreton-in-Marsh, 8.12.51

FS737
No RAF service
To R.Neth.AF 9.46
FS738
20 FTS 4.45- 8.45
6 SFTS [FBI:G] 1.46- 5.47
6 FTS [FBI:S] 5.47- 5.49
FRS 4.50- 4.51
101 FRS 4.51-10.51
7 FTS [O:K] 12.51- 7.53
2 FTS 7.53- 4.54
Sold Hw spares 5.54
FS739
164 Sqdn 4.46-10.46
SF Middle Wallop 10.46- 8.47
1 Sqdn 8.47-10.47
SF Middle Wallop 10.47- 2.48
SF Thorney Island 2.48- 5.48
203 AFS [TO:T/TO:Z] 5.48- 9.49
226 OCU 9.49- 9.51
613 Sqdn [Q3:1] 9.51-10.53
SS (Avex) 5.57
FS740
No RAF service
To R.Neth.AF 10.46
FS741
No service in UK
desp. Algiers 5.44
AB&GS 4.45-11.45
249 Sqdn
cr. ldd. LG H5, Transjordan,29.3.49
FS742
11(P)AFU 1.45- 5.45
7 FIS 5.45-10.46
CFS [FDN:J] 1.47- 1.50
6 FTS [FBJ:L] 1.50
cr. after take-off from Ternhill, Mickley, Salop, 20.8.52
FS743
No RAF service
To R.Neth.AF 9.48
FS744
11(P)AFU 1.45- 6.45
2 FTS [FAK:E] 6.45- 3.46
20 FTS 3.46- 7.49
CFS(EW) 7.49- 3.50
CFS [FDO:U] 3.50- 8.51
CFS(B) [O:U] 8.51-12.53
SOC 19.2.54
FS745
21 FTS 4.45
Spun in, Exhall, Warwicks., 23.4.46
FS746
5(P)AFU 2.45- 4.46
RAFC 8.52
cr. ldd. out of fuel, Packington, Leics., 6.4.53
FS747
No service in UK
desp. Algiers 5.44
11 FIS
cr. on landing, Nicosia, 30.12.46
FS748
11(P)AFU 4.45- 5.45
19 FTS [BF/FAB:F] 5.45-10.46
SOC 30.4.51
FS749
No RAF service
To R.Neth.AF 12.47
FS750
No service in UK
desp. Algiers 5.44
AB&GS 4.45-11.45
SOC 25.4.46
FS751
No RAF service
To R.Neth.AF 10.46
FS752
11(P)AFU 1.45- 4.45
2 FTS 7.45- 7.45
FTCCF [FKN:C] 7.45- 3.53
HCEU 3.53-10.53
HCCS 10.53- 3.54
Nott. UAS 3.54-
SOC 13.12.54

The hot sun of Aden beats down on FS769 of No.8 Squadron at Khormaksar in 1948 *(Vigast via A.Thomas)*

FS753
19 FTS [BK/FAB:K] 5.45- 7.47
1 FTS 7.47- 3.48
CFS [FDN:A] 3.48-12.49
6 FTS [FBG:G] 12.49
cr. during aerobatics 3$\frac{1}{2}$mls NW of Ternhill,22.6.53

FS754
No RAF service
To R.Neth.AF 10.46

FS755
19 FTS [FL/FAC:W] 5.45- 7.47
1 FTS 7.47- 3.48
CFS 3.48- 9.48
RAFC [FAB:L/BL] 9.48- 4.54
SS (AES) 12.56

FS756
2 FTS 4.45- 3.46
20 FTS [FAI:H] 3.46- 9.46
20 SFTS 9.46- 7.47
2 FTS 7.47- 1.50
22 FTS 1.50- 2.50
3 FTS [FBT:Z] 2.50- 1.52
22 FTS 3.53- 9.54
Sold Hw spares 3.55

FS757
5(P)AFU 2.45- 4.45
7 SFTS [FBB:E] 4.45- 1.48
7 FTS 1.48- 5.48
1(P)RFU 5.48-10.48
SF Halton 10.48- 1.49
1(P)RFU [FDA:M] 1.49- 5.49
FRS 5.49- 4.51
101 FRS 4.51-11.51
6 FTS 11.51
cr. on overshoot, Ternhill, 6.5.53

FS758
5(P)AFU 2.45- 6.45
19 FTS [FAA:G] 6.45- 4.47
RAFC 4.47- 8.47
2(P)RFU 8.47- 3.48
7 FTS 3.48- 5.48
SF Wittering 5.48-11.48
2 FTS [FAJ:M] 11.48- 4.49
11 RFS 6.50-11.50
3 FTS 7.51- 2.55
SS (Avex) 9.57

FS759
11(P)AFU 1.45- 5.45
19 FTS [GC] 5.45-11.47
SOC 30.4.51

FS760
NTB 7.45-11.45
To R.Nor.AF 11.45

FS761
54 Sqdn 4.46-10.46
SF Odiham [EC] 10.46- 4.47
SOC 30.4.51

FS762
2 FTS 4.45- 3.46
20 FTS [FAI:J] 3.46- 9.46
20 SFTS 9.46- 7.47
2 FTS 7.47-11.49
desp. S. Rhodesia 11.50
5 FTS 7.51
cr. during aerobatics 8mls SW of Gwelo, 23.4.52

FS763
NTB 7.45-11.45
To R.Nor.AF 11.45

FS764
5(P)AFU 2.45- 4.46
7 SFTS 4.46
cr. during low roll, Hibaldstow, 16.8.46

FS765
No RAF service
To R.Neth.AF 10.47

FS766
9(P)AFU 3.45- 6.45
5(P)AFU [BL] 6.45- 4.46
To R.Dan.AF 12.46

FS767
587 Sqdn [M4:R] 5.45- 6.46
691 Sqdn 6.46- 9.46
595 Sqdn 9.46-10.47
1 FTS 5.51-12.51
3 FTS 12.51- 1.52
Glas. UAS 1.56- 1.56
Edin. UAS 1.56- 5.56
Glas. UAS 5.56- 7.56
Aber. UAS 7.56- 8.56
Glas. UAS 8.56- 2.57
St. And. UAS 2.57- 4.57
SS (Avex) 9.57

FS768
NTB 2.45-11.45
To R.Nor.AF 11.45

FS769
No service in UK
desp. ME 9.44
11 FIS
8 Sqdn 2.48- 7.49
SOC 15.9.50

FS770
587 Sqdn [M4:6] 5.45- 6.46
691 Sqdn [M4:S] 6.46- 8.46
603 Sqdn [RAJ:A] 8.46- 3.48
22 RFS 6.50- 7.50
11 RFS 7.50-10.50
101 RFS 4.51- 9.51
RAFC 9.51- 4.54
SS (Avex) 5.57

FS771
No RAF service
To R.Neth.AF 2.47

FS772
NTB 6.45-11.45
To R.Nor.AF 11.45

FS773
19 FTS 5.45- 4.47
RAFC [FAC:V] 4.47- 6.47
1 FTS 6.47- 1.48
6 FTS [FBH:H] 1.48
cr. 1dd. 4mls W of Ternhill, 28.10.52
FS774
No RAF service
To R.Neth.AF 9.47
FS775
No RAF service
To R.Neth.AF 1.48
FS776
5(P)AFU 2.45- 4.45
7 SFTS [FBB:C] 4.45- 1.48
7 FTS [FBA:L] 1.48-11.48
desp. S. Rhodesia 3.51
5 FTS 6.51- 8.53
4 FTS storage 8.53-12.53
Sold 12.53
FS777
No RAF service
To R.Neth.AF
FS778
Handling Sqdn 10.43- 9.44
To R.Neth.AF 7.47
FS779
28 Sqdn
'Recaptured' by USA 11.47
FS780
151 OTU
SOC 24.4.47
FS781
151 OTU
desp. FE
FECS 10.47-11.48
SF Seletar 11.48-10.49
FECS 10.49
DBR in accident 28.7.50
FS782
India: no record of service
To IAF 9.47
FS783
BAFSEA CS
AFS(I)
To Pak.AF 9.47
FS784
9 Sqdn IAF
SLAIS
8 Sqdn IAF
'Recaptured' by USA 11.47
FS785
Burma CS
'Recaptured' by USA 11.47
FS786
9 Sqdn IAF
cr. during low-level roll, Feni, 21.11.44
FS787
20 Sqdn 8.46- 1.47
To IAF 9.47
FS788
3 RFU
SOC 19.6.47
FS789
3 RFU
BAFSEA CS
1 SFTS(I)
AFS(I)
SOC 24.4.47
FS790
225 Gp. CS
SOC 24.4.47
FS791
India: no record of service
To Pak.AF 9.47
FS792
AFTU(I)
SOC 24.4.47
FS793
BAFSEA CS
ACSEA CS
SOC 30.5.46

FS794
SLAIS (6.45-10.45)
216 Sqdn
357 Sqdn
SOC 24.4.47
FS795
45 Sqdn 1.48-
SOC 25.3.48
FS796
159 Sqdn
SOC 29.8.46
FS797
67 Sqdn
'Recaptured' by USA 11.47
FS798
160 Sqdn
SOC 19.6.47
FS799
28 Sqdn
355 Sqdn
To IAF 9.47
FS800
60 Sqdn
SOC 24.4.47
FS801
194 Sqdn
3 RFU
(319 MU)
U/c collapsed on landing, Bhopal, 28.8.45
FS802
(322 MU)
Spun in during aerobatics, Chakeri, 16.8.46
FS803
India: no record of service
To IAF 9.47
FS804
211 Sqdn
SOC 1.1.45
FS805
353 Sqdn
SOC 24.4.47
FS806
203 Sqdn
222 Gp. CF
20 APC
To IAF 9.47
FS807
151 OTU
SOC 24.4.47
FS808
62 Sqdn
SOC 19.6.47
FS809
22 Sqdn
SOC 31.5.45
FS810
117 Sqdn
SOC 4.10.45
FS811
India: no record of service
SOC 13.6.46
FS812
3 RFU
'Recaptured' by USA 11.47
FS813
5(P)AFU 2.45- 2.45
FTCCF 2.45- 4.45
16 SFTS 4.45-11.45
BAS [FDW:F] 11.45- 2.47
CFS 2.47-12.47
RAFC [AB] 12.47- 6.54
SS (Avex) 5.57
FS814
No RAF service
Became 5208M 4.45
FS815
2 FTS 4.45- 8.45
19 FTS [FAC:Z] 2.46- 4.47
RAFC 4.47-12.50
1 FTS [FCA:R] 12.50
Collided with FE756 in aerobatics 1ml S of Graveley, 2.7.51

FS816
5(P)AFU 2.45- 6.45
19 FTS [FAB:K/FAD:X] 6.45- 4.47
1 FTS [FCD:H] 6.47- 2.48
7 FTS 2.48- 4.49
1 FTS [FCA:F] 5.51
cr. out of fuel 1ml NNW of Shipston on Stour, 2.1.52
FS817
No RAF service
To R.Neth.AF 1.48
FS818
SOC on arrival in UK 22.9.43
FS819
2 FIS [B:U] 4.45- 7.45
7 FIS 7.45- 5.46
CFS [FDN:K] 5.46-12.49
6 FTS [FBJ:K] 12.49- 9.50
22 FTS [Y:O] 5.51- 9.54
Sold Hw spares 3.55
FS820
No RAF service
To R.Neth.AF 3.48
FS821
ECFS 4.45- 5.46
EFS 5.46
cr. on take-off, Hullavington, 6.1.47
FS822
5(P)AFU 2.45- 4.45
7 SFTS [FBB:M] 4.45- 1.48
7 FTS 1.48-10.48
2 FTS [FAJ:N] 10.48- 7.49
CFS(EW) 7.49- 5.50
CFS [FDO:V] 5.50- 9.51
CFS(B) 9.51
Collided with KF948 and cr. 1ml S of Calmsden, Glos., 28.7.52
FS823
ECFS [FCT:R] 2.45- 5.46
EFS 5.46- 6.49
EAAS [FGC:U] 6.49- 8.49
RAFFC 8.49- 7.50
CFS [N:Q] 8.51- 7.54
SS (AES) 9.57
FS824
No RAF service
To R.Neth.AF 5.47
FS825
21 FTS 4.45- 9.46
SOC 8.9.50
FS826
No RAF service
To R.Dan.AF 9.47
FS827
3 SFTS [FBU:O] 3.46- 4.47
3 FTS 4.47- 4.48
SF Feltwell 4.48-11.49
RAFC [FAA:H/AH] 11.49- 4.54
Sold Hw spares 5.54
FS828
2 FIS 2.45- 4.45
3 SFTS [FBT:B] 1.46- 4.47
3 FTS [FBT:B] 4.47
cr. on overshoot, Feltwell, 9.5.47
FS829
ECFS [FCT:J] 6.45- 5.46
EFS 5.46- 2.49
EAAS 6.49- 8.49
RAFFC 8.49- 7.50
3 FTS [FBU:T/P:U] 7.51- 1.55
SS (AES) 12.56
FS830
11(P)AFU 3.45- 4.45
To R.Neth.AF 1.47
FS831
No RAF service
To R.Neth.AF 10.46
FS832
ATA 10.43-
Became 5015M 1.45
SOC 4.10.49
FS833
No RAF service
To R.Neth.AF 2.48

FS834
NTB 2.45-11.45
To R.Nor.AF 11.45
FS835
11(P)AFU 4.45- 6.45
20 FTS 6.45- 9.46
20 SFTS 9.46
Hit by KF198 while awaiting take-off, Church Lawford, 10.7.47
FS836
11(P)AFU 1.45- 5.45
2 FTS 5.45- 3.46
20 FTS 3.46
Hit trees in practice forced land'g Badley, Northants., 22.7.46
FS837
2 FTS 4.45- 3.46
20 FTS 3.46- 9.46
20 SFTS [FAK:S] 9.46- 7.47
CFS(EW) 7.49- 3.50
CFS [FDO:W] 3.50- 9.51
CFS(B) 9.51-11.53
SOC 8.5.54
FS838
No service in UK
desp. Algiers 5.44
73 OTU [C/J]
SOC 26.11.46
FS839
UK: no record of service
To R.Neth.AF
FS840
3 SFTS 3.46- 4.47
3 FTS [FBU:P] 4.47-11.49
RAFC [FAA:D/AD] 11.49- 4.54
Sold Hw spares 6.54
FS841
5(P)AFU 2.45- 5.45
19 FTS 5.45- 7.46
1 BAS 7.46- 2.47
CFS 2.47-12.49
6 FTS 12.49- 1.50
CFS [FDN:J/N:J] 1.50- 7.51
22 FTS 12.52- 7.53
9 FTS 7.53- 3.54
Sold Hw spares 7.54
FS842
NTB 6.45-11.45
To R.Nor.AF 11.45
FS843
6 SFTS [FBJ:K] 3.46- 5.47
6 FTS 5.47- 9.47
22 FTS 7.48- 9.50
2 FTS 9.50- 4.51
1 FTS [P:E] 4.51- 1.55
SS (Avex) 5.57
FS844
130 Sqdn 3.46-10.46
SF Odiham 10.46- 3.49
desp. S. Rhodesia 3.51
5 FTS 6.51
Hit by FT250 after landing, Thornhill, 19.8.52
FS845
ECFS 1.44- 4.45
SF Northolt 4.45- 9.46
desp. FE 1.52
84 Sqdn 5.52- 2.53
SF Tengah 2.53- 5.56
MAAF 5.56-
SOC 10.5.57
FS846
No service in UK
desp. Algiers 5.44
73 OTU [J]
SOC 28.11.46
FS847
19 FTS [EG/FAC:F] 5.45- 4.47
RAFC 4.47- 5.47
6 FTS 3.48- 7.48
22 FTS 7.48
Abandoned in spin 1ml N of Kingston on Soar, 25.2.49
FS848
No RAF service
SOC 20.10.50

FS849
5(P)AFU 12.44- 5.45
7 SFTS [FBC:L] 5.45- 6.48
2 FTS [FAI:D] 6.48- 7.49
CFS(EW) 7.49- 3.50
CFS [FDO:Y] 3.50- 9.51
CFS(B) 9.51- 7.54
SS (H.Bath) 3.57
FS850
21 FTS 5.45- 9.46
7 FTS 7.52- 1.53
22 FTS 1.53- 7.53
9 FTS 7.53- 4.54
SS (H.Bath) 3.57
FS851
21 FTS
To R.Neth.AF 4.47
FS852
2 FIS 2.45- 7.45
7 FIS 7.45- 5.46
CFS 5.46- 6.47
CGS 6.47- 8.48
RAFC [FAB:J] 8.48-12.49
3 FTS [FBT:J] 12.49- 7.50
1 FTS 3.51- 9.51
RAFC 9.51- 4.54
Sold Hw spares 5.54
FS853
ECFS [FCT:S] 7.45- 5.46
EFS 5.46- 6.49
EAAS 6.49- 7.49
6 FTS [FBG:D] 7.49-11.53
SS (Avex) 5.57
FS854
2 FIS 4.45- 7.45
7 FIS 7.45- 5.46
CFS 5.46-12.49
6 FTS 12.49- 1.50
CFS 1.50- 2.50
6 FTS 2.50- 9.50
2 FTS 9.50-11.50
1 FTS [FCA:F/P:H] 11.50-10.54
Sold Hw spares 2.55
FS855
5(P)AFU 2.45- 5.45
19 FTS 5.45- 4.47
RAFC 4.47- 8.47
2(P)RFU 8.47- 4.48
6 FTS 4.48- 7.48
22 FTS [FCJ:J] 7.48- 1.53
desp. Mombasa 8.55
No service in Kenya
To R.Jord.AF 6.56
FS856
5(P)AFU 2.45- 5.45
20 FTS [FAJ:F] 5.45-
RAFC [FAB:E] 9.48- 3.54
Sold Hw spares 7.54
FS857
13 SFTS
To RCAF
FS858
Canada: no record of service
To RCAF
FS859
8 SFTS
DBR in accident 27.1.44
FS860
13 SFTS
8 SFTS
To RCAF
FS861
Canada: no record of service
To RCAF
FS862
Canada: no record of service
To RCAF
FS863
8 SFTS
cr. in Northumberland Strait, 14.9.43
FS864
2 FIS(C)
To RCAF

FS865
Canada: no record of service
To RCAF
FS866
6 SFTS
To RCAF
FS867
6 SFTS
To RCAF
FS868
18 SFTS
DBR in accident 3.12.44
FS869
Canada: no record of service
To RCAF
FS870
13 SFTS
To RCAF
FS871
Canada: no record of service
To RCAF
FS872
Canada: no record of service
To RCAF
FS873
35 SFTS
To RCAF
FS874
13 SFTS
To RCAF
FS875
6 SFTS
To RCAF
FS876
13 SFTS
cr. 2mls E of Delmas, Sas., 4.12.44
FS877
Canada: no record of service
To RCAF
FS878
13 SFTS
To RCAF
FS879
No RAF service
To R.Neth.AF 2.47
FS880
No RAF service
To R.Neth.AF 10.46
FS881
587 Sqdn [M4:T] 2.45- 6.46
691 Sqdn 6.46-10.46
FCCS 10.46- 2.49
612 Sqdn [8W:X] 5.50- 6.53
Sold (Avex) 2.57
To Lebanese AF 6.57
FS882
No RAF service
To R.Neth.AF 7.47
FS883
6 SFTS [FBJ:L] 3.46- 5.47
6 FTS 5.47-12.49
CFS [FDO:Z] 12.49
cr. on take-off, Moreton-in-Marsh, 9.1.51
FS884
2 FIS 4.45- 7.45
7 FIS 7.45- 5.46
CFS [FDN:O] 5.46
DBF on ground, Moreton-in-Marsh, 20.6.51
FS885
No RAF service
To R.Neth.AF 9.47
FS886
19 FTS [FE] 5.45- 4.47
RAFC [FAC:R/CR] 4.47- 5.51
22 FTS 5.51- 4.54
SS (Avex) 5.57
FS887
NTB 6.45-11.45
To R.Nor.AF 11.45

FS892 of No.3 FTS crashed in the centre of Ely on 9 August 1951, narrowly missing the Cathedral (in background). The pilot and one person on the ground were killed *(Cambridgeshire collection)*

FS888
65 Sqdn 3.46-10.46
695 Sqdn 10.46- 8.47
41 Sqdn 8.47-10.47
SF Horsham St. Faith 10.47
cr. on overshoot, Horsham St. Faith 4.2.48
FS889
19 Sqdn 5.46- 9.46
desp. S. Rhodesia 3.51
5 FTS 10.51- 8.53
4 FTS storage 8.53-12.53
Sold 12.53
FS890
21 FTS 5.45- 9.46
600 Sqdn [RAG:C] 7.47- 8.49
2 FTS 10.50- 4.51
1 FTS 4.51- 6.52
Nott. UAS 2.56- 6.56
Birm. UAS 6.56- 8.56
Nott. UAS 8.56- 8.56
Man. UAS 8.56-10.56
Nott. UAS 10.56- 5.57
Became 7554M at CFS 1.58
A&AEE for spares
FS891
20 FTS [FAI:T] 4.45- 9.46
20 SFTS 9.46-
2 FTS [FAI:A] 6.49- 2.51
1 FTS 2.51
cr. ldd. ¼ml short of runway, Oakington, 8.6.51
FS892
ECFS [FCT:P] 7.44- 5.46
EFS 5.46- 9.49
RAFFC 9.49-10.49
3 FTS [FBT:G] 10.49
cr. St. Mary St., Ely, 9.8.51
FS893
No RAF service
To R.Neth.AF 11.47
FS894
7 SFTS [FBB:J] 5.45- 1.48
7 FTS [O:W] 1.48-12.52
6 FTS 12.52- 8.53
Sold Hw spares 3.55
FS895
No service in UK
desp. Algiers 5.44
No record of service in ME
SOC 28.11.46
FS896
No RAF service
To R.Neth.AF 10.46
FS897
NTB 6.45-11.45
To R.Nor.AF 11.45
FS898
2 FTS 4.45- 3.46
21 FTS 3.46- 9.46
6 FTS [O:Z] 8.52-10.53
9 FTS 10.53- 4.54
Sold Hw spares 5.54
FS899
20 FTS [FAI:P] 4.45-
RAFC [FAB:M] 9.48- 6.49
2 FTS 6.49- 7.49
CFS(EW) 7.49- 3.50
CFS [FDO:M] 3.50- 9.51
CFS(B) [O:M/N:M]9.51-11.54
Sold Hw spares 3.55
FS900
20 FTS 4.45- 9.46
20 SFTS 9.46- 7.47
2 FTS [FAI:M] 7.47- 5.51
22 FTS [FCJ:Y] 5.51- 8.51
1 FTS 8.51- 1.52
3 FTS [P:X] 1.52
Lost prop. blade and abandoned 4½mls NW of Downham Market, 5.4.54
FS901
No service in UK
desp. Algiers 6.44
2 FTLU
6 Sqdn
U/c collapsed on landing, Kolundia, Palestine, 4.10.46
FS902
A&AEE 5.44-
1 FTS 4.52- 8.53
CFS 8.53- 7.54
Sold Hw spares 4.55
FS903
2 FIS 4.45- 7.45
7 FIS 7.45- 5.46
CFS 5.46- 7.46
To French AF 5.49
FS904
No RAF service
To R.Neth.AF for spares 10.46
FS905
315 Sqdn 4.46- 5.47
SF Odiham 5.47-
1 Sqdn [JX:D]
desp. S. Rhodesia 6.51
5 FTS 8.51- 8.53
4 FTS storage 8.53-12.53
Sold 12.53
FS906
7 SFTS [FBB:J] 6.45- 8.46
501 Sqdn [RAB:A] 8.46- 5.47
1 FTS [P:V] 7.51- 3.55
SS (Av.Tr.) 6.57
FS907
NTB 6.45-11.45
To R.Nor.AF 11.45

FS908
No RAF service
To R.Neth.AF 4.47
FS909
No RAF service
To R.Neth.AF 3.48
FS910
No RAF service
To R.Neth.AF 8.47
FS911
NTB 6.45-11.45
To R.Nor.AF 11.45
FS912
5(P)AFU 12.44- 4.45
7 SFTS 4.45- 7.45
To R.Neth.AF 5.47
FS913
No RAF service
To R.Neth.AF 2.47
FS914
20 FTS 4.45- 9.46
20 SFTS [FAI:G] 9.46- 7.47
2 FTS [FAI:N] 7.47- 5.51
103 FRS 5.51-11.51
207 AFS [M:37] 11.51- 5.52
1 FTS 5.52
Hit by KF397 on runway, Moreton-in-Marsh, 12.9.52
FS915
No RAF service
To R.Neth.AF 10.46
FS916
NTB 6.45-11.45
To R.Nor.AF 11.45
FS917
NTB 6.45-12.45
To R.Dan.AF 5.47
FS918
NTB 6.45-11.45
To R.Nor.AF 11.45
FS919
No RAF service
To R.Neth.AF 9.47

FS920
ECFS [FCT:G] 6.44- 5.46
EFS 5.46- 6.49
EAAS 6.49- 8.49
RAFFC 8.49- 7.50
103 RFS 7.51-11.51
3 FTS 12.51- 7.53
2 FTS [P:W/N:Q] 7.53- 4.54
SS (Av.Tr.) 10.57
FS921
5(P)AFU 2.45- 4.46
316 Sqdn 4.46-12.46
SF Wattisham 12.46- 5.47
SF Duxford 5.47-12.47
1 Sqdn [JX:G] 12.47- 8.48
RCITF 8.48- 1.50
RCCS [RCA:L] 1.50- 8.50
1 FTS 7.51
cr. on take-off, Oakington, 3.8.51
FS922
5(P)AFU 12.44- 4.46
7 SFTS 4.46- 5.46
To R.Dan.AF 4.47
FS923
3 TAF CS
Burma CF
357 Sqdn
1300 Flt 5.46- 1.47
desp. FE 1.47
18 Sqdn 5.47- 8.47
84 Sqdn 1.48- 6.48
FECS 6.48- 3.50
FEAFExS 3.50-11.50
FECS 11.50-12.54
SOC 4.57
FS924
India: no record of service
'Recaptured' by USA 11.47
FS925
82 Sqdn
45 Sqdn
SOC 23.8.45

FS926
India: no record of service
SOC 13.6.46
FS927
8 Sqdn IAF
To IAF 9.47
FS928
India: no record of service
SOC 13.6.46
FS929
681 Sqdn
45 Sqdn
SOC 30.5.46
FS930
ACSEA CS
BAFSEA CS 10.44-
8 FU
SOC 31.5.45
FS931
27 Sqdn
1 SFTS(I)
To Pak.AF 9.47
FS932
1300 Flt 5.46- 1.47
NFT
FS933
India: no record of service
SOC 13.6.46
FS934
135 Sqdn
34 Sqdn
615 Sqdn
To IAF 9.47
FS935
60 Sqdn
34 Sqdn
228 Gp. CF
U/c collapsed on landing, Ranchi, 9.6.45
FS936
India: no record of service
SOC 26.4.45

FS948 of an unrecorded unit in India. Note the helpfully large serial on the fuselage repeated on the fin (via R.C.Sturtivant)

FS937
India: no record of service
SOC 28.6.45
FS938
670 Sqdn
cr. after take-off, Razmak, 8.5.46
FS939
India: no record of service
To IAF 9.47
FS940
3 RFU
To IAF 9.47
FS941
3 RFU
'Recaptured' by USA 11.47
FS942
SF Koggala
SOC 25.6.46
FS943
India: no record of service
SOC 11.7.46
FS944
AFTU
22 AACU
To IAF 9.47
FS945
45 Sqdn
SOC 27.9.45
FS946
India: no record of service
SOC 13.6.46
FS947
BAFSEA CS 10.44-
ACSEA CS
To Pak.AF 9.47
FS948
DGA CF
To IAF 9.47
FS949
22 AACU
To IAF 9.47
FS950
India: no record of service
SOC 13.6.46
FS951
India: no record of service
SOC 24.4.47
FS952
45 Sqdn
SF Negombo -12.49
desp. FE
SF Kai Tak 10.50- 1.51
HKAAF 1.51
cr. in sea near Hong Kong, 18.7.54
FS953
SLAIS
1(I)Gp. CF
To Pak.AF 9.47
FS954
India: no record of service
SOC 11.7.46
FS955
India: no record of service
SOC 11.7.46
FS956
India: no record of service
To IAF 9.47
FS957
13 SFTS (10.43- 2.44)
To RCAF
FS958
Canada: no record of service
To RCAF
FS959
13 SFTS (10.43- 2.44)
To RCAF
FS960
13 SFTS (1.44-12.44)
To RCAF
FS961
13 SFTS
To RCAF
FS962
13 SFTS
To RCAF

FS963
Canada: no record of service
To RCAF
FS964
13 SFTS
To RCAF
FS965
Canada: no record of service
To RCAF
FS966
13 SFTS
To RCAF
FS967
Canada: no record of service
To RCAF
FS968
13 SFTS (7.44-10.44)
To RCAF
FS969
Canada: no record of service
To RCAF
FS970
Canada: no record of service
To RCAF
FS971
13 SFTS
To RCAF
FS972
14 SFTS
To RCAF
FS973
13 SFTS (11.43-10.44)
To RCAF
FS974
Canada: no record of service
To RCAF
FS975
Canada: no record of service
To RCAF
FS976
Canada: no record of service
To RCAF
FS977
Canada: no record of service
To RCAF
FS978
13 SFTS (11.43-
Collided with RCAF 3296 and crashed
5.1.44
FS979
India: no record of service
SOC 24.4.47
FS980
India: no record of service
SOC 26.6.47
FS981
India: no record of service
SOC 2.8.45
FS982
231 Gp. CF -10.45
SF Jessore 10.45- 1.46
SOC 24.4.47
FS983
India: no record of service
desp. FE by 9.46
1315 Flt 1.48-10.48
SOC 11.10.48
FS984
India: no record of service
Desp. FE by 9.46
1315 Flt
SOC 11.10.48
FS985
231 Gp. CF -10.45
SF Jessore 10.45- 1.46
SOC 24.4.47
FS986
India: no record of service
To IAF 9.47
FS987
2 Sqdn IAF
To IAF 9.47

FS988
India: no record of service
desp. FE by 9.46
1315 Flt
SOC 11.10.48
FS989
357 Sqdn
155 Sqdn
SF Jessore 10.45- 1.46
SOC 1.6.47
FS990
1 SFTS(I)
SOC 2.8.45
FS991
28 Sqdn 6.46-10.46
SOC 28.8.47
FS992
607 Sqdn
SOC 19.6.47
FS993
151 OTU
To Pak.AF 9.47
FS994
1 SFTS(I)
U/c collapsed on landing, Ambala,
13.3.45
FS995
India: no record of service
'Recaptured' by USA 11.47
FS996
52 Sqdn
SOC 27.6.46
FS997
India: no record of service
SOC 28.6.45
FS998
India: no record of service
SOC 19.6.47
FS999
17 Sqdn
84 Sqdn
cr. ldd. in Malaya, 29.10.46

****

FT100
222 Gp. CF
45 Sqdn 1.48- 6.48
SF Negombo 6.48-12.49
SF Kai Tak 10.50-12.50
HKAAF 12.50
Spun in, Aberdeen Is., Hong Kong,
20.5.56
FT101
SF Kohat
TSTU
2(I)Gp. CF 12.46- 7.47
To IAF 9.47
FT102
31 Sqdn
224 Gp. CF
2(I)Gp. CF [E] 12.46- 6.47
SOC 26.6.47
FT103
AHQ India CS 3.46- 7.47
To IAF 9.47
FT104
60 Sqdn (4.45- 6.45)
SOC 24.4.47
FT105
151 OTU
SOC 28.9.44
FT106
1(I)Gp. CF
To IAF 9.47
FT107
India: no record of service
SOC 11.7.46
FT108
21 FC
23 APC
SOC 24.4.47

FT109
India: no record of service
SOC 11.7.46
FT110
151 OTU
SOC 25.9.47
FT111
India: no record of service
SOC 20.9.45
FT112
113 Sqdn
JTRU 3.45- 6.45
34 Sqdn
To IAF 9,47
FT113
221 Gp. CF
PSOC 1.1.47
FT114
99 Sqdn
1331 CU
To IAF 9.47
FT115
India: no record of service
To IAF 9.47
FT116
ACSEA CS
SOC 11.7.46
FT117
India: no record of service
SOC 12.12.46
FT118
India: no record of service
SOC 11.7.46
FT119
India: no record of service
SOC 11.7.46
FT120
India: no record of service
SOC 11.7.46
FT121
1 SFTS (I)
To IAF 9.47
FT122
155 Sqdn
9 Sqdn RIAF
To Pak.AF 9.47
FT123
3 RFU
2(I)Gp. CF [F] 12.46- 7.47
To IAF 9.47
FT124
1315 Flt
SOC 11.10.48
FT125
India: no record of service
SOC 19.6.46
FT126
India: no record of service
SOC 24.4.47
FT127
3 RFU
SOC 24.4.47
FT128
8 FU
1 SFTS (I)
To IAF 9.47
FT129
India; no record of service
SOC 24.4.47
FT130
India: no record of service
'Recaptured' by USA 11.47
FT131
42 Sqdn
To IAF 9.47
FT132
India: no record of service
To IAF 9.47
FT133
7 SFTS 6.45-10.45
SOC 30.4.51
FT134
No RAF service
To R.Neth.AF 2.47

FT135
9(P)AFU 9.44- 6.45
5(P)AFU 6.45- 5.46
To R.Dan.AF 12.46
FT136
No RAF service
To R.Neth.AF 9.47
FT137
ECFS [A] 6.44- 5.46
EFS 5.46
Spun into ground 2mls S of Wooton-under-Edge 3.2.47
FT138
NTB 2.45-10.45
To R.Nor.AF 11.45
FT139
NTB 2.45-10.45
To R.Nor.AF 11.45
FT140
No RAF service
To USAAF, Warton 6.44
FT141
17 SFTS 10.44- 6.47
1 FTS 6.47- 7.47
602 Sqdn [RAI:Z] 7.47
cr. in R. Cart nr. Abbotsinch 24.1.49
FT142
No RAF service
To R.Neth.AF 11.46
FT143
No RAF service
To R.Dan.AF 5.47
FT144
No RAF service
To R.Neth.AF 8.46
FT145
No RAF service
To R.Neth.AF 8.47
FT146
17 SFTS 2.45- 9.45
To R.Neth.AF 3.48
FT147
No RAF service
To USAAF, Warton 6.44
FT148
No RAF service
To R.Neth.AF 8.47
FT149
11(P)AFU 1.45- 5.45
19 FTS [FAA:D] 5.45- 4.47
RAFC [FAA:D] 4.47- 8.47
3 FTS [FBU:J] 8.47- 1.55
SS (Avex) 4.57
FT150
2 FIS 10.44-10.44
9(P)AFU 10.44- 6.45
5(P)AFU 6.45- 4.46
SOC 23.1.51
FT151
No RAF service
To R.Neth.AF 9.46
FT152
12 FU 1.45- 3.45
Yugoslav FTS 4.45-
To Yugo.AF
FT153
9(P)AFU 9.44- 6.45
5(P)AFU 6.45- 1.46
3(P)AFU 1.46- 3.46
3 SFTS 3.46-10.46
7 SFTS 10.46- 1.48
7 FTS [FBB:F] 1.48- 1.51
CFS 1.51-12.53
SOC 30.12.53
FT154
No RAF service
To R.Dan.AF 6.47
FT155
No service in UK
desp. ME 8.44
AB&GS 4.45-11.45
73 Sqdn - 9.50
SOC 10.4.51

FT156
11(P)AFU 1.45- 6.45
2 FTS 6.45- 3.46
21 FTS 3.46- 9.46
1 FTS 9.52- 6.54
SS (Avex) 5.57
FT157
No RAF service
To R.Dan.AF 4.47
FT158
9(P)AFU 9.44- 6.45
5(P)AFU 6.45-10.45
7 FIS 10.45- 5.46
CFS [FDM:C] 5.46-12.49
6 FTS [FBJ:O] 12.49-11.53
SS (Avex) 5.57
FT159
No RAF service
To R.Neth.AF 9.47
FT160
No RAF service
To R.Neth.AF 6.47
FT161
11(P)AFU 1.45- 6.45
To R.Neth.AF 12.46
FT162
5(P)AFU 2.45-10.45
6(P)AFU 10.45-12.45
6 SFTS 12.45-12.46
SOC 25.8.50
FT163
NTB 2.45-10.45
To R.Nor.AF 11.45
FT164
9(P)AFU 9.44- 6.45
5(P)AFU 6.45-10.45
6(P)AFU 10.45-12.45
6 SFTS 12.45- 5.47
6 FTS [FBG:F] 5.47- 2.50
desp. S. Rhodesia 11.50
4 FTS 7.51- 9.52
5 FTS 9.52
Ran into hole on landing and hit by EX777, Heany 13.4.53
FT165
11(P)AFU 1.45- 6.45
20 FTS 6.45- 1.47
6 SFTS 1.47- 5.47
6 FTS [FBJ:D] 5.47-12.49
CFS [N:H] 12.49
Spun into ground, Icomb, Glos. 11.10.51
FT166
NTB 2.45-10.45
SOC 10.10.45
FT167
No RAF service
To R.Neth.AF 8.47
FT168
5(P)AFU 2.45- 6.45
2 FTS 6.45- 3.46
21 FTS 3.46- 9.46
SOC 20.10.50
FT169
ECFS 6.44
Missing 23.7.44
FT170
5(P)AFU 1.45- 6.45
2 FTS 6.45- 3.46
21 FTS 3.46- 9.46
SOC 25.9.50
FT171
No RAF service
To R.Neth.AF 3.48
FT172
ECFS [M/FCT:M] 6.44- 6.45
desp. S. Rhodesia 3.51
5 FTS 7.51- 9.53
4 FTS 9.53-12.53
Sold 12.53
FT173
5(P)AFU 1.45- 6.45
19 FTS 6.45
Collided with FX228 in Cranwell circuit and DBR 18.1.46

FT174
No service in UK
Yugoslav FTS 3.45-
To YugoAF
FT175
5(P)AFU 2.45- 5.45
21 FTS 5.45- 8.46
22 SFTS [FCJ:H] 8.46- 2.49
22 FTS [R:D] 2.49- 5.54
SS (AES) 12.56
FT176
No RAF service
To R.Neth.AF 8.46
FT177
2 FIS
To R.Neth.AF 10.46
FT178
2 FIS 2.45-10.45
To R.Neth.AF 10.46
FT179
5 Sqdn
2(I)Gp. CF 12.46- 7.47
To IAF 9.47
FT180
India: no record of service
To IAF 9.47
FT181
7 Sqdn RIAF
To IAF 9.47
FT182
226 Gp. CF
152 Sqdn
To Pak.AF 9.47
FT183
232 Gp. CF
SOC 30.8.45
FT184
India: no record of service
'Recaptured' by USA 11.47
FT185
India: no record of service
To IAF 9.47
FT186
45 Sqdn 5.49- 6.49
1301 Flt 6.49- 7.49
SF Negombo 12.49- 4.55
SOC 13.4.55
FT187
10 Sqdn RIAF
To IAF 9.47
FT188
India: no record of service
To Pak.AF 9.47
FT189
India: no record of service
SOC 19.6.47
FT190
India: no record of service w. RAF
Transferred to RN 1.45
733 Sqdn 2.45
cr. in sea 25.6.45
FT191
TSTU
To Pak.AF 9.47
FT192
SLAIS 11.44-
AFS (I)
20 Sqdn 8.46- 1.47
To IAF 9.47
FT193
India: no record of service
'Recaptured' by USA 11.47
FT194
6 Sqdn RIAF
To Pak.AF 9.47
FT195
India: no record of service
To IAF 9.47
FT 196
India: no record of service
SOC 11.7.46
FT197
1 AGS (I)
AFS (I)
To IAF 9.47

FT198
8 FU
SOC 24.4.47
FT199
India: no record of service
SOC 11.7.46
FT200
3 RFU 6.45- 8.45
To IAF 9.47
FT201
321 Sqdn 6.45- 8.45
SOC 24.4.47
FT202
India: no record of service
To IAF 9.47
FT203
232 Gp. CS
SOC 25.3.48
FT204
India: no record of service
SOC 19.6.47
FT205
10 FU
SOC 24.4.47
FT206
3 TAF CS
Burma CF
SOC 27.2.47
FT207
SOC on arrival in UK 21.1.44
FT208
1689 Flt [9X:A] 9.45- 2.47
HCEU [J:R] 2.52- 7.53
SS (Avex) 5.57
FT209
5(P)AFU 2.45- 6.45
19 FTS [FAD:C] 6.45- 4.47
RAFC [FAB:U/BU] 4.47
cr. ldd. at night $\frac{3}{4}$m W of Cranwell, 17.3.53
FT210
No RAF service
To R.Neth.AF 11.47
FT211
No RAF service
To R.Neth.AF 2.48
FT212
No RAF service
To R.Neth.AF 5.47
FT213
5(P)AFU 2.45- 6.45
19 FTS 6.45- 7.46
1 BAS 7.46- 2.47
CFS [FDM:E/FDN:L/N:L] 2.47- 7.54
Sold Hw spares 3.55
FT214
2 FIS 2.45- 6.45
20/21 FTS 6.45- 7.45
7 FIS 7.45- 5.46
CFS 5.46- 6.47
CGS [FJX:A] 6.47- 8.48
RAFC [FAA:Z] 8.48-12.49
3 FTS [FBV:F/P:O/P:B]12.49-4.55
SS 12.56
FT215
17 SFTS 8.44- 6.47
1 FTS 6.47- 3.48
CFS 3.48- 9.48
RAFC [FAB:N/BN] 9.48- 3.54
SS 12.56
FT216
No RAF service
To R.Neth.AF 4.48
FT217
No RAF service
To R.Neth.AF 6.47
FT218
5(P)AFU 2.45- 4.45
7 SFTS 4.45- 5.46
1 FU 2.47- 4.47
To R.Dan.AF 4.47
FT219
No RAF service
To R.Neth.AF 3.47

FT220
No RAF service
To R.Neth.AF 10.46
FT221
NTB 2.45-11.45
To R.Nor.AF 11.45
FT222
No RAF service
To R.Neth.AF 5.47
FT223
No RAF service
To R.Neth.AF 7.47
FT224
19 FTS [GN/FAD:M] 9.45-10.46
12 Gp. CF 10.46- 8.47
2(P)RFU 8.47- 3.48
1(P)RFU [FDD:D] 3.48-11.48
2 FTS [FAK:N] 11.48
cr. $1\frac{1}{2}$mls W of Fairford 13.12.48
FT225
No RAF service
To R.Neth.AF 9.47
FT226
No RAF service
To R.Dan.AF 9.47
FT227
No RAF service
To USAAF, Burtonwood 6.44
FT228
No RAF service
To R.Neth.AF 7.47
FT229
No RAF service
To R.Neth.AF 5.47
FT230
No RAF service
To R.Neth.AF 11.47
FT231
No RAF service
To R.Neth.AF 3.47
FT232
ECFS 6.44
DBR in accident 23.4.45
FT233
No RAF service
To R.Neth.AF 9.46
FT234
No RAF service
To R.Neth.AF 3.47
FT235
3 SFTS 3.46- 1.47
22 SFTS 1.47-11.47
SOC 30.4.51
FT236
No RAF service
To USAAF, Burtonwood 6.44
FT237
NTB 2.45-11.45
To R.Nor.AF 11.45
FT238
No RAF service
To R.Neth.AF 10.46
FT239
19 FTS [CN] 9.45- 4.47
RAFC 4.47- 5.47
6 FTS 3.48- 7.48
22 FTS [FCJ:O/R:U] 7.48- 9.54
SS (Avex) 5.57
FT240
No RAF service
To R.Neth.AF 9.46
FT241
No RAF service
To USAAF,Burtonwood 6.44
FT242
No RAF service
To R.Neth.AF 8.47
FT243
No RAF service
To USAAF, Warton 6.44
FT244
No RAF service
To R.Neth.AF 3.48

FT245
5(P)AFU 2.45- 6.45
20/21 FTS 6.45- 6.45
2 FTS 6.45- 3.46
21 FTS 3.46- 9.46
17 SFTS 9.46- 6.47
1 FTS 6.47- 1.48
6 FTS [FBH:K] 1.48-12.49
CFS [FDN:A/N:A] 12.49- 9.54
Sold Hw spares 3.55
FT246
17 SFTS [FCD:H] 8.44-11.46
CFS 11.46-12.46
21(P)AFU 12.46- 7.47
1(P)RFU 7.47- 5.49
FRS 6.49- 4.51
CFS [FDM:X/M:X] 4.51- 7.54
SS (AES) 6.57
FT247
No RAF service
To R.Neth.AF 11.47
FT248
No RAF service
To R.Neth.AF 7.47
FT249
No RAF service
To R.Neth.AF 8.47
FT250
17 SFTS 8.45- 3.46
19 FTS 3.46- 4.47
RAFC [FAB:M] 4.47- 7.47
66 Gp. CF 7.49-11.49
desp. S. Rhodesia 5.51
5 FTS 9.51- 7.53
4 FTS storage 7.53-12.53
Sold 12.53
FT251
2 FIS 2.45- 7.45
To R.Dan.AF 7.47
FT252
NTB 2.45-11.45
To R.Nor.AF 11.45
FT253
No RAF service
To USAAF, Warton 6.44
FT254
6 SFTS [FBI:M] 3.46- 5.47
6 FTS 5.47-10.51
7 FTS [N:L] 12.51- 8.53
2 FTS 8.53- 4.54
11 RFS 4.54- 5.54
Edin. UAS 5.54- 8.54
SOC 31.8.54
FT255
5(P)AFU 11.44- 6.45
19 FTS [CL] 6.45-11.45
7 SFTS [FBB:U] 10.46- 1.48
7 FTS 1.48-10.48
2 FTS [FAJ:L] 10.48- 4.51
22 FTS [FCJ:T/R:S] 4.51- 5.54
SS (AES) 12.56
FT256
No RAF service
To R.Neth.AF 1.47
FT257
16 SFTS 8.45-11.45
To R.Dan.AF 7.47
FT258
3 SFTS 3.46-12.46
22 SFTS [FCI:R] 12.46- 2.49
22 FTS 2.49- 7.49
2 FTS 7.49- 4.51
7 FTS [N:H] 4.51- 5.53
2 FTS 5.53- 5.54
1 FTS 5.54- 2.55
SS (Avex) 5.57
FT259
19 FTS [DN/FAD:N] 9.45- 4.47
RAFC [FAC:A] 4.47- 3.54
SS (AES) 12.56
FT260
5(P)AFU [GL] 9.44- 4.46
desp. S. Rhodesia 6.51
5 FTS 8.51- 8.53
4 FTS storage 8.53-12.53
Sold 12.53
FT261
No RAF service
To R.Neth.AF for spares 10.46
FT262
11(P)AFU 5.45- 6.45
20 FTS 6.45
Hit HT cables, Church Lawford, 23.9.46
FT263
16 SFTS 8.44-12.45
3 SFTS [FBS:J] 1.46- 4.47
3 FTS [FBT:N] 4.47-
Leeds UAS 2.56-
SS (Av.Tr.) 10.57
FT264
NTB 2.45-11.45
To R.Nor.AF 11.45
FT265
Canada: no record of service
To RCAF
FT266
Canada: no record of service
To RCAF
FT267
Canada: no record of service
To RCAF
FT268
No service in Canada
desp. UK 3.44
No service in UK
To R.Neth.AF for spares 12.46
FT269
No service in Canada
desp. UK 5.44
17 SFTS 8.44
cr. on approach to Spitalgate, 21.3.46
FT270
No service in Canada
desp. UK 4.44
17 SFTS 8.44-11.46
CFS 11.46-12.46
21(P)AFU 12.46-
desp. S. Rhodesia 12.50
5 FTS [42] 4.51- 8.53
4 FTS storage 8.53-12.53
Sold 12.53
FT271
No service in Canada
desp. UK 3.44
22 SFTS 11.45- 3.46
21 FTS 3.46- 9.46
1 FTS 4.52
cr. East Noyle, Wilts., 12.12.52
FT272
14 SFTS 11.43-
To RCAF
FT273
14 SFTS 11.43-
To RCAF
FT274
14 SFTS 11.43
To RCAF
FT275
14 SFTS 11.43-
To RCAF
FT276
14 SFTS 11.43
To RCAF
FT277
14 SFTS 11.43-
To RCAF
FT278
14 SFTS 11.43
1 FIS(C)
To RCAF
FT279
No service in Canada
desp. UK 4.44
11(P)AFU 1.45- 6.45
7 FIS 6.45- 5.46
CFS 3.47- 6.47
11 AGS 6.47-11.47
To R.Neth.AF 3.48
FT280
No service in Canada
desp. UK 4.44
No service in UK
To R.Neth.AF 9.46
FT281
No service in Canada
desp. UK
5(P)AFU 11.44- 5.46
7 SFTS 4.46-12.46
22 SFTS [FCI:M] 12.46- 2.49
22 FTS 2.49-12.49
2 FTS 12.49- 6.51
6 FTS [D:Q] 6.51- 8.53
Sold Hw spares
FT282
No service in Canada
desp. UK 4.44
5(P)AFU 11.44- 4.46
7 SFTS 4.46- 8.46
610 Sqdn [RAQ:Y/DW:Y/Y] 8.46- 6.52
Edin. UAS 6.52-11.52
11 RFS 11.52-
St. And. UAS 10.55-
cr. ldd. Perth 27.2.57
FT283
No service in Canada
desp. UK
2 FTS 4.45- 3.46
21 FTS [FAN:E] 3.46- 9.46
SOC 31.10.50
FT284
No service in Canada
desp. UK 4.44
19 FTS [GF] 5.45- 4.47
CFS 4.47- 6.47
17 SFTS 6.47- 6.47
1 FTS 6.47- 8.47
3 FTS [FBU:Q/R:T] 8.47- 4.55
Camb. UAS 1.56- 6.56
HCEU 6.56- 9.56
Camb. UAS 9.56- 4.57
SS (Av.Tr.) 9.57
FT285
No service in Canada
desp. UK
3 FIS [6] 8.44- 8.45
7 FIS 8.45- 1.46
3 SFTS [FBS:E] 1.46- 4.47
3 FTS 4.47-10.47
To French AF 4.49
FT286
No service in Canada
desp. UK
2 FIS 7.44- 7.45
To R.Neth.AF 2.47
FT287
No service in Canada
desp. UK 4.44
9(P)AFU 9.44- 6.45
5(P)AFU 6.45-11.45
7 FIS 11.45- 5.46
CFS 5.46-12.49
6 FTS 12.49- 1.50
CFS [N:G] 1.50- 5.52
22 FTS [Y:T] 5.52- 6.53
9 FTS 6.53- 4.54
SS (H.Bath) 3.57
FT288
No service in Canada
desp. UK 4.44
9(P)AFU 8.44- 6.45
5(P)AFU 6.45- 4.46
21(P)AFU [FDA:K] 12.46- 1.47
604 Sqdn [RAK:Y] 1.47- 7.49
607 Sqdn 7.49-
SOC 31.7.53
FT289
Canada: no record of service
To R.Neth.AF

FT290
No service in Canada
desp. UK
9(P)AFU 9.44- 6.45
5(P)AFU 6.45-12.45
6 SFTS 12.45- 5.47
6 FTS 5.47- 7.47
3 FTS [FBT:P/P:O] 3.48- 2.55
SS (AES) 6.57
FT291
No service in Canada
desp. UK
9(P)AFU 9.44- 6.45
5(P)AFU 6.45- 4.46
7 SFTS 4.46- 5.46
To R.Dan.AF 5.47
FT292
Canada: no record of service
To RCAF
FT293
No service in Canada
desp. UK 4.44
No service in UK
To R.Neth.AF 10.46
FT294
No service in Canada
desp. UK 4.44
No service in UK
To R.Neth.AF 10.46
FT295
No service in Canada
desp. UK
16 SFTS 8.44-11.45
17 SFTS 11.45
cr. on landing, Spitalgate, 2.10.46
FT296
2 FIS(C)
To RCAF
FT297
No service in Canada
desp. UK
16 SFTS 9.44-12.45
7 SFTS 12.45-
Sold Hw spares 4.51
FT298
No service in Canada
desp. UK 4.44
9(P)AFU 12.44- 6.45
5(P)AFU 6.45-11.45
22 SFTS [FCI:A] 11.45- 2.49
22 FTS [FCJ:F] 2.49- 1.51
SS (Avex) 9.57
FT299
No service in Canada
desp. UK 4.44
9(P)AFU 9.44- 6.45
5(P)AFU 6.45- 4.46
7 SFTS 4.46- 5.46
Sold Hw spares 4.51
FT300
No service in Canada
desp. UK
5(P)AFU 12.44- 6.45
2 FTS 6.45- 3.46
21 FTS 3.46- 9.46
SOC 20.10.50
FT301
No service in Canada
desp. India 6.44
3 RFU
'Recaptured' by USA 11.47
FT302
19 FTS [FAD:H] 8.45- 4.47
RAFC [GJ] 4.47- 7.47
To French AF 4.49
FT303
11(P)AFU 5.45- 6.45
2 FTS [FAJ:T] 6.45- 3.46
20 FTS 3.46- 7.47
2 FTS 7.47- 4.51
7 FTS [N:V] 4.51- 5.53
Became 7107M 9.53
FT304
No RAF service
To R.Neth.AF 8.47
FT305
9(P)AFU 9.44- 6.45
5(P)AFU 6.45- 4.46
7 SFTS 4.46- 5.46
To R.Dan.AF 4.47
FT306
No RAF service
To R.Neth.AF 10.48
FT307
No RAF service
To USAAF, Burtonwood 6.44
FT308
No RAF service
To R.Neth.AF 5.47
FT309
NTB 2.45-11.45
To R.Nor.AF 11.45
FT310
ECFS [C] 6.44- 5.46
EFS [FCT:C] 5.46- 6.49
EAAS 6.49- 8.49
RAFFC 8.49-11.49
3 FTS 11.49- 3.55
SS (AES) 6.57
FT311
No RAF service
To R.Neth.AF .48
FT312
No RAF service
To R.Neth.AF 4.48
FT313
19 FTS [AN] 9.45-
7 SFTS
19 FTS 3.46- 7.46
1 BAS 7.46- 2.47
CFS [FDM:O] 2.47- 1.53
RAFC [BP] 1.53- 5.54
SS (Avex) 5.57
FT314
No RAF service
To R.Neth.AF 3.48
FT315
19 FTS [BN] 9.45- 4.47
RAFC 4.47- 8.47
2(P)RFU 8.47- 3.48
1(P)RFU 3.48- 6.49
FRS 6.49- 9.51
RAFC [BV] 9.51- 4.54
Sold Hw spares 5.54
FT316
16 SFTS 8.44-11.45
To R.Neth.AF 10.46
FT317
No RAF service
To R.Neth.AF 10.46
FT318
16 SFTS 9.44-12.45
3(P)AFU 12.45-12.45
3 SFTS [FBP:D] 12.45- 8.47
66 Gp. CF 6.49- 3.50
desp. S. Rhodesia 5.51
5 FTS 8.51- 7.53
4 FTS storage 7.53-12.53
Sold 12.53
FT319
ECFS [N] 6.44- 5.46
EFS [FCT:N] 5.46- 6.49
EAAS 6.49- 7.49
7 FTS [O:M] 7.49- 8.53
2 FTS 8.53- 4.54
Sold Hw spares 6.54
FT320
No RAF service
To R.Neth.AF 12.47
FT321
2 FIS 8.44- 6.45
7 FIS 6.45- 5.46
CFS [FDM:D] 5.46- 2.50
CFS(EW) 2.50- 3.50
CFS 3.50- 5.52
22 FTS 5.52- 8.52
7 FTS 8.52
force-landed 2m NE of Cottesmore, 4.11.52
FT322
16 SFTS [47] 9.44- 1.46
3 SFTS [FBT:M] 1.46- 4.47
3 FTS 4.47- 5.52
22 FTS 5.52- 6.53
9 FTS 6.53- 4.54
SS (Avex) 5.57
FT323
No RAF service
To R.Neth.AF 12.46
FT324
9(P)AFU 10.44- 6.45
5(P)AFU [BD] 6.45- 4.46
7 SFTS 4.46-10.47
22 SFTS [FCI:P] 10.47- 2.49
22 FTS [Y:C] 2.49- 7.54
Sold Hw spares 3.55
FT325
No RAF service
To R.Neth.AF 9.46
FT326
No RAF service
To R.Neth.AF 9.46
FT327
9(P)AFU 9.44- 6.45
5(P)AFU 6.45-11.45
22 SFTS [FCI:J] 11.45- 4.47
Sold Hw spares 4.51
FT328
No RAF service
To R.Neth.AF 10.46
FT329
16 SFTS 9.44-11.45
3(P)AFU 11.45- 3.46
3 SFTS [FBU:K] 3.46- 4.47
3 FTS 4.47
cr. on take-off, Feltwell, 22.4.50
FT330
ECFS [D/FCT:D] 6.44- 9.45
19 FTS 9.45- 1.46
6 SFTS [FBJ:C] 3.46-12.46
CFS [M:N] 12.49- 9.54
Sold Hw spares 3.55
FT331
2 FIS 8.44- 6.45
7 FIS 6.45- 5.46
CFS [FDM:K] 5.46
cr. 1m SE of Little Rissington, 6.12.49
FT332
19 FTS 9.45- 7.46
1 BAS [FDW:K] 7.46- 2.47
CFS [FDW:K] 2.47- 6.47
EFS [FCT:B] 6.47- 6.49
EAAS 6.49- 8.49
RAFFC 8.49- 1.50
RAFC [FAA:F/AF] 1.50- 5.51
22 FTS 5.51- 7.53
9 FTS 7.53- 4.54
Sold Hw spares 6.54
FT333
19 FTS [FAC:X] 9.45- 4.47
RAFC 4.47- 7.47
To French AF 5.49
FT334
9(P)AFU 9.44- 6.45
5(P)AFU 6.45-12.45
22 SFTS [FCI:N] 12.45- 2.49
22 FTS 2.49-12.49
2 FTS [FAJ:M] 2.49
Hit tree on approach to South Cerney at night, 15.3.50
FT335
2 FIS 7.44- 6.45
To R.Nor.AF
FT336
9(P)AFU 10.44- 6.45
5(P)AFU [BW] 6.45-12.45
3(P)AFU 12.45- 3.46
3 SFTS 3.46-12.46
22 SFTS [FCI:J] 1.47- 2.49
22 FTS 2.49- 3.50
3 FTS [FBT:Y] 3.50
Collided with KF372 during formation aerobatics, Feltwell,15.8.52

FT337
19 FTS [FB] 5.45- 4.47
RAFC 4.47- 7.47
1 FTS [FCA:U] 7.47- 2.48
RAFC 2.48- 4.49
5 RFS 7.50-10.50
1 FTS 12.50-10.53
SOC 7.10.53
FT338
19 FTS [DH] 5.45- 4.47
RAFC [FAD:H] 4.47- 6.47
17 SFTS 6.47- 7.47
1 FTS 7.47- 8.47
3 FTS [FBU:R] 8.47-12.49
RAFC [FAA:Z] 12.49-12.50
1 FTS [FCA:S] 12.50- 9.51
RAFC 9.51- 4.54
Sold Hw spares 6.54
FT339
No RAF service
To Yugoslav AF 4.45
FT340
No RAF service
To R.Neth.AF 5.47
FT341
16 SFTS [40] 8.44-11.45
3(P)AFU 11.45- 3.46
3 SFTS [FBT:J] 3.46- 4.47
3 FTS [FBT:J] 4.47-10.47
SOC 4.10.50
FT342
16 SFTS [77] 10.44-12.45
604 Sqdn [RAK:Z] 7.46- 3.49
603 Sqdn [RAJ:B] 3.49- 9.53
SOC 13.10.53
FT343
5(P)AFU 12.44- 4.45
7 SFTS 4.45-12.47
RAFC [FAA:F] 12.47- 6.49
2 FTS 6.49- 5.50
22 FTS [U:D] 5.50- 6.54
1 FTS [P:A] 6.54-11.54
SS (Avex) 5.57
FT344
16 SFTS [49] 9.44- 4.45
SOC 9.4.45
FT345
17 SFTS 7.44- 8.44
2 FIS 8.44- 7.45
To R.Neth.AF 5.47
FT346
16 SFTS [53] 9.44-10.45
7 FIS 10.45- 5.46
CFS [FDM:W] 5.46- 5.47
7 SFTS [FBC:A] 5.47- 1.48
7 FTS 1.48- 1.51
CFS 1.51- 9.51
CFS(B) [O:G/N:G]9.51-10.54
SOC 25.10.54
FT347
No RAF service
To R.Neth.AF 1.47
FT348
9(P)AFU 9.44- 6.45
5(P)AFU 6.45- 1.46
6 SFTS [FBJ:O] 1.46- 5.47
6 FTS 5.47-12.49
CFS [FDN:C] 12.49- 4.52
1 FTS 4.52- 7.53
CFS(B) 7.53- 8.54
Sold Hw spares 3.55
FT349
No RAF service
To R.Neth.AF 8.47
FT350
No RAF service
To R.Dan.AF 12.46
FT351
16 SFTS [76] 10.44- 1.46
3 SFTS 1.46-12.46
22 SFTS [FCJ:D] 12.46- 2.49
22 FTS 2.49-12.53
Man. UAS 3.55-12.55
Durham UAS 12.55- 5.57
SS (Av.Tr.) 10.57

FT352
ECFS [E] 6.44- 5.46
EFS [FCT:E] 5.46- 6.49
EAAS [FGC:P] 6.49- 8.49
RAFFC 8.49- 7.50
605 Sqdn 11.51-10.53
SS (AES) 6.57
FT353
5(P)AFU 9.44- 6.45
19 FTS [BL] 6.45- 4.47
RAFC 4.47- 7.47
1 FTS 7.47
Undershot landing, Folkingham, 26.11.47
FT354
5(P)AFU 1.45- 6.45
20 FTS [FAJ:K] 6.45- 7.47
2 FTS 7.47- 7.49
CFS(EW) 7.49- 3.50
CFS 3.50- 9.51
CFS(B) [O:K] 9.51- 7.54
Sold Hw spares 4.55
FT355
17 SFTS 9.44-11.46
CFS 11.46-12.46
21(P)AFU 12.46- 7.47
1(P)RFU 9.47-12.47
62 Gp. CF 6.49-12.49
desp. S. Rhodesia 5.51
SOC 7.5.53
FT356
9(P)AFU 10.44- 6.45
5(P)AFU 6.45-12.45
Became 5768M 12.45
SOC 20.9.50
FT357
16 SFTS 9.44-11.45
To R.Neth.AF 12.46
FT358
16 SFTS 9.44-10.45
7 FIS 10.45- 5.46
CFS 5.46- 4.48
Sold Hw spares
FT359
5(P)AFU 12.44- 6.45
20/21 FTS 6.45- 3.46
20 FTS 3.46- 8.46
Overshot, Church Lawford, 21.8.46
FT360
ECFS [F] 6.44- 5.46
EFS [FCT:F] 5.46- 6.48
EAAS 6.48- 8.49
RAFFC 8.49- 9.49
1 FTS [FCA:W][K:B/N:O]3.51-10.54
Sold Hw spares 4.55
FT361
3 FIS [4] 8.44- 8.45
7 FIS 8.45- 5.46
CFS [FDN:X] 5.46- 9.51
CFS(B) 9.51- 7.54
SS (Avex) 6.57
FT362
17 SFTS 8.44- 9.45
To R.Neth.AF 11.46
FT363
16 SFTS [6] 8.44-11.45
3(P)AFU 11.45-12.45
3 SFTS [FBS:B] 12.45- 4.47
3 FTS [FBS:A] 4.47
Collided with FT263 and abandoned, 4mls W of Marham, 3.2.49
FT364
9(P)AFU 10.44- 6.45
5(P)AFU 6.45-11.45
6(P)AFU 11.45-12.45
6 SFTS [FBG:G] 12.45- 5.47
6 FTS 5.47-12.49
CFS [FDM:D] 12.49- 5.52
CFS(B) 5.52- 7.54
Sold Hw spares 3.55
FT365
No RAF service
To R.Neth.AF for spares 10.46

FT366
No RAF service
To R.Neth.AF for spares 11.46
FT367
16 SFTS 8.44-10.45
7 FIS 10.45- 5.46
CFS 5.46- 5.47
3 FTS [FBT:B] 5.47- 7.47
22 SFTS 7.47- 9.47
SOC 30.4.51
Sold Hw spares
FT368
No RAF service
To R.Neth.AF 5.47
FT369
17 SFTS 8.44- 6.47
610 Sqdn [DW:Z] 7.47-10.53
SOC 30.12.53
FT370
607 Sqdn
28 Sqdn
Missing nr. Agartala, 14.3.45
FT371
AFS(I)
To IAF 9.47
FT372
India: no record of service
SOC 24.4.47
FT373
SF St. Thomas Mount
To IAF 9.47
FT374
18 Sqdn
155 Sqdn
60 Sqdn 10.46-
28 Sqdn -12.47
FECS 12.47-11.49
FEExS
cr. on landing, Butterworth, 6.2.51
FT375
16 SFTS 8.44-12.45
RAE 5.46-
A&AEE 11.54-pres.
FT376
9(P)AFU 9.44- 6.45
5(P)AFU [BH] 6.45-12.45
3 SFTS 12.45-10.46
7 SFTS [FBB:Q] 10.46
Hit tree while low flying, Normanby, Lincs., 5.1.50
FT377
9(P)AFU 9.44- 6.45
5(P)AFU 6.45- 5.46
To R.Dan.AF 4.47
FT378
9(P)AFU 9.44- 6.45
5(P)AFU 6.45-10.45
19 FTS [FAC:E] 10.45- 4.47
RAFC [CE] 4.47- 4.54
Sold Hw spares 6.54
FT379
17 SFTS 8.44- 6.47
62 Gp. CF 6.49-12.49
desp. S. Rhodesia 5.51
5 FTS .51- 8.53
4 FTS storage 8.53- 9.53
1340 Flt 9.53- 9.55
SOC 31.3.56
FT380
9(P)AFU 9.44- 6.45
5(P)AFU 6.45- 4.46
7 SFTS 4.46- 5.46
To R.Dan.AF 1.47
FT381
No record of any RAF service
To R.Neth.AF
FT382
No RAF service
To R.Neth.AF 6.47
FT383
? FTS 5.45- 3.46
21 FTS [FAN:G] 3.46- 9.46
desp. Singapore 1.52
MAAF 8.52- 4.57
SOC 30.4.57

FT384
No RAF service
To R.Neth.AF 6.47
FT385
16 SFTS [16] 8.44-11.45
To R.Neth.AF 2.47
FT386
12(P)AFU 8.44- 4.45
16 SFTS 4.45-12.45
3 SFTS [FBR:J] 1.46
cr. Downham Market 29.11.46
FT387
19 FTS [EL/FAC:F] 5.45- 7.46
22 SFTS 7.46-11.46
SOC 30.4.51
Sold Hw spares
FT388
19 FTS [ED] 5.45- 4.47
RAFC [FAE:D] 4.47-10.47
SOC 30.4.51
Sold Hw spares
FT389
11(P)AFU 1.45- 6.45
2 FTS 6.45- 3.46
21 FTS 3.46- 9.46
RCCF 7.47- 9.47
610 Sqdn 9.47- 3.48
SOC 30.4.51
Sold Hw spares
FT390
9(P)AFU 9.44-10.44
SOC 26.10.44
Retd. to USA 6.48
FT391
No RAF service
To R.Neth.AF 10.47
FT392
22 RFS [64/B] 6.49-10.49
desp. S. Rhodesia 1.51
5 FTS 4.51- 2.53
1340 Flt 6.53- 9.55
SOC 31.3.56
FT393
7 SFTS 6.45- 1.48
7 FTS [FBB:K] 1.48- 6.48
2 FTS [FAI:G] 6.48- 7.49
CFS(EW) 7.49- 7.50
22 FTS [R:O] 1.51- 4.54
SS (AES) 12.56
FT394
9(P)AFU 10.44- 6.45
5(P)AFU 6.45-11.45
22 SFTS [FCI:D] 11.45- 3.48
7 FTS [P:B/N:B] 5.51- 8.53
2 FTS 8.53- 5.54
1 FTS [N:N] 5.54- 2.55
SS (H.Bath) 3.57
FT395
16 SFTS 8.44
Collided with Oxford EB797 1m S of Newton, 18.2.45
FT396
Crashed in USA before despatch
FT397
19 FTS 5.45- 4.47
RAFC 4.47- 2.48
2 FTS [FAK:P] 11.48- 7.49
CFS(EW) 7.49- 2.50
CFS [FDO:J] 3.50- 9.51
CFS(B) [O:J] 9.51- 8.54
Sold Hw spares 3.55
FT398
9(P)AFU 9.44- 6.45
5(P)AFU [BG] 6.45- 5.46
To R.Dan.AF 5.47
FT399
9(P)AFU 11.44- 6.45
5(P)AFU [BA] 6.45- 4.46
7 SFTS 4.46- 7.47
203 AFS 4.48- 9.49
226 OCU 9.49- 1.50
desp. S. Rhodesia 11.50
5 FTS [54] 3.51- 8.53
4 FTS storage 8.53-12.53
Sold 12.53

Code letter FAO:G signify allocation of FT346 to No.21 SFTS, yet there is no record of its service with this unit! *(via R.C.Sturtivant)*

FT400
9(P)AFU 11.44- 6.45
5(P)AFU 6.45- 3.46
To R.Neth.AF 4.47
FT401
17 SFTS 9.44-11.46
CFS 11.46-12.46
21(P)AFU [FDA:P] 12.46- 7.47
1(P)RFU 9.47-10.48
2 FTS [FAK:J] 10.48- 1.50
22 FTS 1.50- 3.50
3 FTS 3.50- 3.50
22 FTS 3.50- 9.50
2 FTS 9.50-11.50
22 FTS [R:L] 11.50
cr. Broadlaw Hill, Peebles, 17.1.53
FT402
ECFS [O] 6.44- 5.46
EFS [FCT:O] 5.46
cr. Kingscote, Glos., 27.9.48
FT403
5(P)AFU 9.44- 6.45
19 FTS [BH] 6.45- 4.47
RAFC [FAA:U] 4.47-11.47
SOC 30.4.51
Sold Hw spares
FT404
No RAF service
To R.Neth.AF 7.47
FT405
17 SFTS [FCE:J] 2.46- 8.46
604 Sqdn [RAK:X] 7.47-11.50
SS (Av.Tr.) 6.57
FT406
No RAF service
To R.Neth.AF 8.47
FT407
No RAF service
To R.Neth.AF 11.47
FT408
2 FIS 8.44- 7.45
To R.Neth.AF 10.46
FT409
17 SFTS 10.44- 6.47
613 Sqdn [RAT:1/Q3:1] 4.49- 1.52
desp. Kenya 7.54
1340 Flt 9.54- 9.55
To R.Jord.AF 1.56
FT410
2 FIS 8.44- 7.45
To R.Neth.AF 10.46
FT411
2 FIS 7.44- 6.45
7 FIS 6.45- 5.46
CFS 5.46-12.49
6 FTS [FBH:K] 12.49- 8.53
Sold Hw spares 5.54
FT412
17 SFTS [FCE:M] 8.44- 6.47
1 FTS [FCE:M] 6.47- 1.48
7 FTS [FBA:J] 1.48
Hit tree during forced landing, nr. Barsby, Leics., 14.7.50
FT413
16 SFTS [21] 8.44-11.45
6(P)AFU 11.45- 3.46
6 SFTS [FBG:E] 3.46-10.46
7 SFTS [FBB:Y] 10.46- 1.48
7 FTS 1.48- 3.53
6 FTS 3.53- 2.54
SS (AES) 6.57
FT414
16 SFTS 8.44-12.45
600 Sqdn 8.46
Cr. into blast pen and DBF, Biggin Hill, 23.8.51
FT415
17 SFTS 7.44- 6.47
1 FTS 6.47- 2.48
RAFC 2.48- 4.51
22 FTS 4.51
Flew into railway tunnel, Kinder Scout, Derbyshire, 14.1.52
FT416
5(P)AFU 10.44- 5.46
1 FTS [P:B] 4.52- 2.55
SS (Avex) 5.57
FT417
16 SFTS 8.44- 9.45
6 SFTS 3.46- 5.47
6 FTS 5.47-10.47
To R.Neth.AF 11.48
FT418
7(P)AFU 10.44-12.44
EFS [FCT:C]
7 SFTS [FBB:A] 10.47- 1.48
7 FTS [N:G] 1.48- 6.53
2 FTS 6.53- 6.54
SS (Avex) 5.57
FT419
No RAF service
To R.Neth.AF 11.47
FT420
No RAF service
To R.Neth.AF 4.47
FT421
16 SFTS 8.44-10.45
7 FIS 10.45- 5.46
CFS [FDN:F/N:F] 5.46-
RAFC 1.53- 3.54
Sold Hw spares 7.54
FT422
No RAF service
To R.Neth.AF 6.47
FT423
19 FTS [FK] 5.45- 7.46
1 FTS [N:W] 12.52- 1.55
SS(Avex) 6.57

Seen at RNAS Bramcote's Navy Day in June 1949 is Mk.III Harvard FT965 of No.1833 Squadron *(R.C.Sturtivant)*

FT424
2 FIS 5.44- 6.45
7 FIS 6.45- 5.46
CFS [FDM:F] 5.46
Hit trees and cr. during low flying
nr. Stow-on-the-Wold, 22.1.52
FT425
ECFS 6.44- 5.45
To R.Neth.AF 10.46
FT426
17 SFTS 8.44- 6.47
1 FTS 6.47-
SOC 15.9.50
FT427
No RAF service
To R.Neth.AF 30.10.47
FT428
9(P)AFU [T:40] - 6.45
5(P)AFU 6.45-

FT428
9(P)AFU [T:40]
5(P)AFU 10.44-
Collided with Oxford LW955 and cr.,
Oakley Folly, Salop, 27.2.45
FT429
9(P)AFU 9.44-.6.45
5(P)AFU 6.45-11.45
22 SFTS [FCI:E/FCJ:D] 11.45-11.47
Became 6530M 4.48
FT430
17 SFTS 7.44- 8.44
2 FIS 8.44- 7.45
To R.Neth.AF 5.47
FT431
ECFS [K] 6.44- 5.46
EFS [FCT:K] 5.46- 6.49
EAAS 6.49- 7.49
7 FTS [FBA:X][N:K] 7.49-10.53
2 FTS 10.53- 4.54
SS (H.Bath) 3.57
FT432
16 SFTS 8.44-11.45
To R.Dan.AF 6.47

FT433
19 FTS [EB] 5.45- 4.47
RAFC 4.47- 6.47
17 SFTS 6.47- 6.47
RAFC [FAA:P/AP] 2.48- 3.54
SS(AES) 12.56
FT434
9(P)AFU 9.44- 6.45
5(P)AFU 6.45- 4.46
7 SFTS 4.46-10.47
SOC 30.9.50
FT435
5(P)AFU [HX] 9.44- 4.46
7 SFTS [FBC:J] 4.46- 1.48
7 FTS 1.48- 5.48
1(P)RFU 5.48- 5.49
FRS 6.49- 4.51
7 FTS [O:L] 9.51-12.53
SS (AES) 6.57
FT436
17 SFTS 10.44- 9.46
7 FTS 7.52- 1.53
22 FTS 1.53- 7.53
9 FTS 7.53- 6.54
SS (H.Bath) 3.57
FT437
No RAF service
To R.Neth.AF 11.46
FT438
17 SFTS [FCE:R] 10.44- 6.47
SOC 30.9.50
FT439
5(P)AFU 9.44- 6.45
19 FTS [FAA:P] 6.45- 4.47
RAFC 4.47-11.47
Sold Hw spares 4.51
FT440
5(P)AFU 9.44- 6.45
21 FTS 6.45- 8.46
7 SFTS [FBB:W] 8.46- 1.48
7 FTS 1.48
cr. Deeping St. James, Lincs.,
20.2.53

FT441
17 SFTS [FCE:S] 10.44- 6.47
SOC 31.10.50
FT442
5(P)AFU 9.44
cr. Shining Tor 4.4.45
FT443
17 SFTS 10.44- 6.47
To French AF 5.49
FT444
7(P)AFU 10.44- 3.46
7 SFTS 3.46- 8.46
To French AF 5.49
FT445
ECFS [L] 6.44- 5.46
EFS [FCT:L] 5.46- 6.49
EAAS 6.49- 7.49
6 FTS [FBG:A] 7.49- 3.50
1 FTS [N:O] 5.51-10.54
SS (Avex) 6.57
FT446
17 SFTS [FCE:U] 10.44- 6.47
SOC 30.9.50
FT447
No RAF service
To R.Neth.AF 7.47
FT448
No RAF service
To R.Neth.AF 5.47
FT449
9(P)AFU 9.44- 6.45
5(P)AFU 6.45- 4.46
SOC 31.1.51
FT450
3 SFTS [FBR:G] 2.46- 4.47
3 FTS 4.47- 9.47
2 FTS [FAK:H] 11.48- 7.49
CFS(B) [FDO:N] 7.49- 9.52
desp. Malaya 7.53
MAAF 10.53-10.56
SOC 30.4.57
FT451
17 SFTS [FCE:V] 10.44- 6.47
SOC 15.10.50

FT452
No RAF service
To R.Neth.AF 1.47
FT453
17 SFTS 8.44- 4.46
1 FTS 7.51- 1.52
3 FTS [R:S] 1.52
cr. ldd. on approach to Feltwell, 1.2.54
FT454
No RAF service
To R.Neth.AF 7.47
FT455
No RAF service
To R.Neth.AF 12.47
FT456
No RAF service
To R.Neth.AF 9.46
FT457
16 SFTS 8.44- 6.45
19 FTS 6.45- 9.45
16 SFTS 9.45-12.45
7 FTS 12.45- 7.47
608 Sqdn [RAO:N] 4.48- 5.48
504 Sqdn 5.48- 7.48
608 Sqdn [6T:N] 7.48-12.53
SOC 30.12.53
FT458
No RAF service
To R.Neth.AF 8.47
FT459
No RAF service
To R.Neth.AF 11.46
FT460
5(P)AFU 9.44- 6.45
2 FTS 6.45- 9.46
SOC 31.10.50

****

FT955
ECFS 9.44- 7.45
Transferred to RN 7.45
748 Sqdn 11.45-
SOC 14.1.50
FT956
798 Sqdn 5.45-
1830 Sqdn 8.47- 9.48
SOC 8.6.53
FT957
798 Sqdn [L3M]
766 Sqdn 9.46-12.47
NFT
FT958
A&AEE 6.45- 8.45
Transferred to RN
700/799 Sqdn 7.47- 7.49
St. Merryn 10.51- 7.53
SF RNEC 1.54-12.54
SOC 21.1.55
FT959
766 Sqdn 1.46-
NFT
FT960
1832 Sqdn 8.47- 4.48
SOC 10.1.50
FT961
759 Sqdn 11.45- 2.46
SOC 14.1.50
FT962
798 Sqdn [L2W]
NFT
FT963
778 Sqdn
NFT
FT964
Gibraltar 11.44- 1.45
NFT
FT965
780 Sqdn [X] 9.44-12.44
798 Sqdn [L3X] 12.44-
748 Sqdn 6.45-11.45
1833 Sqdn [252:BR] 1.49- 3.50
To Port.AF 3.56

FT966
768 Sqdn 1.44- 7.44
759 Sqdn 2.45-12.45
To Port.AF 3.56
FT967
766 Sqdn [239:LM] 9.46- 3.48
desp. Malta
SF Hal Far 7.49- 5.50
SOC 20.5.55
FT968
RN: no record of service
Transferred to RAF 11.46
NFT
FT969
RN: no record of service
SOC
FT970
RN: no record of service
SOC 14.1.50
FT971
794 Sqdn 11.45- .46
718 Sqdn - 1.48
799 Sqdn 4.51- 7.51
To Port.AF 3.56
FT972
798 Sqdn 5.45-
778 Sqdn 12.47- 2.48
SOC 14.1.50
FT973
798 Sqdn [L3Q] 6.45- 7.45
758 Sqdn 11.45-
1830 Sqdn 7.47-11.47
SOC 14.1.50
FT974
758 Sqdn [U2R] 3.45- 5.46
780 Sqdn [U2R] 5.46- 3.47
desp. Malta
SF Hal.Far 9.49- 1.52
SOC 5.56

Note: of the above, FT966 and FT972, and perhaps others, were fitted with arrestor hooks.

****

FX198
8 RFS 6.50-10.50
1 FTS [FCA:V] 2.51-10.52
desp. Singapore 8.53
HKAAF 8.54- 1.58
SOC 31.1.58
FX199
3 FIS [1] 7.44- 8.45
7 FIS [FDM:P] 8.45- 5.46
CFS 5.46- 5.52
CFS(B) 5.52- 7.52
6 FTS 7.52
Engine cut in circuit; cr. ldd. nr. Ternhill, 13.4.53

FX200
9(P)AFU 9.44-12.45
SOC 21.12.45
RBOC 15.1.46
16 FU 9.46-10.46
St. Mawgan 10.46-11.46
Manston 5.48- 6.48
CFS(EW) 7.49- 4.50
2 FTS [FAJ:X] 4.50- 4.51
101 FRS 4.51-10.51
3 FTS 2.52
cr. ldd. Feltwell 29.1.54
FX201
5(P)AFU [HC] 10.44- 1.46
6 SFTS 1.46- 9.46
To R.Hell.AF 7.47
FX202
2 FTS 10.50- 2.51
1 FTS 2.51
Broke up in dive 4mls WNW of Stow-on-the-Wold, 25.8.54
FX203
9(P)AFU 9.44- 6.45
5(P)AFU [BM] 6.45- 1.46
6 SFTS [FBH:B] 1.46- 5.47
6 FTS 5.47
Stalled and cr. nr. Ternhill,9.5.51
FX204
7 SFTS 6.45- 7.46
To R.Hell.AF 5.47
FX205
16 SFTS 8.44-11.45
615 Sqdn [RAV:Y/V6:Y] 8.46- 6.53
SS (AES) 12.56
FX206
9(P)AFU 9.44- 6.45
5(P)AFU [EB] 6.45-12.45
6 SFTS 12.45-10.46
8 OTU 12.46- 7.47
237 OCU 7.47- 9.48
541 Sqdn 9.48- 3.51
3 FTS [FBU:A] 8.51
cr. ldd. Feltwell 11.5.54
FX207
2 FIS 4.45- 7.45
7 FIS 7.45-10.46
CFS 1.47- 6.47
7 SFTS 6.47-10.47
608 Sqdn [RAO:T/6T:T] 7.48- 6.52
Camb. UAS 6.52- 8.52
Oxf. UAS 8.52
cr. ldd. Kidlington 14.4.53
FX208
5(P)AFU [ET] 2.45- 4.45
7 SFTS 4.45- 7.46
82 Sqdn 12.46-12.47
541 Sqdn 12.47- 9.48
desp. S. Rhodesia 1.51
5 FTS [61] 6.51- 7.53
4 FTS storage 7.53-12.53
Sold 12.53
FX209
9(P)AFU 9.44- 6.45
5(P)AFU 6.45- 4.46
7 SFTS 4.46-10.47
22 SFTS [FCI:H] 10.47- 2.49
22 FTS 2.49- 9.50
2 FTS 9.50-11.50
1 FTS [FCA:A] 11.50- 5.51
22 FTS [R:P] 4.52
cr. Farnsfield, Notts., 4.5.53
FX210
8 OTU 12.46- 7.47
237 OCU 7.47- 5.51
1 FTS 10.52-10.53
CFS(B) 10.53- 8.54
SS (Av. Tr.) 10.57
FX211
No RAF service
SOC 30.6.50
FX212
9(P)AFU 9.44- 6.45
5(P)AFU [BO] 6.45- 4.46
7 SFTS 4.46-11.47
To Belg.AF 9.49

FX213
9(P)AFU 9.44- 6.45
5(P)AFU 6.45-12.45
6 SFTS [FBH:D] 12.45- 5.47
6 FTS 5.47- 6.51
3 FTS 10.52- 4.55
Nott. UAS 2.56- 4.56
Glas. UAS 4.56- 1.57
Aber. UAS 1.57- 2.57
Glas. UAS 2.57- 4.57
SS (AES) 9.57
FX214
2 FTS 10.50- 2.51
1 FTS 2.51-10.54
Glas. UAS 10.55- 4.57
SS (Av.Tr.) 9.57
FX215
16 SFTS [50] 9.44-12.45
3 SFTS 1.46-12.46
22 SFTS 12.46- 7.48
desp. S. Rhodesia 1.51
5 FTS 5.51- 5.52
SOC 7.5.52
FX216
RAE 12.44-10.50
3 FTS 7.51
SOC as DBR after hitting ground, 6.7.54
FX217
No RAF service
SOC 31.7.50
FX218
16 SFTS 9.44-11.45
SOC 30.9.50
FX219
21 Gp. CF [FKO:C] 3.45- 3.46
17 SFTS 3.46- 1.47
Horsham St. Faith 7.47- 5.50
613 Sqdn [Q3:3] 5.50
Overshot, Ringway, 11.11.50
FX220
21 FTS 5.45- 9.46
1 Sqdn 8.47-11.47
22 RFS [B] 6.49-10.49
2 FTS 11.50- 5.51
103 FRS 5.51-11.51
7 FTS [N:A] 3.52- 1.53
1 FTS [P:Z] 1.53-12.54
Sold Hw spares 4.55
FX221
2 FIS 7.44-11.44
7 FIS
CFS
Cat.E 21.7.49
FX222
303 Sqdn 4.46-12.46
691 Sqdn 12.46- 1.47
303 Sqdn 1.47- 8.47
1 Sqdn 8.47-11.47
691 Sqdn 11.47- 2.49
17 Sqdn [UT:M] 2.49- 4.51
502 Sqdn 4.51-12.52
609 Sqdn [Y] 12.52-10.53
SS (Avex) 5.57
FX223
16 SFTS 8.44-11.45
SOC 31.8.50
FX224
122 Sqdn 3.46-10.46
12 Gp. CF 10.46- 8.47
41 Sqdn 8.47-11.47
12 Gp. CF 11.47- 5.49
SOC 15.2.51
FX225
No RAF service
SOC 31.8.50
FX226
9(P)AFU 9.44- 6.45
5(P)AFU [BP] 6.45- 4.46
7 SFTS 4.46-10.47
EAAS [FGC:P] 10.47- 6.49
7 FTS [FBA:K] 6.49- 9.50
2 FTS 9.50- 5.51
102 FRS [M:10] 5.51-12.51
3 FTS 4.52- 5.52
22 FTS [Y:R] 5.52- 4.54
Sold Hw spares 4.55
FX227
5(P)AFU [BX] 11.44- 1.46
6 SFTS [FBH:E] 1.46- 5.47
6 FTS [FBH:E] 5.47- 8.47
CFS [FDN:B/N:B] 12.49- 7.54
Sold Hw spares 3.55
FX228
19 FTS 5.45
Collided with FT173 and cr. near Cranwell, 18.1.46
FX229
A&AEE 4.45-
ETPS - 9.46
SOC 15.9.50
FX230
5(P)AFU 2.45- 6.45
19 FTS [FAD:M/DM] 6.45- 4.47
RAFC 4.47-10.47
SOC 15.7.50
FX231
5(P)AFU 12.44- 6.45
19 FTS 6.45- 4.47
RAFC 4.47- 5.47
22 FTS 3.48- 8.54
SS (Av.Tr.) 10.57
FX232
16 SFTS 8.44-11.45
SOC 8.6.50
FX233
9(P)AFU 9.44- 6.45
5(P)AFU 6.45- 4.46
Sold Hw spares 4.51
FX234
9(P)AFU 9.44- 6.45
5(P)AFU 6.45- 3.46
7 FIS 3.46- 5.46
CFS [FDM:K/N:D] 5.46- 4.52
1 FTS [P:R] 4.52- 2.55
SS (Avex) 5.57
FX235
9(P)AFU 9.44- 6.45
5(P)AFU 6.45- 4.46
To R.Hell.AF 5.47
FX236
135 Wing 11.46-
16 Sqdn
2 Sqdn 8.49-12.50
1 FTS [P:Y] 10.52-10.54
Sold Hw spares 4.55
FX237
20 FTS [FAI:C] 4.45 7.47
2 FTS [FAI:E] 7.47
cr. near South Cerney, 26.5.48
FX238
Inst. of Av. Med. 5.48- 7.53
SS (Avex) 5.57
FX239
11(P)AFU 1.45- 6.45
17 SFTS 6.45- 4.47
To French AF 4.49
FX240
2 FIS 7.44- 6.45
7 FIS 6.45- 5.46
CFS [FDM:S] 5.46- 7.50
7 FTS [FBB:L] 7.51- 5.53
2 FTS 5.53- 6.54
3 FTS 6.54- 3.55
SS (H.Bath) 3.57
FX241
ATA 6.44-
Became 5250M
FX242
Burma CF
SOC 26.6.47
FX243
9(P)AFU 9.44
cr. Balbeggie, Perthshire 26.11.44
FX244
9(P)AFU 9.44- 6.45
5(P)AFU 6.45-11.45
22 SFTS 11.45-11.46
Became 6312M 4.47
FX245
9(P)AFU 9.44- 6.45
5(P)AFU [EH] 6.45-
1 Sqdn [JX:L] 9.47- 8.48
ITF Tangmere 8.48- 1.49
22 RFS 6.50- 6.50
3 FTS [FBT:W] 5.51
Stalled and cr., Waldesea, Cambs., 21.3.52
FX246
2 FIS 7.44- 7.45
SOC 15.9.50
FX247
SOC on arrival in UK 14.5.44
FX248
9(P)AFU 9.44- 6.45
5(P)AFU 6.45- 1.46
6 SFTS 1.46-10.46
1 Sqdn [JX:J] 9.47- 8.48
RCITF 8.48- 8.51
22 FTS [U:I] 11.52
Hit by Very cartridge and DBR while awaiting take-off, Syerston,14.1.54
FX249
16 SFTS [72] 9.44-11.45
3(P)AFU 11.45-12.45
3 SFTS [FBR:B] 3.46- 4.47
3 FTS 4.47-12.47
502 Sqdn [RAC:R] 7.48
cr. Hope Mtn., Flint, 19.3.51
FX250
No RAF service
To French Air Force 18.5.49
FX251
11(P)AFU 1.45- 5.45
17 SFTS 5.45- 4.46
41 Sqdn 8.47- 7.48
203 AFS 7.48- 8.49
desp. S. Rhodesia 1.51
5 FTS 4.51- 8.53
4 FTS (storage) 8.53-12.53
Sold 31.12.53
FX252
5 RFS 7.50-10.50
CFS [M:W] 2.51- 9.54
SS (AES) 12.56
FX253
5(P)AFU 12.44- 6.45
2 FTS 6.45- 3.46
20 FTS 3.46- 1.47
17 SFTS 1.47- 6.47
1 FTS 6.47
Hit tree on approach to Spitalgate, 15.8.47
FX254
2 FIS 8.44- 6.45
7 FIS 6.45- 5.46
CFS 10.46- 7.54
SS (AES) 6.57
FX255
22 RFS 6.49- 8.49
64 Gp. CF 8.49-11.49
desp. S. Rhodesia 5.51
5 FTS .51
Stalled on take-off, Thornhill, 23.1.52
FX256
1 FTS [P:S] 1.51
cr. on take-off, Moreton-in-Marsh, 3.9.54
FX257
9(P)AFU 9.44- 6.45
5(P)AFU 6.45-12.45
3(P)AFU 12.45- 3.46
3 SFTS 3.46-12.46
3 SFTS [FBT:G] 2.47- 4.47
3 FTS 4.47- 9.49
11 RFS 6.50-11.50
101 FRS 4.51- 9.51
RAFC [CC] 9.51- 4.54
Sold Hw spares 5.54
FX258
5(P)AFU 1.45- 1.46
SOC 15.7.50

FX259
16 SFTS 9.44-11.45
3(P)AFU 11.45- 3.46
3 SFTS 3.46-10.46
7 SFTS 10.46
cr. on overshoot, Kirton-in-Lindsey and DBF, 23.7.47
FX260
16 SFTS 8.44-11.45
SOC 15.10.50
FX261
5(P)AFU 2.45- 6.45
19 FTS [FAA:U] 6.45- 4.47
RAFC 4.47- 6.47
RAFC [AU] 3.48- 4.54
Sold Hw spares 6.54
FX262
5(P)AFU 12.44- 5.45
21 FTS 5.45- 9.46
17 SFTS 9.46-11.46
CFS 11.46-12.46
21(P)AFU 12.46- 8.47
1(P)RFU 8.47- 5.49
FRS 6.49- 4.51
101 FRS 4.51-10.51
SS (Av.Tr.) 6.57
FX263
9(P)AFU 9.44- 6.45
5(P)AFU 6.45-12.45
6 SFTS 12.45-10.46
7 SFTS [FBB:X] 10.46- 1.48
7 FTS 1.48- 3.53
FTC CF 3.53-
2 FTS - 5.54
SS (AES) 12.56
FX264
5(P)AFU 2.45- 4.46
Sold Hw spares 4.51
FX265
9(P)AFU 9.44- 6.45
5(P)AFU 6.45-12.45
3 SFTS 12.45-12.46
3 SFTS [FBS:F] 2.47- 4.47
3 FTS 4.47-11.47
APS Acklington 11.47- 9.48
41 Gp. 9.48- 6.49
22 RFS 6.49- 7.49
64 Gp. CF 7.49-11.49
desp. S. Rhodesia 11.51
4 FTS [H:83] 3.52- 9.53
1340 Flt 9.53
cr. 1dd. in clearing 20 mls NW of Nyeri, Kenya, 7.4.55
FX266
9(P)AFU 9.44- 6.45
5(P)AFU [BU] 6.45- 4.46
7 SFTS [FBC:R] 4.46- 1.48
7 FTS 1.48- 5.48
CFS 5.48- 9.48
RAFC [FAB:D] 9.48-12.49
3 FTS [FBP:D/FBU:E/P:H] 12.49
cr. 1dd. Feltwell 22.10.54
FX267
No RAF service
SOC 18.1.51
FX268
16 SFTS [54] 9.44-11.45
6(P)AFU 11.45- 3.46
6 SFTS 3.46-12.46
SOC 25.8.50
FX269
17 SFTS 8.44- 9.44
9(P)AFU 9.44- 6.45
5(P)AFU [BB] 6.45- 1.46
3(P)AFU 1.46- 3.46
3 SFTS [FBR:H] 3.46- 4.47
3 FTS 4.47-10.47
1 PTS 10.47- 6.50
Manston 6.50- 9.50
OFU 9.50- 2.53
167 Sqdn [QO:J] 2.53-11.53
SS (AES) 12.56

FX270
5(P)AFU 11.44- 4.45
7 SFTS 4.45- 5.46
SOC 9.3.51
FX271
19 FTS [FAC:P] 5.45- 9.46
2(P)RFU 8.47- 3.48
1(P)RFU 3.48- 4.48
Manston (for accident prevention film) 4.48- 2.49
SOC 8.2.49
FX272
17 SFTS 8.44- 5.45
SOC 25.9.50
FX273
2 FTS 4.45- 3.46
21 FTS [FAP:S] 3.46- 9.46
SOC 27.6.50
FX274
25 RFS 6.50- 7.50
FRS 3.51- 4.51
101 FRS 4.51-10.51
1 FTS 4.52- 7.53
CFS 7.53- 7.54
SS (AES) 12.56
FX275
9(P)AFU 9.44- 6.45
To R.Hell.AF 9.49
FX276
No RAF service
To Belg.AF
FX277
9(P)AFU 9.44- 6.45
5(P)AFU 6.45- 4.46
Sold Hw spares 4.51
FX278
9(P)AFU 9.44- 6.45
5(P)AFU 6.45-12.45
22 SFTS [FCI:P] 12.45- 9.47
A&AEE 10.48- 4.53
SOC 2.4.53
FX279
9(P)AFU 11.44- 6.45
5(P)AFU 6.45-12.45
22 SFTS [FCI:O] 12.45- 2.49
22 FTS [R:G] 2.49-12.52
SOC after accident 6.10.53
FX280
16 SFTS [3] 8.44-11.45
607 Sqdn [RAN:B] 9.46- 6.48
2 FTS 2.50- 4.51
1 FTS [FCD:P/FCA:J] 4.51- 9.51
overshot and cr., Cranwell village, 6.1.53
FX281
16 SFTS 8.44-11.45
ETPS 8.46- 9.51
1 FTS 10.52- 7.53
CFS (B) [O:L] 7.53- 8.54
SS (Avex) 5.57
FX282
11 RFS 8.50-10.50
desp. FEAF 3.51
MAAF 7.51
cr. on approach, Tiger Lane, Malaya 3.9.52
FX283
3 FIS [7] 8.44- 8.45
7 FIS 8.45- 1.46
3 SFTS 1.46- 4.47
3 FTS 4.47-11.47
612 Sqdn [RAS:S] 11.47- 8.49
3 FTS [FBT:I] 11.50-11.50
1 FTS 11.50-10.51
6 FTS 10.51-10.53
9 FTS 10.53- 4.54
Sold Hw spares 6.54
FX284
9(P)AFU 9.44- 6.45
5(P)AFU 6.45-4.46
7 SFTS [FBA:H/FBA:P] 4.46- 1.48
7 FTS 1.48-10.49
3 FTS 11.50-11.50
1 FTS [FCA:C/K:A] 11.50-11.54
Sold Hw spares 3.55

FX285
ATA 6.44- 7.44
64 Gp. CF 8.49-11.49
desp. S. Rhodesia 1.51
5 FTS 6.51- 8.53
4 FTS storage 8.53-12.53
Sold 31.12.53
FX286
9(P)AFU 9.44- 6.45
5(P)AFU 6.45- 3.46
6 SFTS [FBH:C] 3.46- 5.47
6 FTS 5.47- 9.49
FRS 3.50- 4.51
101 FRS 4.51-10.51
RAFC [BW] 3.53- 4.54
Sold Hw spares 5.54
FX287
No RAF service
SOC 28.6.50
FX288
17 SFTS 8.44- 6.47
1 FTS [P:T/K:A]4.51- 1.55
SS (Avex) 5.57
FX289
9(P)AFU 9.44- 6.45
5(P)AFU 6.45- 4.46
Sold Hw spares 4.51
FX290
No RAF service
Sold Hw spares 4.51
FX291
5(P)AFU 11.44- 5.45
19 FTS [BE] 5.45- 1.46
21 FTS 1.46- 8.46
17 SFTS 8.46- 6.47
1 FTS 6.47- 8.47
3 FTS [FBU:S] 8.47- 7.48
CFS [N:F] 2.51-10.51
CFS (B) [O:F] 10.51-10.54
Sold Hw spares 3.55
FX292
11(P)AFU 4.45- 6.45
20 FTS 6.45- 8.47
3 FTS [FBT:E/P:J] 8.47-11.54
SOC 20.1.55
FX293
9(P)AFU 9.44- 6.45
5(P)AFU 6.45- 1.46
Became 5770M 1.46
SOC 17.9.47
FX294
No RAF service
SOC 12.9.50
FX295
5(P)AFU 9.44- 6.45
19 FTS [BJ] 6.45- 4.47
RAFC 4.47-10.47
SOC 4.10.50
FX296
9(P)AFU 9.44- 6.45
5(P)AFU 6.45- 4.46
7 SFTS 4.46
Hit building while low flying, Stiffkey, Norfolk,22.12.47
FX297
ECFS [S] 3.46- 5.46
EFS [FCT:I] 5.46- 6.49
EAAS [FGC:S] 6.49- 8.49
RAFFC [FGC:S] 8.49- 9.52
6 FTS 9.52-11.53
SS (AES) 5.57
FX298
5(P)AFU 11.44- 4.46
Sold Hw spares 4.51
FX299
5(P)AFU 11.44- 6.45
19 FTS 6.45- 8.46
19 FTS [GK] 11.46- 4.47
RAFC [FAC:K] 4.47-11.47
To Belg. AF 9.49
FX300
5(P)AFU 11.44- 4.46
7 SFTS [FBB:O/FBC:U] 4.46- 6.48
2 FTS [FAI:E] 6.48- 7.49
CFS (EW) 7.49- 5.50

22 FTS [FCI:T] 5.50- 9.50
2 FTS [FAI:Z] 9.50- 4.51
101 FRS 4.51-11.51
Oxf. UAS [K] 8.54- 5.57
SS (Av.Tr.) 10.57
FX301
3 FIS [2] 7.44- 8.45
7 FIS 8.45- 5.46
CFS 5.46-11.47
CFS [FDM:V/FDN:Q/N:Q] 2.48
coll. with FX438 on approach to Moreton-in-Marsh, 26.4.51
FX302
16 SFTS
6(P)AFU 11.45-12.45
6 SFTS 12.45-10.46
To French Air Force 5.49
FX303
16 SFTS [34] 8.44-11.45
Sold Hw spares 4.51
FX304
2 FIS 7.44- 7.45
SOC 15.10.50
FX305
5(P)AFU 2.45- 5.45
19 FTS [GL] 5.45- 4.47
RAFC 4.47- 1.48
EANS 1.48- 3.48
RAFC [FAD:K] 3.48
lost wings in dive, Coleby Hall, 6.1.50
FX306
17 SFTS 10.44- 9.45
3 SFTS [FBR:N] 2.46- 4.47
3 FTS 4.47-11.49
RAFC [FAA:E] 11.49- 7.52
6 FTS 7.52
cr. ldd. Foolow, Derbyshire10.12.52
FX307
17 SFTS 10.44-11.46
CFS 11.46-12.46
21(P)AFU [FDA:S] 12.46- 8.47
1(P)RFU [FDD:S] 8.47-10.48
2 FTS [FAI:D] 10.48- 7.49
CFS (EW) 7.49- 3.50
CFS [FDO:I] 3.50
cr. $\frac{3}{4}$ml S of Pebworth, Warwickshire 24.1.51
FX308
Not used in UK
desp. S. Rhodesia 11.51
4 FTS 3.52 9.52
5 FTS [G:77] 9.52- 8.53
4 FTS storage 8.53-12.53
Sold 31.12.53
FX309
No RAF service
SOC 20.7.50
FX310
9(P)AFU 9.44- 6.45
5(P)AFU 6.45- 4.46
7 SFTS 4.46-10.46
41 Sqdn 8.47- 6.48
12 Gp. CF 6.48-10.48
226 OCU 10.48- 8.49
desp. S. Rhodesia 3.51
5 FTS 7.51
SOC after damage 25.6.53
FX311
17 SFTS 10.44- 4.46
1 Sqdn [JX:G] 12.47- 8.48
ITF Tangmere 8.48- 5.49
22 RFS 6.50- 7.50
11 RFS 7.50-11.50
61 Gp. CF 5.51- 6.51
6 FTS 6.51- 9.53
Sold Hw spares 3.55
FX312
16 SFTS 8.44- 1.46
3 SFTS 1.46-10.46
6 SFTS 10.46- 5.47
6 FTS 5.47-11.47
APS Acklington 11.47- 9.48
To French Air Force 5.49

FX313
5(P)AFU 11.44- 6.45
19 FTS 6.45- 5.46
SOC 14.9.50
FX314
17 SFTS 8.44- 6.47
1 FTS 6.47- 8.47
614 Sqdn 8.47-11.49
desp. S. Rhodesia 6.51
5 FTS 9.51
u/c collapsed, Thornhill 20.5.53
FX315
9(P)AFU 9.44- 6.45
5(P)AFU 6.45- 4.46
SOC 9.3.51
Sold Hw spares
FX316
No RAF service
SOC 30.4.51
Sold Hw spares
FX317
No RAF service
SOC 23.8.50
FX318
2 FIS 7.44- 7.45
SOC 25.9.50
FX319
2 FIS 9.44
cr. on take-off from field 20.1.45*
FX320
2 FIS 10.44-10.44
9(P)AFU 10.44- 6.45
5(P)AFU 6.45-12.45
3 SFTS 12.45- 4.47
3 FTS 4.47
cr. off Norfolk coast 16.1.48
FX321
2 FIS 7.44- 9.44
9(P)AFU 9.44- 6.45
5(P)AFU 6.45- 1.46
Became 5771M 1.46
SOC 13.1.48
FX322
No RAF service
To French Air Force 5.49
FX323
No RAF service
To French Air Force 5.49
FX324
9(P)AFU 9.44- 6.45
5(P)AFU [BF] 6.45- 4.46
7 SFTS [FBC:W] 4.46- 1.48
7 FTS [FBA:M] 1.48- 3.54
Sold Hw spares 7.54
FX325
16 SFTS 8.44-11.45
17 SFTS 11.45- 6.47
1 FTS 6.47- 2.48
RAFC [FAA:L/A:L] 2.48- 4.54
Sold Hw spares 4.55
FX326
No RAF service
SOC 18.1.51
FX327
16 SFTS [2] 8.44-11.45
SOC 31.8.50
FX328
No RAF service
SOC 10.7.50
FX329
No RAF service
SOC 29.8.50
FX330
No RAF service
Sold Hw spares 4.51
FX331
17 SFTS [FCD:X] 8.44- 6.47
1 FTS 6.47- 7.47
SOC 25.8.50
FX332
9(P)AFU 9.44- 6.45
5(P)AFU 6.45-12.45
SOC 4.10.50

Blackness, Midlothian

FX333
2 FIS 7.44- 7.45
SOC 18.9.50
FX334
5(P)AFU 2.45- 4.46
7 SFTS 4.46-12.46
22 SFTS 12.46- 8.48
7 FTS [O:G] 11.50- 6.52
Camb. UAS 1.56- 6.56
Nott. UAS 6.56
cr. ldd. Kinloss 23.7.56
FX335
No service in UK
desp. S. Rhodesia 6.51
To SRAF 8.51
Retd. to RAF 4.53
5 FTS [57] 4.53- 8.53
4 FTS storage 8.53
Sold 12.53
FX336
9(P)AFU 9.44- 6.45
5(P)AFU 6.45-12.45
3 SFTS 12.45
SOC
BBOC 4.47
3 FTS 4.47- 6.47
RCCF/S 6.47-11.47
SOC 30.4.51
Sold Hw spares
FX337
ATA [5] 3.45-12.45
SOC 10.7.50
FX338
9(P)AFU 9.44
spun in, Lindores, Perth 13.10.44
FX339
2 FIS 2.45- 7.45
7 FIS 7.45- 5.46
CFS 5.46- 8.47
3 FTS 3.48- 7.48
RAFC 2.50- 7.50
22 FTS [FCJ:X/Y:F/R:Z] 5.51- 5.54
SS (AES) 12.56
FX340
5(P)AFU 12.44- 5.45
20/21 FTS 5.45- 3.46
21 FTS [FAN:J] 3.46- 8.46
17 SFTS [FCF:C] 8.46- 6.47
1 FTS 6.47- 2.48
RAFC [FAA:N/AN]2.48- 4.54
Sold Hw spares 4.55
FX341
No RAF service
To French Air Force 5.49
FX342
9(P)AFU 9.44- 6.45
5(P)AFU 6.45- 4.46
SOC 30.4.51
Sold Hw spares
FX343
9(P)AFU 9.44- 6.45
5(P)AFU [BV] 6.45- 4.46
7 SFTS 4.46- 8.47
RAFC 3.48-12.49
3 FTS 12.49- 3.55
SS (H. Bath) 3.57

Central Flying School's FX350 coded N:Z at Bristol (Whitchurch) in 1953 (J.J.Halley)

FX344
No RAF service
SOC 15.9.50
FX345
2 FIS 7.44- 7.45
SOC 9.3.51
Sold Hw spares
FX346
No RAF service
SOC 22.6.50
FX347
17 SFTS [FCD:Y] 8.44- 6.47
1 FTS 6.47- 7.47
desp. S. Rhodesia 3.51
5 FTS [G:83] 7.51- 8.53
4 FTS storage 8.53
Sold 31.12.53
FX348
No RAF service
SOC 20.7.50
FX349
17 SFTS 8.44-11.45
BAS 11.45- 4.46
SOC 15.5.46
FX350
5(P)AFU 11.44- 6.45
21 FTS 6.45- 8.46
17 SFTS 8.46- 6.47
1 FTS 6.47- 7.48
3 FTS [FBU:T] 7.48- 8.50
11 RFS 8.50-11.50
CFS [FDM:A/N:Z] 3.51- 7.54
Sold Hw spares 4.55
FX351
5(P)AFU 11.44- 4.46
7 SFTS 4.46- 8.46
1 FU 8.47- 5.48
22 RFS 6.50- 7.50
18 RFS 7.50- 8.50
11 RFS 8.50-11.50
6 FTS 4.51-11.53
Sold Hw spares 5.54
FX352
17 SFTS 8.44- 6.47
1 FTS 6.47- 1.48
6 FTS [FBH:F] 1.48
Overshot, Ternhill 30.10.50
FX353
9(P)AFU 9.44- 6.45
5(P)AFU 6.45- 4.46
7 SFTS 4.46- 8.46
SOC 20.10.50
FX354
A&AEE 5.44-10.45
SOC 30.4.51
Sold Hw spares
FX355
9(P)AFU 9.44- 6.45
5(P)AFU 6.45-12.45
43 OTU 9.46- 8.47
41 Sqdn 8.47-12.47
227 OCU 12.47- 4.49
Booker 6.50-10.50
1 FTS [N:J] 4.51
cr. ldd. ½ml S of Gt. Washbourne, Glos. 23.9.54
FX356
11(P)AFU 1.45- 6.45
20/21 FTS 6.45- 8.46
17 SFTS 8.46-11.46
21(P)AFU [FDA:T] 12.46- 8.47
1(P)RFU 8.47- 5.49
FRS 5.49- 4.51
101 FRS 4.51- 9.51
CFS [N:G] 9.51- 7.54
Sold Hw spares 4.55
FX357
9(P)AFU 9.44- 2.45
NTB 2.45- 6.45
To R.NorAF 11.45
FX358
5(P)AFU 11.44- 1.45
6 FTS 4.51- 9.53
CFS (B) 9.53- 7.54
SS (H.Bath) 3.57
FX359
9(P)AFU 9.44- 6.45
5(P)AFU 6.45- 4.46
7 SFTS 4.46-10.47
SOC 18.9.50
FX360
7 AAU 8.44-
41 OTU - 2.45
61 OTU [TO:P] 2.45- 7.47
203 AFS 7.47- 9.49
226 OCU 9.49- 6.50
614 Sqdn [7A:X] 6.50- 6.52
Aber. UAS 6.52-11.52
11 RFS 11.52- 5.53
22 RFS 5.53- 7.53
SS (Avex) 5.57
FX361
9(P)AFU 9.44- 6.45
5(P)AFU 6.45-12.45
3(P)AFU 12.45-12.45
3SFTS 12.45-10.46
7 SFTS 10.46- 7.47
SOC 30.4.51
Sold Hw spares
FX362
2 FTS 4.45- 3.46
20 FTS [FAI:D] 3.46- 7.47
2 FTS 7.47- 7.49
CFS (EW) 7.49- 3.50
CFS 3.50- 2.52
RAFC 2.52- 4.54
Sold Hw spares 5.54
FX363
No RAF service
SOC 28.8.50
FX364
5(P)AFU 9.44- 4.46
7 SFTS 4.46-10.47
SOC 10.7.50
FX365
RAE 12.44-
ETPS [1] (.46- .49)
SOC 28.2.54
FX366
9(P)AFU 9.44- 2.45
desp. FEAF 2.51
MAAF 4.51- 1.56
SOC 30.7.56
FX367
16 SFTS 8.44- 1.46
3 SFTS [FBR:E] 1.46- 4.47
3 FTS 4.47
cr. after engine failure, Wendling 9.6.47
FX368
16 SFTS 9.44-10.45
7 FIS 10.45- 5.46
CFS 5.46- 5.47
3 FTS [FBT:C] 5.47
cr. ldd. Feltwell 11.8.50
FX369
2 FIS 8.44- 7.45
7 FIS 7.45- 5.46
CFS [FDM:Z] 5.46- 5.47
3 FTS [FBT:D] 5.47- 1.55
SS (H.Bath) 3.57
FX370
9(P)AFU 9.44- 6.45
5(P)AFU [EK] 6.45- 4.46
RCCF [RAG:A] 6.47- 8.52
600 Sqdn 8.52- 8.53
SS (AES) 12.56
FX371
16 SFTS [52] 9.44-11.45
ETPS [11] 8.46-
A&AEE
spun in 2mls N of Amesbury 12.6.52
FX372
No RAF service
SOC 16.6.50
FX373
17 SFTS 8.44- 6.47
1 FTS 6.47- 7.47
A&AEE 9.49-12.49
desp. S. Rhodesia 11.50
5 FTS [G:43] 4.51
collidedwith FX431 in flypast, New Sarum,14.6.53
FX374
No RAF service
SOC 23.8.50
FX375
9(P)AFU 9.44- 6.45
5(P)AFU 6.45- 1.46
22 SFTS [FCJ:V] 1.46- 5.47
SOC 23.1.51
FX376
16 SFTS 9.44- 1.46
3 SFTS 1.46-10.46
7 SFTS [FBB:H] 10.46- 1.48
7 FTS 1.48-10.48
2 FTS [FAJ:F] 10.48- 7.49
CFS (EW) 7.49- 4.50
2 FTS 4.50- 4.51
101 FRS 4.51-10.51
SS (H.Bath) 3.57
FX377
17 FTS 7.44- 9.45
SOC 14.9.50
FX378
9(P)AFU 9.44- 6.45
5(P)AFU 6.45- 4.46
SOC 30.4.51
Sold Hw spares
FX379
16 SFTS [33] 8.44-10.45
7 FIS 10.45-
CFS - 8.48
RAFC [FAB:B] 8.48-12.49
3 FTS [FBU:P/R:E] 12.49
cr. on fire 4mls N of Littleport 30.8.54
FX380
No RAF service
SOC 22.6.50
FX381
16 SFTS [10] 8.44
collided with FT344 nr. Wroot, Yorks.,16.3.45
FX382
17 SFTS 7.44- 8.44
3 FIS [3] 8.44- 8.45
7 FIS [FDN:W] 8.45- 5.46
CFS 5.46- 5.47
6 FTS 5.47- 9.47
609 Sqdn [RAP:X] 4.48- 5.51
615 Sqdn 5.51-12.51
604 Sqdn 12.51- 3.52
SS (Av.Tr.) 6.57
FX383
23 APC
SOC 21.6.45
FX384
17 SFTS 7.44- 6.47
1 FTS 6.47
force-landed out of fuel, Werring-to, Northants 22.7.47
FX385
16 SFTS 8.44-11.45
3(P)AFU 11.45-12.45
3 SFTS 12.45- 4.47
3 FTS 4.47-10.47
2 FTS 10.47-10.50
103 FRS 5.51-12.51
3 FTS 12.51- 1.55
SS (H.Bath) 3.57
FX386
9(P)AFU 9.44- 6.45
5(P)AFU [HG] 6.45
DBR in accident 25.9.45
FX387
16 SFTS 8.44-11.45
601 Sqdn [RAH:U/HT:X] 7.46- 9.51
22 FTS 12.52-12.52
RAFC 12.52- 4.54
Sold Hw spares 6.54

FX388
9(P)AFU 11.44- 6.45
5(P)AFU 6.45- 4.46
7 SFTS [FBB:D] 4.46- 1.48
7 FTS [O:O] 1.48
collided with KF688 in formation and abandoned nr. Folkingham 17.10.52

FX389
16 SFTS 8.44-10.45
7 FIS [FDN:B] 10.45- 5.46
CFS 5.46- 5.47
FTCCF [FKN:B] 5.47
lost wings in spin nr. Blackbushe 14.12.50

FX390
1 Sqdn 3.46-10.48
FCITF 10.48- 1.49
Oxf. UAS 6.50-10.50
609 Sqdn 3.51- 4.52
Camb. UAS 4.52-11.52
22 RFS 11.52- 3.54
Camb. UAS [C] 3.54- 4.57
SS (AES) 9.57

FX391
2 FIS 7.44- 7.45
7 FIS [FDM:G] 7.45- 5.46
CFS 5.46- 9.51
CFS (B) [O:P] 9.51- 8.54
Sold Hw spares 3.55

FX392
No RAF service
SOC 30.4.51
Sold Hw spares

FX393
25 RFS 6.50- 7.50
desp. S. Rhodesia 6.51
4 FTS 5.52- 6.52
1340 Flt 5.53
cr. 60mls N of Mt. Kipipiri, Kenya, 25.2.55

FX394
18 EFTS 7.44- 1.46
22 SFTS [FCI:Q] 1.46- 3.48
2 FTS 7.49- 2.51
1 FTS [FCB:L] 2.51-10.51
22 FTS [U:E] 10.51
SOC after damage 2.10.53

FX395
16 SFTS 9.44-11.45
17 SFTS 11.45-11.46
CFS 11.46-12.46
21(P)AFU [FDD:N/FDA:S] 12.46- 8.47
1(P)RFU 8.47- 5.49
FRS 5.49- 7.50
1 FTS 6.51- 1.55
Nott. UAS 1.55- 5.57
SS (Av.Tr.) 10.57

FX396
No RAF service
SOC 27.6.50

FX397
5(P)AFU 11.44- 4.45
7 SFTS 4.45- 1.48
7 FTS [FBB:B] 1.48- 9.50
2 FTS 9.50-12.50
CFS 12.50- 5.51
7 FTS [O:J] 5.51- 1.53
22 FTS 1.53- 7.53
9 FTS 7.53- 4.54
Sold Hw spares 3.55

FX398
No RAF service
PSOC 21.6.47

FX399
9(P)AFU 9.44- 6.45
5(P)AFU 6.45-10.45
7 SFTS 10.45- 7.46
601 Sqdn [RAH:V/H:V] 1.47- 6.49
desp. S. Rhodesia 3.51
5 FTS 6.51- 7.51
4 FTS 7.51- 1.52
5 FTS 1.52- 8.53
4 FTS storage 8.53
Sold 12.53

FX400
9(P)AFU 11.44- 6.45
5(P)AFU 6.45- 4.46
7 SFTS [FBB:G] 4.46- 1.48
7 FTS 1.48- 5.48
CFS 5.48-12.49
6 FTS [FBH:J] 12.49
cr. 2½mls N of Stone, Staffs10.3.50

FX401
India: no record of use
To IAF 9.47

FX402
17 SFTS [FCE:I] 3.45- 6.47
1 FTS 6.47- 7.47
ETPS 7.47-
A&AEE - 1.49
6 FTS 11.50
cr. ldd. Ternhill 4.12.51

FX403
3 FIS [8] 8.44- 8.45
7 FIS 8.45- 5.46
CFS [FDN:Y] 5.46-10.53
9 FTS 10.53- 4.54
SS (Avex) 5.57

FX404
No RAF service
SOC 29.8.50

FX405
Crashed in USA before delivery

FX406
5(P)AFU [H:L] 2.45-
SOC 30.4.51

FX407
2 FIS 10.44-
9(P)AFU
5(P)AFU 6.45- 4.46
7 SFTS 4.46- 8.46
SOC 25.9.50

FX408
5(P)AFU 11.44- 6.45
21 FTS 6.45- 9.46
SOC 4.10.50

FX409
No RAF service
SOC 3.7.50

FX432 of No.500 Squadron carrying that unit's fuselage markings and code R in the early fifties (via R.C.Sturtivant)

Seen at Wellingore early in 1947 is No.19 FTS's FX441 *(Sqn Ldr Middlebrook via B.Goulding)*

FX410
16 SFTS [64] 9.44-11.45
23 Gp. CF 11.45-12.45
610 Sqdn [RAQ:X/DW:X] 8.46-10.53
SOC 30.12.53
FX411
17 SFTS 8.44- 4.46
1 Sqdn [JX:K] 9.47- 8.48
RCITF 8.48- 8.49
and 12.49-12.50
61 Gp. CF 5.51- 6.51
6 FTS 6.51- 8.51
desp. FEAF 1.53
FECS 3.53- 1.55
MAAF 9.56- 5.57
SOC 10.5.57
FX412
19 FTS 5.45
cr. in sea off Theddlethorpe ranges Lincs., 4.4.46
FX413
9(P)AFU 9.44- 6.45
5(P)AFU 6.45-12.45
22 SFTS 12.45- 6.46
To RHellAF 5.47
FX414
5(P)AFU 2.45- 5.45
19 FTS [FAB:E] 5.45- 4.47
RAFC 4.47-10.47
To Belg.AF 9.49
FX415
16 SFTS [61] 9.44-11.45
SOC 14.9.50
FX416
3 FIS [5] 8.44- 8.45
7 FIS 8.45- 1.46
3 SFTS 1.46- 9.46
1 Sqdn [JX:H] 9.47- 8.48
ITF Tangmere 8.48- 1.49
desp. S. Rhodesia 3.51
5 FTS 7.51
cr. 1½mls S of Indiva, SR, 1.7.52
FX417
16 SFTS 8.44-11.45
23 Gp. CF 11.45-12.45
614 Sqdn [7A:Y] 9.46- 7.54
SS (AES) 12.56

FX418
19 FTS 5.45- 5.46
SOC 18.9.50
FX419
8 RFS 6.50-10.50
1 FTS 12.50- 7.53
CFS [M:P] 7.53- 9.54
SS (Avex) 5.57
FX420
16 SFTS 9.44-11.45
23 Gp. CF [FKP:P] 11.45- 9.47
SF Halton 9.47- 1.49
501 Sqdn [RAB:C/SD:C] 12.49- 6.52
Oxf. UAS 6.52- 7.52
desp. FEAF 7.53
MAAF 9.53-
Lost part of wing and cr., Jugra, Malaya, 7.8.54
FX421
2 FTS 4.45- 3.46
21 FTS 3.46- 9.46
To R.Hell.AF 5.47
FX422
9(P)AFU 9.44- 6.45
5(P)AFU 6.45-12.45
SOC 10.5.46
FX423
16 SFTS 9.44-11.45
SOC 14.9.50
FX424
No RAF service
PSOC 21.6.47
FX425
2 FIS 10.44-
9(P)AFU
5(P)AFU 6.45-10.45
6(P)AFU 10.45-12.45
6 SFTS 12.45- 6.46
RCCF 6.47- 2.48
600 Sqdn 2.48-10.48
604 Sqdn 10.48- 7.52
Camb. UAS 7.52-11.52
22 RFS 11.52- 3.53
Queens UAS [I] 3.53- 2.56
Nott. UAS 2.56- 6.56
Leeds UAS 6.56- 7.56
Nott. UAS 7.56- 5.57
SS (Av.Tr.) 10.57

FX426
No RAF service
SOC 16.6.50
FX427
16 SFTS 9.44-12.45
7 SFTS 12.45- 8.46
613 Sqdn [RAT:2] 8.46- 3.50
610 Sqdn [RAQ:X]
22 FTS [R:K] 1.51- 9.54
SS (Avex) 5.57
FX428
9(P)AFU 9.44- 6.45
5(P)AFU 6.45- 4.46
7 SFTS [FBD:D] 4.46- 1.48
7 FTS 1.48- 4.49
22 RFS 6.50- 7.50
18 RFS 7.50- 8.50
11 RFS 8.50-10.50
6 FTS 5.51
hit ground inverted during Battle of Britain display, Thornaby15.9.51
FX429
5(P)AFU 11.44- 6.45
21 FTS 6.45- 9.46
SOC 25.8.50
FX430
No RAF service
SOC 12.6.50
FX431
No service in UK
desp. S. Rhodesia 12.50
5 FTS [58] 4.51
collided with FX373 in flypast, New Sarum 14.6.53
FX432
5(P)AFU 11.44- 5.45
19 FTS [FAB:B] 5.45- 9.47
500 Sqdn [RAA:R/R] 4.48-10.53
SS (AES) 5.57
FX433
5(P)AFU 11.44- 4.45
7 SFTS 4.45
DBR in accident 8.6.45

FX434
16 SFTS 9.44-11.44
6(P)AFU 11.44-12.45
6 SFTS 12.45- 5.47
6 FTS [FBG:B] 5.47-11.50
1 FTS 11.50-10.51
CFS [FDO:L] 10.51
cr. on take-off, S. Cerney 22.6.53

FX435
No service in UK
desp. S. Rhodesia 12.50
5 FTS 4.51- 8.53
4 FTS storage 8.53-12.53
Sold 12.53

FX436
16 SFTS 9.44-11.45
3(P)AFU 11.45-12.45
3 SFTS 12.45-12.46
22 SFTS [FCJ:C] 12.46- 2.49
22 FTS 2.49- 9.50
2 FTS 9.50-11.50
1 FTS 11.50- 2.52
desp. FEAF 11.52
SF Seletar 1.53- 5.53
MAAF Singapore Ftr. Sqdn 5.53-10.53
SF Tengah 10.53- 9.55
MAAF 9.55- 5.57
SOC 11.12.57

FX437
19 FTS [FAB:T] 5.45- 4.47
RAFC 4.47- 8.47
2(P)RFU 8.47- 3.48
3 FTS [FBT:J] 3.48-12.49
RAFC [FAB:J/B:J] 12.49- 7.52
22 FTS [R:B] 7.52-12.53
SOC 7.4.54

FX438
11(P)AFU 1.45- 5.45
17 SFTS 5.45- 6.47
CFS 6.47-11.50
collided with FX301 on approach to Moreton-in-Marsh 26.4.51

FX439
No RAF service
SOC 23.8.50

FX440
5(P)AFU 11.44- 6.45
21 FTS [FAP:J] 6.45- 9.46
SOC 31.8.50

FX441
5(P)AFU 12.44- 5.45
19 FTS [HN/FAD:Z] 5.45- 4.47
RAFC [FAD:Z] 4.47-10.47
SOC 4.10.50

FX442
61 OTU 2.45- 7.47
203 AFS 7.47- 8.49
226 OCU [TO:M] 8.49-12.50
501 Sqdn [SD:B] 12.50-11.53
SS (Avex) 12.56

FX443
41 OTU 8.44- 2.45
61 OTU 2.45- 7.47
203 AFS 7.47- 9.49
226 OCU [TO:J] 9.49- 4.50
20 Sqdn 4.50-11.51
SS (Av.Tr.) 6.57

FX444
16 SFTS 9.44-12.45
7 SFTS 12.45-12.47
RAFC [FAA:D] 12.47-11.49
3 FTS 11.49
hit windsock on take-off, Feltwell, 19.6.50

FX445
India: no record of use
To IAF 9.47

FX446
No RAF service
SOC 28.8.50

FX447
India: no record of use
To IAF 9.47

FX448
India: no record of use
To IAF 9.47

FX449
India: no record of use
SOC 26.4.45

FX450
EFS [FCT:H] 2.49- 6.49
EAAS 6.49- 8.49
desp. S. Rhodesia
5 FTS 6.52- 6.53
RATG CF 6.53- 8.53
4 FTS storage 8.53-12.53
Sold 12.53

FX451
3 RFU
20 Sqdn (.46- .47)

FX452
19 FTS 5.45- 5.46
SOC 30.4.51
Sold Hw spares

FX453
No RAF service
SOC 12.6.50

FX454
India: no record of use
To IAF 9.47

FX455
117 Wg. CF
To IAF 9.47

FX456
India: no record of use
To Pak.AF 9.47

FX457
India: no record of use
To Pak.AF 9.47

FX458
India: no record of use
To IAF 9.47

FX459
129 Sqdn 4.46-10.46
SF Church Fenton 10.46- 5.47
SF Horsham St. Faith 5.47- 8.47
695 Sqdn 8.47- 8.47
41 Sqdn 8.47-10.47
SF Horsham St.Faith 10.47-12.47
41 Sqdn 12.47- 9.48
HCEU 2.53- 4.54
19 RFS 4.54- 5.54
Liv. UAS 5.54
cr. ldd. Woodvale 6.4.56

FX460
India: no record of use
To IAF 9.47

FX461
27 Sqdn
SOC 12.7.45

FX462
232 Gp. CS (11.44-1.46)
SOC 25.9.47

FX463
4 Sqdn RIAF
SOC 31.12.46

FX464
India; no record of use
To IAF 9.47

FX465
22 APC
3(I)Gp. CF
SOC 1.6.47

FX466
19 FTS [DK] 5.45-10.46
To Belg.AF 9.49

FX467
No RAF service
SOC 10.7.50

FX468
19 FTS [BM/FAD:X] 5.45-12.46
21(P)AFU [FDD:C] 12.46- 8.47
2(P)RFU 8.47- 3.48
1(P)RFU 3.48
hit building on approach, Finningley, 24.11.48

FX469
Lon. UAS 6.50- 7.50
7 FTS [FBA:A] 2.51- 1.53
22 FTS 1.53- 7.53
9 FTS 7.53- 3.54
Sold Hw spares 6.54

FX470
19 FTS [FH] 5.45- 7.47
1 FTS 7.47- 2.48
CFS [FDM:W/N:I/M:J]2.48- 7.54
Sold Hw spares 3.55

FX471
India: no record of use
desp. to FE 3.47
desp. to ME 11.47
SOC 27.5.48

FX472
AFS (I)
To IAF 9.47

FX473
India: no record of use
To IAF 9.47

FX474
117 Sqdn (1.45-7.45)
SOC 25.3.48

FX475
SF Redhills Lake
hit wires on landing and lost u/c, Redhills Lake, 4.2.45

FX476
52 Sqdn
81 Sqdn
SF Tengah 6.48- 5.53
MAAF Singapore Ftr. Sqdn 5.53- 1.54
desp. FE
SF Kai Tak 11.55- 9.56
HKAAF 9.56
cr. ldd. and DBR, Kai Tak 26.1.57

FX477
India: no record of service
desp. FE 3.47
desp. ME 11.47
SOC 27.5.48

FX478
SLAIS (2.45- 4.45)
To IAF 9.47

FX479
India: no record of service
desp. FE 3.47
84 Sqdn 1.48- 6.48
FECS 6.48- 3.50
FEAFExS 3.50- 5.51
FEAFTrS 5.51-10.52
SF Seletar 10.52
DBR in take-off accident, Seletar, 8.2.56

FX480
India; no record of service
desp. FE 3.47
FECS 8.48-11.52
SF Negombo 11.52- 7.57
SOC 29.7.57

FX481
India: no record of service
SOC 30.5.46

FX482
BAFSEA CS
AHQ India CF
To IAF 9.47

FX483
India: no record of service
desp. FE 3.47
FECS 7.48- 7.51
MAAF Penang Ftr. Sqdn 11.51
cr. in sea 5mls WNW of Palautikus, Malaya, during aerobatics 18.5.52

FX484
BAFSEA CS
AHQ India CF
SOC 26.9.46

FX485
India: no record of service
To Pak.AF 9.47

FX486
BAFSEA CS (5.45)
AHQ India CF (3.46- 8.46)
To IAF 9.47

FX487
India: no record of service
desp. FE 3.47
SOC 26.2.48
FX488
India: no record of service
desp. FE 3.47
FECS 6.48- 3.50
FEAFExS 3.50- 5.51
FEAFTrS 5.51- 3.52
SF Kai Tak 11.52- 9.56
HKAAF 9.56- 1.58
SOC 9.1.58
FX489
221 Gp.CF
cr. ldd. 29mls S of Imphal 10.3.45
FX490
117 Wg.CF
To IAF 9.47
FX491
HQ RAF Burma CS - 7.45
27 Sqdn 7.45-
SOC 31.12.46
FX492
India: no record of service
To IAF 9.47
FX493
India: no record of service
desp. FE 3.47
SF Kai Tak 5.48- 5.55
SOC 11.5.55
FX494
India: no record of service
desp. FE 3.47
desp. ME 11.47
SOC 27.5.48
FX495
India: no record of service
desp. FE 3.47
FECS 6.48- 3.50
FEAFExS 3.50-11.50
MAAF 7.51- 1.57
SOC 28.6.57
FX496
BAFSEA CS
84 Sqdn
81 Sqdn 9.48- 4.49
FECS 4.49-11.52
MAAF Singapore Ftr. Sqdn 3.53
cr. ldd. Seletar 13.8.56
FX497
BAFSEA CS - 3.46
AHQ India CS 3.46-
To Pak.AF 9.47

****

KE305
RN: no record of service
KE306
738 Sqdn 2.43-
cr. near Greylock Mtn., Mass., USA 8.5.43
KE307
738 Sqdn 2.43-
cr. Boxrah, Conn., USA, 30.3.43
KE308
RN: no record of service
KE309
738 Sqdn
cr. ldd. Quonset 19.9.43

****

KF100
3 RFU
To IAF 9.47
KF101
India: no record of service
To IAF 9.47
KF102
India: no record of service
To IAF 9.47
KF103
India: no record of service
desp. FE 3.47
84 Sqdn 1.48- 3.48
28 Sqdn 3.48- 4.48
SF Sembawang 4.48- 5.48
28 Sqdn 5.48-
SOC 13.10.52
KF104
India: no record of service
desp. FE 3.47
SF Seletar
FECS 9.48-
SOC 16.11.50
KF105
India: no record of service
desp. FE 3.47
BC Air CS 9.47
SOC 3.12.47
KF106
42 Sqdn
Damaged by Spitfire and cr.ldd., nr. Meiktila, 14.2.45
KF107
42 Sqdn
desp. FE 3.47
27 APC
60 Sqdn 3.50- 6.50
27 APC 6.50- 9.50
SF Butterworth 9.50- 9.54
MAAF 10.54- 3.55
SF Butterworth 3.55-
SOC 2.1.57
KF108
42 Sqdn
PSOC 1.1.47
KF109
261 Sqdn
Collided with Thunderbolt KJ325 and crashed, Myingyan, 25.4.45
KF110
India: no record of service
To Pak.AF 9.47
KF111
India: no record of service
desp. FE 7.44
BC Air CS 3.47-
SOC 25.3.48
KF112
India: no record of service
desp. FE 3.47
FECS 7.48- 5.51
MAAF 10.51-12.55
SOC 30.4.57
KF113
India: no record of service
desp. FE
BC Air CS 3.47-
To RNZAF 6.48
KF114
India: no record of service
cr. on take-off, Kohat, 5.5.47
KF115
India: no record of service
To IAF 9.47
KF116
India: no record of service
To Pak.AF 9.47
KF117
India: no record of service
To IAF 9.47
KF118
11 Sqdn
SOC 25.9.47
KF119
20 Sqdn
To IAF 9.47
KF120
India: no record of service
SOC 11.7.46
KF121
India: no record of service
To IAF 9.47
KF122
1 SFTS (I)
To IAF 9.47
KF123
India: no record of service
To IAF 9.47
KF124
225 Gp. CS 9.45-
SOC 27.6.46
KF125
India: no record of service
To Pak.AF 9.47
KF126
India: no record of service
desp. FE
209 Sqdn
SF Seletar 6.48- 3.50
FEAFExS 3.50- 5.50
FECS 8.50- 3.52
FEAF CS 6.52-
267 Sqdn 2.54
cr. ldd. Butterworth 3.5.55
Allocated 7229M but n.t.u.
KF127
16 SFTS 9.44-10.45
7 FIS 10.45- 5.46
CFS [FDM:A] 5.46-12.48
6 FTS [FBJ:I] 12.48
Collided with FS753 and cr. 3mls N of Ledbury, 18.5.51
KF128
5(P)AFU 2.45- 5.45
21 FTS [FAN:P] 5.45- 9.46
FTC CF 9.46- 1.47
41 Sqdn 9.47- 7.48
691 Sqdn 7.48- 2.49
17 Sqdn 2.49- 4.50
22 FTS [Y:D][R:C] 2.51- 9.54
SS (AES) 12.56
KF129
India: no record of service
desp. FE
1315 Flt
SF Iwakuni <u>or</u> BC Air CS 1.48-
SOC 25.3.48
KF130
22 FTS [U:V] 1.51
cr. ldd. Syerston 19.5.54
KF131
India: no record of service
desp. FE
1315 Flt
SOC 24.6.48
KF132
India: no record of service
desp. FE 3.47
SF Sembawang 8.47- 5.49
60 Sqdn 5.49- 2.51
MAAF 2.51-
SOC 19.2.57
KF133
CFS [N:Y] 2.51- 7.54
SS (Avex) 4.57
KF134
India: no record of service
desp. FE
HK CS 9.46- 3.47
BC Air CS 3.47-
SOC 24.6.48
KF135
India: no record of service
To IAF 9.47
KF136
9(P)AFU 9.44- 7.45
SOC 25.8.50
KF137
India: no record of service
To IAF 9.47

KF138
16 SFTS 8.44- 1,46
3 SFTS [FBT:Q] 1.46- 4.47
3 FTS 4.47
cr. in sea 12mls N of Kings Lynn, 17.10.52
KF139
India: no record of service
desp UK
5(P)AFU 2.45- 6.45
19 FTS [FAA:H] 6.45- 8.47
2(P)RFU 8.47- 3.48
1(P)RFU [FDA:O] 3.48- 5.49
3 FTS 5.49- 7.49
2 FTS [FAI:C] 7.49- 1.50
22 FTS [U:Q] 1.50- 8.54
SS (Avex) 4.57
KF140
ATA 7.44- 5.45
19 FTS [HM] 9.45- 4.47
RAFC [FAD:Y] 4.47
Abandoned out of fuel, Brant Broughton, Lincs., 4.11.49
KF141
India: no record of service
desp. FE 3.47
27 APC
45 Sqdn 7.49- 8.49
267 Sqdn [D] 5.55- 3.57
SOC 9.4.57
KF142
16 SFTS [45] 9.44-11.45
6(P)AFU 11.45-12.45
6 SFTS [FBG:J] 12.45-12.49
CFS [FDM:B] 12.49- 4.51
7 FTS [N:J] 4.51- 2.53
CFS 2.53-
SOC 24.3.54
KF143
India: no record of service
desp. FE 3.47
27 APC
33 Sqdn 2.50- 7.50
SF Seletar 12.50-10.52
MAAF 1.53- 9.54
SF Butterworth 9.54- 3.55
MAAF 3.55- 1.57
SOC 4.57
KF144
India: no record of service
To Pak.AF 9.47
KF145
16 SFTS 8.44- 1.46
3 SFTS [FBU:H] 1.46- 4.47
3 FTS 4.47-11.47
605 Sqdn [RAL:M/P] 5.48-10.53
SS (AES) 5.57
KF146
No RAF service
SOC 28.4.49
KF147
No RAF service
SOC 30.4.51
Sold Hw spares
KF148
16 SFTS [44] 9.44-11.45
6(P)AFU 11.45- 3.46
6 SFTS 3.46- 5.47
6 FTS 5.47- 7.47
RAFC [FAA:X/AX] 3.48- 4.54
SS (AES) 12.56
KF149
16 SFTS [24] 8.44-11.45
614 Sqdn [RAU:2] 9.46-10.53
SS (H.Bath) 3.57
KF150
CFS [N:T] 7.51-11.53
SOC 30.12.53
KF151
601 Sqdn [RAH:S/HT:Z] 7.47- 1.53
desp. Kenya
1340 Flt 8.54- 9.55
SOC 23.3.56
KF152
16 SFTS 9.44-11.45
SOC 25.9.50
KF153
16 SFTS [41] 8.44- 1.46
3 SFTS 1.46- 4.47
3 FTS [FBU:G] 4.47- 7.48
7 FTS [FBA:H][P:A] 3.50- 1.53
22 FTS 1.53- 7.53
9 FTS 7.53-
Sold Hw spares 6.54
KF154
16 SFTS [25] 8.44-11.45
SOC 4.10.50
KF155
17 SFTS 10.44- 9.45
3 SFTS 2.46-12.46
22 SFTS 12.46- 6.47
695 Sqdn [8Q:6] 4.48- 2.49
34 Sqdn 2.49- 6.49
London UAS 7.50-
23 RFS
501 Sqdn 10.50- 1.51
502 Sqdn 1.51- 8.51
504 Sqdn 8.51-
SS (AES) 12.56
KF156
2 FIS 4.45- 7.45
7 FIS 7.45- 6.47
7 SFTS [FBB:V] 6.47- 1.48
7 FTS 1.48- 6.48
2 FTS [FAI:C] 6.48- 7.49
CFS(EW) [FDM:B] 7.49- 5.50
3 FTS [FBU:O/P:L] 5.50- 2.55
SS (Avex) 4.57

KF183, one of the venerable Boscombe Down Harvard IIb's *(G.J.Cruickshank)*

KF157
ATA 7.44- 5.45
6 FTS [FBJ:N/O:U] 1.49- 1.54
SS (AES) 5.57
KF158
No RAF service
SOC 18.1.51
KF159
5(P)AFU 2.45- 4.46
SOC 26.4.51
Sold Hw spares
KF160
19 FTS [HF] 5.45- 6.47
1 FTS [FCE:V] 6.47-10.47
605 Sqdn [RAL:O/NR:D] 4.48- 2.52
Man. UAS 5.54
cr. ldd. Woodvale 11.1.55
KF161
20 FTS 3.46- 7.47
2 FTS 7.47- 8.47
3 FTS [FBT:F] 8.47
cr. on landing, Feltwell, 8.4.48
KF162
16 SFTS 9.44- 1.46
3 SFTS [FBS:D] 1.46- 4.47
3 FTS 4.47- 1.52
22 FTS 1.53- 7.53
9 FTS 7.53- 4.54
SS (AES) 9.57
KF163
ATA 8.44- 5.45
2 FTS 11.48- 1.50
22 FTS [FCI:R] 1.50- 5.54
Sold Hw spares 7.54
KF164
16 SFTS 8.44- 9.44
SOC 8.9.44
KF165
16 SFTS 9.44-11.45
6(P)AFU 11.45-12.45
6 SFTS [FBG:K] 12.45- 5.47
6 FTS [O:E] 5.47- 2.54
2 FTS 2.54- 6.54
SS (AES) 5.57
KF166
66 Gp. CF 6.49- 3.50
desp. S. Rhodesia 3.51
5 FTS 5.51
cr. 17mls S of Thornhill, 31.3.53
KF167
No RAF service
SOC 12.9.50
KF168
No RAF service
SOC 9.3.51
KF169
CFS 11.50- 9.51
CFS(B) [O:A/N:A] 9.51-10.54
Sold Hw spares 4.55
KF170
19 FTS [FAA:J] 5.45- 4.47
RAFC 4.47-10.47
SOC 12.9.50
KF171
No RAF service
SOC 3.7.50
KF172
CFS [N:W] 2.51- 1.55
SS (Avex) 4.57
KF173
9(P)AFU 9.44- 6.45
5(P)AFU 6.45-11.45
22 SFTS [FCI:B] 11.45- 2.49
22 FTS 2.49
Iced up and abandoned, Swinford, Warwicks., 8.3.51
KF174
11(P)AFU 1.45- 5.45
17 SFTS 5.45- 6.47
1 FTS 6.47- 7.47
SOC 4.10.50
KF175
ATA 9.44-10.45
SOC 14.2.51

KF176
No RAF service
SOC 26.4.51
Sold Hw spares
KF177
A&AEE
ETPS .44-12.45
16 FU 9.46-11.46
1 FU 11.46-
Pershore - 4.48
3 FTS [FBT:B/R:G] 3.50
cr. 6mls NW of Edzell, 7.9.54
KF178
No RAF service
SOC 26.4.51
Sold Hw spares
KF179
11(P)AFU 1.45- 7.45
20 FTS [FAJ:R] 6.45- 1.50
22 FTS [FCI:K] 1.50- 9.50
2 FTS 9.50
engine cut on approach to Kemble, 23.10.50
KF180
No RAF service
SOC 26.4.51
Sold Hw spares
KF181
No RAF service
SOC 14.2.51
KF182
5(P)AFU 2.45- 5.45
19 FTS [DC] 5.45- 6.47
17 SFTS 6.47- 6.47
1 FTS 6.47- 2.48
CFS [FDM:H] 2.48- 1.50
6 FTS 1.50- 1.54
SS (AES) 5.57
KF183
7(P)AFU 12.44-12.44
7 SFTS 12.44-10.45
3 SFTS [FBU:L] 2.46- 4.47
3 FTS 4.47-11.47
ATDU 11.47-
A&AEE -pres.
KF184
5(P)AFU 4.45- 6.45
ORTU
SOC 24.7.50
KF185
9(P)AFU 3.45- 6.45
5(P)AFU [B:N] 6.45-10.45
7 FIS 10.45- 6.47
7 SFTS [FBD:O] 6.47- 1.48
7 FTS [FBA:Q] 1.48- 4.53
2 FTS 4.53- 5.54
1 FTS 5.54- 2.55
SS (AES) 5.57
KF186
19 FTS 5.45- 8.47
2(P)RFU 8.47- 3.48
1(P)RFU 3.48- 5.49
FRS 5.49-10.51
22 RFS 6.53- 3.54
Camb. UAS 3.54-11.55
London UAS 11.55-10.56
SS(Av.Tr.) 6.57
KF187
5(P)AFU [11] 9.44- 4.45
7 SFTS 4.45- 5.46
SOC 26.4.51
Sold Hw spares
KF188
6 FTS [O:D] 11.50- 9.53
CFS(B) 9.53- 8.54
SS (AES) 9.57
KF189
No RAF service
To R.Hell.AF 8.49
KF190
No RAF service
SOC 22.6.50
KF191
11(P)AFU 1.45- 6.45
20 FTS 6.45- 1.47
19 FTS [FAB:H] 1.47- 8.47
3 FTS [FBU:C] 8.47-11.49
RAFC [FAB:O/B:O] 11.49- 4.54
Sold Hw spares 5.54
KF192
11(P)AFU 12.44- 5.45
2 FTS [FAJ:L] 5.45- 3.46
20 FTS [FAJ:L] 3.46- 7.47
2 FTS [FAJ:L] 7.47- 9.48
RAFC [FAB:C] 9.48
cr. during aerobatics, Cranwell, 11.9.51
KF193
9(P)AFU 9.44- 6.45
5(P)AFU 6.45-11.45
22 SFTS 11.45- 7.46
607 Sqdn [RAN:C/LA:C] 7.47-10.53
Sold Hw spares 5.54
KF194
9(P)AFU 9.44- 6.45
5(P)AFU 6.45-12.45
3 SFTS [FBR:C] 12.45
cr. on overshoot, Feltwell, 8.9.47
KF195
22 FTS [FCI:J] 3.50- 8.54
SS (AES) 12.56
KF196
ATA [4] 8.44- 4.46
SOC 24.7.50
KF197
5(P)AFU 12.44- 5.45
19 FTS [EF] 5.45- 1.46
6 SFTS 1.46- 5.47
6 FTS 5.47- 8.47
22 FTS [FCJ:P/U:I/R:W] 4.49
SOC after damage 15.9.53
KF198
2 FIS 4.45- 7.45
7 FIS 7.45- 8.46
20 FTS 8.46- 7.47
2 FTS [FAJ:M] 7.47-10.48
Booker 6.50- 8.50
11 RFS 8.50-10.50
22 FTS 3.51- 8.51
3 FTS 8.51-12.54
SS (AES) 12.56
KF199
No RAF service
SOC 3.7.50
KF200
11(P)AFU 12.44- 5.45
17 SFTS 5.45- 6.47
1 FTS 6.47- 7.47
615 Sqdn [RAV:X/V6:X] 7.47- 3.52
Camb. UAS 5.52-11.52
22 RFS 11.52
cr. 3mls E of Waterbeach, 2.6.53
KF201
41 OTU 8.44- 1.45
61 OTU 1.45- 7.47
203 AFS [TO:R] 7.47- 9.49
226 OCU 9.49- 9.51
600 Sqdn [B] 9.51- 8.53
SS (Avex) 5.57
KF202
11(P)AFU 12.44- 6.45
21 FTS 6.45- 9.46
SOC 25.9.50
KF203
No RAF service
To R.Hell.AF 7.49
KF204
11(P)AFU 12.44- 4.45
22 FTS [R:F] 1.51- 4.54
SS (Avex) 5.57
KF205
11(P)AFU 12.44
DBR in accident 29.4.45

Code letter LA:C replaced Reserve Command code RAN:C on No.607 Squadron Harvard KF193 in 1951. Note the Tempest behind the Harvard in this air-show picture *(via R.C.Sturtivant)*

KF206
11(P)AFU 12.44- 5.45
7 FIS 5.45- 5.46
CFS [FDM:F] 5.46- 6.47
7 SFTS [FBD:N] 6.47- 6.48
2 FTS [FAI:F] 6.48- 2.51
1 FTS 2.51- 3.55
SS (Avex) 5.57

KF207
11(P)AFU 1.45- 5.45
19 FTS [GB/FAD:A] 5.45- 5.47
To Belg.AF 9.49

KF208
41 OTU 8.44- 1.45
61 OTU 1.45
cr. Wootton Bassett, 27.6.46

KF209
9(P)AFU 9.44-10.44
2 FIS 10.44- 6.45
19 FTS 6.45- 7.45
22 SFTS [FCI:Z] 2.46- 2.49
22 FTS 2.49- 7.53
9 FTS 7.53-12.54
Became 7116M 12.54

KF210
No RAF service
SOC 20.7.50

KF211
11(P)AFU 1.45- 6.45
20 FTS 6.45- 3.46
21 FTS 3.46- 8.46
17 SFTS 8.46-
CFS -12.46
21(P)AFU 12.46- 7.47
1(P)RFU 7.47- 3.48
FRS 3.50-10.51
CFS [N:Q] 10.51
Spun in, 3½mls N of Naunton, Glos., 4.2.53

KF212
41 OTU 8.44- 5.45
61 OTU 5.45- 7.47
203 AFS [TO:G] 7.47
cr. in sea 3mls N of Lynmouth, 16.1.48

KF213
16 SFTS 10.44- 6.45
19 FTS 6.45-11.45
SOC 25.8.50

KF214
5(P)AFU 9.44- 6.45
2 FTS 6.45- 7.45
7 FIS 7.45- 3.46
20 FTS 3.46- 1.47
19 FTS [FAB:R] 1.47- 4.47
RAFC [B:R] 4.47-
CFS - 3.54
Sold Hw spares 6.54

KF215
11(P)AFU 1.45- 5.45
19 FTS [H:D] 5.45- 4.47
RAFC 4.47-10.47
SOC 26.4.51

KF216
3 Sqdn 3.49- 8.50
6 FTS [P:C] 6.51- 9.53
SS (AES) 5.57

KF217
17 SFTS 10.44- 9.45
SOC 4.10.50

KF218
No RAF service
SOC 10.7.50

KF219
5(P)AFU 1.45- 4.45
7 SFTS 4.45
Hit control van on take-off, Kirton-in-Lindsey, 17.9.46

KF220
5(P)AFU 9.44- 4.46
7 SFTS 4.46-10.47
22 SFTS 10.47-12.47
RAFC [FAA:A] 12.47-11.49
3 FTS [FBT:H] 11.49- 4.55
SS (AES) 5.57

KF221
9(P)AFU 9.44- 6.45
5(P)AFU [EP] 6.45- 3.46
22 SFTS 3.46- 2.49
22 FTS [FCI:C] 2.49-12.50
1 FTS 6.51
DBR when it hit tree, 4.9.53

KF222
ME: no record of service
SOC 18.8.49

KF223
611 Sqdn [RAR:Y] 10.46-12.50
desp. S. Rhodesia 11.51
4 FTS 4.52- 6.52
1340 Flt 6.53
cr. Aberdare Forest, Kenya, 19.1.54

KF224
5(P)AFU 9.44- 4.46
7 SFTS [FBC:C] 4.46- 1.48
7 FTS [FBA:V] 1.48- 9.50
2 FTS [FAI:P] 9.50- 2.51
1 FTS [N:V/P:U] 2.51- 3.55
SS (Avex) 5.57

KF225
No RAF service
SOC 26.4.51
Sold Hw spares

KF226
5(P)AFU 12.44- 4.45
7 SFTS 4.45- 8.46
AFEE 10.48-
SOC 19.10.50

KF227
41 OTU 8.44-10.44
61 OTU 10.44- 7.47
203 AFS 7.47- 9.49
226 OCU [TO:S] 9.49- 8.50
CFS 7.51- 7.51
1 FTS [P:G] 4.52- 3.55
SS (Avex) 5.57

KF228
17 SFTS 10.44
Undershot landing and collided with hut, Wellingore, 5.2.45

KF229
5(P)AFU 10.44- 4.46
SOC 26.4.51
Sold Hw spares

KF230
21 FTS 5.45- 9.46
SOC 4.10.50
KF231
5(P)AFU 9.44- 5.45
19 FTS 5.45-11.46
" 3.47- 4.47
RAFC [FAB:Y/BY]4.47- 4.54
Sold Hw spares 6.54
KF232
No RAF service
SOC 25.9.50
KF233
9(P)AFU 9.44- 6.45
5(P)AFU [EP] 6.45- 5.46
7 FTS 11.50-11.50
1 FTS [P:M] 11.50
cr. ldd. Moreton-in-Marsh, 1.12.54
KF234
7 FIS 10.45- 3.46
SOC 26.4.51
Sold Hw spares
KF235
No RAF service
SOC 16.6.50
KF236
cr. in USA before delivery
KF237
5(P)AFU 2.45- 5.45
20 FTS [FAJ:A] 5.45- 7.47
2 FTS [FAJ:A] 7.47- 8.47
3 FTS [FBT:Q/O:P] 8.47- 5.55
SS (AES) 5.57
KF238
5(P)AFU 12.44- 4.46
7 SFTS [FBD:F] 4.46- 7.47
7 FTS [FBA:S/P:A] 7.47-10.53
2 FTS 10.53- 4.54
Sold Hw spares 4.55
KF239
5(P)AFU 12.44- 5.45
19 FTS [DA] 5.45- 1.46
6 SFTS 1.46
Force-landed, Copster Green, Lancs. 5.11.46
KF240
5(P)AFU 11.44- 6.45
2 FTS [FAK:B] 6.45- 3.46
20 FTS 3.46- 1.50
22 FTS [FCI:A] 1.50- 4.54
Sold Hw spares 3.55
KF241
5(P)AFU 9.44- 1.45
19 FTS [GD/FAA:L] 5.45-10.46
20 FTS [FAK:C] 1.47- 8.47
2(P)RFU 8.47- 7.49
CFS(EW) 7.49- 3.50
CFS [O:E] 3.50- 2.54
SOC 19.3.54
KF242
5(P)AFU 9.44- 4.46
7 SFTS 4.46-10.47
SOC 25.8.50
KF243
9(P)AFU 9.44- 6.45
5(P)AFU 6.45- 4.46
7 SFTS [FBA:Z] 4.46-10.47
EAAS 10.47- 5.49
7 FTS [N:D] 5.49-11.53
9 FTS 11.53
cr. ldd. during aerobatics practice Toddington, Glos., 14.1.54
KF244
17 SFTS 10.44- 6.47
1 FTS 6.47- 2.48
CFS [FDM:S] 2.48- 2.53
Edin. UAS [56] 5.54- 5.57
SS (Av.Tr.) 10.57
KF245
9(P)AFU 9.44- 6.45
5(P)AFU 6.45- 1.46
22 SFTS [FCI:N] 1.46- 4.46
41 Sqdn 8.47
Spun in, Whitley Bridge, Yorks., 16.4.48
KF246
No RAF service
SOC 22.6.50
KF247
11 RFS 6.47-12.47
66 Gp. CF 12.47- 3.49
SOC 14.2.51
KF248
9(P)AFU 11.44- 3.45
2 FTS 7.45- 7.45
FTC CF [FKN:D/D] 7.45- 6.47
SOC 25.9.50
KF249
No RAF service
SOC 14.2.51
KF250
5(P)AFU 9.44- 6.45
2 FTS [FAK:J] 6.45- 3.46
20 FTS 3.46- 9.46
20 SFTS 9.46- 7.47
2 FTS 7.47- 9.48
RAFC [FAB:G/BG] 9.48- 5.54
SS (Avex) 5.57
KF251
17 SFTS [FCB:B] 10.44
cr. ldd. Spitalgate, 17.1.47
KF252
17 SFTS 10.44- 6.45
ECFS 6.45- 9.45
SOC 14.9.50
KF253
No RAF service
SOC 3.7.50
KF254
5(P)AFU 10.44- 5.45
20 FTS [FAJ:B] 5.45- 9.46
20 SFTS 9.46- 7.47
2 FTS 7.47- 9.48
RAFC [FAB:D] 9.48
DBR in accident 18.10.49

Snowy fields are seen below No.2 FTS Harvard KF250, flying from Church Lawford in December 1947
(Sqn Ldr A.B.Walker via B.Goulding)

Early-morning view of the apron at Ternhill, with No.6 FTS Harvard KF268 prominent *(via R.C.Sturtivant)*

Unit	Code	Dates
KF255		
611 Sqdn	[RAR:Z]	10.46- 6.52
Oxford UAS		6.52- 5.57
SS (Av.Tr.)		10.57
KF256		
9(P)AFU		9.44- 6.45
5(P)AFU		6.45-10.45
7 FIS		10.45- 5.46
11 AGS		6.47-11.47
CFS		5.46- 6.47
11 AGS		6.47-11.47
62 Gp. CF		6.49-12.49
desp. S. Rhodesia		12.50
5 FTS		5.51- 7.53
4 FTS storage		7.53-12.53
Sold		12.53
KF257		
5(P)AFU		12.44- 5.45
19 FTS	[FF]	5.45- 1.46
6 SFTS		1.46- 5.47
6 FTS		5.47- 8.47
To French AF		4.49
KF258		
5(P)AFU		11.44- 4.45
7 SFTS		4.45
DBR in accident		12.5.45
KF259		
5(P)AFU		1.45- 6.45
19 FTS	[GE]	6.45- 6.47
1 FTS		6.47- 2.48
SF Wittering		2.48-11.48
2 FTS		11.48- 1.50
22 FTS	[U:T]	1.50- 7.54
SS (Av.Tr.)		6.57
KF260		
5(P)AFU		11.44
DBR in accident		31.12.44
KF261		
ETPS	[10]	
desp. FE		3.51
MAAF		6.51
cr. ldd. Bayan Lepas		30.9.51
KF262		
2 FIS		2.45- 9.45
SOC		3.7.50
KF263		
2 FTS		11.48- 4.51
22 FTS	[FCJ:S/Y:I]	4.51- 5.54
SS (Avex)		5.57
KF264		
5(P)AFU		11.44- 6.45
21 FTS		6.45- 8.46
17 SFTS		8.46- 6.47
1 FTS		6.47- 2.48
RAFC	[FAA:T]	2.48- 1.51
22 FTS	[R:J]	1.51- 8.54
SS (AES)		12.56
KF265		
5(P)AFU		1.45- 5.45
19 FTS	[FAA:C]	5.45- 6.47
1 FTS	[FCD:A]	6.47- 2.48
7 FTS	[FBA:P]	2.48-11.48
2 FTS	[FAK:T]	11.48- 1.50
22 FTS		1.50- 4.50
3 FTS	[FBT:R]	4.50- 2.55
SS (Avex)		4.57
KF266		
5(P)AFU		12.44- 5.45
19 FTS	[BA]	5.45- 4.47
RAFC		4.47- 6.47
7 FTS	[FBA:G/N:G]	2.48- 3.53
FTC CF		3.53- 3.53
CFS		3.53- 8.54
SS (Av.Tr.)		10.57
KF267		
5(P)AFU	[ET]	2.45- 4.46
SOC		26.4.51
Sold Hw spares		
KF268		
2 FIS		2.45- 7.45
7 FIS		7.45- 5.46
CFS		5.46-12.49
6 FTS	[FBJ:C/P:W]	12.49- 4.53
2 FTS		2.54- 4.54
SS (H.Bath)		3.57
KF269		
41 OTU		8.44-11.44
53 OTU		11.44- 2.45
61 OTU	[TO:L]	2.45- 7.47
203 AFS		7.47- 9.49
226 OCU		9.49- 4.50
APS Acklington		4.50- 2.51
3 FTS		10.52
DBR		3.12.53
KF270		
5(P)AFU		10.44- 5.45
20 FTS	[FAJ:E]	5.45- 9.46
20 SFTS	[FAJ:E]	9.46 7.47
2 FTS	[FAJ:D]	7.47- 2.51
1 FTS	[N:D]	2.51- 2.55
SS (AES)		5.57
KF271		
5(P)AFU		12.44- 5.45
19 FTS	[AL]	5.45- 4.47
RAFC		4.47-10.47
SOC		26.4.51
Sold Hw spares		
KF272		
11(P)AFU		1.45- 5.45
2 FTS		5.45- 3.46
20 FTS	[FAJ:H]	3.46- 9.46
20 SFTS		9.46- 7.47
2 FTS		7.47- 9.48
RAFC	[FAB:K]	9.48
cr. 2mls SW of Barkston Heath,		12.6.53
KF273		
5(P)AFU		1.45- 5.45
21 FTS		5.45- 9.46
SOC		25.9.50
KF274		
17 SFTS		10.44-11.46
CFS		11.46-12.46
21(P)AFU		12.46- 7.47
1(P)RFU		7.47-12.47
22 FTS		3.51- 9.51
1 FTS	[N:F]	9.51-11.54
Sold Hw spares		4.55

KF275
11(P)AFU 12.44- 6.45
2 FTS 6.45-10.45
21 FTS 3.46- 8.46
17 SFTS 8.46- 6.47
1 FTS 6.47- 1.48
6 FTS [FBH:A] 1.48-11.48
RAFC [FAB:D/BD] 2.50- 4.54
Sold Hw spares 5.54

KF276
11(P)AFU 12.44- 6.45
21 FTS 6.45- 8.46
17 SFTS 8.46- 6.47
1 FTS 6.47- 2.48
CFS [FDM:X] 2.48- 4.51
7 FTS 4.51- 1.53
3 FTS 1.53- 3.55
SS (Av.Tr.) 6.57

KF277
5(P)AFU 2.45-11.45
22 SFTS 11.45- 2.49
22 FTS [FCI:G] 2.49- 9.50
2 FTS 9.50-11.50
1 FTS 11.50-10.51
22 FTS [U:R] 10.51
DBR in accident 17.5.54

KF278
No RAF service
SOC 23.8.50

KF279
No RAF service
SOC 13.6.50

KF280
11(P)AFU 1.45- 6.45
21 FTS 6.45- 8.46
17 SFTS [FCD:U] 8.46- 6.47
1 FTS 6.47- 3.48
RAFC [FAA:W] 3.48- 1.50
3 FTS 10.50-11.50
1 FTS [FCA:I/N:Q]11.50
cr. ldd. Moreton-in-Marsh, 31.12.54

KF281
5(P)AFU 12.44- 4.45
7 SFTS 4.45- 5.46
SOC 26.4.51
Sold Hw spares

KF282
17 SFTS 10.44-11.46
CFS 11.46-12.46
21(P)AFU 12.46- 7.47
1(P)RFU 7.47- 5.49
FRS 5.49- 1.50
CGS [FJX:K/FJU:V] 1.50- 2.51
22 FTS 2.51
cr. ldd. Syerston, 24.2.54

KF283
12 FU 1.45- 4.45
To Yugo.AF 4.45

KF284
11(P)AFU 1.45
DBR in accident 7.4.45

KF285
11(P)AFU 1.45- 6.45
20 FTS 6.45- 3.46
21 FTS 3.46- 9.46
SOC 20.10.50

KF286
No RAF service
SOC 24.7.50

KF287
5(P)AFU 12.44- 4.45
7 SFTS 4.45- 5.46
desp. ME 5.48
32 Sqdn
213 Sqdn 3.49- 2.50
MEITF [F] 2.50-12.51
To Leb.AF 1.54

KF288
5(P)AFU 11.44- 3.45
7 SFTS [FBA:B] 3.45- 1.48
7 FTS 1.48- 1.51
CFS 1.51- 4.51
7 FTS [O:E/N:F] 4.51- 4.53
2 FTS 4.53- 4.54
Sold Hw spares 5.54

KF289
9(P)AFU 9.44- 6.45
5(P)AFU 6.45- 4.46
7 SFTS [FBD:J] 4.46- 1.48
7 FTS [FBA:U] 1.48- 9.50
2 FTS 9.50-12.50
CFS [O:B] 12.50-10.54
SS (AES) 5.57

KF290
7 FTS [O:U] 7.51- 1.53
22 FTS 1.53- 7.53
9 FTS [M:E] 7.53
DBR in accident 5.11.53

KF291
5(P)AFU 1.45- 5.45
19 FTS [BC] 5.45- 5.46
SOC 4.10.50

KF292
17 SFTS 10.44- 6.45
2 FTS 6.45- 3.46
17 SFTS 3.46-11.46
CFS 11.46-12.46
21(P)AFU 12.46- 8.47
1(P)RFU 8.47-12.47
RAFC 12.47-11.49
3 FTS [FBT:K] 11.49- 4.55
SS (Av.Tr.) 6.57

KF293
5(P)AFU 11.44- 1.46
6 SFTS 1.46
DBR in accident 22.5.47

KF294
No RAF service
SOC 16.6.50

KF295
No RAF service
To R.Hell.AF 7.49

KF296
17 SFTS 10.44- 6.47
1 FTS 6.47- 2.48
RAFC [FAA:R/AR] 2.48- 4.54
Sold Hw spares 6.54

KF297
No RAF service
SOC 29.8.50

No.2 FTS Harvard KF270 [FAJ:E] at Church Lawford *(M.Gray via R.C.Sturtivant)*

KF289 oi CFS Litle Rissington *(via R.C.Sturtivant)*

KF298
9(P)AFU 9.44- 6.45
5(P)AFU 6.45- 4.46
7 SFTS 4.46-10.47
22 SFTS 10.47-12.47
RAFC [FAA:C] 12.47-12.49
3 FTS [FBU:M/R:L]12.49
cr. 1dd. on overshoot, Methwold, 5.4.54
KF299
No RAF service
SOC 14.2.51
KF300
5(P)AFU 2.45- 5.45
21 FTS 5.45- 8.46
17 SFTS [FCE:L] 8.46- 6.47
1 FTS 6.47- 2.48
7 SFTS [FBA:F] 2.48- 7.49
CFS(EW) 7.49- 3.50
CFS 3.50- 7.50
22 FTS [FCJ:Q/Y:H] 4.51
cr. 7mls NE of Newark, 6.5.53
KF301
5(P)AFU 1.45- 5.45
19 FTS [CC/FAC:C] 5.45- 9.46
1 FTS 7.47- 2.48
CFS 2.48- 2.48
3 FTS [FBT:V] 3.50- 1.55
SS (AES) 5.57
KF302
12 FU 1.45- 3.45
To Yugo.AF 4.45
KF303
11(P)AFU 1.45- 5.45
19 FTS [HC] 5.45-11.47
SOC 26.4.51
Sold Hw spares
KF304
No RAF service
SOC 27.6.50
KF305
12 FU 2.45- 3.45
To Yugo.AF 4.45
KF306
SF Celle 10.46- 3.47
123 Wing 3.47- 4.47
80 Sqdn 4.47- 6.49
26 Sqdn 1.50- 5.50
2 Sqdn 5.50- 1.51
1 FTS 1.51- 3.51
CFS [O:V] 9.52-10.54
SS (Avex) 5.57
KF307
11(P)AFU 1.45- 6.45
2 FTS 6.45- 3.46
20 FTS 3.46- 9.46
20 SFTS 9.46- 3.47
CFS 3.47-10.53
9 FTS 10.53- 3.54
Sold Hw spares 3.55
KF308
11(P)AFU 1.45- 6.45
20 FTS 6.45- 3.46
21 FTS 3.46- 8.46
17 SFTS 8.46- 6.47
1 FTS 6.47- 3.48
RAFC [FAA:V/AV] 3.48- 4.54
Sold Hw spares 6.54
KF309
No RAF service
SOC 20.7.50
KF310
22 RFS [F] 6.49- 8.49
600 Sqdn [RAG:C/C] 8.49- 2.52
RAFC [AO] 1.53- 5.54
SS (Avex) 5.57
KF311
No RAF service
SOC 22.6.50
KF312
No RAF service
SOC 29.8.50
KF313
9(P)AFU 11.44- 6.45
5(P)AFU 6.45-11.45
22 SFTS [FCJ:B] 11.45- 2.49
22 FTS 2.49-12.49
2 FTS [FAJ:J] 12.49- 4.51
22 FTS [R:Q] 4.51- 5.54
SS (Avex) 5.57
KF314
A&AEE 2.49
cr. $2\frac{1}{2}$mls NE of Chilmark, Wilts., 22.2.82
KF315
41 OTU 8.44- 2.45
61 OTU [TO:O] 2.45- 7.47
203 AFS 7.47- 9.49
226 OCU 9,49- 1.50
613 Sqdn 1.50- 1.50
CFS 1.51- 9.51
CFS(B) [O:C] 9.51- 7.54
3 FTS 7.54- 7.56
Edin. UAS 7.56- 7.56
Camb. UAS 7.56- 4.57
SS (AES) 9.57
KF316
No RAF service
To French AF 4.49
KF317
No RAF service
SOC 26.4.51
Sold Hw spares
KF318
No service in UK
desp. FE 3.51
MAAF 8.51
DBR in accident 16.8.52
KF319
2 FIS 4.45- 7.45
7 FIS 7.45- 5.46
CFS 5.46- 7.46
22 SFTS [FCJ:H] 7.46- 2.49
22 FTS 2.49
Overshot at night, Newton, 25.3.49
KF320
101 FRS 4.51- 9.51
CFS [M:V] 9.51
DBR in accident 16.4.54

KF321
2 FIS 4.45- 7.45
7 FIS 7.45- 5.46
CFS [FDM:U] 5.46- 5.52
Camb. UAS 1.56- 6.56
Bris. UAS 6.56- 4.57
SS (Av.Tr.) 10.57

KF322
2 FTS 10.50- 5.51
6 FTS 5.51
cr. ldd. 4mls SW of Ternhill 1.8.52

KF323
No RAF service
SOC 3.7.50

KF324
No service in UK
desp. S. Rhodesia 5.51
5 FTS [87] 8.51- 7.53
4 FTS storage 7.53-12.53
Sold 12.53

KF325
5(P)AFU 11.44
DBR in accident 3.7.45

KF326
No service in UK
desp. S. Rhodesia 5.51
4 FTS 5.52- 6.52
1340 Flt 6.53- 9.55
SOC 23.3.56

KF327
No RAF service
SOC 22.6.50

KF328
5(P)AFU 2.45- 6.45
19 FTS [BG/FAB:G] 6.45- 7.47
1 FTS 7.47- 3.48
CFS 3.48- 9.48
RAFC [FAB:M/BM] 9.48- 4.54
Sold Hw spares 5.54

KF329
No service in UK
desp. ME 5.48
6 Sqdn 7.48- 2.50
MEITF [E] 2.50- 1.52
107 MU 1.52
Abandoned in spin, $\frac{3}{4}$ml S of Geneifa 11.8.53

KF330
No service in UK
desp. S. Rhodesia 5.51
5 FTS 8.51- 7.53
4 FTS storage 7.53-10.53
Sold 10.53

KF331
587 Sqdn 2.45-
695 Sqdn [4M:Q]
691 Sqdn 9.46- 1.47
Became 6316M 1.47
Reverted to airworthy 5.47
22 RFS 6.49- 7.49
64 Gp. CF 7.49-11.49
desp. S. Rhodesia 11.51
4 FTS 3.52- 6.52
5 FTS [40] 8,52- 8.53
4 FTS storage 8.53-12.53
Sold 12.53

KF332
No service in UK
desp. ME 5.48
32 Sqdn 10.48- 1.50
MEITF [D] 1.50-10.51
MEAF CF 2.52-11.52
SOC 22.7.53

KF333
5(P)AFU 11.44- 4.45
7 SFTS 4.45- 8.45
A&AEE 1.46-
ETPS - 6.47
1 Sqdn [JX:E] 1.48- 7.48
FCCS 7.48- 2.49
FRS [FDA:U] 3.50-11.51
7 FTS 11.51- 3.53
2 FTS 3.53- 6.54
3 FTS [R:L] 6.54-12.54
SS (AES) 5.57

KF334
5(P)AFU 2.45- 5.45
19 FTS [FAB:S] 5.45- 4.47
RAFC 4.47- 8.47
2(P)RFU 8.47- 3.48
1(P)RFU [FDA:T/FDD:K] 3.48- 5.49
FRS 5.49- 4.51
101 FRS 4.51
Abandoned in spin 2mls E of Breighton, 12.9.51

KF335
21 FTS [FAN:D] 5.45- 9.46
SOC 14.9.50

KF336
No RAF service
SOC 23.8.50

KF337
66 Gp. CF 6.49-10.49
612 Sqdn 10.49- 5.50
1 FTS [FCB:C] 1.51- 8.51
22 FTS [U:P] 10.52- 5.54
SS (Avex) 5.57

KF338
2 FIS 2.45- 7.45
7 FIS 7.45- 5.46
CFS [FDM:T] 5.46
cr. on take-off, Little Rissington, 21.7.52

KF339
2 FIS 2.45- 7.45
7 FIS 7.45- 5.46
CFS 5.46
cr. on take-off, Little Rissington, 16.9.47

KF340
No RAF service
SS (BKLA) 8.49

The standard post-war colour scheme, an all-silver finish with yellow trainer bands, is illustrated on KF308 of the RAF College, Cranwell *(Air-Britain)*

An aggressive Harvard Mk.IIb: KF348 of No.1340 Flight carries 20-lb bombs during the anti-Mau Mau campaign (E.W.Hughes)

KF341
5(P)AFU 2.45- 4.45
7 SFTS 4.45- 8.45
22 SFTS [FCI:Y] 2.46- 2.49
22 FTS 2.49- 7.54
1 FTS [P:T] 7.54- 3.55
SS (AES) 5.57

KF342
2 FIS 2.45- 6.45
5(P)AFU 6.45- 7.45
7 FIS 7.45- 1.46
3 SFTS [FBT:P] 1.46- 4.47
3 FTS 4.47-11.47
APS Acklington [81:S] 11.47- 5.50
3 FTS 12.50- 2.51
22 FTS 4.51- 7.51
1 FTS 7.51-10.51
6 FTS 10.51- 9.53
Sold Hw spares 3.55

KF343
RCCF 2.49- 2.50
RCCS 2.50- 9.50
6 FTS 5.51-11.53
22 FTS 11.53- 6.54
1 FTS [P:C] 6.54- 1.55
SS (Avex) 2.57

KF344
No RAF service
To R.Hell.AF 7.49

KF345
9(P)AFU 9.44- 6.45
5(P)AFU 6.45-11.45
22 SFTS [FCI:K] 11.45- 2.49
22 FTS 2.49-12.49
2 FTS 12.49-10.50
6 FTS 6.51- 2.54
Sold Hw spares 3.55

KF346
3 FTS 2.51
Engine cut during practice forced landing; hit HT cables and DBR, 14.1.55

KF347
No RAF service
SOC 18.1.51

KF348
No service in UK
desp. S. Rhodesia 4.51
5 FTS 8.51- 6.53
1340 Flt 6.53
cr. ldd. Aberdare Mountains, Kenya, 19.4.54

KF349
5(P)AFU 2.45- 5.45
19 FTS [BD] 5.45- 4.47
RAFC 4.47-10.47
SOC 31.10.50

KF350
No service in UK
desp. ME 5.48
84 Sqdn 5.49-10.49
SF Shallufa 10.49-12.49
208 Sqdn 4.50- 9.50
MEAF CF 1.52-10.52
To Leb.AF 1.54

KF351
5(P)AFU 9.44- 1.46
Became 5769M 1.46
SOC 11.5.50

KF352
9(P)AFU 9.44- 6.45
5(P)AFU 6.45-12.45
6 SFTS [FBH:J] 12.45- 5.47
6 FTS 5.47-12.49
CFS [FDM:A] 12.49- 7.54
SS (AES) 5.57

KF353
No service in UK
desp. S. Rhodesia 3.51
5 FTS [44] 6.51
cr. 14mls SSW of Thornhill, 18.6.53

KF354
6 FTS 11.50- 9.53
Sold Hw spares 4.54

KF355
2 FTS 10.50- 5.51
6 FTS 5.51-11.53
22 FTS 11.53
cr. S. Collingham, Lincs., 6.5.54

KF356
3 FTS 12.50- 5.52
22 FTS 5.52- 8.52
7 FTS 8.52- 1.53
1 FTS [P:D] 1.53- 3.55
SS (AES) 5.57

KF357
No service in UK
desp. FE 3.51
FECS 7.51- 2.54
267 Sqdn 2.54-12.56
SOC 4.57

KF358
9(P)AFU 9.44- 6.45
5(P)AFU 6.45- 1.46
6 SFTS [FBH:I] 1.46- 5.47
6 FTS [FBH:X] 5.47- 2.54
Sold Hw spares 4.55

KF359
17 SFTS [FCE:D] 10.44- 6.47
SOC 25.8.50

KF360
2 FTS 10.50- 7.51
1 FTS [N:P] 7.51- 2.55
SS (AES) 6.57

KF361
6 FTS [FBJ:F] 1.49-10.53
SS 12.53

KF362
7 FTS 11.50-11.50
1 FTS 11.50- 1.52
CFS 1.52- 2.52
CFS(B) [O:S] 2.52-11.54
SS (Av.Tr.) 10.57

KF363
No service in UK
desp. S. Rhodesia 3.51
4 FTS 6.51- 7.52
5 FTS 3.53- 8.53
4 FTS storage 8.53-12.53
Sold 12.53

KF364
7 FTS 12.48- 2.49
2 FTS 2.49- 4.49
7 FTS [FBA:F/N:C] 4.49- 6.53
2 FTS 6.53- 5.54
1 FTS 5.54- 2.55
SS (Av.Tr.) 6.57

KF365
No RAF service
SOC 12.6.50
KF366
16 SFTS 10.44
DBR inaccident 21.4.45
KF367
RAFC [FAB:S/BS] 2.50- 3.54
SS (Avex) 5.57
KF368
RAE
desp. S. Rhodesia 3.51
4 FTS 7.51- 1.52
5 FTS [41] 1.52- 8.53
4 FTS storage 8.53-12.53
Sold 12.53
KF369
No service in UK
desp. FE 5.49
28 Sqdn 7.49- 4.51
80 Sqdn 4.51- 7.52
SF Kaitak 7.52-10.52
HKAAF 10.52-11.52
SF Kaitak 11.52- 3.53
HKAAF 3.53
SOC 9.1.58
KF370
No service in UK
desp. S. Rhodesia 3.51
4 FTS 7.51- 1.52
5 FTS [56] 1.52- 8.53
4 FTS storage 8.53-12.53
Sold 12.53
KF371
16 RFS 7.50-10.50
CFS 2.51- 7.54
Sold Hw spares 4.55
KF372
20 SFTS [FAJ:F]
2 FTS [FAJ:P] 7.47- 5.51
3 FTS [P:P] 5.51- 3.55
SS (AES) 5.57
KF373
607 Sqdn [RAN:A/LA:A]8.46- 2.51
611 Sqdn 2.51-10.53
SS (Avex) 5.57
KF374
602 Sqdn [RAI:Y/LO:Y] 8.46-
609 Sqdn [PR:B] -
SOC 27.10.53
KF375
22 RFS 6.50- 7.50
18 RFS 7.50- 8.50
11 RFS 8.50-11.50
1 FTS 3.51-12.51
3 FTS [R:X] 12.51- 1.55
SS (Avex) 5.57
KF376
No RAF service
To French AF 4.49
KF377
2 FTS [FAJ:B] 11.48- 4.51
22 FTS [FCJ:P/Y:E] 4.51- 7.53
9 FTS 7.53-
SS (AES) 12.56
KF378
No service in UK
desp. FE 5.49
SF Kaitak 5.52
Flew into hill, Tin Ma Swaw, Hong Kong, 1.5.52
KF379
London UAS 6.47- 6.47
22 RFS 6.47-11.47
1 FTS [FCB:E] 1.51- 3.55
SS (Av.Tr.) 10.57
KF380
123 Wing 7.46- 4.47
3 Sqdn 4.47- 2.49
desp. FE 3.51
MAAF (SF Sqdn) 6.51- 7.53
MAAF (KL Sqdn) 11.53- 4.57
SOC 11.12.57
KF381
No service in UK
desp. S. Rhodesia 3.51
5 FTS 5.51
cr. on take-off, Thornhill, 21.6.51
KF382
No service in UK
desp. S. Rhodesia .51
5 FTS 6.51- 8.53
1340 Flt 9.53
cr. ldd., Aberdare Mountains, Kenya 19.4.54
KF383
501 Sdqn [RAB:B/SD:B]8.46- 1.50
610 Sqdn [DW:W] 1.50- 1.51
613 Sqdn [Q3:3] 1.51-10.53
SS (AES) 5.57
KF384
Booker 6.50-10.50
1 FTS [N:F] 10.52- 3.55
SS (Av.Tr.) 10.57
KF385
No service in UK
desp. S. Rhodesia 3.51
5 FTS 5.51- 8.53
4 FTS storage 8.53-12.53
Sold 12.53
KF386
22 RFS 6.50- 7.50
11 RFS 7.50-10.50
1 FTS 2.51
SOC 16.2.54

No.1340 Flight KF395 in trouble in Kenya *(E.W.Hughes)*

KF402 of No.601 Squadron, North Weald around 1950 *(Harry Holmes via R.C.Sturtivant)*

KF387
602 Sqdn 8.46- 8.46
613 Sqdn [RAT:1] 8.46
cr. on take-off, Ringway, 4.8.49
KF388
7 FTS 11.50-11.50
1 FTS [FCA:K] 11.50-10.51
3 FTS 10.51-11.51
6 FTS [O:J] 11.51-11.53
SS (Avex) 2.57
KF389
609 Sqdn [RAP:Y] 12.48- 7.49
602 Sqdn [RAI:Z/LO:X] 7.49
SOC 27.10.53
KF390
7 SFTS -12.47
desp. S. Rhodesia 3.51
5 FTS [53] 5.51- 6.53
1340 Flt 6.53- 9.55
SOC 23.3.56
KF391
No service in UK
desp. ME 11.49
32 Sqdn 1.50- 7.50
MEAF CF 1.52-10.52
To Leb.AF 1.54
KF392
FTC CF [A] 1.51- 3.53
HCExU 3.53-10.53
HCCS 10.53- 4.54
Bris. UAS [B] 4.54-11.56
SS (Av.Tr.) 10.57
KF393
No RAF service
SOC 22.6.50
KF394
5(P)AFU -11.45
22 SFTS 11.45- 1.46
20 SFTS 1.46- 3.46
desp. ME 11.49
MEITF [B] 2.50-10.51
MEAF CF 4.52-10.52
To Leb.AF 1.54
KF395
1 OFU 10.49- 9.50
OFU [QO:A] 9.50- 1.53
desp. Kenya
1340 Flt 9.54- 9.55
SOC 23.3.56
KF396
2 FTS 10.50- 5.51
102 FRS 5.51-11.51
7 FTS 11.51- 4.53
2 FTS 4.53- 4.54
Sold Hw spares 5.54
KF397
2 FTS [FAK:J] 10.50- 4.51
1 FTS 4.51- 9.52
desp. FE
FECS 3.54- 4.56
267 Sqdn 4.56- 3.57
SOC 28.6.57
KF398
64 Gp. CF 6.49- 1.50
desp. S. Rhodesia 6.51
4 FTS 5.52- 8.52
1340 Flt 3.53- 9.55
SOC 23.3.56
KF399
London UAS 6.47- 6.47
22 RFS 6.47-
SF Biggin Hill -11.47
SOC 9.3.51
KF400
22 FTS [FCI:L/U:G] 1.49- 7.54
SS (H.Bath) 3.57
KF401
16 Sqdn 6.49- 7.50
desp. S. Rhodesia 12.51
4 FTS 5.52- 6.52
5 FTS [G:45] 4.53- 8.53
4 FTS storage 8.53-12.53
Sold 12.53
KF402
601 Sqdn [HT:Y/Y] 6.49- 9.53
SOC 27.10.53
KF403
Direct to RNZAF 10.44
KF404
No service in UK
desp. S. Rhodesia 3.51
5 FTS 5.51-11.51
SOC 7.5.53
KF405
34 Sqdn [8Q:6] 7.49- 6.52
Camb. UAS 6.52-11.52
22 RFS 11.52- 1.54
SS (Avex) 2.57
KF406
NO service in UK
desp. FE 5.49
80 Sqdn 5.50
DBR in accident 27.11.50
KF407
Direct to RNZAF 10.44
KF408
6 FTS [FBJ:A] 1.49-11.53
22 FTS 11.53- 7.54
Sold Hw spares 4.55
KF409
6 SFTS [FBH:G] 3.46- 5.47
6 FTS 5.47-10.53
9 FTS 10.53- 4.54
Sold Hw spares 5.54
KF410
Direct to RNZAF 10.44
KF411
6 FTS [FBH:A] 12.48- 5.50
22 FTS [FCK:A/U:A] 5.51- 9.54
SS (Avex) 5.57
KF412
RAFC [FAB:S/BS] 2.49-10.49
desp. S. Rhodesia 12.50
5 FTS 4.51
DBR in accident 22.11.51
KF413
5(P)AFU 12.44- 5.45
19 FTS [FAB:L] 5.45- 4.47
RAFC 4.47- 5.47
33 Sqdn 6.48- 8.49
1 FTS [FCB:D] 1.51
cr. $3\frac{3}{4}$mls SSW of Kimbolton, Hunts., and DBF, 23.7.51

KF414
5(P)AFU 11.44- 6.45
21 FTS 6.45- 9.46
SOC 20.10.50

KF415
5(P)AFU 12.44- 6.45
19 FTS [FG/FAB:A] 6.45- 4.47
To Belg.AF 9.49

KF416
5(P)AFU 1.45- 6.45
19 FTS [EJ] 6.45
cr. on overshoot, Cranwell, 23.3.47

KF417
5(P)AFU 11.44- 6.45
20 FTS 6.45- 5.46
17 SFTS 8.46-11.46
CFS 11.46-12.46
21(P)AFU 12.46- 7.47
1(P)RFU 7.47- 5.49
FRS 5.49-10.51
SS (Av.Tr.) 6.57

KF418
5(P)AFU 11.44- 4.46
SOC 23.1.51

KF419
5(P)AFU 1.45- 6.45
2 FTS [FAI:A] 6.45- 3.46
20 FTS [FAJ:K] 3.46- 9.46
20 SFTS [FAK:K] 9.46- 7.47
1 FTS 4.51-12.52
Oxford UAS 7.54- 9.55
Birm. UAS 9.55
cr. ldd. Castle Bromwich, 24.10.55

KF420
11(P)AFU 1.45- 5.45
19 FTS 5.45- 1.46
6 SFTS 1.46- 5.47
6 FTS 5.47- 8.47
desp. S. Rhodesia 11.51
1340 Flt 3.53
cr. on approach to Eastleigh, Kenya 9.5.53

KF421
No RAF service
SS (BKLA) 8.49

KF422
5(P)AFU 12.44- 4.45
7 SFTS 4.45- 6.45
SOC 25.8.50

KF423
11(P)AFU 1.45- 5.45
2 FTS 5.45- 3.46
20 FTS 3.46- 9.46
20 SFTS 9.46- 7.47
2 FTS 7.47- 8.47
500 Sqdn [RAA:B] 4.48-10.53
SS (Av.Tr.) 6.57

KF424
11(P)AFU 1.45- 6.45
20 FTS 6.45- 3.46
21 FTS 3.46- 9.46
SOC 20.10.50

KF425
11(P)AFU 1.45- 6.45
21 FTS 6.45- 9.46
SOC 20.10.50

KF426
309 Sqdn 4.46- 8.46
613 Sqdn 8.46-12.46
22 SFTS [FCI:A] 12.46-12.49
2 FTS 12.49- 4.51
101 FRS 4.51-10.51
CFS [M:B] 11.52-10.53
9 FTS 10.53- 4.54
Sold Hw spares 5.54

KF427
RAE 12.44-10.50
6 FTS 8.52- 8.53
SS (Av.Tr.) 6.57

KF428
5(P)AFU 11.44-11.45
22 SFTS 11.45
cr. Hexham, Northumberland,19.12.46

KF429
12 FU 1.45-
To Yugo.AF 4.45

KF430
5(P)AFU 2.45- 5.45
20 FTS 5.45- 9.46
20 SFTS 9.46- 7.47
2 FTS 7.47- 8.47
3 FTS [FBT:K] 8.47-11.49
RAFC [FAA:G/AG] 11.49-11.51
22 FTS [U:K] 2.52- 4.54
Sold Hw spares 2.55

KF431
5(P)AFU 11.44- 4.45
7 SFTS 4.45
DBF in accident 1.9.45

KF432
5(P)AFU 12.44- 6.45
2 FTS *[FAJ:C] 6.45- 3.46
20 FTS *[FAK:C] 3.46- 9.46
20 SFTS *[FAK:F] 9.46- 7.47
2 FTS 7.47
cr. near South Cerney, 15.4.50

*sequence not known

KF433
5(P)AFU 11.44- 6.45
20 FTS 6.45- 4.46
605 Sqdn [RAL:N] 5.48- 5.52
Birm. UAS 5.52-11.52
5 RFS 11.52- 5.53
19 RFS [R] 5.53- 5.54
Man. UAS [R] 5.54- 4.57
SS (AES) 9.57

KF434
11(P)AFU 1.45- 5.45
20 FTS 5.45- 6.45
2 FTS 6.45- 3.46
CFE 9.47- 5.49
SOC 14.2.51

KF435
11(P)AFU 12.44- 6.45
2 FTS [B:Q] 6.45- 3.46
20 FTS 3.46- 9.46
22 SFTS 11.46- 7.47
2 FTS [FAI:R] 7.47- 2.51
1 FTS [N:G] 2.51- 3.55
SS (Skylines) 9.57

KF436
5(P)AFU 2.45- 5.45
19 FTS [CD/FAC:D] 5.45- 6.47
To French AF 5.49

KF437
11(P)AFU 1.45- 6.45
20 FTS [FAI:Q] 6.45- 9.46
20 SFTS 9.46- 7.47
2 FTS [FAI:T] 7.47
cr. during low aerobatics $1\frac{1}{2}$mls N of Cricklade, 7.11.49

KF438
5(P)AFU 12.44-10.45
2 FTS [FAI:B] 10.45-
CFS(EW) 7.49- 4.50
2 FTS [FAJ:W] 4.50- 4.51
22 FTS [FCJ:M] 4.51-12.51
3 FTS 12.51- 2.55
SS (AES) 5.57

All-yellow Harvard IIb KF432 of No.2 FTS, Church Lawford *(Sqn Ldr A.B.Walker via B.Goulding)*

KF439
3 FTS 2.51- 7.53
2 FTS 7.53- 1.54
Sold Hw spares 6.54
KF440
5(P)AFU 12.44- 4.46
7 SFTS 4.46- 9.47
SOC 25.8.50
KF441
No RAF service
SOC 20.7.50
KF442
5(P)AFU 12.44- 5.45
19 FTS 5.45- 1.46
6 SFTS [FBI:J] 1.46- 5.47
6 FTS 5.47- 8.47
602 Sqdn 4.49- 9.49
SOC 13.2.50
KF443
5(P)AFU 11.44- 6.45
20 FTS [FAJ:N] 6.45- 9.46
20 SFTS 9.46- 7.47
2 FTS 7.47- 9.48
RAFC [FAB:F] 9.48
Spun in ½ml SW of Navenby, Lincs., 5.2.49
KF444
5(P)AFU 11.44- 5.45
7 SFTS 4.45- 7.46
SOC 20.10.50
KF445
5(P)AFU 12.44- 4.46
7 SFTS 4.46- 8.46
SOC 3.7.50
KF446
11(P)AFU 1.45
Engine cut on take-off, Calveley, 26.3.45
KF447
11(P)AFU 12.44- 5.45
19 FTS [AM] 5.45- 7.46
22 SFTS [FCI:I] 7.46- 2.49
22 FTS [U:L] 2.49- 7.54
Sold Hw spares 5.55
KF448
5(P)AFU 2.45- 5.45
19 FTS [FAA:A] 5.45- 4.47
RAFC 4.47 8.47
3 FTS [FBU:F] 8.47-12.49
RAFC [FAA:Y] 12.49- 1.51
22 FTS [R:T] 1.51- 3.53
Hull UAS 1.56- 5.57
SS (Av.Tr.) 10.57
KF449
5(P)AFU 12.44- 4.45
7 SFTS 4.45- 8.46
603 Sqdn [RAJ:B] 8.46- 4.52
2 FTS 3.53- 5.54
1 FTS 5.54-11.54
SS (AES) 12.56
KF450
63 Gp. CF 7.49- 3.50
desp. S. Rhodesia 11.50
5 FTS [G:47] 4.51- 2.53
1340 Flt 3.53
Spun in 10mls N of Nyeri, Kenya, 6.2.54
KF451
5(P)AFU 11.44- 6.45
21 FTS 6.45- 9.46
SOC 25.9.50
KF452
11(P)AFU 1.45- 4.45
ECFS 6.45- 5.46
EFS 5.46- 6.46
SOC 26.4.51
Sold Hw spares
KF453
RCITF 7.49-12.50
desp. FE 2.52
MAAF 8.52- 1.57
SOC 4.57
KF454
11(P)AFU 1.45- 6.45
20 FTS 6.45-

Manchester UAS's KF433 at Woodvale *(A.P Ferguson)*

2 FTS [FAK:A] 7.47
cr. on take-off from Blakehill Farm 9.1.51
KF455
11(P)AFU 1.45- 6.45
20 FTS 6.45- 3.46
21 FTS [FAN:S] 3.46- 9.46
SOC 20.10.50
KF456
No RAF service
SOC 3.7.50
KF457
5(P)AFU 2.45- 6.45
19 FTS [FAC:G] 6.45-11.47
SOC 26.4.51
Sold Hw spares
KF458
5(P)AFU 11.44-11.45
22 SFTS [FCJ:S/FCI:M] 11.45- 2.49
22 FTS [Y:D] 2.49-10.54
Sold Hw spares 4.55
KF459
19 FTS [FG] 5.45- 4.47
RAFC [FAF:M] 4.47
DBR in accident 8.3.54
KF460
5(P)AFU 12.44- 6.45
21 FTS [FAP:H] 6.45- 9.46
SOC 8.9.50
KF461
No RAF service
SOC 3.7.50
KF462
5(P)AFU 11.44
DBR in accident 16.5.45
KF463
5(P)AFU 11.44- 6.45
20 FTS 6.45- 9.46
20 SFTS 9.46- 6.47
Oxford UAS 6.47-11.47
To Belg.AF 8.49
KF464
11(P)AFU 1.45- 5.45
19 FTS [HB] 5.45- 6.47
541 Sqdn 1.49- 3.51
237 OCU 3.51- 7.51
1689 Flt 11.51- 5.52
CFS(B) 11.52- 5.54
SOC 14.6.54

KF465
11(P)AFU 12.44- 6.45
20 FTS [FAJ:S] 7.45- 9.46
20 SFTS [FAJ:S] 9.46- 7.47
2 FTS [FAJ:S] 7.47- 3.51
Liv. UAS 4.56- 4.57
SS (Avex) 9.57
KF466
5(P)AFU 12.44- 1.46
6 SFTS 1.46- 5.47
6 FTS 5.47- 7.48
22 FTS 7.48- 7.49
2 FTS [FAJ:K] 7.49- 4.51
22 FTS [FCJ:K/U:M/Y:C] 4.51- 9.54
Sold Hw spares 3.55
KF467
5(P)AFU 2.45- 4.45
7 SFTS 4.45
cr. 4mls S of Harlaxton, 30.1.46
KF468
11(P)AFU 1.45- 5.45
2 FTS 5.45- 7.45
7 FIS 7.45- 3.46
20 FTS [FAJ:J] 3.46- 7.47
2 FTS 7.47- 7.49
CFS(EW) 7.49- 3.50
CFS 3.50-11.51
CFS(B) [FDO:Q] 11.51- 8.54
SS (Avex) 5.57
KF469
11(P)AFU 1.45- 6.45
21 FTS [FAP:E] 6.45- 9.46
SOC 8.9.50
KF470
11(P)AFU 1.45- 5.45
17 SFTS 5.45- 7.47
613 Sqdn [RAT:2/Q3:2] 7.47-10.53
SS (AES) 9.57
KF471
12 FU 1.45
To Yugo.AF 3.45
KF472
5(P)AFU 2.45- 6.45
19 FTS [FA] 6.45- 4.47
RAFC 4.47- 7.47
7 FTS [FBB:L/O:T]4.49-12.52
6 FTS [P:L] 12.52- 2.54
2 FTS 2.54- 5.54
1 FTS 5.54-11.54
SS (Avex) 5.57

Very FAI:R shot of KF435 of No.2 FTS at Church Lawford around 1946! *(via R.C.Sturtivant)*

KF473
11(P)AFU 12.44- 6.45
2 FTS 6.45- 3.46
20 FTS 3.46- 9.46
20 SFTS 9.46- 7.47
2 FTS 7.47- 7.49
CFS(EW) 7.49- 3.50
CFS [O:H/N:H] 3.50- 9.53
CFS(B) 9.53-10.54
SS (H.Bath) 3.57
KF474
12 FU 1.45
To Yugo.AF 3.45
KF475
612 Sqdn 10.46- 5.52
Aber. UAS 5.52-11.52
11 RFS 11.52- 5.53
22 RFS 5.53- 3.54
Camb. UAS [D] 3.54-11.55
London UAS 11.55- 5.56
SOC 20.9.56
KF476
11(P)AFU 1.45- 5.45
19 FTS [HA] 5.45- 4.47
RAFC [FAD:N] 4.47- 7.47
22 FTS [FCI:W] 4.49- 9.50
2 FTS 9.50- 6.51
6 FTS 6.51-11.53
Sold Hw spares 4.54
KF477
12 FU 1.45
To Yugo.AF 3.45
KF478
No RAF service
SOC 28.4.49
KF479
ATA [25] 2.45- 2.45
To French AF 5.49
KF480
5(P)AFU 2.45- 4.46
To R.Hell.AF 5.47
KF481
5(P)AFU 1.45- 6.45
21 FTS 6.45- 8.46
17 SFTS [FCF:J] 8.46- 6.47
1 FTS 6.47- 2.48
7 FTS [FBA:C/N:Q] 2.48- 8.53
2 FTS 8.53- 4.54
SS (AES) 5.57
KF482
63 Gp. CF 7.49- 1.50
desp. S. Rhodesia 6.51
5 FTS 9.51
cr. near Thornhill on overshoot, 25.9.52
KF483
5(P)AFU 2.45- 6.45
19 FTS [FAC:G] 6.45- 4.47
RAFC 4.47-11.47
To Belg.AF 9.49
KF484
No RAF service
SOC 16.6.50
KF485
2 FTS [FAK:L] 1.49- 7.49
CFS(EW) 7.49- 4.50
2 FTS 4.50- 2.51
1 FTS [N:X] 2.51- 3.55
SS (Av.Tr.) 10.57
KF486
No RAF service
SOC 14.2.51

A more unusual form of code, Q3:2, carried by KF470 of No.613 Squadron, photographed at Ringway in June 1950 *(R.A.Scholefield)*

KF487
66 Gp. CF 6.49- 3.50
1 FTS [FCA:T/N:T]12.50-1.55
SS (Avex) 12.56
KF488
No RAF service
SOC 20.7.50
KF489
2 FIS 2.45- 7.45
7 FIS 7.45- 1.46
3 SFTS 1.46
u/c retracted too soon on take-off
Feltwell 16.1.47
KF490
5(P)AFU 2.45- 4.46
7 SFTS 4.46-10.47
To Belg.AF 8.49
KF491
11(P)AFU 1.45- 6.45
2 FTS [FAI:E] 6.45- 3.46
20 FTS 3.46- 9.46
20 SFTS 9.46- 7.47
2 FTS [FAK:M] 7.47- 5.51
6 FTS 5.51-11.53
SS (H.Bath) 3.57
KF492
5(P)AFU 12.44- 6.45
21 FTS 6.45- 9.46
SOC 25.9.50
KF493
798 Sqdn 10.45-
766 Sqdn 12.46- 1.47
736 Sqdn 2.48- 1.49
780 Sqdn 7.49- 9.49
1832 Sqdn 1.52- 2.54
SOC 22.2.54
KF494
729 Sqdn 5.45- 4.46
desp. UK
799 Sqdn [207:MA] 5.51- 8.52
Admiralty Flt 9.54- 6.55
SOC 30.8.56
KF495
780 Sqdn 1.47-
790 Sqdn 1.48- 5.48
780 Sqdn 9.48- 7.49
781 Sqdn [L] 1.52- 2.54
SOC 20.2.54
KF496
11(P)AFU 1.45- 6.45
20 FTS 6.45- 9.46
20 SFTS 9.46- 3.47
CFS 3.47- 6.47
7 SFTS [FBD:R] 6.47- 1.48
7 FTS [FBA:T] 1.48- 1.51
CFS 1.51
cr. ldd. and DBF, Moreton-in-Marsh, 26.2.51
KF497
11(P)AFU 1.45- 5.45
19 FTS [AF] 5.45- 4.47
RAFC 4.47- 6.47
17 SFTS 6.47- 6.47
1 FTS 6.47- 2.48
RAFC [FAA:K] 2.48-
SOC 21.4.54
KF498
63 Gp. CF 7.49-12.49
desp. S. Rhodesia 5.51
5 FTS 8.51
cr. 1953S 3015E 25.9.52
KF499
733 Sqdn 10.47-
desp. UK
799 Sqdn 3.49- 5.50
767 Sqdn 7.50-
1833 Sqdn [256:BR] 7.52-12.53
SOC 4.12.53
KF500
758 Sqdn 5.45-10.45
780 Sqdn 8.46-12.46
1832 Sqdn [203:CH] 7.47-
781 Sqdn [267:LP] 1.49- 9.49
1831 Sqdn [203:JA/ 203:ST] 1.51- 9.51
SOC 23.10.54
KF501
794 Sqdn 7.45-
799 Sqdn 4.47-
cr. 1½mls S of Long Sutton, Hants., 4.6.48
KF502
798 Sqdn [L3Z] 5.45- 6.45
NFT
KF503
1840 Sqdn [220] 1.52- 2.54
SOC 22.2.54
KF504
India: no record of RN service
desp. UK
FF Anthorn 8.49-
781 Sqdn [267:LP] 5.50- 2.54
SOC 20.2.54
KF505
758 Sqdn 6.45-10.45
SF Syerston (RN) 1.49- 1.54
SOC 17.2.54

Fleet Air Arm Harvard Mk.IIb KF500 of No.1831 Squadron at Stretton around 1951 *(Ray Williams via R.C.Sturtivant)*

Harvard IIb KF550 operated by the Fleet Air Arm *(G.J.Cruickshank)*

KF506
798 Sqdn [L3Y] 6.45- 3.46
780 Sqdn 3.46-11.46
1830 Sqdn 3.48- 1.49
767 Sqdn 3.49-
781 Sqdn 5.49- 9.51
SOC 15.10.51
KF507
798 Sqdn [L3B] .45-
4 FF 2.47- 3.47
1831 Sqdn [203:JA] 1.49-11.49
SOC 19.5.50
KF508
758 Sqdn 8.45- 9.45
780 Sqdn 8.46- 9.46
NFT
KF509
India: no record of RN service
desp. UK
799 Sqdn 10.47-10.50
SF Anthorn 10.50- 5.51
799 Sqdn [205:MA] 5.51- 8.52
1832 Sqdn [278] 10.54- 4.55
SOC 30.8.56
KF510
FP Yeovilton 11.45- 7.46
NFT
KF511
719 Sqdn 4.47- 5.47
798 Sqdn [L3C] 5.45- 4.47
SF Eglinton 5.47-11.48
1831 Sqdn [201:JA] 5.50-10.51
799 Sqdn 10.51- 1.52
SOC 20.1.52
KF512
S. Africa: no used by RN
desp. UK
SF Arbroath [901:AO] 10.50- 5.51
799 Sqdn [201:MA] 5.51- 5.52
SOC 30.8.56
KF513
Not used by RN (damaged in transit)
Transferred to RAF 3.46
3 SFTS [FBT:H] 3.46- 4.47
3 FTS 4.47-11.49
RAFC [AA] 11.49- 4.51
22 FTS 4.51- 1.52
3 FTS 1.52
DBR in accident 28.10.53
Became 7113M
KF514
758 Sqdn 5.45- 5.46
780 Sqdn 5.46-12.46
771 Sqdn 1.48-
781 Sqdn [268:LP] 12.48- 1.49
1840 Sqdn [219:FD] 7.51-10.53
SOC 22.2.54
KF515
758 Sqdn
NFT
KF516
799 Sqdn 5.46- 9.47
1830 Sqdn [211:AC] 1.49-11.53
SOC 21.11.53
KF517
758 Sqdn 7.45-
799 Sqdn 11.47- 1.49
1830 Sqdn [239:AC/ 239:DO] 10.50-11.53
SOC 21.11.53
KF518
Damaged in transit to RN in UK
SOC by RAF 1.45
KF519
702 Sqdn 1.46-
NFT
KF520
732 Sqdn 10.45-
1833 Sqdn [251:BR] 1.49- 6.52
" 2.54- 7.54
SOC 20.7.54
KF521
758 Sqdn 4.45- 6.45
727 Sqdn [201:GJ] 8.47- 9.47
1833 Sqdn [257:BR] 5.52-12.53
SOC 4.12.53
KF522
794 Sqdn [A] 5.45- 1.46
780 Sqdn [U2R] 7.46- 7.49
799 Sqdn 7.49- 6.50
764 Sqdn [266:VL] 2.54- 9.54
SOC 30.8.56
KF523
758 Sqdn 8.45- 5.46
1830 Sqdn [237:AC] 7.53- 7.54
SOC 10.9.54
KF524
798 Sqdn 3.45- 7.45
799 Sqdn 5.46- 6.47
1832 Sqdn [206:CH] 7.47- 4.51
1840 Sqdn 5.51- 7.52
SOC 15.12.52
KF525
702 Sqdn 1.46-
799 Sqdn [757] 6.47- 5.48
782 Sqdn 1.49-
1831 Sqdn [202:JA] 7.50
cr. $1\frac{1}{2}$mls N of Woodford, 12.5.54
KF526
791 Sqdn 1.46- 5.47
SF Sembawang 9.47-
desp. UK
781 Sqdn 3.50- 4.50
1832 Sqdn 4.50- 4.51
1840 Sqdn [217:FD] 5.51
cr. ldd. Ford 14.2.54
KF527
798 Sqdn [L3G] 3.45- 7.45
NFT
KF528
758 Sqdn [U3XX] 3.45- 4.45
799 Sqdn 9.46-11.47
" 6.51- 6.52
1831 Sqdn 6.54-11.54
1834 Sqdn [277] 11.54- 4.55
SOC 30.8.56
KF529
22 FTS 3.49- 4.54
SOC 7.5.54
KF530
702 Sqdn 1.46- 2.46
799 Sqdn 9.47- 4.48
SOC 15.4.48
KF531
702 Sqdn 2.46-
799 Sqdn 7.51- 1.52
1834 Sqdn 7.54
cr. Ilchester, 21.8.54

Unit	Code	Dates
KF532		
758 Sqdn		5.45-
799 Sqdn	[751:LP]	7.47- 8.47
727 Sqdn		7.49- 1.50
799 Sqdn	[203:MA]	9.51- 7.52
781 Sqdn	[269:LP]	12.53- 2.54
SOC		29.4.54
KF533		
799 Sqdn		6.47- 3.49
SOC		17.4.50
KF534		
729 Sqdn		9.45-12.45
desp. Malaya		
HMS Indefatigable	[273:S]	
791 Sqdn		12.45- 8.46
desp. UK		
799 Sqdn	[204:MA]	5.51- 8.52
1834 Sqdn	[276]	10.54- 4.55
SOC		30.8.56
KF535		
758 Sqdn		7.45- 8.45
NFT		
KF536		
Sembawang		5.46-
NFT		
KF537		
1833 Sqdn	[252:BR]	7.50- 4.52
1842 Sqdn		3.53
cr. ldd. Ford		4.3.54
KF538		
19 FTS		5.45- 1.46
6 SFTS	[FBH:L]	1.46- 5.47
6 FTS		5.47- 7.48
22 SFTS	[FCI:X]	7.48- 2.49
22 FTS		2.49- 4.55
SS (H. Bath)		3.57
KF539		
19 FTS	[FAD:G]	5.45- 8.47
3 FTS	[FBR:D]	8.47-12.49
RAFC	[FAB:B/BB]	12.49-4.54
SS (AES)		5.57
KF540		
1832 Sqdn	[202:CH]	7.47-
1840 Sqdn		5.51- 6.51
1832 Sqdn		8.51
Cr. on take-off, Culham,		24.8.51
KF541		
1 BAS	[B:C/FDW:D]	6.45- 2.47
CFS		2.47- 6.47
EFS	[FCT:A]	6.47- 6.49
EAAS		6.49- 9.49
desp. S. Rhodesia		1.51
5 FTS/3 ANS		4.51- 8.53
4 FTS storage		8.53
Sold		11.53
KF542		
733 Sqdn		11.45-
desp. UK		
1833 Sqdn	[258:BR]	5.52- 7.54
SOC		9.11.54
KF543		
1830 Sqdn	[237:DO]	3.50- 5.53
SOC		12.5.53
KF544		
SF Colombo		5.45- 9.45
desp. UK		
1831 Sqdn	[201:JA]	9.51- 4.54
SOC		11.10.54
KF545		
757 Sqdn		6.45-
desp. UK		
1832 Sqdn		7.50- 1.53
1834 Sqdn		7.53- 1.54
SOC		22.2.54
KF546		
RN: no record of service		
SOC		
KF547		
No RAF service		
To R.Hell.AF		7.49
KF548		
733 Sqdn		10.45-11.45
NFT		
KF549		
FF Coimbatore		6.45- 8.45
desp. UK		
1833 Sqdn	[253:BR]	9.50- 5.52
1830 Sqdn	[239:AC]	3.54-10.54
SOC		30.8.56
KF550		
SF Tambaran		11.45-
desp. UK		
780 Sqdn	[204:CW]	6.48-11.49
Admiralty Flt		11.49- 6.51
799 Sqdn	[206:MA]	6.51- 8.52
SOC		30.8.56
KF551		
794 Sqdn		6.45-
715 Sqdn		8.45-
799 Sqdn		5.46- 5.47
NFT		
KF552		
757 Sqdn	[P:93]	7.45-11.45
desp. UK		
799 Sqdn	[208:MA]	6.51- 8.52
1834 Sqdn	[265:VL]	7.54- 3.55
SOC		30.8.56
KF553		
702 Sqdn		2.46-
SF St. Merryn		.47-
799 Sqdn		5.48-
1832 Sqdn	[200:CH]	2.49
cr. ldd. Culham,		17.2.50
KF554		
798 Sqdn		5.45-
799 Sqdn		5.46-10.46
"		1.50- 4.50
1832 Sqdn		8.52- 7.54
SOC		7.10.54
KF555		
798 Sqdn	[L3D]	6.45- 7.45
799 Sqdn		5.46- 6.49
1834 Sqdn		7.53-10.54
SOC		7.10.54

Above the Surrey countryside in 1956 ia KF565 of London University Air Squadron *(N.D.Welch)*

KF556
794 Sqdn 6.45-
715 Sqdn 11.45-
799 Sqdn 8.46-10.46
1830 Sqdn 6.48- 1.50
SOC 19.3.50
KF557
715 Sqdn 6.45-
NFT
KF558
794 Sqdn 11.45- 1.46
799 Sqdn 9.46- 6.48
736 Sqdn 12.48- 1.49
780 Sqdn [206:CW] 2.49-11.49
Admiralty Flt 11.49- 1.52
SOC 21.6.54
KF559
709 Sqdn [S3V] .45- 1.46
780 Sqdn 4.47- 2.48
790 Sqdn 3.48- 5.48
799 Sqdn 1.49- 6.50
1834 Sqdn [265:VL] 1.54- 7.54
SOC 2.7.54
KF560
2 FTS 4.45-10.45
603 Sqdn [RAJ:C] 4.47- 5.52
St.And. UAS 5.52-11.52
11 RFS 11.52- 6.53
SS (Avex) 5.57
KF561
2 FTS 4.45- 3.46
20 FTS 3.46- 9.46
20 SFTS 9.46- 7.47
2 FTS [FAI:N] 7.47- 9.47
226 OCU 10.48- 9.49
20 Sqdn [TH:Z] 9.49- 9.50
1 FTS 5.51- 3.52
3 FTS 3.52- 5.52
22 FTS [Y:S] 5.52- 7.54
SS (AES) 12.56
KF562
A&AEE 9.49- 9.51
3 FTS 9.52- 2.55
SS (Avex) 5.57
KF563
2 FIS 4.45- 7.45
7 FIS 7.45- 5.46
CFS [FDN:C] 5.46-12.49
6 FTS [FBH:E] 12.49-11.50
1 FTS [FCA:L] 11.50-11.51
22 FTS 11.51- 3.52
6 FTS 1.53-12.53
SS (Av.Tr.) 6.57
KF564
2 FIS 4.45- 7.45
7 FIS 7.45- 5.46
CFS [FDN:D] 5.46-12.49
6 FTS 12.49- 1.50
CFS 1.50- 2.50
6 FTS 2.50
cr. 4mls N of Pershore, 22.10.51
KF565
3 FTS 1.49- 9.50
2 FTS 9.50- 4.51
7 FTS [O:Y] 4.51- 4.53
2 FTS [N:P] 4.53- 6.54
London UAS [Y] 5.56-10.56
SS (Avex) 5.57
KF566
No RAF service
SOC 2.6.50
KF567
No RAF service
To French AF 5.49
KF568
6 SFTS 3.46- 5.47
6 FTS 5.47- 1.48
1 Sqdn 1.48- 8.48
ITF Tangmere 8.48- 5.49
To Belg.AF 10.49
KF569
123 Wing 11.46-
80 Sqdn - 2.48
33 Sqdn 2.48
SOC 29.4.48
KF570
6 SFTS 3.46
cr. Postern Hill, Derbyshire, 16.1.47
KF571
No RAF service
SOC 10.7.50
KF572
17 SFTS 8.45- 3.46
19 FTS [CJ] 3.46- 4.47
RAFC [FAB:J] 4.47- 6.48
2 FTS [FAJ:U] 2.50- 2.51
1 FTS 2.51-10.51
CFS [N:O] 10.51-10.54
SS (Av.Tr.) 10.57
KF573
20 FTS 6.45- 9.46
SOC 10.7.50
KF574
7 FIS 8.45- 5.46
CFS 5.46- 6.47
CGS [FJX:B] 6.47- 8.48
RAFC [FAB:A/BA] 8.48-12.50
1 FTS 12.50- 9.51
RAFC 9.51- 4.54
SS (AES) 12.56
KF575
No RAF service
SOC 12.6.50
KF576
6 FTS [P:U] 5.51- 9.53
SS (AES) 5.57
KF577
No RAF service
To French AF 5.49
KF578
SF Celle 10.46- 5.47
2 Sqdn 5.47- 2.48
26 Sqdn 2.48- 5.50
6 FTS 4.51
Spun in near Ternhill, 16.11.51
KF579
1 BAS 6.45- 3.47
17 SFTS 3.47- 6.47
1 FTS 6.47- 8.47
504 Sqdn [RAD:X] 4.48-10.52
Nott. UAS 10.52-11.52
16 RFS 11.52- 5.53
desp. Kenya
1340 Flt 8.54- 9.55
To R.Jord.AF 1.56
KF580
6 FTS 2.49- 9.50
2 FTS 9.50- 5.51
102 FRS 5.51-12.51
6 FTS [FBJ:Q] 12.51-11.53
SS (H.Bath) 3.57
KF581
No RAF service
To French AF 4.49
KF582
No RAF service
SOC 22.6.50
KF583
63 Gp. CF 7.49-10.49
RCITF 10.49- 4.51
CFS(B) 10.52- 7.54
SS (Avex) 5.57
KF584
7 SFTS 8.45- 8.46
602 Sqdn [RAI:X/LO:X] 8.46- 7.51
613 Sqdn 7.51- 9.51
CFS 7.52
DBR in accident 11.12.53
KF585
No RAF service
SOC 20.7.50
KF586
No RAF service
SOC 3.7.50
KF587
6 FTS [FBJ:P/P:M] 1.49- 9.53
SS (Av.Tr.) 6.57
KF588
7 FTS [FBB:G/N:R] 5.51- 2.53
CFS [N:E] 2.53
cr. 4mls SE of Thame, 14.12.54
KF589
No RAF service
SOC 22.6.50
KF590
7 FTS [FBA:E/N:E] 12.48- 3.53
2 FTS 3.53- 5.54
1 FTS 5.54
cr. Broadway, Worcs., 31.8.54
KF591
No RAF service
SOC 13.6.50
KF592
ETPS [12]
SOC 2.6.50
KF593
No RAF service
SOC 25.5.50
KF594
No RAF service
SOC 14.2.51
KF595
No RAF service
To French AF 4.49
KF596
19 FTS [HH/FAA:J] 5.45- 4.47
RAFC 4.47- 7.47
1 FTS 7.47-12.47
EFS 12.47- 2.48
RAFC 2.48- 3.54
SS (AES) 12.56
KF597
NO RAF service
To French AF 4.49
KF598
No RAF service
SOC 10.7.50
KF599
2 FTS 5.45
DBR in accident 1.9.45
KF600
No RAF service
SOC 10.7.50
KF601
RCCF 6.47- 2.48
SOC 14.2.51
KF602
No RAF service
SOC 14.2.51
KF603
No RAF service
SOC 20.7.50
KF604
Manston 9.49- 9.50
OFU 9.50- 9.52
FTU 9.52- 2.53
167 Sqdn [QO:N] 2.53- 8.53
Sold Hw spares 5.54
KF605
6 SFTS [FBG:K] 3.46- 9.50
7 FTS [FBA:O] 12.50-12.53
SS (AES) 5.57
KF606
No RAF service
SOC 16.6.50
KF607
No RAF service
SOC 20.7.50
KF608
No RAF service
To French AF 4.49
KF609
11 RFS 6.50- 8.50
FRS 4.51-10.51
CFS 9.52-10.52
22 FTS 10.52-12.52
RAFC 12.52- 3.54
Sold Hw spares 6.54
KF610
21 FTS [FAN:B] 5.45- 9.46
SOC 25.8.50
KF611
No RAF service
SOC 16.6.50

Seen at Sherburn-in-Elmet in June 1950 is No.604 Squadron's KF709 from Hendon (A.M.G.Armstrong via R.A.Scholefield)

KF612
6 FTS 5.51- 9.53
CFS(B) [N:E] 9.53-10.54
SS (H.Bath) 3.57
KF613
NO RAF service
SOC 3.7.50
KF614
NO RAF service
SOC 20.7.50
KF615
No RAF service
SOC 13.6.50
KF616
35 Wing 6.46- 7.47
501 Sqdn [RAB:B/SD:B] 7.47
Spun in, Filton, 10.9.50
KF617
No RAF service
SOC 2.6.50
KF618
No RAF service
SOC 24.7.50
KF619
No RAF service
SOC 3.7.50
KF620
No RAF service
SOC 27.6.50
KF621
No RAF service
cr. Araxos, Greece while on delivery to R.Hell.AF, 9.7.49
KF622
No RAF service
SOC 5.6.50
KF623
No RAF service
SOC 23.6.50
KF624
No RAF service
SOC 25.5.50
KF625
No service in UK
desp. S. Rhodesia 11.51
4 FTS 3.52- 9.52
1340 Flt 3.53- 9.55
SOC 23.3.56
KF626
No service in UK
desp. FE 2.51
Sing.AAF 5.51- 5.53
MAAF 9.53
overturned on landing, Kuala Lumpur, 16.4.55
KF627
165 Sqdn 4.46-10.46
631 Sqdn 10.46-10.46
66 Sqdn 10.46- 8.47
41 Sqdn 8.47-11.47
631 Sqdn 11.47- 2.49
20 Sqdn 2.49- 9.49
6 FTS 5.51
Hit by KF959 in formation and cr. near Ternhill, 28.6.52
KF628
No RAF service
SOC 23.6.50
KF629
No RAF service
SOC 3.7.50
KF630
No RAF service
SOC 12.6.50
KF631
No RAF service
To R.Hell.AF 8.49
KF632
No RAF service
SOC 2.6.50
KF633
7 FTS 12.48- 2.49
2 FTS 2.49- 4.49
7 FTS [FBA:R] 4.49- 9.50
desp. FE 1.52
MAAF 8.52- 7.56
SOC 4.57
KF634
No RAF service
SOC 13.6.50
KF635
No RAF service
SOC 12.6.50
KF636
NO RAF service
SOC 26.5.50
KF637
No RAF service
SOC 29.6.50
KF638
No RAF service
SOC 22.6.50
KF639
7 SFTS 6.45- 8.46
615 Sqdn [RAV:Z] 8.46- 3.53
SS (Skyline) 4.54
KF640
17 SFTS 6.45- 6.47
611 Sqdn [RAR:X/FY:X] 7.47-10.53
SS (AES) 12.56
KF641
No RAF service
SOC 2.6.50
KF642
No RAF service
SOC 5.6.50
KF643
No RAF service
SOC 24.7.50
KF644
No RAF service
SOC 10.7.50
KF645
7 SFTS 6.45- 8.46
600 Sqdn [RAG:A] 8.46- 9.47
609 Sqdn [RAP:X] 4.48- 7.53
SS (AES) 12.56
KF646
No RAF service
SOC 13.6.50

KF647
7 SFTS 11.45-
SOC 2.6.50
KF648
No RAF service
SOC 16.6.50
KF649
No RAF service
SOC 22.6.50
KF650
2 FTS [FAJ:G] 11.48- 1.51
22 FTS [Y:M] 1.51
cr. ldd. Syerston 14.5.54
KF651
35 Wing 7.46- 5.47
84 Gp. CS 5.47- 7.47
1(P)RFU 2.49- 5.49
FRS 5.49- 2.51
22 FTS [R:A] 2.51- 7.54
SS (Avex) 5.57
KF652
No RAF service
SOC 22.6.50
KF653
2 FTS 7.45- 7.45
FTCCF [FKN:E] 7.45- 5.47
6 FTS [FBJ:E] 3.48
cr. ldd. Ternhill 15.3.51
KF654
7 FIS 8.45- 9.45
7 SFTS 9.45
cr. on approach to Kirton-in-Lindsey and DBF, 22.7.47
KF655
No RAF service
To R.Hell.AF 8.49
KF656
No RAF service
To French AF 5.49
KF657
No RAF service
SOC 27.6.50
KF658
No RAF service
To French AF 4.49
KF659
16 SFTS [49] 8.45-11.45
6(P)AFU 11.45-12.45
6 SFTS [FBH:H] 12.45- 9.50
2 FTS 9.50
cr. 9mls SE of Cranwell, 28.2.51
KF660
No RAF service
SOC 26.5.50
KF661
35 Wing 6.46- 8.46
135 Wing 8.46-
26 Sqdn - 2.48
2 Sqdn 2.48- 1.51
1 FTS 1.51-
22 FTS
7 FTS 1.53- 7.53
9 FTS 7.53- 4.54
SS (AES) 5.57
KF662
6 SFTS [FBG:C] 3.46- 5.47
6 FTS 5.47-12.53
SS (AES) 5.57
KF663
6 SFTS 3.46- 5.47
6 FTS [FBJ:M] 5.47-12.53
desp. S. Rhodesia 11.50
5 FTS 3.51
Spun induring aerobatics $1\frac{1}{2}$mls NE of Senale, 20.4.51
KF664
604 Sqdn 7.46- 7.46
SOC 1.6.50
KF665
22 SFTS [FCJ:W] 10.46-12.48
2 FTS 12.48- 4.51
7 FTS [N:U] 4.51- 8.53
2 FTS 8.53- 6.54
3 FTS 6.54
cr. 6mls NNW of Downham Market, 17.9.54

KF666
612 Sqdn [RAS:R] 4.47-
63 Gp. CF
Abandoned out of fuel nr. Topcliffe 25.1.49
KF667
No RAF service
To French AF 5.49
KF668
7 FTS 12.48- 7.52
CFS [N:G] 7.52-10.53
9 FTS 10.53- 4.54
SS (Av.Tr.) 9.57
KF669
1 FTS 7.51- 8.53
CFS 8.53-10.53
9 FTS 10.53- 4.54
SS (Av.Tr.) 10.57
KF670
501 Sqdn [RAB:A/SD:A] 4.47-11.53
SS (Avex) 5.57
KF671
No RAF service
SOC 20.7.50
KF672
No RAF service
SOC 24.6.50
KF673
No RAF service
SOC 3.7.50
KF674
No service in UK
desp. S. Rhodesia 1.51
5 FTS 5.51
cr. ldd. on road 1ml N of Shangani, 17.3.53
KF675
135 Wing 10.46-
33 Sqdn
DBR in accident on ground 19.8.47
SOC 13.7.48
KF676
No RAF service
SOC 5.6.50
KF677
No RAF service
To French AF 4.49
KF678
3 FTS 6.51- 7.53
2 FTS 7.53- 4.54
SS (Av.Tr.) 6.57
KF679
No RAF service
SOC 12.6.50
KF680
7 FTS 8.45- 9.45
2 FTS 9.45-12.45
Sold Rollasons 9.50
To Belg.AF
KF681
6 SFTS 3.46- 5.47
6 FTS [FBJ:J] 5.47-12.48
desp. S. Rhodesia 3.51
5 FTS 7.51- 8.53
4 FTS storage 8.53-12.53
Sold 12.53
KF682
6 SFTS 3.46- 5.47
6 FTS [FBJ:I] 5.47-12.49
CFS [N:K] 12.49- 9.54
Sold Hw spares 3.56
KF683
No RAF service
SOC 16.6.50
KF684
2 FTS 7.45- 8.45
FTCCF [FKN:F] 8.45- 7.46
SOC 13.6.50
KF685
No RAF service
SOC 25.5.50
KF686
No RAF service
SOC 24.7.50

KF687
No RAF service
SOC 12.6.50
KF688
7 FTS [FBA:C] 12.48
Collided with FX388 and abandoned near Folkingham, Lincs, 17.10.52
KF689
No RAF service
SOC 23.6.50
KF690
601 Sqdn 7.46- 7.46
SOC 16.6.50
KF691
247 Sqdn 4.46-10.46
SF Duxford 10.46-12.47
1 Sqdn 12.47-11.48
16 RFS 7.50- 7.50
7 FTS 11.50- 1.53
22 FTS 1.53- 7.53
9 FTS 7.53- 4.54
SS (H.Bath) 3.57
KF692
No RAF service
SOC 10.7.50
KF693
22 SFTS 1.47- 2.49
22 FTS 2.49- 7.49
2 FTS [FAJ:S] 7.49- 6.51
6 FTS [P:U] 6.51- 2.54
SS (AES) 12.56
KF694
7 FIS 8.45- 9.45
7 SFTS 9.45-12.47
RAFC 12.47-11.49
3 FTS [FBR:N/P:Q] 11.49- 1.55
SS (AES) 12.56
KF695
7 SFTS 8.45- 1.48
7 FTS 1.48-
CFS [FDM:H/MH] - 9.54
Sold Hw spares 3.55
KF696
No RAF service
SOC 16.6.50
KF697
No RAF service
To R.Hell.AF 9.49
KF698
7 SFTS [FBC:V] 11.46- 1.48
7 FTS [FBA:L] 1.48- 7.52
CFS 7.52- 7.54
SS (Av.Tr.) 10.57
KF699
11 RFS 6.47- 8.47
603 Sqdn [RAJ:A] 1.48-10.53
SS (H.Bath) 3.57
KF700
19 FTS [FAB:O] 8.45- 8.47
2(P)RFU 8.47- 3.48
1(P)RFU [FDD:L] 3.48- 5.49
FRS 5.49-10.51
CFS 10.51- 5.52
22 FTS 5.52-12.52
RAFC 12.52- 4.54
Sold Hw spares 4.55
KF701
No RAF service
SOC 3.7.50
KF702
7 SFTS 8.45- 4.46
20 FTS [FAI:K] 4.46- 9.46
20 SFTS 9.46- 7.47
2 FTS 7.47- 7.49
CFS(EW) 7.49- 3.50
CFS [M:Q] 3.50-12.54
Sold Hw spares 4.55
KF703
No RAF service
SOC 3.7.50

KF704
2 FTS [FAJ:C] 4.45- 3.46
20 FTS [FAJ:C] 3.46- 9.46
20 SFTS 9.46- 7.47
2 FTS [FAJ:A] 7.47- 5.51
22 FTS 5.51- 8.51
1 FTS 8.51-12.51
3 FTS 12.51
cr. 1ml S of Downham Market airf'ld 18.7.52
KF705
3 FTS 12.48- 1.49
6 FTS [FBJ:J] 1.49- 9.50
2 FTS 9.50- 4.51
1 FTS 4.51-10.51
6 FTS 10.51-10.53
SOC 1.12.53
KF706
612 Sqdn [RAS:T] 11.46-11.49
SOC 24.2.50
KF707
502 Sqdn [V9:Q/V] 7.48- 2.54
Sold Hw spares 6.54
KF708
41 Gp. Trg. Flt
RAFC 12.48-10.49
desp. S. Rhodesia 5.51
5 FTS 8.51- 8.53
4 FTS storage 8.53-12.53
Sold 12.53
KF709
604 Sqdn [RAK:Y] 10.48- 6.52
S'ton UAS 6.52-11.52
14 RFS 11.52- 4.53
Bristol UAS [B] 4.53- 9.55
S'ton UAS 9.55- 2.56
SOC 18.2.56
KF710
41 Gp. Trg. Flt
1689 Flt [9X:B] 6.50- 4.53
FTU 4.53- 9.53
SS (AES) 3.57
KF711
61 OTU 9.45- 7.47
203 AFS 7.47- 9.49
226 OCU [TO:D] 9.49-10.49
2 FTS 10.50- 5.51
6 FTS 5.51- 8.51
22 FTS [R:E] 1.53- 9.54
SS (AES) 12.56
KF712
41 Gp. Trg. Flt 11.45- 1.46
1689 Flt [9X:C] .46- .47
1 FTS [N:K] 7.51- 2.55
SS (Av.Tr.) 6.57
KF713
6 FTS 6.51
Broke up in air, 1ml SW of Meir, Staffs., 17.2.53
KF714
6 FTS [FBJ:J] 11.50- 9.51
7 FTS [N:T] 9.51- 4.53
2 FTS [N:O] 5.53- 4.54
SS (AES) 12.56
KF715
No RAF service
Sold Rollasons 9.50
To Belg.AF
KF716
No RAF service
Sold Rollasons 9.50
To Belg.AF
KF717
502 Sqdn 7.48- 7.54
Camb. UAS 8.56- 4.57
SS (Avex) 9.57
KF718
500 Sqdn [S7:S/S] 5.48- 6.52
Oxford UAS 6.52
cr. 1ml S of Bretherton, Yorkshire, 1.7.54
KF719
No RAF service
Sold Rollasons 9.50
To Belg.AF
KF720
616 Sqdn 5.48- 6.48
609 Sqdn 6.48- 6.48
616 Sqdn [RAW:3] 6.48-11.53
SS (Avex) 5.57
KF721
1 FTS 1.53
cr. in forced landing 2mls NE of Redditch, 5.8.53
KF722
608 Sqdn [RAO:R/6T:R] 6.48-11.55
SS (AES) 5.57
KF723
1(P)RFU 12.48- 5.49
3 FTS [FBT:X] 5.49
Hit HT wires 7½mls SW of South Luffenham, Northants., 14.1.52
KF724
No RAF service
Sold Rollasons 13.9.50
To Belg.AF
KF725
7 FTS 11.48- 7.49
CFS(EW) 7.49- 5.50
3 FTS 5.50- 8.50
2 FTS [FAI:X] 8.50-11.50
1 FTS [FCA:M] 11.50- 2.52
3 FTS [P:Z] 2.52
cr. ldd. Methwold 21.8.53
KF726
3 FTS 1.53-12.54
SS (Avex) 9.57

KF722 of No.608 Squadron, Royal Auxiliary Air Force *(G.J.Cruickshank)*

A fine view of His Royal Highness the Duke of Edinburgh flying solo in KF729, an aircraft allocated to the Home Command Examining Unit at White Waltham and not used until 1953 (Charles E.Brown/RAF Museum)

Serial / Unit	Code	Dates
KF727		
No RAF service		
Sold Rollasons		9.50
KF728		
No RAF service		
To R.Hell.AF		7.49
KF729		
HCEU		2.53- 5.57
SS (Av.Tr.)		10.57
KF730		
6 FTS	[P:Z]	8.52- 2.54
SS (Av.Tr.)		6.57
KF731		
1 FTS	[N:C]	5.51- 3.55
SS (Av.Tr.)		6.57
KF732		
1 FTS	[P:P]	5.51- 3.55
Queens UAS		3.55- 9.55
Glas. UAS		9.55- 4.57
SS (AES)		9.57
KF733		
616 Sqdn	[RAW:B/RAW:4]	5.48- 5.51
Leeds UAS		5.52-11.52
25 RFS		11.52- 2.53
SS (H.Bath)		3.57
KF734		
No RAF service		
Sold Rollasons		9.50
To Belg.AF		
KF735		
22 RFS		7.53- 3.54
Camb. UAS	[A]	3.54- 4.57
SS (Av.Tr.)		9.57
KF736		
RAFC		8.52- 4.54
SS (H.Bath)		3.57
KF737		
607 Sqdn	[RAN:A]	
Sold Rollasons		9.50
To Belg.AF		
KF738		
No RAF service		
Sold Rollasons		9.50
To Belg.AF		
KF739		
Queens UAS		7.54- 2.56
Nott. UAS		2.56- 6.56
Durham UAS		6.56- 7.56
Nott. UAS		7.56- 5.57
SS (Av.Tr.)		10.57
KF740		
No RAF service		
SS (AES)		9.57
KF741		
3 FTS		1.52- 4.55
SS (AES)		9.57
KF742		
No RAF service		
To R.Hell.AF		8.49
KF743		
No RAF service		
To R.Hell.AF		8.49
KF744		
7 SFTS		1.46
DBR in accident		20.8.46
KF745		
No service in UK		
desp. FE		1.53
MAAF		2.53- 2.57
SOC		11.12.57
KF746		
RAFC	[BJ]	2.53- 4.54
SS (Avex)		9.57
KF747		
6 FTS		8.52- 9.53
Aber. UAS		10.55- 5.57
SS (Av.Tr.)		10.57
KF748		
1 FTS	[N:U]	7.51- 3.55
SS (Av.Tr.)		10.57
KF749		
6 FTS		9.52- 8.53
SS (CS)		9.57
KF750		
3 FTS	[R:C]	10.52- 4.53
SS (H.Bath)		3.57
KF751		
6 FTS		6.51- 7.51
502 Sqdn		2.52- 5.52
Queens UAS	[Q]	5.52
cr. Loughgall, Armagh,		30.5.54
KF752		
No RAF service		
To R.Hell. AF		8.49
KF753		
7 SFTS	[FBB:P]	12.45- 1.48
7 FTS		1.48- 5.48
SF Wittering		5.48-11.48
2 FTS		11.48-11.49
11 RFS		6.50- 8.50
2 FTS		10.50
cr. near South Cerney,		29.11.50
KF754		
3 SFTS		1.46- 1.47
22 SFTS		1.47-10.47
504 Sqdn	[RAD:Y]	6.48- 9.53
SS (AES)		12.56
KF755		
CFS	[O:T]	9.52-10.54
Glas. UAS		3.56- 6.56
Liv. UAS		6.56- 8.56
Glas. UAS		8.56- 5.57
SS (Av.Tr.)		10.57
KF756		
CFS(B)	[O:X/N:X]	2.52-10.54
Birm. UAS		2.56- 4.57
SS (Av.Tr.)		9.57
KF757		
22 FTS	[FCJ:V/Y:P]	5.51- 7.53
9 FTS		7.53- 3.54
Sold Hw spares		5.54

****

An * marked against serial numbers between KF901 and KF999 indicates Mk.TT.IIb target-tug aircraft.

****

KF901
6 SFTS 3.46-10.46
SOC 24.7.50
KF902
2 FTS [FAJ:H] 11.48- 2.51
1 FTS 2.51
Spun in, Little Staughton, 20.9.51
KF903*
ME: no record of service
SOC 26.6.47
KF904*
ME: no record of service
SOC 26.6.47
KF905
No RAF service
SOC 14.2.51
KF906
1 FU 7.46- 8.46
SOC 26.7.50
KF907
3 SFTS 1.46-12.46
22 SFTS 12.46- 2.49
22 FTS 2.49- 7.49
2 FTS 7.49
Overshot, South Cerney, 24.1.50
KF908*
ME: no record of service
To R.Hell.AF 3.47
KF909*
cr. in USA 31.7.45
KF910
19 FTS [FAC:Y] 2.46- 4.47
RAFC [FAC:Y] 4.47- 6.54
S'ton UAS 3.56- 5.57
KF911
22 SFTS [FCI:T] 1.46- 2.49
22 FTS 2.49-12.49
2 FTS 12.49- 5.51
3 FTS [FBB:T/R:Q] 5.51
DBR in accident 12.10.53
KF912*
293 Sqdn
desp. UK 6.47
SOC 12.6.50
KF913
ME: no record of service
To R.Hell.AF 3.49
KF914*
ME: no record of service
desp. UK 6.47
SOC 20.10.50
KF915*
ME: no record of service
desp. UK 6.47
SOC 20.10.50
KF916*
2 FU
Undercarriage raised in error while taxying, 23.5.45
KF917*
ME: no record of service
desp. UK 6.47
SOC 25.9.50
KF918*
ME: no record of service
desp. UK 6.47
SOC 12.6.50
KF919
22 SFTS [FCI:R] 1.46
cr. on overshoot, Ouston, 14.10.46
KF920
595 Sqdn [7B:R] 8.47- 2.49
5 Sqdn [7B:R] 2.49-
602 Sqdn [LO:Z]
600 Sqdn 3.51- 5.52
Glas. UAS 5.52-11.52
11 RFS 11.52
cr. on approach, Perth, 7.2.53

KF921*
ME: no record of service
desp. UK 6.47
SOC 22.6.50
KF922
6 SFTS 3.46-10.46
7 SFTS 10.46- 1.48
7 FTS [FBB:Z] 1.48
cr. 3mls NE of Cottesmore, 26.9.52
KF923*
ME: no record of service
SOC 29.5.47
KF924
19 FTS [CF/FAC:E] 9.45- 8.47
2(P)RFU 8.47- 3.48
7 FTS 3.48- 5.48
1(P)RFU 5.48- 5.49
FRS 5.49- 4.51
101 FRS 4.51-11.51
7 FTS [N:K] 11.51- 4.53
2 FTS 4.53- 4.54
SS (AES) 5.57
KF925
6 SFTS 3.46- 5.47
504 Sqdn [RAD:Z/TM:Z] 7.48
cr. on fire, Breighton, 10.8.51
KF926*
ME: no record of service
SOC 18.8.49
KF927*
ME: no record of service
DBR in accident 11.7.46
KF928*
ME: no record of service
SOC 18.8.49
KF929*
MEITF [A] 12.47-
SOC 24.11.50
KF930*
324 Wing
SOC 14.2.46
KF931*
ME: no record of service
SOC 10.2.49
KF932*
MEITF 12.47- 9.49
73 Sqdn 10.49-12.49
SOC 30.11.50
KF933*
ME: no record of service
To R.Hell.AF 2.47
KF934*
ME: no record of service
SOC 18.8.49
KF935*
ME: no record of service
SOC 18.8.49

KF936*
ME: no record of service
SOC 18.8.49
KF937
6 FTS [FBJ:K] 1.49-12.49
CFS [N:M] 12.49
Spun in during BoB display, St. Athan, 15.9.51
KF938*
ME: no record of service
SOC 18.8.49
KF939*
ME: no record of service
To R.Hell.AF 2.47
KF940*
ME: no record of service
SOC 18.8.49
KF941*
ME: no record of service
SOC 18.8.49
KF942*
ME: no record of service
SOC 18.8.49
KF943
306 Sqdn 4.46- 5.46
22 SFTS [FCI:V/U:N]12.46- 7.54
Sold Hw spares 3.55
KF944
No RAF service
SOC 13.6.50
KF945*
8 Sqdn - 8.49
SOC 15.9.50
KF946*
SF Nicosia - 7.48
SF Ismailia 7.49- 1.50
73 Sqdn 1.50- 8.50
SOC 30.11.50
KF947
No RAF service
SOC 10.7.50
KF948
1 FTS 7.51- 1.52
CFS(B) 1.52
Collided with FS822 and cr. near Calmsden, Glos., 28.7.52
KF949
No RAF service
SOC 25.5.50
KF950
No RAF service
SOC 10.7.50
KF951*
ME: no record of service
SOC 18.8.49

KF918 was a Harvard modified for target-towing as TT.Mk.IIb, seen here at an unidentified location in the Middle East. Note the black and yellow striped colour scheme ("Roundel" magazine)

Displaying a yellow colour scheme, early postwar roundels and code 9X:E, KF998 was the penultimate RAF Harvard
(Bruce Robertson)

KF952*
ME: no record of service
SOC 18.8.49
KF953
22 SFTS [FCI:S] 1.46
Cr. during aerobatics, Blyton, 27.11.51
KF954
6 SFTS 4.46- 5.47
6 FTS 5.47- 8.47
607 Sqdn [RAN:B/LA:B] 7.48- 5.52
Durham UAS 5.52-11.52
23 RFS 11.52- 5.53
Oxford UAS 5.53
cr. ldd. Woodvale, 22.6.54
KF955
6 SFTS 1.46-10.46
7 SFTS [FBC:Q] 10.46- 1.48
7 FTS [FBB:R] 1.48- 3.54
3 FTS 3.54- 2.55
ss (AES) 12.56
KF956*
ME: no record of service
TO R.Hell.AF 2.47
KF957*
ME: no record of service
To R.Hell.AF 2.47
KF958
RAE (?)
SOC 4.10.50
KF959
1 BAS [FDW:G] 1.46- 2.47
CFS 2.47- 6.47
7 SFTS [FBB:W] 6.47- 1.48
7 FTS [FBA:W] 1.48- 9.50
2 FTS 9.50-11.50
1 FTS [FCA:N] 11.50-10.51
6 FTS 10.51- 2.54
SS (AES) 5.57
KF960
22 SFTS 1.46-10.47
609 Sqdn [RAP:Z] 6.48-10.53
ss (AES) 12.56

KF961*
ME: no record of service
SOC 27.2.47
KF962
No RAF service
To R.Hell.AF 7.49
KF963
22 SFTS 3.46- 4.46
To R.Hell.AF 5.47
KF964
No RAF service
SOC 23.6.50
KF965*
ME: no record of service
SOC 10.2.49
KF966
3 SFTS [FBR:M/FBT:F] 2.46- 4.47
3 FTS [R:R] 4.47
cr. ldd. Methwold, 6.9.54
KF967
No RAF service
To R.Hell.AF 8.49
KF968*
336 Sqdn
cr. on landing, Sedes, Greece, 17.12.46
KF969*
ME: no record of service
SOC 18.8.49
KF970*
ME: no record of service
SOC 18.8.49
KF971*
ME: norecord of service
SOC 10.2.49
KF972
6 SFTS [FBJ:B] 3.46-11.50
1 FTS 11.50-10.51
22 FTS 10.51- 1.52
3 FTS 1.52- 2.55
SS (Avex) 5.57

KF973*
ME: no record of service
To R.Hell.AF 2.47
KF974
41 Gp. Trg. Flt 10.45- 1.46
1689 Flt [9X:D] - 4.53
FTU 4.53- 8.53
Sold Hw spares 4.54
KF975*
ME: no record of service
SOC 26.6.47
KF976
No RAF service
SOC 2.6.50
KF977
BLEU 2.46-
ETPS
BLEU - 9.47
3 FTS 3.48- 3.49
2 FTS 3.49- 4.49
3 FTS [FBT:A] 4.49- 7.53
2 FTS [N:N] 7.53- 4.54
Sold Hw spares 4.55
KF978
6 SFTS 4.46- 5.47
6 FTS [FBG:J] 5.47
cr. ldd. Ternhill, 5.3.53
KF979
No RAF service
To French AF 4.49
KF980
No RAF service
SOC 27.6.50
KF981
NO RAF service
SOC 10.7.50
KF982
22 SFTS [FCI:W] 1.46
Abandoned after control lost, near Ouston, 3.8.46
KF983
No RAF service
SOC 16.6.50

KF984
3 SFTS [FBU:E] 2.46
cr. during aerobatics, Feltwell, 17.9.48

KF985
7 SFTS [FBB:S] 1.46- 1.48
EFS 2.49- 6.49
EAAS 6.49- 8.49
desp. S. Rhodesia 5.51
5 FTS 8.51- 8.53
4 FTS storage 8.53- 9.53
1340 Flt 9.53
Force-landed, Aberdare Mountains, Kenya,19.4.54

KF986
19 FTS [FAD:L] 9.45- 4.47
21(P)AFU [FDD:B] 12.46-
2(F)RFU 8.47- 3.48
1(P)RFU 3.48- 5.49
FRS 5.49-10.50
102 FRS 7.51-12.51
RAFC [BH] 12.51- 3.54
Sold Hw spares 6.54

KF987
2 FTS 2.49- 6.49
desp. S. Rhodesia 11.50
5 FTS 3.51- 8.53
4 FTS storage 8.53-12.53
Sold 12.53

KF988
No RAF service
To French AF 4.49

KF989
EFS [FCT:D] 2.49- 6.49
EAAS 6.49- 8.49
desp. S. Rhodesia 5.51
5 FTS 8.51- 8.53
4 FTS storage 8.53-12.53
Sold 12.53

KF990
3 SFTS 2.46-12.46
22 SFTS [FCJ:I] 12.46- 3.50
3 FTS 3.50- 1.51
RAFC 12.52- 3.54
SS (AES) 12.56

KF991
CGS 8.46-11.46
FRS 4.50- 4.51
101 FRS [FDA:O] 4.51-10.51
RAFC 12.52- 4.54
Sold Hw spares 6.54

KF992
6 SFTS 3.46
cr. near Malpas, Cheshire, 22.11.46

KF993
No RAF service
SS (BKLA) 8.49

KF994
No RAF service
SOC 1.6.50

KF995
3 SFTS 1.46- 4.47
3 FTS [FBU:M] 4.47-12.49
RAFC [FAA:C/AC] 12.49- 3.54
Sold Hw spares 7.54

KF996
66 Gp. CF 6.49-10.49
612 Sqdn 10.49- 3.54
SS (Avex) 5.57

KF997
616 Sqdn [RAW:5/RAW:C/YQ:C] 6.48- 9.53
SS (Avex) 9.57

KF998
41 Gp. Trg. Flt
1689 Flt [9X:E] 10.45-12.47
25 RFS 7.50- 8.50
11 RFS 8.50-10.50
1 FTS 5.51- 2.55
SS (Avex) 5.57

KF999
3 SFTS [FBU:N] 1.46- 4.47
3 FTS 4.47
cr. 5mls NNW of Feltwell, 22.2.50

****

A correct, and early, application of a four-letter code on KF561 of No.20 SFTS, Church Lawford in September 1946 (M.P.March via D.J.Smith)

CODE MARKINGS

A NOTE ON CODE MARKINGS CARRIED BY RAF AND RN HARVARDS

As might be expected when dealing with a type of aircraft used in many different theatres of operation, code markings applied by the RAF and Royal Navy to their Harvards conformed to a variety of schemes. It was not until the early post-War period that Flying Training and Reserve Commands indulged in an overall coding system for their aircraft.

In the United Kingdom, Mk.I Harvards, if they carried any codes at all, sported local schemes consisting of letters or numerals. When the same aircraft later found themselves in Southern Rhodesia they carried pairs of letters, while Mk.II aircraft in the same area showed numerlas and Mk.IIa either single letters or numerals.

Canadian-based Harvards Mk.II usually carried numbers of up to three digits, each SFTS having its own series. Aircraft of all marks in the Middle East used codes conforming with local ad-hoc systems, usually a single letter or numeral.

When the Mk.IIb Harvards began to arrive in the UK in 1944 and were taken on charge by (P)AFUs a variety of locally-designed systems of letters and/or numerals began to appear. However, by the time these units had been modified to become SFTSs and FTSs a centralised system was considered necessary, so the famous four-letter codes came into being in 1946. Flying Training Command units, which employed most of the UK-based Harvards, used a series of letters beginning with F, e.g. FDM at Central Flying School, followed by an individual aircraft letter. The three 'unit' letters were intended to be marked on one side of the fuselage roundel and the individual letter on the other side, but in practice the letters were applied as space dictated. Reserve Command used a similar system beginning with the letter R and Technical Training Command used letter T, although as far as is known no Harvards carried the latter. This system lasted until the Spring of 1951, when two-letter codes were substituted, and these were used until Harvards were finally withdrawn from the FTSs. The strange thing is that the two-letter codes of one FTS often compromised those of other Schools.

In the post-War Rhodesian Air Training Group, Harvard aircraft of 5 FTS carried two-letter codes for a period, later using the letter G plus a two-digit numeral. 4 FTS also used two-letter codes at first, often with the letters SE painted on the engine cowling, but later changed to the letter H with a numeral.

The many squadrons which used Harvards in either the training role or as hacks often applied code letters in conformity with the letters carried by the squadron's main aircraft type. Individual letters used on such Harvards were often grouped near either the beginning or the end of the alphabet, or numerals were used, e.g. M4:6.

Harvards used by the Fleet Air Arm of the Royal Navy during and just after the War carried the letter/numeral combination codes of the period, e.g. Y6, followed by an individual letter. Subsequently, letters denoting the aircraft's base, e.g. VL for Yeovilton, were carried on the aircraft's tail fin, with a three-digit numeral adjacent to the roundel.

There follows in tabulated form details known to the author of four-letter codes, squadron codes and later two-letter codes used on RAF Harvards. Spaces have been left for the reader to insert further code tie-ups which may come to light, and it would be appreciated if the author could be advised, via Air Britain, of any such additions.

FOUR-LETTER CODES

	19 FTS/RAFC					20 SFTS/2 FTS		
	FAA	FAB	FAC	FAD	FAE	FAI	FAJ	FAK
A	KF220 KF448	KF415 KF574	FT259	KF207		FS891 KF419	KF237 KF704	KF454
B		FX379 FX432 KF539				KF438	KF254 KF377	KF240
C	KF265 KF298 KF995	KF192	KF301	FT209		FX237 KF139 KF156	KF432 KF704	KF241 KF432
D	FS840 FT149 FX444	FX266 KF254 KF275	KF436		FT388	FS849 FX307 FX362	KF270	KF454
E	FX306	FS856 FX414	FT378 KF924			FX237 FX300 KF491	KF270	FS744
F	FT332 FT343	FS748 KF443	FS847 FT387			FS725 KF206	FS856 FX376 KF372	KF432
G	FS758 KF430	KF250 KF328	KF457 KF483	KF539		FS914 FT393	KF650	KF240
H	FS827 KF139	FS899 KF191		FT302 FT338		FS756	KF272 KF902	FT450
J	KF170 KF596	FS852 FX437 KF572				FS762	KF313 KF468	FT401 KF250 KF397
K	KF497 FS816	FS753 FS816 KF272	FX299	FX305		KF702	FT354 KF419 KF466	KF419
L	KF241	FS755 KF413		KF986			FT255 KF192	KF485
M	KF459	FS899 FT250 KF328		FT224 FX230		FS900	FS758 FT334 KF198	KF491
N	FX340	FT215		FT259 KF476		FS914 KF561	FS822 KF443	FT224
O		KF191 KF700						
P	FT433 FT439		FX271			FS899 KF224 KF437	KF372	FT397
Q								
R	KF296	KF214	FS886			KF435	KF179	
S	KF334	KF367				KF473	KF465 KF693	FS837
T	KF264	FX437				FS891 KF435 KF437	FT303	KF265
U	FT403 FX261	FT209					KF572	
V	KF308		FS773	FS855				
W	KF280		FS755				KF438	
X	KF148		FT333	FS816 FX468		KF725	FX200	
Y	KF448	KF231	KF910	KF140				
Z	FT214 FT338		FS815	FX441		FX300		

Typical livery of the early 'fifties is seen on KF977 [N:N] of No.2 FTS at Cluntoe. Note individual letter repeated on cowling. (R.Rayner via "Roundel" magazine)

21 SFTS

	FAN	FAP
A		
B	KF610	
C		
D	KF335	
E	FT283	KF469
F		
G	FT383	
H		KF460
J	FX340	FX440
K		
L		
M		
N		
O		
P	KF128	
Q		
R		
S	KF455	FX273
T		
U		
V		
W		
X		
Y		
Z		

7 SFTS/7 FTS

	FBA	FBB	FBC	FBD
A	FT346	FT153	FT346	
	FX469	FT418		
B	KF288	FX397		
C	KF481	FS776	KF224	
	KF688			
D	KF481	FX388		FX428
E		FS757		
F	KF300	FT153		KF238
	KF364	FT413		
G	KF266	FX400		
		KF588		
H	FX284	FX376		
	KF153			
J	FT412	FS894	FT435	KF289
		FS906		
K	FX226	FT393		
L	FS776	FX240	FS849	
	KF698	KF472		
M	FX324	FS822		
N				KF206
O	KF605	FX300		KF185
P	FX284	KF753		
	KF265			
Q	KF185	FT376	KF955	
R	KF955	KF955	FX266	KF496
S	KF238	KF985		
T	KF496			
U	KF289	FT255	FX300	
V	KF224	KF156	KF698	
W	KF959	FT440	FX324	
		KF959		
X	FT431	FX263		
Y		FT413		
Z	KF243	KF922		

Numerical codes were usual in Canada. Here Mk.IIb FE277 of No.31 SFTS carries number 105 and sports a part-chequered cowling
(Capt T.W.Harrington, DFC, RN(Rtd) via R.C.Sturtivant)

6 SFTS/6 FTS

	FBG	FBH	FBI	FBJ
A	FT445	KF275		KF408
		KF411		
B	FX434	FX203		KF972
C	KF662	FX286		FT330
				KF268
D	FS853	FX213		FT165
				KF182
E	FT413	FX227		KF653
		KF563		
F	FT164	FX352		KF361
G	FT364	FS753	FS738	
		KF409		
H		FS773		
		KF659		
I	FE910	KF358	FS513	KF127
				KF682
J	KF142	FX400	KF442	KF681
	KF978	KF352		KF705
				KF714
K	KF165	FT245		FS819
	KF605	FT411		FS843
				KF937
L		KF538		FS743
				FS883
M			FT254	KF663
N				KF157
O				FT158
				FT348
P				KF587
Q				KF580
R				
S			FS738	
T				
U				
V				
W				
X		KF358		

3 SFTS/3 FTS

	FBP	FBR	FBS	FBT	FBU
A			FT363	KF977	FX206
B		FX249	FT363	FS828	
				FT367	
				KF177	
C		KF194		FX368	KF191
D	FT318		KF162	FX369	
	FX266				
E		FX367	FT285	FT292	FX266
					KF984
F			FX265	KF161	FT214
				KF966	KF448
G		FT450		FS892	KF153
				FX257	
H		FX269		KF220	KF145
				KF513	
I				FX283	
J		FT386	FT263	FS852	FT149
				FT341	
				FX437	
K				KF292	FT329
				KF430	
L				FS735	KF183
M		KF966		FT322	KF298
					KF995
N		FX306		FT263	KF999
O				KF138	FS827
					KF156
P				FT290	FS840
				KF342	FX379
Q				KF138	FT284
				KF237	
R				KF265	FT338
S					FX291
T				KF911	FS829
					FX350
U					
V				KF301	
W				FX245	
X				KF723	
Y				FT336	
Z				FS756	

1 FTS

	FCA	FCB
A	FX209	
B		KF251
C	FX284	KF337
D		KF413
E		KF379
F	FS816	
	FS854	
G		
H		
I	KF280	
J	FX280	
K	KF388	
L	KF563	FX394
M	KF725	
N	KF959	
O		
P		
Q		
R	FS815	
S	FT338	
T	KF487	
U	FT337	
V	FX198	
W	FT360	
X		
Y	FX288	
Z		

	17 SFTS/1 FTS			22 SFTS/22 FTS			
	FCD	FCE	FCF	FCI	FCJ	FCK	FCM
A	KF265			FT298		KF411	
				KF240			
				KF426			
B				KF173	KF313		
C			FX340	KF221	FX436		
D		KF359		FT394	FT351		
					FT429		
E				FT429			?FX289
F					FT298		
G				KF277	FT175		
H	FS816			FX209	FT175		
	FT246			KF319			
I		FX402		KF447	KF990		
J		FT405	KF481	FT327	FS855		
				FT336			
				KF195			
K				KF179	KF466		
				KF345			
L		KF300		KF400			
M		FT412		FT281	KF438		
				KF458			
N				FT334	KF665		
				KF245			
O				FX279	FT239		
P	FX280			FT324	KF197		
	KF266			FX278	KF377		
Q				FX394	KF300		
R		FT438		FT258			
				KF163			
				KF919			
S		FT441		KF953	KF263		
					KF458		
T				FX300	FT255		
				KF911			
U	KF280	FT446					
V		FT451		KF943	FX375		
		KF160			KF757		
W				KF476			
				KF982			
X	FX331			KF538			
Y	FX347			KF341	FS900		
Z				KF209			

	CFS			BAS/CFS	EAAS/RAFFC
	FDM	FDN	FDO	FDW	FGC
A	FX350	FS753			
	KF127	FT245			
	KF352				
B	KF142	FX227			
	KF156	FX389			
C	FT158	FT348			
		KF563			
D	FT321	KF564		KF541	
	FT364				
E	FT213				
F	FT424	FT421		FS813	
	KF206				
G	FX391		?FT346	KF959	
H	KF182				
	KF695				
I			KF307		
J		FS841	FT397		
K	FT331	FS819		FT332	
	FX234				
L		FT213	FX434		
M			FS899		
N			FT450		
O	FT313	FS884			
P	FX199				FT352
					FX226
Q		FX301	KF468		
R					
S	FX240				FX297
	KF244				
T	KF338				
U	KF321		FS744		FS823
V	FX301		FS822		
	KF321				
W	FT346	FT361	FS837		
	FX470	FX382			
X	FT246	FT361			
	KF276				
Y		FX403	FS849		
Z	FX369		FS883		

	ECFS/EFS/RAFFC	21(P)AFU/1(P)RFU/FRS		
	FCT	FDA	FDC	FDD
A	KF541			
B	FT332			KF986
C	FT310			FX468
	FT418			
D	FT330			FT224
	KF989			
E	FT352			
F	FT360			FS770
G	FS920			
H	FX450			
I	FT401			
	FX297			
J	FS829			
K	FT431	FT288		KF334
L	FT445			KF700
M	FT172	FS757		
N	FT319			FX395
O	FT402	KF139		
		KF991		
P	FS892	FT401	FT401	
Q	..859			
R	FS823			
S	FS853	FX307		FX307
		FX395		
T		FX356		
		KF334		
U		KF333		
V				
W				
X				
Y				
Z		KF417		

	CGS	FTCCF	21 Gp. CF	23 Gp. CF
	FJX	FKN	FKO	FKP
A	FT214			
B	KF574	FX389		
C		FS752	FX219	
D		KF248		
E		KF653		
F		KF684		
G				
H				
I				
J				
K	KF282			
L				
M				
N				
O				
P				FX420
Q				
R				
S				
T				
U				
V	KF282			
W				
X				
Y				
Z				

TWO-LETTER CODES

	500 Sqdn	501 Sqdn	502 Sqdn	504 Sqdn	600 Sqdn	601 Sqdn	602 Sqdn	603 Sqdn
	RAA	RAB	RAC	RAD	RAG	RAH	RAI	RAJ
A		FS906 KF670			FX370 KF645			FS770 KF699
B	KF423	KF383 KF616			FT414			FT342 KF449
C		FX420 KF616			FS890 KF310			KF560
R	FX432		FX249					
S						KF151		
T	KF423							
U						FX387		
V						FX399		
W								
X				KF579			KF584	
Y							KF374	
Z				KF925			FT141	

	604 Sqdn	605 Sqdn	607 Sqdn	608 Sqdn	609 Sqdn	610 Sqdn	611 Sqdn	612 Sqdn
	RAK	RAL	RAN	RAO	RAP	RAQ	RAR	RAS
A			KF373 KF737					
B			FX280 KF954					
C			KF193					
D								
E								
F								
G								
H								
I								
J								
K								
L								
M		KF145						
N		KF433		FT457				
O		KF160						
P								
Q								
R				KF722				KF666
S								FX283
T								KF706
U								
V								
W								
X	FT405				FX382 KF645	FX427 FX410	KF640	
Y	FT288 KF709				KF389	FT282	KF223	
Z	FT342				KF960		KF255	

	613 Sqdn	614 Sqdn	615 Sqdn	616 Sqdn	RCCS
	RAT	RAU	RAV	RAW	RCA
A					
B				KF733	
C				KF997	
L					FS921
X			KF200		
Y		KF149			
Z		KF149			
1	FT409 KF387				
2	FX427 KF470				
3				KF720	
4				KF733	
5				KF997	

	1 FTS			2 FTS		3 FTS		
	K	N	P	N	P	O	P	R
A	FX284 FX288		FT343					
B	FT360		FT416					
C		KF731	KF343					KF750
D		KF270	KF356					
E			FS843					FX379
F		KF274 KF384						
G		KF435	KF227					KF177
H			FS854				FX266	
I								
J							FX292	
K								
L							KF156	KF298 KF333
M			KF233					
N		FT394	FE948	KF977				
O		FT360		KF714				
P		KF360	KF732	KF565		KF237	KF372	
Q		KF280		FS920			KF694	KF911
R			FX234					KF966
S			FX256					
T		KF487	FX288 KF341					FT284
U		KF748	KF224				FS829	
V		KF224	FS906					
W		FT423			FS920			
X		KF485					FS900	KF375
Y			FX236					
Z			FX220				KF725	

	6 FTS		7 FTS			9 FTS
	O	P	N	O	P	M
A			FX220	KF153 KF238		
B						
C		KF216	KF364			
D	KF188		KF243			
E	KF165		KF590			KF290
F			KF288	KF288		
G			KF266	FX334		
H				KF955		
I						
J	KF388		KF142	FX397		
K			KF924	FS738		
L		KF472				
M		KF587				
N						
O				FS894 FX388		
P						
Q			KF481	FE948		
R			KF588			
S						
T			KF714	KF472		
U	KF157	KF576 KF693	KF665	KF290		
V						
W		KF268				
X						
Y				KF565		
Z	FS898	KF730				

19 FTS

	A	B	C	D	E	F	G	H
A	KF513	KF266		KF239				KF476
B		FE909 KF539					KF207	KF464
C		KF291	KF301	KF182			FS759	KF303
D		KF349	KF436				KF241	KF215
E		FX291				FS886	KF259	
F	KF497	FS748	KF924		KF197	KF257		KF160
G		KF328			FS847	KF415 KF459		
H						FX470		KF596
I								
J		FX295	KF572		KF416		FT302	
K		FS753		FX466			FX299	
L	KF271					FS735	FX305	
M	KF447	FX468		FX230				KF140
N								FX441
O								
P								
Q								
R								
S		KF367 KF412						

	CFS			RAFC		
M		FS899 KF172 KF937	FS899		KF328	
N	FT330			FX340	FT215	
O		FS823 KF572		KF310	KF191	
P	FX419		FX391	FT433		
Q	KF702	FS823 FX301 KF211				
R				KF296	KF214	FS886
S			KF362			
T		KF150	KF755			
U			FS744	FX261	FT209	
V	KF320		KF306	KF308		
W	FX252	KF172			FX286	
X		KF756	KF756	KF148		
Y		KF133			KF231	
Z		FX350				

22 FTS

	R	U	Y
A	KF651	KF411	
B	FX437		
C	KF128	KF341	
D			KF128 KF458
E	KF711	FX394	KF377
F	KF204		FX339
G	FX279	KF400	KF466
H			KF300
I		FX248 KF197	KF263
J	KF264		
K	FX427	KF430	
L		KF447	
M		KF466	KF650
N			
O			FS819
P	FX209	KF337	KF757
Q	KF313	KF139	
R		KF277	FX226
S	FT255		
T	KF448	KF259	
U	FT239		
V		KF130	
W	KF197		
X			
Y			
Z	FX339		

5(P)AFU

	B	E	H
B	FX269	FX206	
C			FX201
F	FX324		
G			FX386
H		FX245	
K		FX370	
L	FS766		FX406
M	FX203		
N	KF185		
O	FX212		
P	FX226	KF221 KF233	
T		FX208 KF267	
U	FX266		
V	FX343		
X	FX227		

CFS

	M	N	O
A	KF352	KF169	KF169
B	KF426	FX227	KF289
C			KF315
D		FX234 KF572	
E		KF588 KF612	KF241
F		FX291	FX291
G		FT346 FX356 KF668	
H	KF695	KF473	KF473
I		FX470	
J	FX470	FS841	
K		KF682	
L			FX281

RAFC

	A	B	C
A		KF574	
B	FS813		
C	KF995		FX257
D	FS840	KF275	
E			FT378
F	FT332		
G	KF430	KF250	
H	FS827	KF986	
J		FX437 KF746	
L	FX325	FS755	

SQUADRON CODES

1 Sqdn:	JX:D	FS905
	JX:E	KF333
	JX:G	FS921 FX248 FX311
	JX:H	FX416
	JX:J	FX248
	JX:K	FX411
	JX:L	FX245
5 & 595 Sqdns:	7B:R	KF920
17 Sqdn:	UT:M	FX222
20 Sqdn:	TH:Z	KF561
34 Sqdn:	8Q:6	KF155 KF405
167 Sqdn:	QO:A	KF395
	QO:J	FX269
	QO:N	KF604
500 Sqdn:	S7:S	KF718
501 Sqdn:	SD:A	KF670
	SD:B	FX442 KF383
	SD:C	FX420 FX442
502 Sqdn:	V9:Q	KF707
504 Sqdn:	TM:Z	KF155 KF925
587 Sqdn:	M4:R	FS767
	M4:S	FS770
	M4:T	FS881
601 Sqdn:	HT:V	FX399
	HT:X	FX387
	HT:Y	KF402
	HT:Z	KF151
602 Sqdn:	LO:X	KF389 KF584
	LO:Y	KF374
	LO:Z	KF920
605 Sqdn:	NR:D	KF160
607 Sqdn:	LA:A	KF373
	LA:B	KF954
	LA:C	KF193
608 Sqdn:	6T:N	FT457
	6T:R	KF722
	6T:T	FX207
609 Sqdn:	PR:B	KF374
610 Sqdn:	DW:W	KF383
	DW:X	FX410
	DW:Y	FT282
	DW:Z	FT369
611 Sqdn:	FY:X	KF640
612 Sqdn:	8W:X	FS881
613 Sqdn:	Q3:1	FS739
	Q3:2	KF470
	Q3:3	FX219 KF383
614 Sqdn:	7A:X	FX360
	7A:Y	FX417
615 Sqdn:	V6:X	KF200
	V6:Y	FX205
616 Sqdn:	YQ:C	KF997
695 Sqdn:	4M:Q	KF331
1689 Flt:	9X:A	FT208
	9X:B	KF710
	9X:C	KF712
	9X:D	KF974
	9X:E	KF998
61 OTU/203 AFS/226)OCU	TO:D	KF711
	TO:G	KF212
	TO:J	FX443
	TO:L	KF269
	TO:N	KF315
	TO:O	KF315
	TO:P	FX360
	TO:R	KF201
	TO:S	KF227
	TO:T	FS739
	TO:Z	FS739

FTSs in Rhodesian Air Training Group:

	4 FTS					5 FTS
	B	D	F	G	H	X
A	EX358	EX514			EX161	EX521
B	EX375	EX518	EX385		EX359	EX510
C		EX523		EX245		EX405
		EX528				
D	EX401	EX675				EX518
E	EX830	EX707		EX420		EX420
F	EX436			EX437	EX418	EX530
G		EX786				EX523
H		EX832				EX707
I			EX510			
J		EX845	EX529			EX753
K	EX753	EX416			EX416	EX832
L	EX411				EX510	EX773
M			EX700	EX522		EX765
N	EX437	EX522		EX159	EX533	EX514
O	EX534					EX513
	EX673					
P	EX517					EX532
Q						
R	EX419					
S	EX373					
T	EX411					
U	EX405					
V	EX765					
W	EX842					
X						
Y						
Z	EX818					

Reserve Command code RAP:X on Harvard IIb of No.609 Squadron *(via R.C.Sturtivant)*

DISPOSALS

BELGIAN AIR FORCE

The first batch of Harvards transferred from the RAF to the Belgian Air Force comprised 56 Mk.IIa and Mk.III aircraft supplied between February and May 1947. Of these ten were not allocated FAB serials and were used as a source of spare parts. All 56 aircraft had seen wartime service in South Africa before being shipped to the UK in late 1946 and put into storage.

A further 24 Harvards Mk.IIa were supplied in November 1953 for use in the Belgian Congo; these were aircraft for which the RAF had no further use after the closeure of the Rhodesian Air Training Group.

Between August and October 1949 ten Mk.IIb Harvards with previous service in the United Kingdom were supplied to the FAB, and ten more followed in September/October 1950, this time via Rollason Aircraft. The final batch of ten Mk.IIb Harvards of RAF origin arrived in Belgium from the Royal Netherlands Air Force between October 1952 and March 1953 to join one which had been in Belgium since 1949.

Mk.IIa and Mk.III

FAB serial	RAF serial	SAAF serial	
H.1	EZ162	7548	became F-BJBA
H.2	EX974	7531	
H.3	EZ335	7632	became F-BJBB
H.4	EX660	7309	became F-BJBC
H.5	EX937	7493	
H.6	EZ174	7555	became F-BJBD
H.7	EZ186	7563	
H.8	EX476	7295	became F-BJBE
H.9	EX959	7509	became F-BJBF
H.10	EX438	7027	
H.11	EX239	7094	
H.12	EX544	7268	
H.13	EX551	7239	
H.14	EX993	7527	became F-BJBG
H.15	EZ310	7625	to SAAF (7729) 1.61
H.16	EZ214	7578	became F-BJBH
H.17	EX542	7269	became OO-GEM
H.18	EX181	7045	became OO-GEQ
H.19	EZ210	7605	to SAAF (7731) 10.61
H.20	EX230	7007	
H.21	EZ256	7630	
H.22	EX264	7107	to FAC 1962
H.23	EZ292	7622	to FAC 1962
H.24	EX295	7077	
H.25	EX303	7043	
H.26	EX371	7187	became OO-GEN
H.27	EX439	7282	
H.28	EX461	7210	became OO-GEO
H.29	EX633	7349	became F-BJBI
H.30	EX602	7384	became F-BJBJ
H.31	EX661	7315	became OO-GER
H.32	EX760	7400	
H.33	EX823	7468	became F-BJBK
H.34	EX910	7476	to FAC 1962
H.35	EX939	7505	to FAC 1962
H.36	EX273	7184	became OO-GES
H.37	EX305	7115	became OO-GDK
H.38	EX946	7501	
H.39	EX292	7182	Preserved
H.40	EX318	7128	became F-BJBL
H.41	EX567	7232	
H.42	EX623	7344	became OO-GDL
H.43	EX779	7409	became OO-GDM
H.44	EZ307	7623	
H.45	EX680	7329	became OO-GEP
H.46	EX994	7528	

FAB serial	RAF serial	SAAF serial	
--	EX251	7141	For use as spares
--	EX254	7098	"
--	EX275	7164	"
--	EX393	7179	"
--	EX448	7030	"
--	EX546	7286	"
--	EX547	7288	"
--	EX550	7236	"
--	EX821	7470	"
--	EX940	7494	"
H.201	EX419	--	
H.202	EX534	--	
H.203	EX788	--	to FAC 1962
H.204	EX682	--	
H.205	EX655	--	
H.206	EX656	--	
H.207	EX699	--	
H.208	EX678	--	to FAC 1962
H.209	EX525	--	
H.210	EX753	--	
H.21	EX671	--	
H.212	EX374	--	
H.213	EX245	--	
H.214	EX379	--	
H.215	EX420	--	
H.216	EX405	--	to SAAF (7732) 2.61
H.217	EX528	--	
H.218	EX698	--	
H.219	?	--	
H.220	EX771	--	
H.221	EX784	--	to SAAF (77..) .62
H.222	EX651	--	
H.223	EX657	--	to SAAF (7730) 2.61
H.224	EX436	--	

Mk.IIb

FAB serial	RAF serial	
H.47	FS820	ex R.NethAF (B-120) .49
H.49	KF490	
H.50	KF463	
H.51	KF207	
H.52	KF415	became OO-GDO
H.53	FX212	
H.54	FX414	
H.55	FX466	
H.56	FX299	
H.57	KF483	
H.58	KF568	became OO-AAR
H.64	FX276	
H.65	KF738	
H.66	?	
H.67	KF715	became OO-GDP
H.68	KF724	
H.69	KF716	
H.70	KF737	
H.71	KF719	
H.72	KF680	
H.73	KF734	became OO-GDQ
H.74	FT247	ex R.NethAF (B-99)
H.75	FT430	ex R.NethAF (B-47)
H.76	FT381	ex R.NethAF (B-131)
H.77	FT410	ex R.NethAF (B-37)
H.78	FT142	ex R.NethAF (B-20)
H.79	FT210	ex R.NethAF (B-105)
H.80	FS885	ex R.NethAF (B-89)
H.81	FS730	ex R.NethAF (B-128)
H.82	FT286	ex R.NethAF (B-58)
H.83	FT390	ex R.NethAF (B-139)

Belgian Air Force H.49 still carrying RAF serial KF490. Note unusual black/yellow/red rudder markings, which were restricted to a few aircraft supplied by Rollasons (V.Kenens)

H.207 of Belgian Air Force (formerly EX699) is assessed as Cat.5 after crashing in the Congo (V.Kenens)

CONGOLESE AIR FORCE

The Congolese Air Force inherited a number of former Belgian Air Force Harvards in 1962, but full details are unknown. BAF serials of the aircraft included H.22, H.23, H.34, H.35, H.203 and H.208.

L'ARMEE DE L'AIR (French Air Force)

Thirty Harvards Mk.IIb, many previously unused, were supplied to France in April/May 1949 from RAF stocks in the United Kingdom. They were supplemented later by 17 ex-RAF Mk.II aircraft from Canada. All these aircraft probably retained their original RAF serials while in French service.

Mk.IIb

FS903, FT285, FT302, FT333, FT443, FT444, FX239, FX250, FX302, FX312, FX322, FX323, FX341, KF257, KF316, KF376, KF436, KF479, KF567, KF577, KF581, KF595, KF597, KF608, KF656, KF658, KF667, KF677, KF979, KF988.

Mk.II

AH191, AJ550, AJ561, AJ650, AJ654, AJ662, AJ753, AJ790, AJ801, AJ827, AJ831, AJ897, AJ918, AJ937, AJ950, BW199, BW203.

INDIAN AIR FORCE

On the partition of India in Sept. 1947, the new India received 82 Harvards Mk.IIb from remaining RAF stocks in that country. They were renumbered into the IAF's HT series but details are not known.

FE354	FS782	FT115	FX455
FE374	FS787	FT121	FX458
FE424	FS799	FT123	FX460
FE429	FS803	FT128	FX464
FE482	FS806	FT131	FX472
FE483	FS927	FT132	FX473
FE597	FS934	FT179	FX478
FE616	FS939	FT180	FX482
FE664	FS940	FT181	FX486
FE685	FS944	FT185	FX490
FE711	FS948	FT187	FX492
FE775	FS949	FT192	KF100
FE883	FS956	FT195	KF101
FE952	FS986	FT202	KF102
FE954	FS987	FT371	KF115
FE974	FT101	FX401	KF119
FH113	FT103	FX445	KF122
FS693	FT106	FX447	KF123
FS697	FT112	FX448	KF135
FS700	FT114	FX451	KF137
FS707		FX454	

ISRAELI DEFENCE FORCE AIR FORCE

The Israeli Defence Force Air Force used a number of Harvards, but only one is positively identified: FE452, a Mk.IIb from Canadian stocks. This aircraft later became 4X-ARA.

ITALIAN AIR FORCE

Italy received 13 Mk.IIa Harvards from UK stocks in May 1949 following their 'recapture' by the USA. These aircraft had been among the many shipped from South Africa in 1946. One Mk.II aircraft was also supplied, from surplus RCAF stocks, and the 14 aircraft were numbered MM53038-53051 in the IAF, though not necessarily strictly in order.

RAF serial	SAAF serial	RAF serial	SAAF serial
EX258	7101	EX466	7038
EX269	7112	EX489	7221
EX278	7169	EX504	7258
EX301	7083	EX581	7247
EX332	7151	EX731	7375
EX390	7189	EX835	7458
EX397	7180		
		AJ564	--

JORDANIAN AIR FORCE

The Royal Jordanian Air Force purchased three of the RAF's Mk.IIb Harvards which had been used by the anti-Mau-Mau 1340 Flight in Kenya. They were received in Jordan in January and February 1956 and were given new serials such as T207, but no details are known.

FS855, FT409, KF579.

LEBANESE AIR FORCE

It is known that the Lebanese Air Force operated at least sixteen Harvards serialled L121 to L136. Some of them were ex-RAF aircraft purchased from Airwork Ltd. in 1952 (e.g. L125); others, including the four listed below were well-used aircraft from RAF units based in the Middle East. These went to Lebanon in January 1954.

KF287, KF350, KF391, KF394.

MARINE LUCHTVAARTDIENST (Royal Dutch Navy)

The MLD (Marine Luchtvaartdienst), the Royal Dutch Navy's aviation service, received six Harvards Mk.IIb on loan from the Royal Netherlands Air Force in 1946. They were returned in 1949, and it was 1958 before four more Harvards were transferred from the Air Force, probably also on loan. The final four aircraft arrived at de Kooy in 1965/66.

MLD serial	R.NethAF serial	RAF serial	t.o.c.	ret'd
L-1	B-63	FT316	10.46	4.49
L-2	B-62	FT326	9.46	7.48
L-3	B-61	FT233	8.46	9.48
L-4	B-60	FT456	9.46	2.49
L-5	B-59	FT144	8.46	4.49
L-6	B-64	FE907	8.46	9.48
043	B-56	FT176	1.65	
044	B-57	FE980	1.65	
098	B-84	FT454	3.66	
099	B-164	FE821	3.66	
	B-101	FT407	.58	
	B-134	FS777	.58	
	B-136	FS913	.58	
	B-155	FE947	.58	

PAKISTAN AIR FORCE

Twenty-nine Harvards Mk.IIb were handed over to the Pakistan Air Force on formation in Sept. 1947, as listed below; PAF serials, if any, are unknown.

FE373	FS711	FT122	FX485
FE413	FS783	FT182	FX497
FE472	FS791	FT188	KF110
FE687	FS931	FT191	KF116
FE708	FS947	FT194	KF121
FE766	FS953	FX456	KF125
FE879	FS993	FX457	KF144
FS702			

PORTUGUESE AIR FORCE

The Portugeuse Air Force took delivery of sixteen Harvards Mk.III from the Royal Navy in March 1956, and numbered them 1654 to 1669. 59 more Harvards, this time Mk.IIa, were supplied to Portugal by the South African Air Force at the end of 1969 and were numbered 1501 to 1559 by the FAP.

Seven more Mk.IIa and three Mk.IIb Harvards were handed over to the FAP by the Belgian Air Force

Seven more Mk.IIa and three Mk.IIb Harvards were supplied to the FAP from Belgium in 1962, latterly having carried Belgian civil registrations. Prior to that they had seen service with the Belgian Air Force and South African Air Force.

FAP serial	RAF serial	
1654		
1655	EZ421	
1656	EZ407	Under restoration for RN Hist. Aircraft Flt.
1657	EX976	Preserved at FAA Museum
1658	FT965	
1659	FT966	
1660	EZ403	
1661	FT971	Became G-BGOW
1662	EZ341	Stored at Sintra
1663	EZ303	
1664	EZ401	
1665	EZ451	
1666	EZ312	
1667	EZ281	
1668	EZ438	
1669	EZ420	

FAP serial	SAAF serial	RAF serial	
	7004	EX211	
	7020	EX227	
	7022	EX229	
	7029	EX446	
1551	7039	EX467	
	7043	EX408	
	7051	EX182	
	7052	EX196	
	7060	EX205	
1545	7084	EX302	Became G-BICE
	7096	EX117	
1558	7103	EX260	
	7106	EX263	
1519	7110	EX267	
	7124	EX314	
	7131	EX169	
	7132	EX170	
	7133	EX171	
1532	7142	EX252	
	7150	EX330	
1560	7168	EX287	Became G-RCAF
	7171	EX271	
	7174	EX361	
1554	7185	EX392	Became G-BGOU
	7202	EX443	
	7220	EX488	
1538	7223	EX495	
	7224	EX561	
	7243	EX582	
1522	7244	EX584	
	7248	EX580	
	7296	EX475	
	7301	EX472	
	7319	EX634	
1523	7333	EX688	
	7334	EX693	
	7335	EX599	
	7350	EX636	
	7363	EX695	
1559	7382	EX600	Became G-BGOV
	7388	EX608	
	7407	EX706	
	7428	EX841	
1506	7424	EX881	Became G-SUES

L.125 of Lebanese Air Force, a former RAF Harvard IIb (K.M.Robertson collection)

FAP serial	SAAF serial	RAF serial	
1513	7426	EX884	Returned to UK; under rebuild at Cranfield
	7430	EX873	
	7431	EX892	
1502	7439	EX915	Became G-JUDI
1504	7441	EX894	Became G-ELLY
	7445	EX890	
	7450	EX869	
	7485	EX911	
1508	7504	EX935	Became G-BGOR
	7518	EX973	
	7571	EZ144	
	7588	EZ201	
	7591	EZ207	
	7613	EZ226	
	7614	EZ224	

FAP serial	Civil serial	Belg.AF serial	SAAF serial	RAF serial
	OO CDL	H.42	7344	EX623
	OO-GDM	H.43	7409	EX779
	OO-GDO	H.52	--	KF415
	OO-GDP	H.67	--	KF715
	OO-GEN	H.26	7187	EX371
	OO-GEO	H.28	7210	EX461
	OO-GEQ	H.18	7045	EX181
	OO-GER	H.31	7315	EX661
	OO-GES	H.36	7184	EX273
1794	D-FIBU/ OO-AAR	H.58	--	KF568

Belgian Air Force Harvard H.35 demonstrating the under-wing stores carried during the Congo campaign (V.Kenens)

ROYAL CANADIAN AIR FORCE

When the RAF elements completed their withdrawal from the Commonwealth Air Training Scheme in Canada in 1944, hundreds of RAF-serialled Harvards, together with a great deal of other equipment, were left behind to become RCAF property. As such, they retained their original RAF serial numbers, as listed below, and continued in service at the RCAF's training schools. Subsequently, transfers were made to a number of European air arms; these are indicated below.

Mk.II (224 aircraft)

AH185-189	AJ723 (?)	AJ913-915
191-194	724	917-926
198-200	726	927-945
203,204	729-731	947-952
AJ539-541	733-736	954,955
544-546	753,754	957,958
550-555	756-758	960-965
557,558	760	967-969
560-562	762	971
564-568	764,765	973,974
570,571	788	976-978
573-589	790-792	979-981
591-596	794,795	983,984
644	798,799	985 (?)
647,648	801,802	986
650	823-825	987 (?)
652-656	827	BW184
658-662	829-835	186
685,686	847-849	188-190
688,689	851-853	195-197
692	893	199-204
696	895-897	206,207
700	900-910	

Sales and other transfers of Mk.II Harvards were subsequently made as follows:

To Turkish Air Force:	AH187, AJ565, AJ791, AJ848, AJ940, AJ970, BW188, BW207.
To French Air Force:	AH191, AJ550, AJ561, AJ650, AJ654, AJ662, AJ753, AJ790, AJ801, AJ827, AJ831, AJ897, AJ918, AJ937, AJ950, BW199, BW203.
To Italian Air Force:	AJ564.
To Royal Canadian Navy:	AH200.

Mk.IIb (494 aircraft)

FE269-283	FE456,457	FE863-865
285-287	460	869-877
289,290	462-465	902
292-296	467	905
299,300	499,500	912-915
302	502-505	917-920
306,307	507-527	922-942
309,310	554-557	944,945
312-317	559,560	947
319,320	562-572	949-951
322,323	574-581	976,977
325-328	583-585	979-982
330,331	588-592	984-994
333	618,619	996-999
335	621-634	FH100-106
337-339	636-646	117-119
341,342	648	121-127
344	650-661	129-160
346-348	688-695	162,163
350,351	722-730	165,166
383 (?)	733-738	FS661
384,385	739 (?)	663
388	741-743	665-681
390,391	745-749	857,858
392 (?)	751-754	860-862
396	762-764	864-878
400-402	790-797	957-977
404-410	801	FT265-267
412	803,804	272-278
433-438	807-818	289
440-443	820-837	292
445-447	839-858	296
449-454	860,861	

Subsequent sales and transfers of Mk.IIb Harvards were as follows:

To Swedish Air Force:	FE272, FE276, FE312, FE327, FE328, FE335, FE344, FE385, FE400, FE401, FE437, FE464, FE500, FE502, FE503, FE509, FE511, FE513, FE518, FE520, FE524, FE525, FE554, FE555, FE562, FE564, FE565, FE568, FE577, FE580, FE585, FE589, FE619, FE625, FE628, FE630, FE632, FE633, FE637, FE638, FE646, FE648, FE651, FE653, FE654, FE657, FE658, FE660, FE661, FE688, FE689, FE691-695, FE722-724, FE726, FE734, FE741-743, FE752, FE753, FE792, FE795, FE796, FE803, FE812, FE823, FE831-837, FE842, FE844, FE845, FE851-853, FE856, FE861, FE863, FE902, FE918, FE920, FE927, FE928, FE932, FE934, FE940, FE950, FE987, FE991, FE992, FH100, FH104, FH122, FH125, FH127, FH132, FH137, FH138, FH140, FH148, FH154, FH156-158, FH163, FH166, FS666, FS672, FS673, FS681, FS862, FS867, FS870, FS871, FS873, FS875, FS878, FS957, FS958, FS961, FS962, FS966, FS968, FS972, FT266, FT272, FT274-277, FT292, FT296.
Royal Netherlands A.F:	FE307, FE505, FE517, FE519, FE521, FE745, FE797, FE809, FE821, FE919, FE930, FE931, FE933, FE942, FE947, FE951, FE976, FE977, FE980, FE982, FE984-986, FE990, FE994, FE996, FE998, FE999, FH105, FH106, FH117, FH119, FH126, FH129-131, FH133, FH136, FH139, FH150, FH153, FH159, FS661, FS667, FS668, FS857, FS874, FS960, FT289.
Royal Danish Air Force:	FE391, FE623, FE804, FE905.
Royal Norwegian A.F:	FE296, FE435, FE460, FE621, FE992, FS959, FS965.
Swiss Air Force:	FE590, FE824.
Israeli Defence Force:	FE452.

ROYAL DANISH AIR FORCE

Denmark was another country which received ex-RAF Harvards in the immediate post-war years, 27 Mk.IIb aircraft being flown from the UK between December 1946 and September 1947 and four shipped from Canada. In addition three Mk.IIa and four Mk.III Harvards were supplied for use as technical training airframes and as a source of spare parts; these had seen service with the SAAF before being shipped to the UK for disposal.

RDAF serial	RAF serial	
301	FE760	
302	FE798	
303	FE800	
304	FE867	
305	FH109	
306	FH114	preserved and on display at Stauning
307	FS721	
308	FS766	
309	FS826	preserved
310	FS917	became LN-BNN
311	FS922	
312	FT135	became TF-ERN
313	FT143	
314	FT154	
315	FT157	
316	FT218	
317	FT226	

RDAF serial	RAF serial	
318	FT251	
319	FT257	
320	FT291	
321	FT305	
322	FT350	
323	FT377	
324	FT380	
325	FT398	
326	FT432	
327	FE391	ex RCAF
328	?	
329	FE905	ex RCAF; became LN-BNM
330	FE623	ex RCAF
331	FE804	ex RCAF

The Mk.IIa /III aircraft used as instructional air-frames were:

RDAF serial	RAF serial	SAAF serial
351	EX895	7434
352	EX925	7489
353	EZ339	7629
354	EX400	7178
355	EX279	7195
356	EX285	7075
357	EZ221	7594
358	EZ150	7537
359	EZ152	7538
360	EZ220	7582

ROYAL HELLENIC AIR FORCE

Greece received 35 Harvards Mk.IIa from the United Kingdom between March and August 1947. These were all aircraft which had seen service in South Africa before being shipped to the UK in the winter of 1946/47. They probably retained their RAF serial numbers in R.HellAF service.

RAF serial	SAAF serial	RAF serial	SAAF serial
EX177	7136	EX431	7275
EX221	7014	EX441	7274
EX223	7016	EX442	7207
EX228	7021	EX471	7298
EX236	7089	EX486	7218
EX249	7139	EX494	7222
EX253	7097	EX552	7229
EX257	7100	EX558	7235
EX259	7102	EX568	7285
EX282	7196	EX579	7249
EX291	7199	EX612	7389
EX299	7081	EX615	7339
EX308	7118	EX617	7341
EX313	7123	EX624	7345
EX320	7130	EX647	7358
EX340	7071	EX729	7373
EX347	7158	EX736	7370
EX382	7175		

Concurrently with the transfer to Greece of the Mk. IIa Harvards, thirty Mk.IIb aircraft began to arrive. 23 of these were sent from the UK (7 in July/August 1947 and 16 between July and September 1949) and of these fifteen had never seen active service. All but one of the other seven, which were sent from the Middle East in 1947 and 1949, were target-tug aircraft.

despatched from the UK		despatched from the ME
FX201	KF621	KF908*
FX204	KF631	KF913
FX235	KF655	KF933*
FX275	KF697	KF939*
FX413	KF728	KF956*
FX421	KF742	KF957*
KF189	KF743	KF973*
KF203	KF752	
KF295	KF962	
KF344	KF963	
KF480	KF967	
KF547		

* Mk.TT.IIb

Jerome Geeson of No.3 FP, Hawarden, poses with a Harvard IIb destined for the Royal Netherlands Air Force in 1946 (J.Geeson via D.J.Smith)

ROYAL NETHERLANDS AIR FORCE

Between August 1946 and November 1948 193 Harvards Mk.IIb in airworthy condition were handed over by the RAF and RCAF to the Royal Netherlands Air Force and a further seven aircraft were provided for use as a source of spare parts.

Of the 200 aircraft, fifty (B-151 to 200) were shipped from Canada after wartime use in the Flying Training Schools of the Commonwealth Air Training Scheme, while at least 115 of the 150 sent from the United Kingdom had not seen any previous service, having spent several years in storage in various Maintenance Units.

In addition to the Mk.IIb aircraft, 13 Mk.IIa and 7 Mk.III Harvards were shipped from South Africa in February 1947 for use as spare parts.

Mk.IIb

Dutch serial	RAF serial	
B-1	FT240	
B-2	FT238	
B-3	FT293	
B-4	FT317	
B-5	FT151	
B-6	FS754	
B-7	FS737	
B-8	FS896	
B-9	FE888	
B-10	FT178	
B-11	FT280	
B-12	FT459	
B-13	FS751	
B-14	FS831	
B-15	FT325	became PH-NIF
B-16	FT328	became PH-NIZ
B-17	FS740	
B-18	FT362	
B-19	FT323	became PH-SKK
B-20	FT142	to Belgian Air Force (H.78)
B-21	FT456	
B-22	FT256	
B-23	FT452	
B-24	FS716	
B-25	FS830	
B-26	FT234	
B-27	FT231	
B-28	FT161	
B-29	FT408	
B-30	FT400	
B-31	FE758	
B-32	FS851	
B-33	FS908	
B-34	FT420	
B-35	FT340	
B-36	FT134	
B-37	FT410	to Belgian Air Force (H.77)
B-38	FT425	

Dutch serial	RAF serial	
B-39	FT437	
B-40	FT177	
B-41	FS915	
B-42	FE750	
B-43	FE787	
B-44	FT212	
B-45	FT229	became PH-SKM
B-46	FT345	
B-47	FT430	to Belgian Air Force (H.75)
B-48	FS912	
B-49	FT222	
B-50	FT308	
B-51	FT448	
B-52	FS824	
B-53	FE332	
B-54	FT384	
B-55	FT385	
B-56	FT176	to MLD (043) 1.65
B-57	FT220	to MLD (044) 1.65
B-58	FT286	to Belgian Air Force (H.82)
B-59	FT144	to MLD
B-60	FT357	to MLD
B-61	FT233	to MLD (12.3)
B-62	FT326	to MLD
B-63	FT316	to MLD (12.1)
B-64	FE907	to MLD
B-65	FT160	
B-66	FT382	
B-67	FT422	
B-68	FT217	
B-69	FT223	
B-70	FT368	
B-71	FT404	became PH-MLM
B-72	FS778	
B-73	FT228	preserved at Schipol Aviodome
B-74	FT248	
B-75	FT447	
B-76	FS882	
B-77	FS839	
B-78	FT304	
B-79	FT145	
B-80	FT349	
B-81	FS726	
B-82	FT148	
B-83	FT406	
B-84	FT454	to MLD (098) 3.66
B-85	FT458	
B-86	FT242	
B-87	FT249	
B-88	FS910	
B-89	FS885	to Belgian Air Force (H.80)
B-90	FT136	
B-91	FT225	
B-92	FS774	
B-93	FS919	
B-94	FT159	
B-95	FS733	
B-96	FS724	
B-97	FT391	became PH-HON
B-98	FT230	
B-99	FT247	to Belgian Air Force (H.74)
B-100	FT347	
B-101	FT407	to MLD
B-102	FS765	
B-103	FT419	
B-104	FS728	
B-105	FT210	to Belgian Air Force (H.79)
B-106	FS719	
B-107	FS893	
B-108	FT320	
B-109	FS749	
B-110	FT167	
B-111	FS775	
B-112	FS817	
B-113	FS723	
B-114	FT244	
B-115	FT211	
B-116	FS727	
B-117	FS717	
B-118	FT427	became PH-TOO
B-119	FS731	
B-120	FS820	to Belgian Air Force (H.47)
B-121	FS909	

Dutch serial	RAF serial	
B-122	FT314	
B-123	FT279	
B-124	FT219	
B-125	FS833	
B-126	FT146	
B-127	FT171	
B-128	FS730	to Belgian Air Force (H.81)
B-129	FT312	
B-130	FH108	
B-131	FT381	to Belgian Air Force (H.76)
B-132	FT216	
B-133	FT311	
B-134	FS777	to MLD
B-135	FS880	became PH-BKT
B-136	FS913	to MLD
B-137	FS771	
B-138	?	
B-139	FT390	to Belgian Air Force (H.83)
B-140	FS743	
B-141	FT306	
B-142	FT455	
B-143	FT417	
B-151	FE521	became PH-NIA
B-152	FE505	
B-153	FE745	
B-154	FE519	
B-155	FE947	to MLD
B-156	FE517	
B-157	FE980	
B-158	FH153	became PH-PPS
B-159	FE951	
B-160	FT289	
B-161	FS857	
B-162	FE933	
B-163	FE930	
B-164	FE821	to MLD (099) 3.66
B-165	FH130	
B-166	FE976	
B-167	FE982	
B-168	FE984	
B-169	FH150	
B-170	FE977	
B-171	FE931	
B-172	FH129	
B-173	FH119	
B-174	FE986	
B-175	FH131	
B-176	FE985	became PH-NID
B-177	FE999	
B-178	FH105	
B-179	FS667	
B-180	FH133	
B-181	FE809	under restoration to flying condition at Fokker Tech. Scl.
B-182	FS668	preserved at Schipol Aviodome
B-183	FE998	
B-184	FS960	
B-185	FH139	
B-186	FE996	became PH-NIC
B-187	FE990	became PH-NIB
B-188	FH106	
B-189	FS874	
B-190	FH159	
B-191	FH126	
B-192	FE994	
B-193	FH136	
B-194	FS661	
B-195	FE307	
B-196	FE919	
B-197	FE797	
B-198	FH117	
B-199	FE876	
B-200	FE942	

The Mk.IIa and III aircraft acquired from South Africa for spare parts were:

RAF serial	SAAF serial
EX114	7095
EX256	7264
EX261	7104
EX262	7105

RAF serial	SAAF serial
EX350	7157
EX445	7201
EX638	7351
EX659	7311
EX730	7374
EX737	7393
EX750	7398
EX808	7500
EX819	7466
EX885	7433
EX893	7446
EX898	7447
EX916	7478
EX917	7479
EX922	7469
EX954	7498

The Mk.IIb aircraft obtained for spares were:

FS904; FT261; FT268; FT294; FT365; FT366; FE395

ROYAL NEW ZEALAND AIR FORCE

After receiving 67 Mk.II Harvards purchased direct from the United States, the RNZAF took delivery in 1942 of 38 similar aircraft diverted from British Purchasing Commission contracts. These were followed by 52 Mk.IIa aircraft and 42 of the largely similar Mk.III version. Finally, three Mk.IIb Harvards joined the RNZAF in 1944 and one more in 1948, this one probably for use by RNZAF personnel in Japan.

All these Harvards (except KF113) were allocated and carried RNZAF serial numbers from their arrival in New Zealand and were formally transferred to RNZAF ownership in September 1946.

RNZAF serials	RAF serials	Mark	Arrival in NZ
NZ968-1005	AJ855-892	II	.42
1006-1017	EX184-195	IIa	9.42
1018-1021	EX326-329	"	12.42
1022-1029	EX421-428	"	2.43- 3.43
1030-1037	EX585-592	"	5.43
1038-1-45	EX741-748	"	8.43
1046-1053	EX789-796	"	8.43
1054-1057	EX825-828	"	9.43
1058-1061	EX865-868	III	11.43
1062-1065	EX941-944	"	12.43
1066-1069	EX905-908	"	1.44
1070	EX783	IIa	12.43
1071-1073	EX997-999	III	12.44
1074-1078	EZ242-246	"	?
1079	EZ177	"	12.44
1080-1084	EZ297-301	"	8.44
1085-1089	EZ329-333	"	8.44
1090-1094	EZ359-363	"	7.44
1095	EZ439	"	11.44
1096	EZ449	"	11.44
1097	EZ453	"	11.44
1098	EZ455	"	11.44
1099	EZ456	"	11.44
1100	KF403	IIb	11.44
1101	KF407	"	11.44
1102	KF410	"	11.44
?	KF113	"	6.48

NZ1015 is currently operated by the RNZAF Historic Flight; NZ1056 became ZK-ENL; NZ1085 became ZK-EMN; NZ1007 became VH-HAR.

RNZAF Harvard III NZ1094, originally EX363, at Wigram *(N.D.Welch)*

ROYAL NORWEGIAN AIR FORCE

On the closure of the Norwegian Training Base (NTB) at Winkleigh in November 1945, the unit's 23 Harvards Mk.IIb (and its Cornells) were flown to Norway for continued use by the Royal Norwegian Air Force. They were joined later by seven similar aircraft from Canada. Subsequently, many were sold to the Turkish Air Force for yet more service.

R.NorAF serial	RAF serial	
M-AB	FS734	To Turkish Air Force
M-AC	FS760	"
M-AD	FS763	"
M-AE	FS768	
M-AF	FS772	To Turkish Air Force
M-AG	FS834	"
M-AH	FS842	
M-AI	FS887	To Turkish Air Force
M-AK	FS897	
M-AL	FS907	TO Turkish Air Force
M-AM	FS911	
M-AN	FS916	
M-AO	FS918	
M-AP	FT138	To Turkish Air Force
M-AR	FT139	
M-AS	FT163	To Turkish Air Force
M-AT	FT221	"
M-AU	FT237	"
M-AV	FT252	"
M-AW	FT264	"
M-AX	FT309	"
M-AY	FT335	
M-AZ	FX357	To Turkish Air Force
M-BA	FE435	ex RCAF
M-BB	FE460	"
M-BC	FS965	" ; to Turkish Air Force
M-BD	FE296	" "
M-BE	FE621	"
M-BF	FS959	"
?	FE992	"

SOUTH AFRICAN AIR FORCE

A major user of the Harvard to the present day, the South African Air Force received its first three Mk.I aircraft direct from the second RAF contract in March 1940, the aircraft being renumbered as SAAF 1301-1303 on arrival.

At the end of 1942 the main influx of Harvards into South Africa began, and between then and June 1944 436 Mk.IIa and 197 Mk.III aircraft were delivered. On arrival at Cape Town or Durban, SAAF serial numbers were applied in place of the RAF serials and the aircraft were allocated to Air Schools and other SAAF training units. Accidents took their inevitable toll, but large numbers of each Mark remained in service at the end of the War.

Disposals began in the winter of 1946/47, when 178 Mk.IIa and 102 Mk.III aircraft given back their original RAF serial numbers, put in crates and shipped to the UK to be resold or scrapped. (Why, one wonders, could they not have been scrapped in South Africa?). The remainder were 'recaptured' by the USA in 1947, effectively staying put as SAAF property. Further disposals included 11 to the Southern Rhodesian Air Force in March 1949; 20 to the Royal Netherlands Air Force for use as spares in February 1947; and, much later, in 1969, 59 aircraft to the Portuguese Air Force.

Several Harvards Mk.IIa and III were taken on charge by the SAAF in the early sixties after service with the Belgian Air Force in the Congo. Some of them were ex-SAAF aircraft coming full circle! They were not given back their earlier SAAF serials, but were allocated new ones instead. Ironically, they were never used again!

The SAAF continued to use their remaining Harvards intensively, and even as this book is being compiled, in mid-1988, no less than 75 of them are still in service at South Africa's CFS. The oldest example is SAAF 7012 (RAF EX219), which arrived in South Africa in November 1942! With a working life of 46 years this must surely be the oldest Harvard, or even the oldest aircraft of any type, in military service anywhere.

Mk.I

SAAF serial	RAF serial	
1301	P5928 or P5931	
1302	P5921	
1303	P5928 or P5931	
1304	N7002	ex S. Rhodesia as instructional airframe 9.43; renumbered IS349

Mk.I instructional airframes

SAAF serial	RAF serial	
IS341	N7091	
IS342	N7079	
IS343	N7185	
IS344	N7193	
IS345	N7103	
IS346	P5966	
IS347	N7046	
IS348	N7042	
IS349	N7002	(temporarily SAAF 1304)

Mk.IIa/III

SAAF serial	RAF serial	
7001	EX208	
7002	EX209	to UK 11.46
7003	EX210	to SRAF 3.49
7004	EX211	to Port.AF
7005	EX213	to SRAF 3.49
7006	EX214	to UK 12.46
7007	EX217	to UK 11.46
7008	EX215	
7009	EX216	
7110	EX217	to UK1.47
7011	EX218	
7012	EX219	
7013	EX220	to UK 1.47
7014	EX221	to UK 10.46
7015	EX222	
7016	EX223	to UK 11.46
7017	EX224	
7018	EX225	to UK 10.46
7019	EX226	to UK 10.46
7020	EX227	to Port.AF
7021	EX228	to UK 11.46
7022	EX229	to Port.AF
7023	EX352	
7024	EX355	
7025	EX356	to UK 11.46
7026	EX417	to UK 12.46
7027	EX438	to UK 11.46
7028	EX444	
7029	EX446	to Port.AF
7030	EX448	to UK 10.46
7031	EX452	to UK 12.46
7032	EX454	
7033	EX455	
7034	EX457	
7035	EX458	to UK 11.46
7036	EX459	
7037	EX462	
7038	EX466	to UK 10.46
7039	EX467	to Port.AF
7040	EX468	
7041	EX473	
7042	EX477	to UK 12.46
7043	EX408	to Port.AF
7044	EX474	
7045	EX181	to UK 9.46
7046	EX178	
7047	EX179	
7048	EX206	
7049	EX183	
7050	EX180	became instructional airframe
7051	EX182	to Port.AF
7052	EX196	to Port.AF
7053	EX198	
7054	EX199	to UK 1.47
7055	EX200	to UK 1.47

7166 (EX277) still exists after 40 years service *(A.Heape)*

SAAF serial	RAF serial	
7056	EX201	
7057	EX202	to UK 11.46
7058	EX203	
7059	EX204	
7060	EX205	to Port.AF
7061	EX207	to UK 10.46
7062	EX342	
7063	EX367	
7064	EX366	to UK
7065	EX338	to UK
7066	EX364	
7067	EX349	to UK
7068	EX351	
7069	EX337	to UK
7070	EX339	to UK 11.46
7071	EX340	to UK 10.46
7072	EX335	
7073	EX331	
7074	EX334	
7075	EX285	to UK 10.46
7076	EX294	
7077	EX295	to UK 10.46
7078	EX296	
7079	EX297	to UK 11.46
7080	EX298	
7081	EX299	to UK 10.46
7082	EX300	
7083	EX301	to UK
7084	EX302	to Port.AF
7085	EX232	
7086	EX233	
7087	EX238	to UK 11.46
7088	EX234	to UK 12.46
7089	EX236	to UK 11.46
7090	EX237	to UK 1.47
7091	EX240	to SRAF 3.49
7092	EX231	
7093	EX235	to UK 11.46
7094	EX239	to UK 11.46
7095	EX114	to R.NethAF for spares 2.47
7096	EX117	to Port.AF
7097	EX253	to UK 11.46

SAAF serial	RAF serial	
7098	EX254	to UK 11.46
7099	EX255	to UK 11.46
7100	EX257	to UK 11.46
7101	EX258	to UK 11.46
7102	EX259	to UK 11.46
7103	EX260	to Port.AF
7104	EX261	to R.NethAF for spares 2.47
7105	EX262	to R.NethAF for spares 2.47
7106	EX263	to Port.AF
7107	EX264	to UK 10.46
7108	EX265	
7109	EX266	to UK 11.46
7110	EX267	to Port.AF
7111	EX268	
7112	EX269	to UK 11.46
7113	EX270	to UK 10.46
7114	EX304	
7115	EX305	to UK 10.46
7116	EX306	to UK 10.46
7117	EX307	to UK 10.46
7118	EX308	to UK 11.46
7119	EX309	
7120	EX310	
7121	EX311	
7122	EX312	
7123	EX313	to UK 1.47
7124	EX314	to Port.AF
7125	EX315	
7126	EX316	
7127	EX317	
7128	EX318	to UK 9.46
7129	EX319	to UK 1.47
7130	EX320	to UK 10.46
7131	EX169	to Port.AF
7132	EX170	to Port.AF
7133	EX171	to Port.AF
7134	EX173	
7135	EX176	
7136	EX177	to UK 10.46
7137	EX247	
7138	EX248	
7139	EX249	to UK 10.46

SAAF serial	RAF serial	
7140	EX250	
7141	EX251	to UK 11.46
7142	EX252	to Port.AF
7143	EX303	to UK 10.46
7144	EX380	
7145	EX381	
7146	EX341	
7147	EX333	
7148	EX336	
7149	EX353	to UK 1.47
7150	EX330	to Port.AF
7151	EX332	to UK
7152	EX365	
7153	EX343	
7154	EX346	
7155	EX345	
7156	EX354	
7157	EX350	to R.NethAF for spares 2.47
7158	EX347	to UK
7159	EX368	
7160	EX348	to UK
7161	EX344	
7162	EX363	to UK 11.46
7163	EX283	to UK 11.46
7164	EX275	to UK 11.46
7165	EX272	to UK 11.46
7166	EX277	
7167	EX280	to UK 11.46
7168	EX287	to Port.AF
7169	EX278	to UK 11.46
7170	EX286	
7171	EX271	to Port.AF
7172	EX281	
7173	EX360	to UK
7174	EX361	to Port.AF
7175	EX382	to UK 11.46
7176	EX398	
7177	EX276	
7178	EX400	to UK 10.46
7179	EX393	to UK 10.46
7180	EX397	to UK 11.46
7181	EX288	to UK 11.46
7182	EX292	to UK 10.46
7183	EX289	to UK 10.46
7184	EX273	to UK 10.46
7185	EX392	to Port.AF
7186	EX362	to UK 12.46
7187	EX371	to UK 10.46
7188	EX372	
7189	EX390	to UK 11.46
7190	EX391	to UK 11.46
7191	EX394	to UK 10.46
7192	EX395	to UK 10.46
7193	EX399	
7194	EX274	to UK 11.46
7195	EX279	to UK 10.46
7196	EX282	to UK 11.46
7197	EX284	became instructional airframe
7198	EX290	
7199	EX291	to UK 11.46
7200	EX293	
7201	EX445	to R.NethAF for spares 2.47
7202	EX443	to Port.AF
7203	EX407	
7204	EX429	
7205	EX460	
7206	EX447	
7207	EX442	to UK 10.46
7208	EX450	to UK 12.46
7209	EX449	to UK 12.46
7210	EX461	to UK 10.46
7211	EX451	
7212	EX480	
7213	EX481	to UK 10.46
7214	EX482	
7215	EX483	to UK 12.46
7216	EX484	to UK 12.46
7217	EX485	
7218	EX486	to UK 11.46
7219	EX487	to UK
7220	EX488	to Port.AF
7221	EX489	to UK 10.46
7222	EX494	to UK 12.46

SAAF serial	RAF serial	
7223	EX495	to Port.AF
7224	EX561	to Port.AF
7225	EX562	to UK 11.46
7226	EX556	to UK 11.46
7222	EX560	
7228	EX559	
7229	EX552	to UK 11.46
7230	EX554	
7231	EX570	
7232	EX567	to UK 9.46
7233	EX557	to UK 1.47
7234	EX569	to UK 11.46
7235	EX558	to UK 10.46
7236	EX550	to UK 12.46
7237	EX574	to UK 1.47
7238	EX566	
7239	EX551	to UK 10.46
7240	EX565	
7241	EX572	
7242	EX573	to UK 11.46
7243	EX582	to Port.AF
7244	EX584	to Port.AF
7245	EX578	to UK 12.46
7246	EX583	
7247	EX581	to UK 1.47
7248	EX580	to Port.AF
7249	EX579	to UK 11.46
7250	EX577	
7251	EX575	
7252	EX576	
7253	EX499	
7254	EX503	to UK 11.46
7255	EX496	
7256	EX497	
7257	EX502	to UK 12.46
7258	EX504	to UK 11.46
7259	EX505	
7260	EX507	
7261	EX508	to UK 1.47
7262	EX506	
7263	EX509	to UK 12.46
7264	EX256	to R.NethAF for spares 2.47
7265	EX440	to UK 11.46
7266	EX453	
7267	EX434	to UK 10.46
7268	EX544	to UK 10.46
7269	EX542	to UK 10.46
7270	EX540	to UK 1.47
7271	EX545	
7272	EX433	to SRAF 3.49
7273	EX469	
7274	EX441	to UK 10.46
7275	EX431	to UK 11.46
7276	EX432	
7277	EX464	
7278	EX463	to SRAF 3.49
7279	EX465	to UK 11.46
7280	EX543	
7281	EX541	
7282	EX439	to UK 10.46
7283	EX456	
7284	EX539	
7285	EX568	to UK 11.46
7286	EX546	to UK 12.46
7287	EX555	to UK 11.46
7288	EX547	to UK 11.46
7289	EX553	
7290	EX563	to UK 12.46
7291	EX571	
7292	EX548	
7293	EX549	
7294	EX564	
7295	EX476	to UK 11.46
7296	EX475	to Port.AF
7297	EX479	to UK 10.46
7298	EX471	to UK 11.46
7299	EX470	
7300	EX478	to UK
7301	EX472	to Port.AF
7302	EX593	to UK 11.46
7303	EX610	
7304	EX625	
7305	EX396	

SAAF serial	RAF serial	
7306	EX626	
7307	EX637	
7308	EX644	
7309	EX660	to UK 9.46
7310	EX668	
7311	EX659	to UK 12.46
7312	EX667	
7313	EX662	
7314	EX665	
7315	EX661	to UK 12.46
7316	EX635	
7317	EX604	
7318	EX663	
7319	EX634	to Port.AF
7320	EX687	
7321	EX692	to SRAF 3.49
7322	EX713	
7323	EX733	
7324	EX735	
7325	EX627	to UK 12.46
7326	EX628	to UK 10.46
7327	EX629	
7328	EX679	
7329	EX680	to UK 10.46
7330	EX681	
7331	EX685	
7332	EX686	
7333	EX688	to Port.AF
7334	EX693	to Port.AF
7335	EX599	to Port.AF
7336	EX603	to UK 10.46
7337	EX611	to UK 10.46
7338	EX614	to UK 11.46
7339	EX615	to UK 11.46
7340	EX616	to UK 12.46
7341	EX617	to UK 10.46
7342	EX619	
7343	EX621	
7344	EX623	to UK 10.46
7345	EX624	to UK 10.46
7346	EX630	
7347	EX631	
7348	EX632	
7349	EX633	to UK 11.46
7350	EX636	to Port.AF
7351	EX638	to R.NethAF for spares 2.47
7352	EX639	
7353	EX640	
7354	EX642	
7355	EX643	
7356	EX645	
7357	EX646	
7358	EX647	to UK 10.46
7359	EX648	
7360	EX666	
7361	EX664	
7362	EX694	
7363	EX695	to Port.AF
7364	EX701	
7365	EX704	
7366	EX715	to UK 10.46
7367	EX716	
7368	EX717	
7369	EX732	
7370	EX736	to UK 11.46
7371	EX739	to UK 11.46
7372	EX718	
7373	EX729	to UK 11.46
7374	EX730	to R.NethAF for spares 2.47
7375	EX731	to UK 11.46
7376	EX734	to UK 11.46
7377	EX740	
7378	EX594	
7379	EX595	
7380	EX596	to UK 11.46
7381	EX597	to UK 10.46
7382	EX600	to Port.AF
7383	EX601	
7384	EX602	to UK 10.46
7385	EX605	
7386	EX606	
7387	EX607	to UK
7388	EX608	to Port.AF

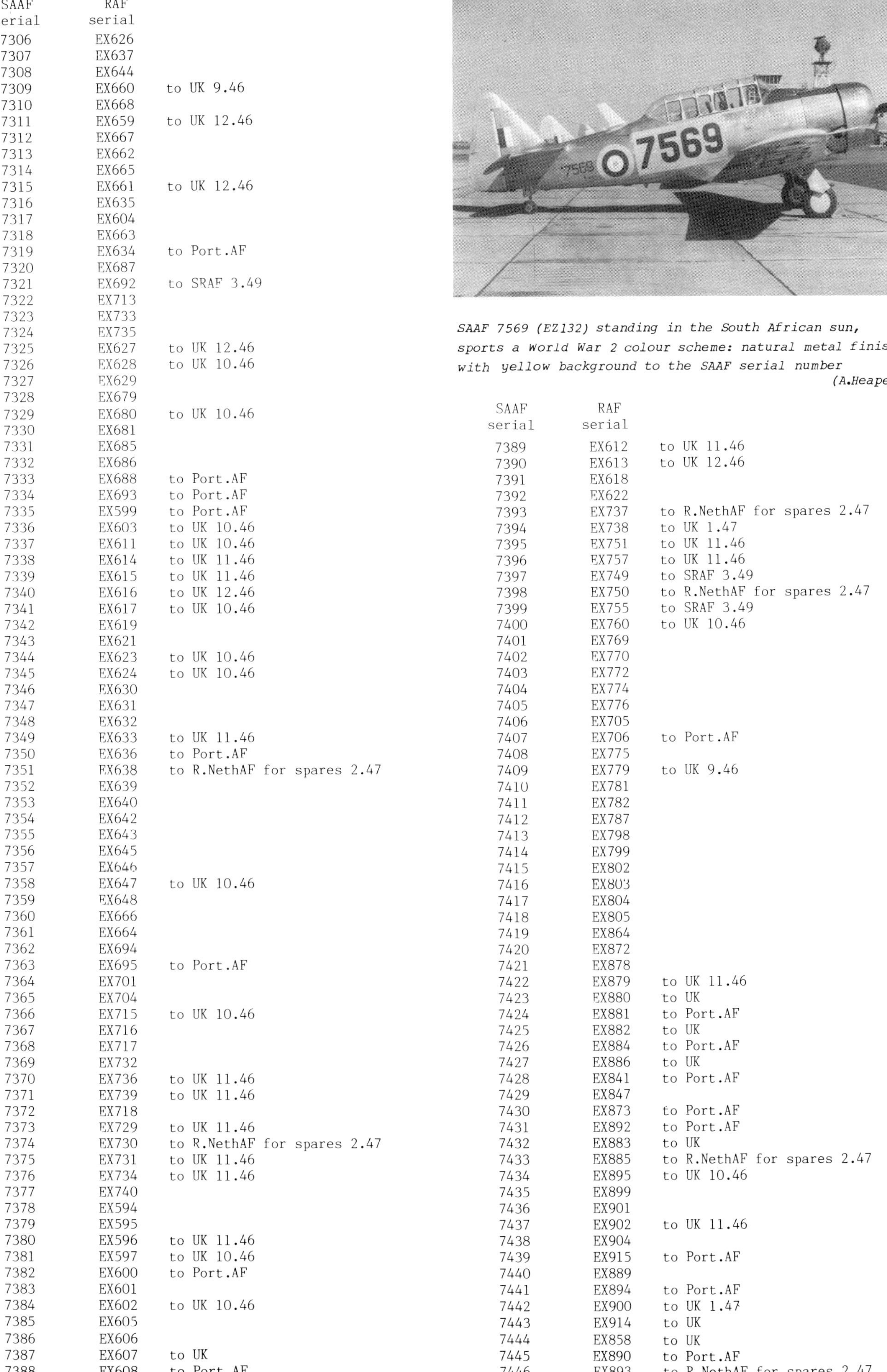

SAAF 7569 (EZ132) standing in the South African sun, sports a World War 2 colour scheme: natural metal finish with yellow background to the SAAF serial number *(A.Heape)*

SAAF serial	RAF serial	
7389	EX612	to UK 11.46
7390	EX613	to UK 12.46
7391	EX618	
7392	EX622	
7393	EX737	to R.NethAF for spares 2.47
7394	EX738	to UK 1.47
7395	EX751	to UK 11.46
7396	EX757	to UK 11.46
7397	EX749	to SRAF 3.49
7398	EX750	to R.NethAF for spares 2.47
7399	EX755	to SRAF 3.49
7400	EX760	to UK 10.46
7401	EX769	
7402	EX770	
7403	EX772	
7404	EX774	
7405	EX776	
7406	EX705	
7407	EX706	to Port.AF
7408	EX775	
7409	EX779	to UK 9.46
7410	EX781	
7411	EX782	
7412	EX787	
7413	EX798	
7414	EX799	
7415	EX802	
7416	EX803	
7417	EX804	
7418	EX805	
7419	EX864	
7420	EX872	
7421	EX878	
7422	EX879	to UK 11.46
7423	EX880	to UK
7424	EX881	to Port.AF
7425	EX882	to UK
7426	EX884	to Port.AF
7427	EX886	to UK
7428	EX841	to Port.AF
7429	EX847	
7430	EX873	to Port.AF
7431	EX892	to Port.AF
7432	EX883	to UK
7433	EX885	to R.NethAF for spares 2.47
7434	EX895	to UK 10.46
7435	EX899	
7436	EX901	
7437	EX902	to UK 11.46
7438	EX904	
7439	EX915	to Port.AF
7440	EX889	
7441	EX894	to Port.AF
7442	EX900	to UK 1.47
7443	EX914	to UK
7444	EX858	to UK
7445	EX890	to Port.AF
7446	EX893	to R.NethAF for spares 2.47

SAAF serial	RAF serial	
7447	EX898	to R.NethAF for spares 2.47
7448	EX855	to UK 10.46
7449	EX857	
7450	EX869	to PortAF
7451	EX850	to UK 12.46
7452	EX921	
7453	EX875	to UK
7454	EX887	
7455	EX816	
7456	EX829	
7457	EX831	
7458	EX835	to UK
7459	EX836	to UK 1.47
7460	EX837	
7461	EX838	to SRAF 3.49
7462	EX809	to UK
7463	EX811	
7464	EX813	
7465	EX815	
7466	EX819	to R.NethAF for spares 2.47
7467	EX820	to UK 10.46
7468	EX823	to UK 10.46
7469	EX922	to R.NethAF for spares 2.47
7470	EX821	to UK 12.46
7471	EX817	
7472	EX871	
7473	EX874	
7474	EX903	
7475	EX909	
7476	EX910	to UK 11.46
7477	EX912	
7478	EX916	to R.NethAF for spares 2.47
7479	EX917	to R.NethAF for spares 2.47
7480	EX918	
7481	EX920	
7482	EX924	
7483	EX923	to UK
7484	EX876	
7485	EX911	to PortAF
7486	EX919	
7487	EX929	to UK
7488	EX932	
7489	EX925	to UK 10.46
7490	EX927	to UK
7491	EX931	
7492	EX934	
7493	EX937	to UK 9.46
7494	EX940	to UK 11.46
7495	EX950	to UK 10.46
7496	EX952	
7497	EX953	to UK 11.46
7498	EX954	to R.NethAF for spares 2.47
7499	EX955	
7500	EX808	to R.NethAF for spares 2.47
7501	EX946	to UK 10.46
7502	EX947	to UK 1.47
7503	EX948	to UK 10.46
7504	EX935	to PortAF
7505	EX939	to UK 10.46
7506	EX960	
7507	EX964	to UK 11.46
7508	EX969	
7509	EX959	to UK 10.46
7510	EX970	
7511	EX986	to UK
7512	EX987	to UK 10.46
7513	EX988	to UK 10.46
7514	EX945	to UK 12.46
7515	EX963	
7516	EX967	to UK 1.47
7517	EX972	to RN in S. Africa
7518	EX973	to PortAF
7519	EX975	
7520	EX977	to UK 12.46
7521	EX978	to UK 1.47
7522	EX979	to UK 1.47
7523	EX980	
7524	EX981	to UK 10.46
7525	EX985	to UK 11.46
7526	EX990	
7527	EX993	to UK 10.46
7528	EX994	to UK 10.46
7529	EZ138	

SAAF serial	RAF serial	
7530	EX989	
7531	EX974	to UK 9.46
7532	EX991	to UK 10.46
7533	EZ131	to UK 1.47
7534	EZ136	to UK 1.47
7535	EZ137	to RN in S. Africa 2.45
7536	EZ142	to UK 1.47
7537	EZ150	to UK 10.46
7538	EZ152	to UK 10.46
7539	EZ134	to UK 12.46
7540	EZ154	
7541	EZ135	
7542	EZ169	to UK
7543	EZ172	to UK 12.46
7544	EZ173	
7545	EZ180	to UK
7546	EZ159	to UK 10.46
7547	EZ161	to UK
7548	EZ162	to UK 9.46
7549	EZ163	
7550	EZ164	
7551	EZ165	
7552	EZ166	to UK 1.47
7553	EZ168	to UK 1.47
7554	EZ171	to RN in S. Africa 1.45
7555	EZ174	to UK 9.46
7556	EZ175	to UK 1.47
7557	EZ176	
7558	EZ178	to RN in S. Africa 2.45
7559	EZ179	
7560	EZ181	to UK 1.47
7561	EZ182	to UK 12.46
7562	EZ183	to UK 12.46
7563	EZ186	to UK 9.46
7564	EZ193	to UK 12.46
7565	EZ195	to UK 1.47
7566	EZ118	to UK
7567	EZ119	to UK 1.47
7568	EZ123	to RN in S. Africa 2.45
7569	EZ132	
7570	EZ143	
7571	EZ144	to PortAF
7572	EZ145	
7573	EZ146	
7574	EZ147	to UK 10.46
7575	EZ149	to UK 1.47
7576	EZ155	
7577	EZ158	to UK 1.47
7578	EZ214	to UK 9,46
7579	EZ215	to UK
7580	EZ216	
7581	EZ217	
7582	EZ220	to UK 10.46
7583	EZ230	to UK 9,46
7584	EZ184	
7585	EZ185	to UK 10.46
7586	EZ196	to UK
7587	EZ200	to UK 12.46
7588	EZ201	to PortAF
7589	EZ203	to UK
7590	EZ206	to UK 1.47
7591	EZ207	to PortAF
7592	EZ213	
7593	EZ219	to UK 1.47
7594	EZ221	to UK 10.46
7595	EZ231	to UK 12.46
7596	EZ235	to UK 12.46
7597	EZ240	to RN in S. Africa 1.45
7598	EZ247	to UK 1.47
7599	EZ191	to UK 1.47
7600	EZ192	
7601	EZ194	
7602	EZ197	to UK 1.47
7603	EZ199	to UK 10.46
7604	EZ205	to UK
7605	EZ210	to UK 10.46
7606	EZ229	
7607	EZ237	to UK 1.47
7608	EZ232	
7609	EZ236	
7610	EZ209	to UK 1.47
7611	EZ294	to UK 1.47
7612	EZ289	to UK 12.46

SAAF serial	RAF serial	
7613	EZ226	to PortAF
7614	EZ224	to PortAF
7615	EZ189	
7616	EZ198	to UK 1.47
7617	EZ187	to UK 1.47
7618	EZ315	
7619	EZ254	to RN in S. Africa 1.45
7620	EZ211	to RN in S. Africa 1.45
7621	EZ251	
7622	EZ292	to UK 10.46
7623	EZ307	to UK 10.46
7624	EZ309	to UK 10.46
7625	EZ310	to UK 9.46
7626	EZ314	
7627	EZ321	to UK 12.46
7628	EZ338	
7629	EZ339	to UK 10.46
7630	EZ256	to UK 10.46
7631	EZ259	to RN in S. Africa 1.45
7632	EZ335	to UK 9.46
7633	EZ336	

SAAF serial	RAF serial	orig. SAAF serial	BAF serial
7729	EZ310	7625	H.15
7730	EX657	--	H.223
7731	EZ210	7605	H.19
7732	EX405	--	H.216
77..	EX784	--	H.221

One more Harvard Mk.III with British origins found its way to the SAAF: this was KE308, which had seen service with the RN in the United States and been civilianised as N69675 before becoming SAAF 7663 in August 1952.

SOUTHERN RHODESIAN AIR FORCE

Twelve Harvards Mk.II were the first of the type to be taken on charge by the newly re-formed Southern Rhodesian Air Force in February 1949, and were transferred from redundant RAF stocks after use in the Commonwealth Air Training Scheme in Rhodesia during the War. As far as can be determined, only two of these aircraft were allocated SRAF serials SR42 and SR43, but which they were is not known. Nine Mk.IIa aircraft from the South African Air Force were next to arrive, in April 1949, and these were given SRAF serials SR44 to SR52, but again only a few serial tie-ups are known.

The next batch of Harvards to join the SRAF were Mk. IIb aircraft, eleven of which were shipped out from the United Kingdom, arriving in Rhodesia from August 1951. These were only on loan to the SRAF, but were allocated SRAF serials SR69 to SR79. They were returned to the RAF in 1952/53 for use in the Rhodesian Air Training Group, and were then exchanged for a similar number of Mk.IIa Harvards which were given the same SRAF serial numbers. One of these was also returned to the RAF. Again, serial number tie-ups are almost unknown.

Mk.II

SRAF serial	RAF serial	SRAF serial	RAF serial
	AJ607		AJ741
	AJ621		AJ752
	AJ667		BD131
	AJ706		BD132
	AJ718		BD134
	AJ720		DG430

Mk.IIa aircraft of the SAAF being crated at No.3 Air Depot, Brooklyn, Capetown for repatriation to the United Kingdom, 1946 *(R.Moulton)*

SR69 of the SRAF over typical scenery *(via R.F.Coombs)*

Mk.IIa ex SAAF

SRAF serial	SAAF serial	RAF serial
	7003	EX210
	7005	EX213
	7091	EX240
	7272	EX433
	7278	EX463
SR50	7321	EX692
SR48	7397	EX749
	7399	EX755
	7461	EX838

Mk.IIb

SRAF serial	RAF serial	t.o.c.	ret'd to RAF
	FX265	12.51	3.52
	FX308	11.51	3.52
SR70	FX335	8.51	4.53
	FX393	8.51	5.52
	KF223	12.51	4.52
	KF326	8.51	5.52
	KF331	12.51	3.52
	KF398	8.51	5.52
	KF401	2.52	5.52
SR77	KF420	12.51	2.53
	KF625	11.51	3.52

Mk.IIa

SRAF serial	RAF serial	t.o.c.	
	EX160	5.52	
	246	5.52	
	373	3.52	
SR70	385	2.53	
	401	4.53	
SR75	414	4.52	
	519	5.52	
	520	7.52	
	522	7.52	
	753	3.52	returned to RAF 6.52
	786	3.52	
	845	3.52	

SWEDISH AIR FORCE

The Swedish Air Force, one of the major users of the Harvard in Europe, took delivery of 144 examples of the type from the Royal Canadian Air Force; all were Mk.IIb aircraft.

SwAF serial	RAF serial	SwAF serial	RAF serial
Fv16001	FT296	Fv16073	FS958
16002	FE743	16074	FE638
16003	FS875	16075	FE630
16004	FE657	16076	FE795
16005	FE852	16077	FS966
16006	FH158	16078	FS961
16007	FH166	16079	FS673
16008	FE753	16080	FS962
16009	FE401	16081	FS666
16010	FE831	16082	FS681
16011	FS968	16083	FH154
16012	FH137	16084	FS873
16013	FE691	16085	FS878
16014	FS870	16086	FE928
16015	FH104	16087	FE312
16016	FS967	16088	FT292
16017	FE927	16089	FE723
16018	FH122	16090	FE856
16019	FH157	16091	FE851
16020	FE861	16092	FE726
16021	FE619	16093	FE661
16022	FE742	16094	FE344
16023	FH132	16095	FE327
16024	FE934	16096	FE580
16025	FE920	16097	FE837
16026	FE648	16098	FE689
16027	FE812	16099	FE844
16028	FE991	16100	FE734
16029	FH148	16101	FE502
16030	FE565	16102	FE385
16031	FT266	16103	FE554
16032	FE849	16104	FE940
16033	FH138	16105	FE695
16034	FE653	16106	FE832
16035	FE633	16107	FE555
16036	FE694	16108	FE835
16037	FS867	16109	FE632*
16038	FH163	16110	FE646
16039	FT277	16111	FE834
16040	FS672	16112	FT272
16041	FE902	16113	FE842
16042	FE524	16114	FE503
16043	FE577	16115	FE335
16044	FE651	16116	FS972
16045	FE987	16117	FE625
16046	FE796	16118	FE400
16047	FE992*	16119	FE500
16048	FS957	16120	FE518
16049	FT275	16121	FE509
16050	FT276	16122	FE688
16051	FE658	16123	FE724
16052	FE918	16124	FE660
16053	FE654	16125	FE585
16054	FE863	16126	FE692
16055	FS871	16127	FE513
16056	FE722	16128	FE511
16057	FS862	16129	FE628
16058	FH140	16130	FE437
16059	FE823	16131	FE464
16060	FE637	16132	FE564
16061	FE836	16133	FE589
16062	FE853	16134	FE833
16063	FE950	16135	FE693
16064	FE525	16136	FE741
16065	FT274	16137	FE276
16066	FH100	16138	FE562
16067	FE803	16139	FE520
16068	FE752	16140	FE272
16069	FE568	16141	FH125
16070	FE932	16142	FE328
16071	FH127	16143	FE845
16072	FH156	16144	FE792*

* Fv16047 became G-BDAM; Fv16109 is preserved at the Swedish Air Force Museum, Linkoping; Fv16144 became SE-FUZ.

SWISS AIR FORCE

It is known that a number of Harvards Mk.IIb of RAF origin were sold to the Swiss Air Force by the RCAF, but little is known about individual aircraft apart from the following two.

Swiss AF serial	RAF serial
U-322	FE590
U-328	FE824

SYRIAN AIR FORCE

Ten Harvards Mk.IIb with RAF origins arrived in Syria from Field Aircraft Services (SA) Pty. Ltd. in South Africa during 1956. They had been allocated South African civil registrations but little is known of their original identities other than two which started life as FT392 and KF151.

TURKISH AIR FORCE

Seventeen former RAF Harvards Mk.IIb were supplied to the Turkish Air Force by the Royal Norwegian Air Force in 1955/56 and these were supplemented by eight Mk.II aircraft which were struck off RCAF charge between November 1957 and March 1958.

Mk.IIb			Mk.II	
TAF serial	RNorAF serial	RAF serial	TAF serial	RAF/RCAF serial
	M-AB	FS734		AH187
	M-AC	FS760		AJ565
	M-AD	FS763		AJ791
	M-AF	FS772		AJ848
	M-AG	FS834		AJ940
	M-AI	FS887		AJ970
	M-AL	FS907		BW188
	M-AP	FT138		BW207
	M-AS	FT163		
	M-AT	FT221		
	M-AU	FT237		
	M-AV	FT252		
	M-AW	FT264		
	M-AX	FT309		
	M-AZ	FX357		
	M-BC	FS965		
	M-BD	FE296		

YUGOSLAVIAN AIR FORCE

Ten Harvards Mk.IIb were supplied to the Yugoslavian Air Force in March/April 1945 for use at the Yugoslav Flying Training School, then operating under the control of the Mediterranean Allied Air Forces. All were in 'as new' condition and were flown out by 12 FU from Melton Mowbray. No YAF serial numbers are known for these aircraft.

FT152, FT174, FT339, KF283, KF302, KF305, KF429, KF471, KF474, KF477.

CIVILIANISED HARVARDS

NOTE: The listings in this Chapter include, for the benefit of the many enthusiasts interested particularly in civil aircraft, Harvards/T-6's which did not have RAF origins as well as those which did. Information on Harvards and T-6's registered in the USA and Canada is sadly lacking, and these countries are therefore not included.

Part 1: European civil-registered Harvards/T-6's

G-AXCR AT-16 Mk 2B, c/n 14-324, ex 42-787, FE590, Swiss AF U-322. Regd 27.3.69 to Mrs L.A.Osborne, Blackbushe. No C of A issued. Regn cld 9.69 as sold in West Germany. Regd D-FHGK 11.69 to Flugzeug-Handels GmbH, Karlsruhe. Regd .71 to G.Roth, Neckarelz. To W.Eichhorn, Breitscheid.

G-AZBN See PH-HON

G-AZJD See F-BJBF

G-AZKI See PH-SKM

G-AZSC See PH-SKK

G-BAFM See PH-SKL

G-BBHK See PH-HTC

G-BDAM See LN-MAA

G-BDZZ T-6G, c/n 182-720, ex 51-15033, Fr AF 115033. Regd 15.6.76 to R.Lamplough. No C of A issued. Regn cld 20.12.76. Sold to Israeli Air Force Museum in exchange for Yak C.11 G-KYAK plus 3 P-51 fuselages. Repainted as "001".

G-BGGR AT-6A, c/n 77-4176, ex 41-217, FAP 1608. Regd 17.1.79 to Euroworld Ltd, Biggin Hill. No C of A issued. Regn cld 20.4.79 as sold in West Germany. Regn D-FOBY reserved .79 to Air Classik GmbH, Dusseldorf; not taken up but displayed as "Firebird" at Dusseldorf.

G-BGHU T-6G, c/n 182-729, ex 51-15042, Fr AF 115042, FAP 1707. Regd 22.1.79 to Gladaircraft Co Ltd, Biggin Hill. C of A permit issued 11.3.79. Regd 12.11.81 to S.M. & P.S.Warner, Wellesbourne Mountford. Painted in USAF c/s as "115042" .84. Regd 29.12.86 to C.E.Bellhouse, Shoreham.

G-BGOR AT-6D Mk III, c/n 88-14863, ex 41-33908, EX935, SAAF 7504, FAP 1508. Regd 28.3.79 to Euroworld International Airline Operations Ltd, Biggin Hill. C of A permit issued 1.10.80. Regd 24.10.80 to P.Mercer, Hurn. Regd 15.11.82 to M.L.Sargeant, Headcorn.

G-BGOS AT-6, ex FAP 1529. Reservation for Euroworld International Airline Operations Ltd; not taken up.

G-BGOT AT-6C Mk IIA, c/n 88-10560, ex 41-33440, EX467, SAAF 7039, FAP 1551. Regd 28.3.79 to Euroworld International Airline Operations Ltd, Biggin Hill. No C of A issued. Regn cld 16.4.80 as sold in USA. Regd N37642 6.80

G-BGOU AT-6C Mk IIA, c/n 88-10108, ex 41-33365, EX392, SAAF 7185, FAP 1554. Regd 28.3.79 to Euroworld International Airline Operations Ltd, Biggin Hill. C of A permit issued 5.9.80. Regd 7.10.80 to A.P.Snell & P.A.Wood, Audley End.

Martin Sergeant's immaculate Harvard Mk.III G-BGOR (Kent & Sussex Courier *via M.Sergeant*)

Regd 21.1.83 to A.P.Snell. Painted in SAAF c/s as 7185 .83. Crashed Bourn 7.9.85 killing owner/pilot.

G-BGOV AT-6C Mk IIA, c/n 88-12044, ex 41-33573, EX600, SAAF 7382, FAP 1559. Regd 28.3.79 to Euroworld International Airline Operations Ltd, Biggin Hill. Regd 5.11.80 to Aces High Ltd, Duxford. C of A permit issued 7.1.81. Regn cld 17.5.83 as sold in USA. Regd N4434N 11.8.83.

G-BGOW AT-6D Mk III, c/n 88-14748, ex 42-44554, FT971, FAP 1661. Regd 28.3.79 to Euroworld International Airline Operations Ltd, Biggin Hill. No C of A issued. Regn cld 16.4.80 as sold in USA. Nothing known since.

G-BGPB T-6J, c/n CCF4-538, ex 53-4619, AA+050, BF+050, FAP 1747. Regd 4.4.79 to A.G.Walker & R.Lamplough, Duxford (later North Weald). C of A permit issued 13.8.80. Painted in RCAF c/s as 20385 "385".80.

G-BHTH T-6G, c/n 168-176, ex 49-3072, N2807G. Regd 20.5.80 to Keenair Services Ltd, Speke. C of A permit issued 6.8.80.Painted in USN c/s as "2807/V-103". Regd 28.10.86 to B.R.Rossiter, Booker. Regd 30.4.87 to A.Reynard, Booker.

G-BHXF See G-RBAC

G-BICE AT-6C Mk IIA, c/n 88-9755, ex 41-33275, EX302, SAAF 7084, FAP 1545. Regd 3.9.80 to C.M.L.Edwards, Ipswich. C of A permit issued 29.4.83. Painted in US Army c/s as "CE".

G-BIHS T-6G, c/n 182-29,(regd with c/n 182-28) ex 51-14342, Fr AF 114342, FAP 1715. Regd 7.11.80 to Aces High Ltd, Fairoaks. No C of A issued. Regd cld 17.5.83 as sold in USA. Regd N4434M 11.83.

G-BIWX Harvard IV, c/n CCF4-..., ex 51-17..., MM53846 "RM-22". Regd 29.4.81 to R.Lamplough, Duxford. C of A permit issued 9.6.81. Painted in RAF c/s as FT239 .83. Regd 22.3.83 to Aero Vintage Ltd. Regd 30.6.83 to A.E.Hutton, White Waltham.

G-BJMS Harvard IV, c/n CCF4-..., ex MM53802. Regd 5.10.81 to N.Grey, Booker. C of A permit issued 16.10.81. Regn cld 4.3.82; sold in France. Regd F-AZCM 9.82 to J.David.

G-BJST Harvard IV, c/n CCF4-..., ex MM53795 "SC-66".(Parts from MM53796/"SC-52") Regd 21.12.81 to V.Norman & M.Lawrence, Kemble.

G-BKCK Harvard IV, c/n CCF4-77, ex RCAF 20286, N13631. Regd 8.3.83 to E.T. & T.C.Webster. Not imported; regn cld 6.1.87. Restored to N13631 1.87.

G-BKRA T-6G, c/n 188-90, ex 51-15227, MM53664 "RM-9". Regd 19.8.83 to T.S.Warren, Sandown. Regd 13.6.84 to Andrew Edie Aviation Ltd, Shoreham. Painted in USN c/s as "51-15227" .84. Regd 21.10.85 to Pulsegrove Ltd, Shoreham. Regd 10.8.87 to M.D.Faiers, Nympsfield.

G-BMJW AT-6D Mk III, c/n 88-15963, ex 42-84182, EZ259. Regd 28.11.85 to J.Woods, Bracknell. On rebuild from components. Note : Also quoted as ex SAAF 7631 - believed unlikely.

G-CTKL Harvard IV, c/n CCF4-... ex 51-17..., MM54137. (Allegedly rebuild of c/n 76-80). Regd 22.11.83 to C.T.K.Lane, Dorchester. Painted in USN c/s as "54136". C of A permit issued 9.7.87. Regd 8.9.87 to J.A.Carr, Dunkeswell.

G-ELLY AT-6D Mk III, c/n 88-14661, ex 41-33867, EX894 SAAF 7441, FAP 1504. Regd 17.1.79 to Euroworld Ltd, E.White & E.D.Sallingboe, Biggin Hill. Regd 4.9.80 to E.D.Sallingboe. C of A permit issued 5.6.81 and repainted in USAF c/s as "133867". Destroyed in fatal crash Nr.Rabat, Malta 22.6.82.

G-JUDI AT-6D Mk III, c/n 88-14722, ex 41-33888, EX915, SAAF 7439, FAP 1502. Regd 17.11.78 to Norfolk Aerial Spraying Ltd, Foulsham. C of A permit issued 17.12.78. Painted in RAF c/s as FX301 .78. Regd 10.1.80 to A.Haig-Thomas, Duxford/Ipswich.

G-RBAC AT-6C Mk IIA, c/n 88-10677, ex 41-33557, EX584, SAAF 7244, FAP 1522 (Note : identities prior to FAP are unconfirmed). Regd 25.1.79 to GRB Aviation Co Ltd, Biggin Hill. C of A permit issued 5.3.79. Regn G-BHXF reserved 6.80 but not taken up. Re-regd G-VALE 17.9.80 to Kayvale Finance Ltd, Shobdon. Painted in USAF c/s as "8810677/LTA-584" .81. Regd cld 12.11.85; to USA. Regd N36CA 11.85.

G-RCAF AT-6C Mk IIA, c/n 88-9723, ex 41-33260, EX287 SAAF 7168, FAP 1560. Regd 6.3.79 to Euroworld International Airline Operations Ltd, Biggin Hill. C of A permit issued 23.8.79. Regn cld 16.4.80; to USA. Regd N42BA 14.7.80.

G-SUES AT-6D Mk III, c/n 88-14552, ex 41-33854, EX881, SAAF 7424, FAP 1506. Regd 18.1.79 to Mark Campbell Airfreight Charters Ltd, Biggin Hill. C of A permit issued 5.3.79. Painted in USAF c/s as EX881 .81. Regd 2.6.81 to B.Willmot. Regd 18.6.81 to PW Leaney Automatic Transmissions Ltd, Biggin Hill. Painted in USN c/s as 133854 .83. Regd cld 10.2.84; to Norway. Regn LN-LFW reserved but not taken up. Regd LN-WNH 11.7.86 to Nordic Air Service A/S, Sandefjord.

G-SURF T-6G, c/n 182-750, ex 51-15063, Fr AF 115063, FAP 1710. Regd 28.3.79 to Euroworld International Airline Operations Ltd, Biggin Hill. No C of A issued. Regn cld 16.4.80; to USA. Nothing known subsequently.

G-TEAC AT-6C Mk IIA, c/n 88-9696, ex 41-33253, EX688, SAAF 7333, FAP 1523 (Note : Identities unconfirmed and originally quoted as ex EX280). Regd 18.1.79 to Trans Europe Air Charter Ltd, Biggin Hill/Bicester. C of A permit issued 5.3.79. Painted in RAF c/s as MC280. Regd 12.7.83 to E.C.English, Bourn. Repainted as EX280 .84.

G-TIDE AT-6A, c/n 78-6698, ex 41-16320, FAP 1620. Regd 28.3.79 to Euroworld International Airline Operations Ltd, Biggin Hill. No C of A issued. Regn cld 16.4.80; sold in USA. Regd N3762J 5.80.

G-TSIX AT-6C Mk IIA, c/n 88-9725, ex 41-33262, EX289 SAAF 7183, FAP 1535. (Note : All identities unconfirmed). Regd 19.3.79 to D.Taylor, East Midlands for Loughborough & Leicester Aircraft Museum, Tollerton/Tatenhill. Painted in RAF c/s as 'G-T6" .83.

G-VALE See G-RBAC

D-FABA Mk IV, c/n CCF4-550, ex 53-4631 (Regd as 54-4631), AA+635. Regd 10.7.63 to Bundesrepublik Deutschland. Regd N73687 (but not taken up). Regn F-BRGB reserved 7.73 for J.Blondel, Beauvais. Not certified as such and regd F-AZAT 12.79 (reserved .78).

D-FABE Mk IV, c/n CCF4-499, ex 52-8578, AA+624. Regd 19.11.63 to Bundesrepublik Deutschland. To R.Strossenreuther, Rosenthal-Field. To K.H.Brader, Wilhelmshaven. To Flugdienst J.Koch KG, Augsburg.

D-FABI Mk IV, c/n CCF4-537, ex 53-4618, AA+628. Regd 10.63 to Bundesrepublik Deutschland. Regn cld.71. Regd N73688 (but not taken up). Regn F-BRGA reserved 7.73 for Institute Aeronautique Amaury de la Grange, Merville. Not certified as such. To J.Salis, La Ferte Alais .82 and for rebuild. Regd F-AZFC .87.

D-FABO Mk IV, c/n CCF4-514, ex 52-8593, AA+603. Regd 30.7.63 to Bundesrepublik Deutschland. To Flying School R.Strossenreuther, Rosenthal-Field.

D-FABU Mk IV, c/n CCF4-465, ex 52-8544, AA+615. Regd 21.8.63 to Bundesrepublik Deutschland. Regn cld .71 To Luftwaffen Museum, Uetersen .73.

D-FABY See F-BJBL.

D-FACA Mk IV, c/n CCF4-484, ex 52-8563, AA+678. Reservation not taken up.

D-FACE Mk IV, c/n CCF4-524, ex 52-8603, AA+629. Reservation not taken up.

D-FACI Mk IV, c/n CCF4-509, ex 52-8588, AA+633. Reservation not taken up; derelict Dusseldorf.

D-FAMA AT-6A, c/n 121-42459, ex 44-81737. Regd .57 to Deutscher Luftfahrt-Beratungsdienst, Wiesbaden. Destroyed in fatal crash nr.Traunstein 12.8.57.

D-FAMO See PH-UEM

D-FAMU AT-6F, c/n 121-42507, ex 44-81785. Regd .57 to Deutscher Luftfahrt-Beratungsdienst, Wiesbaden. Regd to Bundesrepublik Deutschland. Damaged in belly landing Munich 20.1.62. Regn cld 7.63.

D-FATI AT-6F, c/n 121-42449, ex 44-81727. Regd .57 to Deutscher Luftfahrt-Beratunsdienst, Wiesbaden. Crashed Kirchheim 21.3.60.

D-FBEC See SE-CAR

PH-BKT basking in the afternoon sunshine at the Harvard fly-in at Bassingbourn in May 1978 *(author)*

D-FDDD T-6D c/n "43642" Regn reserved 11.81 to H.Dittes, Mannheim. Not taken up; to N2960T but crashed on delivery Dillenburg 22.5.83.

D-FDEM See D-IDEM

D-FDOK See D-IDOK

D-FGAL See OY-DYE

D-FHGK See G-AXCR

D-FIBA AT-6A, c/n 121-42433, ex 44-81711. Regd .57 to Deutscher Luftfahrt-Beratungsdienst, Wiesbaden. Hit trees low flying and destroyed Isny, Nr.Kempten 3.10.57.

D-FIBU See OO-AAR

D-FIII T-6D, c/n "51819". Regn reserved 11.81 by H.Dittes, Mannheim. Not taken up; to N2965S .83.

D-FOBY See G-BGGR

D-FOTO AT-6A, c/n 121-42517, ex 44-81795. Regd .57 to Deutscher Luftfahrt-Beratungsdienst, Wiesbaden. Regn cld .64.

D-IBEC See SE-CAR

D-IDEM AT-6F, c/n 121-42500, ex 44-81778, Bu.90690. Regd 1.58 to H.Weekamp, Dusseldorf. Re-regd D-FDEM 7.58. Regd .71 to J.Hossl, Strasskirchen. Regn PH-HAR reserved 17.9.76 by Fraco BV but not taken up. To J.Sauermann/Nordseeflug GmbH, Munchen. Wfu Leutkirch; to Hermeskeil Museum .82.

D-IDOK AT-6F, c/n 121-42441, ex 44-81719. Regd .57 to Overseas Motor-Sales GmbH, Frankfurt. Re-regd D-FDOK 9.57. Regn cld 3.62.

D-IGAL See OY-DYE

EC-DUM T-6G, ex 51-14904, Fr AF, E16-198. Regd 2.7.84 to Club de Deporte Aereo JL Aresti, Cuatro Vientos.

EC-DUN T-6G, ex 52-8216, Fr AF, E16-201. Regd 2.7.84 to Club de Deporte Aereo JL Aresti, Cuatro Vientos.

F-AZAS See F-BMJP

F-AZAT See F-BRGB

F-AZAU See F-BNAU

F-AZAY T-6G, c/n 182-477, ex 51-14790, Fr AF. Regd 11.79 (reserved 10.78) to J.Decoop, La Ferte Alais (later Mulhouse). Painted in USAF c/s as "BA-132". Crashed Longuyon 9.6.85.

F-AZBE See F-BJBI

F-AZBK See F-BVQD

F-AZBL AT-6G, ex 42-85886, Bu90669. Regd 8.80 (reserved 7.79) to J.Bourret/Aero Retro, St Rambert d'Albon.

F-AZBQ See F-BOEO

F-AZCM See G-BJMS

F-AZCQ T-6G, c/n 168-140, ex 49-3037, Sp AF E16-193. Regd 8.83 (reserved .82) to L.Cazades/Association pour Preservation Avions Historiques Le Maupas, Frontenas.

F-AZCV T-6G, c/n 182-142, ex 51-14456, Sp AF E16-191. Regd 2.84 to L.Cazades/Association pour Preservation Avions Historiques Le Maupas, Frontenas.

F-AZDK See F-BJBE

F-AZDM T-6G, ex Bu43642, N2960T. Regd .84 to Association Air Memorial. Painted in RAF c/s as "JC-N". Destroyed in crash Coulommiers 11.6.84.

F-AZDS See G-AZKI

F-AZDU See F-BJBF

F-AZEF T-6G, ex 51-14387, Fr AF. Regd .86 to D.Chable, Etampes.

F-AZEZ T-6G, ex 51-14674, Fr AF. Regd .87

F-AZFC See D-FABI

F-BJBA AT-6D, c/n 88-15352, ex EZ162, SAAF 7548, Belg AF H-1. Regd 21.5.59 to Cie Air France, Cormeilles. Regd 3.65 to M.Poinsot. Regn cld .65; scrapped.

F-BJBB AT-6D, ex 42-84549, EZ335, SAAF 7632, Belg AF H-3. Regd 20.7.59 to Cie Air-France, Cormeilles. To M.Poinsot 3.65. Regn cld .65.

F-BJBC AT-6C Mk IIA, c/n 88-12326, ex 41-33633, EX660, SAAF 7309, Belg AF H-4. Regd 25.6.59 to Cie Air-France, Cormeilles. Regd 11.64 to Ste Avions Meyer et Air Cameroun, Douala. Regd 9.71 to J.Dere, Douala. Regn cld .77. Reportedly stored Chavenay, (but see F-BJBD).

F-BJBD AT-6D, c/n 88-15564, ex EZ174, SAAF 7555, Belg AF H-6. Regd 19.8.59 to Cie Air-France, Cormeilles (later Toussus). To Aero Club Air France 2.64. To Ets Godet 9.67. Regn cld .70. To M.Chassagnard 9.72. Believed to Collection Aero Club Jean Bertin, Chavenay (but see F-BJBC)

F-BJBE AT-6C, c/n 88-10570, ex 41-33449, EX476, SAAF 7295, Belg AF H-8. Regd 21.5.59 to Cie Air-France, Cormeilles. Regn cld .64. Used as instructional airframe by Air France at Vilgenis. Regd F-AZDK 3.85 (reserved .83) to Aero Retro, St.Rambert.

F-BJBF AT-6D Mk III, c/n 88-14948, ex 41-33931, EX959, SAAF 7509, Belg AF H-9. Regd 19.8.59 to Cie Air-France, Cormeilles. Regd 5.65 to G.Urbain, Cannes. Regn cld 1.71; to UK. Regd G-AZJD 30.11.71 to Sir W.J.D.Roberts. C of A issued 17.8.72. Regd 23.8.77 to Gladaircraft Co Ltd, Biggin Hill. Regd 6.7.83 to Meridian Drilling Co Ltd), Biggin Hill. Regn cld 10.84. To France, initially as F-WZDU .84. Regd F-AZDU 6.85 to G.Robert. Note: RAF serial previously quoted as EX958.

F-BJBG AT-6D, c/n 88-16151, ex EX993, SAAF 7527, Belg AF H-14. Regd 21.5.59 to Cie Air-France, Cormeilles. Damaged Pontoise 21.11.61. Regn cld 7.65. Used as instructional airframe by Air France at Vilgenis. Later to instructional airframe at Cerny La Ville, Essonne; present 1.87.

F-BJBH AT-6D, c/n 88-15778, ex EZ214, SAAF 7578, Belg AF H-16. Regd 16.7.59 to Cie Air-France, Cormeilles. Regn cld 2.66. Used as instructional airframe by Air France at Vilgenis.

F-BJBI AT-6C Mk IIA, c/n 88-12127, ex 41-33606, EX633, SAAF 7349, Belg AF H-29. Regd 25.6.59 to Cie Air-France, Cormeilles. Regd 11.63 to P.Mercier, Cormeilles. Re-regd F-WJBI .69. Restored as F-BJBI .74 to Aero Club de Neuilly, Les Mureaux. Re-regd F-AZBE 8.80 (reserved 4.79) to Salis Aviation, La Ferte Alais. To Amicale J.B.Salis and painted in Fr Navy c/s as "41-F-4".

F-BJBJ AT-6C, c/n 88-12046, ex EX602, SAAF 7384, Belg AF H-30. Regd 29.4.59 to Cie Air-France, Cormeilles. Regn cld 2.66. Used as instructional airframe by Air France at Vilgenis.

F-BJBK AT-6C, c/n 88-14173, ex EX823, SAAF 7468, Belg AF H-33. Regd 29.4.59 to Cie Air-France, Cormeilles. Regd 4.65 to Aero Club Airnautic, Nice. Regn cld .68.

F-BJBL AT-6C, c/n 88-9811, ex EX318, SAAF 7128, Belg AF H-40. Regd 17.6.59 to Cie Air-France, Cormeilles. Regn cld 8.64; to W.Germany. Regn D-FABY reserved but not taken up. Stored by W.Hoft in garden at Hilden.

F-BJBM AT-6D, c/n 88-14510. Regd 20.10.59 to Cie Air-France, Cormeilles. Regd .67 to Societe Gle d'Exploitation Aeronautique (SOGEA), Troyes. Regn cld .70. To Collection Robert Denizot, Pont-sur-Yonne .76. Stored for rebuild.

F-BJBN AT-6D, ex 42-86351. Regd 25.6.59 to Cie Air France, Cormeilles. Regn cld .65.

F-BJBO AT-6D,ex 42-44446. Regd 20.7.59 to Cie Air-France, Cormeilles. Regn cld .65

F-BJBP AT-6F, c/n 121-42480, ex 44-81758. Regd 20.4.59 to Cie Air-France, Cormeilles. Regd 3.7.63 to CEDEA, Cormeilles. Regn cld .65. Regd OO-JBP 18.8.65 to COGEA Nouvelle, Ostend. Regd 15.2.66 to J.Thiel, Wevelgem. Sold to Mr.Honkoop, Veen, Netherlands 7.70. Regn cld 8.70. Stored at Tyre-Firemat premises, Aalburg, Netherlands .71.

F-BJBQ AT-6F, c/n 121-42512, ex 44-81790. Regd 20.4.59 to Cie Air-France, Cormeilles. Regd 3.7.63 to CEDEA, Cormeilles. Regn cld .65. Regd OO-JBQ 24.8.65 to COGEA Nouvelle, Ostend. Regd 11.10.66 to J.Thiel, Wevelgem. Sold to Mr.Honcoop, Veen, Netherlands 7.70. Regn cld 8.70; scrapped.

F-BJBR AT-6F, c/n 121-42513, ex 44-81791. Regd 20.4.59 to Cie Air-France, Cormeilles. Regd 3.7.63 to CEDEA, Cormeilles. Regn cld .65. Regd OO-JBR 20.8.65 to COGEA Nouvelle, Ostend. Regd 11.10.66 to J.Thiel, Wevelgem. Sold to Mr.Honcoop, Veen, Netherlands 7.70. Regn cld 8.70; scrapped.

F-BJBS AT-6F, c/n 121-42497, ex 44-81775. Regd 20.4.59 to Cie Air-France, Cormeilles. Regd 3.7.63 to CEDEA, Cormeilles. Regd cld .65. Regd OO-JBS 10.8.65 to COGEA Nouvelle, Ostend. Regd 11.10.66 to J.Thiel, Wevelgem. Sold to Mr.Honcoop, Veen, Netherlands 7.70. Regn cld 8.70. To scrapyard Bergen op Zoom .71.

F-BJBT AT-6F, c/n 121-42412, ex 44-81690. Regd 20.4.59 to Cie Air-France, Cormeilles. Regd 3.7.63 to CEDEA, Comeilles. Regd cld .65. Regd OO-JBT 20.8.65 to COGEA Nouvelle, Ostend. Regd 11.10.66 to J.Thiel, Wevelgem. Sold to Mr.Honcoop, Veen, Netherlands 7.70. Regn cld 8.70. To scrapyard Bergen op Zoom .71.

F-BJBU AT-6F, c/n 121-42452, ex 44-81730. Regd 20.4.59 to Cie Air-France, Cormeilles. Regd 18.6.63 to CEDEA, Cormeilles. Regn cld .65. Regd OO-JBU 8.65 to COGEA Nouvelle, Ostend. Regd 11.10.66 to J.Thiel, Wevelgem. Sold to Mr.Honcoop, Veen, Netherlands 7.70. Regn cld 8.70. To scrapyard Bergen op Zoom .71.

F-BJBV AT-6F, c/n 121-42511, ex 44-81789. Regd 20.4.59 to Cie Air-France, Cormeilles. Regd 3.7.63 to CEDEA, Cormeilles. Regn cld .65. Regd OO-JBV 27.8.65 to COGEA Nouvelle, Ostend. Regd 11.10.66 to J.Thiel, Wevelgem. Sold to Mr.Honcoop, Veen, Netherlands 7.70. Regn cld 8.70. To scrapyard Bergen op Zoom .71.

F-BMJO T-6G, c/n 88-42005, ex 51-14696, Fr AF Reservation; not certified. Spares in rebuild of F-BMJP as F-AZAS. Rebuilt by Air Classik and painted as "Y-34"; Displayed at Berlin-Tegel,later Vienna-Schwechat.

F-BMJP T-6G, c/n 182-736, ex 51-15049, Fr AF Reservation; not certified. Rebuilt, composite with F-BMJO, and regd F-AZAS 8.80 (regn reserved 3.78) to J.Salis, La Ferte Alais. Painted in USN c/s.

F-BMJQ T-6G, c/n 182-585, ex 51-14898, Fr AF 14898 "KW". Regn reserved 6.74 for Institute Aeronautique Amaury de la Grange, Merville. Not certified and used as instructional airframe.

F-BNAU AT-6G, c/n 182-800, ex 51-15113, Fr AF 15113. Regd 4.7.67 to Y.Collin, Troyes. Regd .68 to A.Butel, Toulouse. Regd .73 to J.Decoop, La Ferte Alais. Painted as Fr AF "71". Re-regd F-AZAU 11.79. Repainted in USAF c/s "MH-038".

F-BOEN T-6G, c/n 182-1, ex 51-14314, Fr AF 14314. Regn reserved 6.74 to Institute Aeronautique Amaury de la Grange, Merville. Not certified and used as instructional airframe.

F-BOEO T-6G, c/n 182-535, ex 51-14848, Fr AF 14848. Regn reserved 6.74 to Institute Aeronautique Amaury de la Grange, Merville. Not certified. Regd F-AZBQ 8.84 (reserved 7.82) to Amicale J-B Salis, La Ferte Alais.

F-BRGA See D-FABI

F-BRGB See D-FABA

F-BVQD T-6G, ex 51-14367, Fr AF 14367. Regn reserved 11.78 by Salis Aviation, La Ferte Alais. Not certified and re-regd F-AZBK 9.81 (reserved 7.79). To P.Zmiro, Pontivy.

F-WJBI See F-BJBI

F-WZDU See F-BJBF

I-TSEI AT-6G, ex 49-3342, Sp AF E16-71. Regd 6.8.86 to Ass.Amatori di Aerei d'Epoca, Treviso.

LN-BNM AT-16 Mk IIB, c/n 14-639, ex 42-12392, FE905, RDAF 31-329. Regd 5.1.61 to Fjellfly S Kjetilson, Skien. C of A lapsed 31.12.68. Regn cld 29.1.73. To Historic Acft Museum, Southend 5.72, repainted in USAF c/s as "12392/TA-392". To RAF Museum, Cardington for storage/rebuild.

LN-BNN AT-16 Mk IIB, c/n 14A-1057, ex 43-12758, FS917, RDAF 31-310. Regd 5.1.61 to Fjellfly S

Kjetilson, Skien. C of A lapsed 31.12.68. Regn cld 14.6.71. Stored until sold to Sweden, and to playground use. Later to Hillerstorp for display purposes.

LN-LFW See G-SUES

LN-MAA AT-16 Mk IIB, c/n 14-726, ex 42-12479, FE992, Fv.16047. Regd 12.9.72 to J.Murer, Oslo. Regn cld 1.4.75; sold in UK. Regd G-BDAM 10.4.75 to D.G.Jones, Swansea. C of A issued 27.6.75. Painted in R.Nor.AF c/s as "216". Regd 4.7.79 to R.H.Reeves, Manchester. Repainted in RAF c/s as FE992 .80. Regd 22.10.81 to M.V.Gauntlett, Goodwood. Regd 15.4.85 to M.V.Gauntlett, E.C.English and N.A.Lees, Goodwood/North Weald.

LN-MAN SNJ-4, c/n 88-11545, ex Bu 26861, NC58273. Regd 10.1.48 to Thor Solberg Flyveselskap, Bergen. Regn cld 9.11.48; to R Nor AF as "MB-G". Later to Turkish AF.

LN-TEX See OO-AAR

LN-WNH See G-SUES

LX-PAE T-6G, ex 49-3453, Sp AF E16-106. Regd 2.9.87 to Luxembourg Association for Vintage Aircraft.

OO-AAR AT-16 Mk IIB, c/n 14A-2268, ex KF568, Belg AF H-58. Regd 1.10.58 to H De Paepe, Borgerhout. Regn cld 11.9.59; to West Germany. Regd D-FIBU 12.59 to RM Overseas Motorsales GmbH, Frankfurt. Regd to Bundesrepublik Deutschland. Regd cld .64. To Portuguese AF as FAP 1794. Regd LN-TEX 3.8.79 to J.Murer & ptnrs, Oslo.

OO-ABD AT-6F, c/n 121-42438, ex 44-81716. Regd 31.5.61 to Automotive Industries Inc NV, Moorsele. Regn cld 5.6.61, sold in France. Regd N9752F to H.L.Knight, Evreux Eure, France but delivered painted as N9852F. Impounded (for smuggling) Barcelona, Spain 8.64. (Extant 7.71). Note: Not ex KF716 as quoted officially on US regn. .

OO-DAF AT-16 Mk IIB, c/n 14A-1494, ex 43-13195, FT454, R Neth AF B-84, MLD 098. Regd 4.8.72 to E.Voormezeele, Braaschaat. To Auto und Technik Museum, Sinsheim; painted as FT454.

OO-GDD See PH-UEK

OO-GDK AT-6C Mk IIA, c/n 88-9778, ex 41-33278, EX305, SAAF 7115, Belg AF H-37. Regd 25.1.62 to COGEA Nouvelle, Ostend. Regn cld 29.10.62; to Belgian Congo.

OO-GDL AT-16 Mk IIB, ex 41-33596, EX623, SAAF 7344, Belg AF H-42. Regd 25.1.62 to COGEA Nouvelle, Ostend. Regn cld 24.5.62; to Portuguese AF.

OO-GDM AT-6C Mk IIA, c/n 88-13598, ex 41-33752, EX779, SAAF 7409, Belg AF H-43. Regd 25.1.62 to COGEA Nouvelle, Ostend. Regn cld 24.5.62; to Portuguese AF.

OO-GDN AT-6A Mk IIA, c/n 78-6562, ex 41-16184, Belg AF H-48. Regd 25.1.62 to COGEA Nouvelle, Ostend. Regn cld 24.5.62; to Portuguese AF.

OO-GDO AT-16 Mk IIB, c/n 14A-2115, ex KF415, Belg AF H-52. Regd 25.1.62 to COGEA Nouvelle, Ostend. Regn cld 24.5.62; to Portuguese AF.

OO-GDP AT-16 Mk IIB, c/n 14A-2415, ex KF715, Belg AF H-67. Regd 25.1.62 to COGEA Nouvelle, Ostend. Regn cld 24.5.62; to Portuguese AF.

OO-GDQ AT-16 Mk IIB, c/n 14A-2434, ex KF734, Belg AF H-73. Regd 25.1.62 to COGEA Nouvelle, Ostend. Regn cld 4.2.70; wfu.

OO-GEM AT-6C Mk IIA, c/n 88-10635, ex 41-33515, EX542, SAAF 7269, Belg AF H-17. Regd 11.10.58 to COGEA Nouvelle, Ostend. Regn cld 22.10.62; to Belgian Congo.

OO-GEN AT-6C Mk IIA, c/n 88-10014, ex 41-33344, EX371, SAAF 7187, Belg AF H-26. Regd 11.10.58 to COGEA Nouvelle, Ostend. Regn cld 24.5.62; to Portuguese AF.

OO-GEO AT-6C Mk IIA, c/n 88-10554, ex 41-33434, EX461, SAAF 7210, Belg AF H-28. Regd 11.10.58 to COGEA Nouvelle, Ostend. Regn cld 24.5.62; to Portuguese AF.

SE-FUZ and friends relax at Bassingbourn, May 1978 *(author)*

OO-GEP AT-6C Mk IIA, c/n 88-12546, ex 41-33653, EX680, SAAF 7329, Belg AF H-45. Regd 11.10.58 to COGEA Nouvelle, Ostend. Regd cld 22.10.62; to Belgian Congo.
OO-GEQ AT-6C Mk IIA, c/n 88-9260, ex 41-33154, EX181, SAAF 7045, Belg AF H-18. Regd 11.10.58 to COGEA Nouvelle, Ostend. Regn cld 24.5.62; to Portuguese AF.
OO-GER AT-6C Mk IIA, c/n 88-12327, ex 41-33634, EX661, SAAF 7315, Belg AF H-31. Regd 11.10.58 to COGEA Nouvelle, Ostend. Regn cld 24.5.62; to Portuguese AF.
OO-GES AT-6C Mk IIA, c/n 88-9689, ex 41-33246, EX273, SAAF 7184, Belg AF H-36. Regd 11.10.58 to COGEA Nouvelle, Ostend. Regn cld 24.5.62; to Portuguese AF.
OO-JBP See F-BJBP
OO-JBQ See F-BJBQ
OO-JBR See F-BJBR
OO-JBS See F-BJBS
OO-JBT See F-BJBT
OO-JBU See F-BJBU
OO-JBV See F-BJBV
OO-JBW See PH-UEI
OY-DYE AT-6A, c/n 78-6992, ex 41-16544, Fv.16291. Regd 26.5.55 to A.P.Botved, Copenhagen. Regn cld 24.4.56. Regd in West Germany as D-IGAL .56 to Deutscher Luftfahrt-Beratungsdienst, Wiesbaden. Re-regd D-FGAL 5.58. Regd PH-NKD 16.6.61 to J.Daams. Regd 23.6.76 to NV Skylight. (Note : Also reported as c/n 78-6922 ex 41-16291/NC52694 - believed unlikely)
PH-BKT AT-16 Mk IIB, c/n 14A-1020, ex 43-12721, FS880, R Neth AF B-135. Regd 14.6.71 to J.A.H.M.Thurling & ptnrs. Regd 4.9.80 to Mrs H.Toren, Hilversum.
PH-HAR See D-IDEM
PH-HON AT-16 Mk IIB, c/n 14A-1431, ex 43-13132, FT391, R Neth AF B-97. Regd 10.7.70 to C.Honcoop, Veen. Regn cld 8.7.71. Regd G-AZBN 13.7.71 to Sir W.J.D.Roberts, Shoreham (later Strathallan). C of A issued 18.1.72. Painted in RAF c/s as FT391 .78. Regd 10.11.81 to The Colt Car Co Ltd, Staverton. Regd 10.1.85 to CE Aviation Ltd, Staverton. Regd 5.9.85 to Ashbon Associates Ltd, Duxford. Regd 26.2.87 to The Old Flying Machine Co Ltd, Duxford.
PH-HTC AT-16 Mk IIB, c/n 14-787, ex 42-12540, FH153, R Neth AF B-158. Regn reserved for C.Honcoop .71 but not taken up. Regd PH-PPS 18.12.72 to J.Daams. Regn cld 20.8.73. Regd G-BBHK 7.9.73 to T.D.L.Rose. C of A issued 28.9.73. Regd 19.6.74 to R.Lamplough, Duxford. Regd 21.1.80 to R.F.Warner, Long Marston/Cardiff. Painted in RAF c/s as FH153 .84.
PH-IIB AT-16 Mk IIB, c/n 14A-1467, ex 43-13168, FT427, R Neth AF B-118. Regd 31.7.79 to H.B. van Meelis & ptnrs, Gilze-Rijen. Painted in R Neth AF c/s as B-118.
PH-KLU AT-16 Mk IIB, c/n 14A-1184, ex 43-12885, FT144, MLD L-., R Neth AF B-59. Regd 23.8.74 to J.A.H.M.Thurling. Regd 12.12.78 to A.C.Groeneveld, Lelystad. Note : Officially regd as 14-664 which was B-163/FE930/42-12417.
PH-KMA See PH-SAZ
PH-MLM AT-16 Mk IIB, c/n 14A-1444, ex 43-13145, FT404, R Neth AF B-71. Regd 5.7.85 to Stichting Vliegsport Gilze Rijen. Painted in R Neth AF c/s as B-71.
PH-NGR AT-16 Mk IIB, c/n 14A-1273, ex 43-12974, FT233, MLD L-3/12-3, R Neth AF B-61. Regd 15.10.56 to Schreiner & Co. Regn cld 10.7.57, reverted to B-61. Regd PH-NIE 25.1.60 to Schreiner & Co. Regn cld 27.1.65, reverted to B-61.
PH-NIA AT-16 Mk IIB, c/n 14-255, ex 42-718, FE521, R Neth AF B-151. Regd 19.8.57 to Schreiner & Co. Crashed 29.9.60 and regn cld 28.5.62 as reverted to B-151.
PH-NIB AT-16 Mk IIB, c/n 14-724 ex 42-12477, FE990, R Neth AF B-187. Regd 24.7.57 to Schreiner & Co. Crashed Den Helder 17.8.59. Regn cld 22.1.60.
PH-NIC AT-16 Mk IIB, c/n 14-730, ex 42-12483, FE996, R Neth AF B-186. Regd 2.8.57 to Schreiner & Co. Regn cld 2.3.64, reverted to R Neth AF and broken up.
PH-NID AT-16 Mk IIB, c/n 14A-807, ex 43-12508, FS667, R Neth AF B-179. Regd 30.7.57 to Schreiner & Co. Regn cld 22.1.60 as reverted to B-179. Note : Official c/n is 14-765 which was B-175; above believed correct. Also reported as R Neth B-176 /FE985.
PH-NIE See PH-NGR
PH-NIF AT-16 Mk IIB, c/n 14A-1365, ex 43-13066, FT325, R Neth AF B-15. Regd 25.1.60 to Schreiner & Co. Regn cld 2.4.64 as reverted to B-15. Subsequently broken up.
PH-NIZ AT-16 Mk IIB, c/n 14A-1368, ex 43-13069, FT328, R Neth AF B-16. Regd 11.8.60 to Schreiner & Co. Regn cld 23.12.64 as reverted to B-16.
PH-NKD See OY-DYE
PH-PPS See PH-HTC
PH-SAZ AT-16 Mk IIB, c/n 14A-1216, ex 43-12917, FT176, R Neth AF B-56. Regn reserved 12.6.64 by Schreiner Aerocontractors; not taken up. To MLD as 043 1.65; wfu 31.3.71. Regd PH-KMA 9.11.71 to C.Honcoop. Regd 20.2.74 to W.Daams. Destroyed in ground collision with Spitfire AB910 at Bex, Switzerland 20.8.78. Regn cld 9.10.78. Remains stored Hilversum.
PH-SKK AT-16 Mk IIB, c/n 14A-1363, ex 43-13064, FT323, R Neth AF B-19. Regd 10.2.70 to J.Daams. Regn cld as sold to USA 19.11.71 but not delivered and restored 5.1.72 to R.N.Rijken. Regn cld 14.1.72 on proposed sale to Switzerland but not delivered because of noise regulations and sold instead in UK. Regd G-AZSC 7.4.72 to Fairoaks Aviation Services Ltd. C of A issued 23.6.72. Painted in RAF c/s as FT830 .77. Regd 2.11.77 to M.W.Stow, Wroughton/Blackbushe. Repainted as FT323 .78. Regd 5.1.81 to D.W.Arnold, Blackbushe. Regd 28.2.84 to Machine Music Ltd, Fairoaks/White Waltham. Repainted in Japanese AF c/s .84.
PH-SKL AT-16 Mk IIB, c/n 14A-868, ex 43-12569, FS728, R Neth AF B-104. Regd 10.2.70 to J.Daams. Regn cld 15.9.72. Regd G-BAFM 16.10.72 to The Hon P.Lindsay, Booker. C of A issued 4.5.73. Regd 9.8.83 to J.Parks, Hamble. Painted as FS728 .84. Regd 28.10.86 to Parker Airways Ltd, Denham. (Note : Also incorrectly quoted as ex B-105, Belg AF H-79 and FT210)
PH-SKM AT-16 Mk IIB, c/n 14A-1269, ex 43-12970, FT229, R Neth AF B-45. Regd 10.2.70 to J.Daams. Regn cld 2.12.71, sold in UK. Regd G-AZKI 8.12.71 to Fairoaks Aviation Services Ltd. C of A issued 17.3.72. Painted in RAF c/s as FT239 .72. Regd 15.11.73 to A.E.Hutton, Wroughton/Duxford. Repainted as FT229 .78. Regd 24.11.81 to T.S.Warren, Sandown. Regd 12.10.82 to A.D.M.Edie, Shoreham. Regd 17.12.82 to Noblair Ltd, Pontoise, France. Regn cld .85. Regd in France as F-AZDS .84 to SLCA, Avignon.
PH-UBD AT-6A, c/n 78-6714, ex 41-16336. Regd 31.7.46 to RLS. Collided with PH-UBO Gilze Rijen 8.5.50. Regn cld 10.5.50.
PH-UBE AT-6A, c/n 78-6556, ex 41-16178. Regd 31.7.46 to RLS. Regn cld 23.9.60. To Avifauna Zoo, painted as "PH-AVI". Broken up .66.
PH-UBF AT-6A (identity not known). Regd 6.9.46 to RLS. Regn cld 30.8.60. Scrapped.
PH-UBG AT-6A, c/n 77-4295, ex 41-336. Regd 17.9.46 to RLS. Crashed Warga 16.10.46. Regn cld 8.11.46.
PH-UBH AT-6A, c/n 78-7154, ex 41-16776. Regd 17.9.46 to RLS. Crashed in North Sea off Texel 2.12.58. Regn cld 7.1.59.
PH-UBI AT-6A, c/n 77-4532, ex 41-503. Regd 6.9.46 to RLS. Regn cld 30.8.60. Broken up.
PH-UBK AT-6A, c/n 78-6580, ex 41-16202. Regd 16.8.46 to RLS. Regn cld 30.8.60. Broken up.
PH-UBL AT-6A, c/n 78-6044, ex 41-758. Regd 17.9.46 to RLS. Regn cld 30.8.60. Broken up.
PH-UBM AT-6A, c/n 78-6599, ex 41-16221. Regd 6.9.46 to RLS. Regn cld 30.8.60. Broken up.
PH-UBN AT-6A, c/n 78-5955, ex 41-689. Regd 16.8.46 to RLS. Regn cld 30.8.60. Broken up.
PH-UBO AT-6A, c/n 78-6384, ex 41-16006. Regd 17.9.46 to RLS. Regn cld 23.9.60. Stored and scrapped Hornhuizen late .78.
PH-UBP AT-6A, c/n 78-6538, ex 41-16160. Regd 6.9.46 to RLS. Badly damaged Gilze Rijen 25.7.49 and regn

The former FH153, G-BBHK is seen at Cranfield in September 1975 *(R.C.Sturtivant)*

cld 29.7.49. Restored 31.8.49. Crashed Wouw 13.1.54. Regn cld 30.3.54.

PH-UBZ AT-6A, c/n 78-4641, ex 41-682. Regd 12.8.47 to RLS. Crashed Veghel 11.11.49. Regn cld 19.11.49. Note : Official c/n is "7857148"; above identity unconfirmed.

PH-UDF AT-6A, c/n 78-7104, ex 41-16726. Regd 23.10.47 to RLS. Regn cld 30.8.60. Broken up.

PH-UEI AT-16 Mk IIB, c/n 14-190, ex 42-653, FE456. Regd 13.6.50 to RLS. Regn cld 23.9.60, sold in Belgium. Regd OO-JBW 8.65 to COGEA Nouvelle, Ostend. Regd 15.2.66 to J.Thiel, Wevelgem. Sold to Mr.Honkoop, Veen, Netherlands. Regn cld 8.70. Stored displayed on garage Boxmeer, Netherlands .71.

PH-UEK AT-16 Mk IIB, c/n 14-143, ex 42-606, FE409. Regd 16.6.50 to RLS. Regn cld 30.8.60. Regd OO-GDD 26.10.60 to COGEA Nouvelle, Ostend. Regn cld 29.10.62; probably to Katanga AF.

PH-UEL AT-16 Mk IIB, c/n 14-779, ex 42-12532, FH145. Regd 3.7.50 to RLS. Regd cld 23.8.60; broken up.

PH-UEM AT-16 Mk IIB, c/n 14-174 ex 42-637, FE440. Regd 3.7.50 to RLS. Regd 21.7.60 to J.Daams. Regd cld 15.6.61 to W.Germany. Regd D-FAMO 7.61 to Deutscher Luftfahrt-Beratungsdienst, Wiesbaden. Regn cld .64. To Portuguese AF as FAP 1791.

PH-UEN AT-16 Mk IIB, c/n 14-185, ex 42-468, FE451. Regd 26.8.50 to RLS. Regn cld 30.8.60; broken up.

PH-UEO AT-16 Mk IIB, c/n 14-541, ex 42-12294, FE807. Regd 2.8.50 to RLS. Regn cld 24.7.58; broken up.

PH-UEP AT-16 Mk IIB, c/n 14-548, ex 42-12301, FE814. Regd 2.8.50 to RLS. Regn cld 30.8.60; broken up.

PH-UER AT-16 Mk IIB, c/n 14-556, ex 42-12309, FE822. Regd 26.8.50 to RLS. Regn cld 30.8.60; broken up.

SE-CAR AT-6A, c/n 77-4259 (also quoted as c/n 121-42449 ex 41-300). Regd .55 to Svensk Flygtjanst AB, Goteborg. Regd D-IBEC .56 to Deutscher Luftfahrt-Beratungsdienst, Wiesbaden. Re-regd D-FBEC .57. Regn cld 7.63.

SE-CHK AT-6, c/n 14-362, ex FE628. Regd 10.59 to Kungl Mal : t och Kronan,Stockholm. Regn cld pre.66

SE-CHO AT-6A, c/n 77-4586. Regd .58 to Svensk Flygtjanst AB, Stockholm. Regn cld pre.66

SE-CHP AT-6A, c/n 77-4524, ex 41-16443, Fv.16269. Regd 10.58 to Svensk Flygtjanst AB, Stockholm. Regd pre.70 to O.H.Ahnstrand, Vallingby. Regd .71 to B.O.Lowgren, Bromma.

SE-CHR AT-6A, c/n 78-7341. Regd .58 to Svensk Flygtjanst AB, Stockholm. Regn cld pre.64.

SE-CHS AT-6A, c/n 78-7367. Regd .58 to Svensk Flygtjanst AB, Stockholm. Regn cld pre.64.

SE-CHT AT-6A, c/n 77-4637. Regd .58 to Svensk Flygtjanst AB, Stockholm. Regn cld pre.64.

SE-CHU AT-6A, C/n 78-6251. Regd .58 to Svensk Flygtjanst AB, Stockholm. Regn cld pre.64.

SE-CHW AT-6A, c/n 77-4244. Regd .58 to Svensk Flygtjanst AB, Stockholm. Regn cld pre.64.

SE-CHX AT-6A, c/n 78-6788. Regd 11.58 to Svensk Flygtjanst AB, Stockholm. Regn cld pre.64.

SE-FUY AT-6A, c/n 14-460, ex 42-923, FE726, Fv.16092. Regd 6.72 to S.H.Hansson, Hoganas. Crashed Arboga 25.5.76; regn cld 22.12.76.

SE-FUZ AT-6A, c/n 14-526, ex 42-12279, FE792, Fv.16144. Regd 2.73 to Sterner Aero AB, Borlange. Regd to B.Lowgren .78.

SX-AEA AT-6G. Regd to A.Potamianos. Regn cld .86

SX-AEB AT-6G. Regd to A.Potamianos. Regn cld .86.

TF-ERN AT-6, ex FT135, RDAF 31-312. Regd 5.61 to Mrs S.Eggertsdottir, Keflavik. Regn cld pre.66.

TF-FSA AT-6F, ex 44-82028. Regd 4.47. Regn cld 10.53; sold to Babb Co, New Jersey, USA.

Part 2: Commonwealth civil-registered Harvards/T-6's (excluding Canada)

VH-HAR AT-6D, ex EX185, NZ1002
VH-HVD See ZK-ENI
VH-NAH See ZK-ENL
VH-PEM See ZK-ENH
VH-SNJ See ZK-ENM
VH-TEX AT-6C, ex 41-33157, EX184, NZ1006. Regd 2.5.86 to R.MacFarlane, Bankstown.
VR-HDC AT-6F Mk II, c/n 121-42502, ex 44-81780. Regd 10.46 to Lee Kim Bun. Regd 22.4.48 to J.H.Fleming.
VT-AVA AT-6F, c/n 121-42506, ex 44-81784. Regd 3.46 to M.Singh, Delhi. Derelict Patiala 12.67.
VT-AXS AT-6F, c/n 121-42776, ex 44-82054. Regd 2.46 to HH Maharaja Jam Sahib of Nawangar, Jamnagar. To HH Maharaja of Jaipur 22.3.49. Current .79.
VT-AYR AT-6F, c/n 121-42509, ex 44-81787. Regd 3.46 to R.Mistri, Bombay. To A.C.P.Wadia 24.2.50. Regn cld
VT-CAW AT-6, c/n 14-420, ex 42-883, FE686. (identities unconfirmed) Regd 3.46 to Indian Overseas Airlines Ltd. To Metcaero Engineers Ltd, Bombay 24.5.51.
VT-CAX AT-6, c/n 14-1086, ex 43-12787, FS946. Regd 3.46 to Indian Overseas Airlines Ltd.
VT-CHR AT-6G, c/n 121-42852, ex 44-82130. Regd 11.46 to J.R.H.Bartlett, Calcutta. Regn cld 30.5.59; scrapped.
VT-CHW AT-6G, c/n 121-42650. Regd 11.46 to G.D.Mukherjee, Calcutta.
VT-CQC AT-6A, c/n 14-288. Regd 11.47 to D.H.Wood, Juhu.
VT-CQD AT-6A, c/n 14-706, ex FE972. Regd 11.47. To A.Zampolmo, Bangalore 2.12.49. To R.S.Cambata, Bombay.
VT-CQN AT-6A, c/n 14-205, ex 42-668, FE471. Regd 12.47 to F.J.Mobsby. To Baroda Rayon Corp, Juhu. Crashed Nr.Boisar 3.9.77.
(NOTE: The identities of all Indian Harvards must be considered unconfirmed).
ZK-ELN Mk III, c/n 88-16143, ex 42-84362, EZ299, NZ1082. Regd 11.80 to Confederate Air Force, NZ Wing, Dairy Flats.
ZK-ENA Mk IIA, c/n 88-12036, ex 41-33565, EX572, NZ1037. Regd 6.78 to J.Matthewson, Ardmore.
ZK-ENB Mk III, c/n 88-15871, ex 41-34117, EZ244, NZ1076. Regd 6.78 to R.Brereton, Dunedin.
ZK-ENC Mk IIA, c/n 88-16505, ex 42-84724, EZ360, NZ1091. Regd 6.78 to W.J.D & S.M.A.Williams, Mount Maunganui.
ZK-END Mk IIA, c/n 88-17004, ex 42-85223, EZ449, NZ1096. Regd 6.78 to W.S.Bell & R.O.Dahlberg, Mount Maunganui.
ZK-ENE Mk III, c/n 88-14762, ex 41-33878, EX905, NZ1066. Regd 6.78 to M.C.Christopherson, Mount Maunganui.
ZK-ENF Mk III, c/n 88-14889, ex 41-33920, EX944, NZ1065. Regd 6.78 to E.J.Adams, W.S.Bell, D.J.Phillips, M.C.Christopherson & R.O.Dahlberg, Mount Maunganui.
ZK-ENG Mk III, c/n 88-15873, ex 41-34119, EZ246, NZ1078. Regd 6.78 to G.A.Martin & D.J.Dalliess, Blenheim.
ZK-ENH Mk III, c/n 88-14494, ex 41-33841, EX868, NZ1061. Regd 8.78 to W.Greville, Broken Hill, NSW. Regn cld .80. Regd VH-PEM 7.80 to W.Greville, Broken Hill.
ZK-ENI Mk III, c/n 88-15870, ex 41-34116, EZ243, NZ1075. Regd 8.78 to D.G.Reidpath, Auckland. Regn cld 6.82. Regd VH-HVD 21.6.82 to H.Brunton, Narromine, NSW.
ZK-ENJ Mk III, c/n 88-17010, ex 42-85229, EZ455, NZ1098. Regd 9.78 to D.G.Reidpath, Auckland.
ZK-ENK Mk III, c/n 88-17011, ex 42-85230, EZ456, NZ1099. Regd 9.78 to D.G.Reidpath, Auckland.
ZK-ENL Mk III, c/n 88-14177, ex 41-33800, EX827, NZ1056. Regd 10.78 to D.G.Reidpath, Auckland. Regn cld .80; sold in Australia. Regd VH-NAH 9.2.84 to Mt Carli Pty Ltd, Moorabbin.
ZK-ENM Mk III, c/n 88-16324, ex 42-84543, EZ329, NZ1085. Regd 10.78 to D.G.Reidpath, Auckland. Regn cld .80. Regd VH-SNJ 4.80.
ZK-ENN Mk IIA, c/n 88-10254, ex 41-33397, EX424, NZ1025. Regd 6.80 to D.M.Diamond & ptnrs, Pleasant Point.
ZK-SGQ Mk IIA, c/n 88-12032, ex 41-33561, EX588, NZ1033. Regd 2.81 to S.G.Quill, Palmerston North.
ZK-WAR Mk III, c/n 88-16506, ex 42-84725, EZ361, NZ1092. Regd 9.78 to G.S.Smith, Auckland.
ZS-DMF AT-6 Mk IIB, c/n 14-1832, ex KF151. Regd 9.55 to Field Aircraft Services (SA) Pty Ltd, Germiston. To Syrian AF 6.56.
ZS-DMG AT-6 Mk IIB, c/n 14-2433. Regd 9.55 to Field Aircraft Services (SA) Pty Ltd, Germiston. To Syrian AF 6.56.
ZS-DMH AT-6 Mk IIB, c/n 14-2502. Regd 9.55 to Field Aircraft Services (SA) Pty Ltd, Germiston. To Syrian AF 6.56.
ZS-DMI AT-6 Mk IIB, c/n 14-2107. Regd 9.55 to Field Aircraft Services (SA) Pty Ltd, Germiston. To Syrian AF 6.56.
ZS-DMJ AT-6 Mk IIB, c/n 14-2162. Regd 9.55 to Field Aircraft Services (SA) Pty Ltd, Germiston. To Syrian AF 6.56.
ZS-DMK AT-6 Mk IIB, c/n 14-1362. Regd 9.55 to Field Aircraft Services (SA) Pty Ltd, Germiston. To Syrian AF 6.56.
ZS-DML AT-6 Mk IIB, c/n 14-1432, ex 43-13133, FT392. Regd 9.55 to Field Aircraft Services (SA) Pty Ltd, Germiston. To Syrian AF 6.56.
ZS-DMM AT-6 Mk IIB, c/n 14-2036. Regd 9.55 to Field Aircraft Services (SA) Pty Ltd, Germiston. To Syrian AF 6.56.
ZS-DMN AT-6 Mk IIB, c/n 14-1124. Regd 9.55 to Field Aircraft Services (SA) Pty Ltd, Germiston. To Syrian AF 6.56.
ZS-DMO AT-6 Mk IIB, c/n 14-2149. Regd 9.55 to Field Aircraft Services (SA) Pty Ltd, Germiston. To Syrian AF 6.56.
(NOTE: The identities of the batch of South African Harvards have previously been misquoted, probably by erroneous extrapolation from c/n's. Only that for ZS-DMF and DML are believed accurate; the batch came from RAF Kenyan sources, including 1340 Flt.)

OTHER SURVIVORS

NON-AIRWORTHY HARVARDS EXTANT IN THE UNITED KINGDOM

EX884 ex PortAF (1513)/SAAF (7426)/EX884; under rebuild at Cranfield -- painted as FT323
EX976 ex PortAF (1657)/EX976; on display at FAA Museum, Yeovilton
EZ407 ex PortAF (1656)/EZ407; undergoing restoration for RN Historic Aircraft Flight at Lee-on-Solent
FE905 ex RCAF (FE905); undergoing restoration
FE905 ex Southend Museum (42-12392)/LN-BNM/R.DanAF (329) FE905; undergoing restoration at Cardington for RAF Museum
FX442 privately owned, Bournemouth
KF435 owned by Barry Parkhouse; at Booker Aircraft Museum

More of the mass formation over Farnborough c.1950 *(Gp.Capt. J.R.Goodman DFC AFC RAF Retd.)*

The final ignominy! Harvard Mk.III EZ259 in a scrap yard; this aircraft is now the subject of long-term restoration *(K.Ellis)*